Republicanism in Nineteenth-Century France, 1814–1871

PAMELA M. PILBEAM

MACMILLAN

First published 1995 by
MACMILLAN PRESS LTD
Houndmills, Basingstoke, Hampshire RG21 2XS
and London
Companies and representatives
throughout the world

ISBN 0–333–56671–8 hardcover
ISBN 0–333–56672–6 paperback

A catalogue record for this book is available
from the British Library

10 9 8 7 6 5 4 3 2 1
04 03 02 01 00 99 98 97 96 95

Printed in Malaysia

To the memory of
Professor Alfred Cobban

To be governed is to be kept in sight, inspected, spied upon, directed, law-driven, numbered, enrolled, indoctrinated, preached at, controlled, estimated, valued, censured, commanded by creatures who have neither the right, nor the wisdom, nor the virtue to do so.

(P.J. Proudhon, *Idée générale de la Révolution*)

Contents

List of Illustrations

Plates

Maps

Preface

British observers of France are inclined to approach the story of the repeated political upheaval of the nineteenth century with a certain puzzled superiority. Marxist historiography used to appear to explain the successive revolutions which followed 1789. French republican historians have always been confident of the inevitability of the triumph or the republic. But which republic? And why three attempts over nearly a century before a permanent republican regime could be established?

This investigation is based on archival research in Paris and a number of departments and on printed material, including an invaluable, if not always well reproduced, multi-volume collection of reprints of republican and socialist pamphlets. It is an attempt to synthesize these findings with the ever-growing number of specific, particularly regional, monographs I make no pretence that my reading is exhaustive. My own life-long preference for republicanism will be transparent. I am indebted to archivists and librarians in Paris, provincial France and in London. I am grateful to the French government for an award which allowed me to do research in France in the summer of 1985 and to the Research Committee of the Department of History of my own college, Royal Holloway and Bedford New College, University of London, which provided me with a grant for research in Paris and the provinces in the summer of 1991.

I thank the many colleagues in French history who listened to and offered constructive criticism of aspects of this book, in particular the Society for the Study of French History in 1992, French Historical Studies and the Western Society for French History in 1992. My gratitude is also offered to the British Academy which made my two American visits possible. Above all I thank my students and friends in the Modern French History Research Seminar at the Institute of Historical Research, University of London, and the *Institut Français*, who have given excellent advice. In 1991–2 this seminar ran a year-long celebration of the declaration of the First Republic, and my debt to our many speakers from France and Britain is recorded throughout this volume in the Notes. Undergraduates in the colleges of London University, in Ontario and Vancouver, extra-mural, sixth-form and other audiences, have generously challenged me to clarify my ideas and justify my preoccupation with France. Above all, this volume has been refined and completed thanks to the patience and self-sacrifice of my own family, who have even come to enjoy (?) research/camping trips to France. If there are any lucid snatches herein recorded, they owe much to the comments of my husband Stephen and daughter Ashka, the latter of whom, a critical and busy undergraduate, simplified a little of my more wordy prose.

Hampstead
April 1993

Plate 1 The First Seal of the First Republic
(see page 6)

Plate 2 The Seal of the Second Republic
(see page 6)

Plate 3 La France Républicaine
(see page 6)

Thermidor

Fructidor

Vendémiaire

Brumaire

Frimaire

Nivôse

Pluviôse

Ventôse

Germinal

Floréal

Prairial

Messidor

Plate 4 The Republican Calendar
(see page 7)

Plate 5 The Republic, by Honoré Daumier
(see page 8)

Plate 6 Liberty guiding the people (1830), by Eugène Delacroix
(see page 8)

Plate 7 The Bastille – the Annual Procession
(see page 9)

Plate 8 The Republic (*Image d'Epinal, Pellerin* – 8 June 1794)
(see page 9)

Plate 9 The Tree of Liberty
(see page 10)

1   The Republic: Idea and Image

France was the only major European state to attempt to replace monarchical with republican government at the end of the eighteenth century. It took three revolutions, two monarchies, two empires and defeat in the war of 1870 before a republic proved sustainable. The purpose of this book is to try to explain why it took so long for a republic to become tolerable to the majority of the French.

'Republicans are men full-grown, Slaves are but children'[1] proclaimed the 'Chant de Départ', the song which became almost a second revolutionary anthem in the 1790s. For republicans a republic came to epitomize the final spiritual and institutional triumph of man in society. The idea of the republic developed in France as a compound of inspiration from the philosophers of the Enlightenment, the emergency of 1792 when the attempt to remodel society was in crisis and, later, in response to the social impact of economic change.

. The bicentenary celebrations of the First Republic were rather modest in comparison with those held to commemorate the 1789 Revolution.[2] Today the republic is depicted as the inheritance of all citizens, whatever their political leanings. Indeed the Fifth Republic is commonly seen as a consensus or compromise, representing the 'centre'.[3] It was not always so and the complacency of today may prove to be misplaced; few compromises are permanent. During the nineteenth century the republic was neither the middle ground, nor was it an anodyne uncontroversial inheritance. Republicans variously honoured and argued over two flags, one tricoloured, one red. Both were flags not of truce, but of conflict. The phrygian red bonnet, the potent symbol of liberty of the 1790s, was rejected in the following century as much by conservative friends of the republic as by monarchist denigrators.

1

At the most basic level of constitutional law a republic is simply an established form of government with neither a monarch nor a dictator. Such a definition tells us little about what the idea means to the French, for whom the republic is a compound of emotional commitment and ideology. What has the idea of the republic signified in France since the eighteenth century? Before the Revolution the concept of a republic conjured up a number of rather contradictory images for the French. The vocabulary of the revolutionaries of the 1790s, their iconography, statuary and architecture, even fashions in furniture and in dress, indicated the inspiration of the Ancient World. The dominance of Greek and Roman history, culture and language in the education of France's elite was reflected in the political forms invented to replace those of the old regime. Republican terminology, as well as direct references to the classical past in speeches, displays the ways in which, to some degree, the new republicans sought to validate and sanctify their own political innovations in the institutions of ancient Greece and Rome.

Curiously, the ambiguity of the First Republic itself could be seen as a mirror of the classical world. In part the Republic was envisaged as the manifestation of ideals of justice and virtue, echoing theoretical concepts like those of Plato's *Republic*. On the other hand the political developments of the 1790s, especially increasingly oligarchical and dictatorial tendencies, were linked by contemporaries with quite different classical antecedents. Napoleon was compared to republican dictators in the ancient world, both in print and most vividly on the canvases of David and others. The further the Republic departed from the principles of the Declaration of Rights, the more strident and emphatic its classicism; unfree institutions were disguised with names like Consulate and Tribunate.

The writers of the eighteenth-century Enlightenment found much to admire in the ancient world. They would habitually use 'republic' neutrally simply to mean a legally constituted political organization, in the way Aristotle had defined *polis*, although the term was also employed more specifically. Montesquieu described a republican government as one in which all or part of the people exercised sovereign power,[4] while Rousseau in saying 'all legitimate government is republican',[5] meant nothing more inflammatory than that a republic was any state ruled by a regular system of law, with or without a monarch. The term continued to be used in this way on occasions well into the nineteenth century.

The tenets of the Enlightenment permeate the debates and policies of the revolutionary period. Those who supported the 1789 Revolution, whether they favoured liberal monarchy or tried to construct a republic, were imbued with the basic optimistic and progressive presumptions of the *philosophes*. Like them they believed that people's selfish instincts could be subdued by enlightened education and that society could be raised to perfection by rational institutional change. This belief in progress, fundamental to nineteenth-century republicans, from Blanqui to Gambetta, was also shared by liberal monarchists such as Guizot and Thiers. The detailed recommendations of the *philosophes* were so varied that their admirers could always find a thinker who reflected the current political fashion. Montesquieu's doctrine of the separation of powers was much quoted in the first phase of the Revolution and the constitution of 1791. When the experiment in constitutional monarchy gave way to a republic, he found less favour, although during the Third Republic he was sometimes referred to as the father of the Republic, when the issue of power-sharing was again relevant.

The more conservative revolutionaries honoured Voltaire who inspired Condorcet's faith in the ameliorating influence of education and science. In 1791 Voltaire's ashes were moved to the Panthéon. At a more popular level, Philippe Curtius made a wax model of Voltaire for his acclaimed waxworks in the Palais Royal. Rousseau apparently exercised his greatest influence through Robespierre and nineteenth-century Jacobin republicans also liked to quote snippets from his work.

To what extent were modern republics an inspiration to the French? European republics such as Cromwell's Britain, or Holland and Switzerland were traditional enemies of France and therefore repellent. Through them republicanism was associated with Protestantism and the rise of capitalism. Commentators sometimes linked the idea of a republic to the Huguenot experience. Madame de Stael and Benjamin Constant stressed personal and ideological connections between the 1789 Revolution and Protestantism. The rationalizing and individualistic aspects of revolutionary ideas certainly appealed to Protestants, and a tolerant political framework offered them the novel opportunity of government employment.

The American Declaration of Independence gave a new specificity to republicanism. The American republic was born of rebellion and revolution, but unlike European republics, it had a more positive image for the French. The rebels and the French were allies in their fight against the British government, ensuring a double seal of approval for the new republic. How important was the American example? A number of leading figures, especially Lafayette, who was to play a long-running role in the French Revolution, had participated in the recent American revolt. The French appeared to imitate the Americans by publishing, like them, a Declaration of the Rights of Man. Philippe Curtius, a showman sensitive to the popular mood, displayed a model of Benjamin Franklin alongside Voltaire in his waxworks.

However, trans-Atlantic fraternity was not to last. During the 1789 Revolution the French never acknowledged an ideological debt to America. In the 1960s historians began to depict the American and French republics of the 1790s and their attendant revolutions as leading elements in an 'Atlantic Revolution'. Godechot and Palmer on either side of the ocean sketched the common features of the genesis and development of revolutionary movements in both continents.[6] Worldwide social and political unrest in 1968/9 gave such analyses immediacy to a generation of graduate students. However, detailed studies of individual revolutions in areas such as the Rhineland, Spain and the Italian states revealed differences rather than common features.[7] In *Sister Republics* Higonnet compared the American and French experiences from the perspective of an American historian of France. He noted that at its inception the French Revolution upheld the rights of the individual against corporative authority, while under the Committee of Public Safety such individualism was overturned in the attempt to avert economic collapse. The American Revolution manifested the opposite tendencies, asserting the pre-eminence of communitarian virtue, while actively pursuing capitalist enterprise. In this sense, he perceives the one republic to be the opposite mirror-image of the other. The attempt to find valid comparisons proved so artificial, that for the rest of the book the author dealt with the two republics in separate chapters.[8]

The 'Atlantic Revolution' seems to have vanished without trace in a welter of empirical research, with predictable conflicting indicators. Cross-fertilization or exportability were minimal. However, a recent French survey claims that the America of Jefferson (Tom Paine is added for good measure) had more impact on France than did the Enlightened writers.[9] One might conclude rather astringently that the only real link between the American and French experience was the cost of the American War, which rendered the French monarchy financially more vulnerable.

In 1792 a republic signified little that was specific, even to educated Frenchmen. It meant nothing to the uneducated. The First Republic had to develop both concept and symbols. It had to try to represent the nation and to create an appeal that was both cerebral and emotional. Symbols which would be used to unite different provinces and peoples of varying religious beliefs, degrees of education, wealth and knowledge of French itself were vital in the uphill struggle to attempt to create and capture a national imagination and leave a favourable imprint on long-term memory. In recent years historians, perhaps made more aware of the appeal of visual symbolism by today's media-dominated politics, have given increasing attention to such issues as statuary, ceremonies and other components of what has come to be called national memory.[10] The politicians of the 1790s displayed living allegories in processions and ceremonies, and commissioned statues in wax, papier-mâché or more durable materials if they could agree on the desired image for long enough for a model to be completed. The contemporary craze for wax was fortuitous. Curtius's pupil, later Madame Tussaud, claimed that she modelled from life or after the guillotine had done its work. Flags, verses and songs simple enough to be committed to memory were vital, especially in the attempt to mould a national conscript army for the first time.

The most permanent symbol devised was the tricolour flag, hastily improvised in the summer of 1789 from the white flag of the Bourbons and the blue and red of the coat of arms of Paris. This revolutionary flag was adopted successively by Republic and Empire. Between 1814/15 and 1830 tricoloured flags and *cocardes* were tucked away in cupboards in sufficient numbers for massed ranks to flutter out in 1830 to replace the white or fleur-de-lys standards of the restored Bourbons. The Orleanist monarchy appointed in 1830 took great care to justify and legitimate its compromise identity by associating itself with the revolutionary flag. This left republicans in a quandary. A red flag had been displayed at times during the First Republic, but although its supporters claimed that it symbolized the blood of the nation and patriotic unity, it was associated with popular radicalism and sectarian, specifically lower-class spilling of the blood of wealthier fellow-citizens. In 1848 most republicans were glad to retain the tricoloured flag, even though Louis Blanc assured them that the red flag had been the standard of the Gauls in the Hundred Years War. The red flag was flown by some who hoped for a social as well as a democratic republic between 1848 and 1851 and again in the Paris Commune of 1871. Divided loyalties about which flag was truly republican effectively signalled more than symbolic differences.

The phrygian cap, almost as uncontroversial today as the tricolour, was a divisive symbol of revolutionary liberty in the nineteenth century. In ancient Rome it was worn by freed slaves, in the First Republic it became the most important radical emblem, favoured during the Convention, disdained by the Directory, abandoned by Napoleon. Its ambiguous status is revealed in the official seal of the First Republic which was used in the more moderate 'Girondin' phase of the Republic from the autumn of 1792 (see Plate 1 on p. xiii), where the comfortably proportioned female representing the Republic does not wear the cap but carries it atop a pike. The fasces she holds symbolized unity in Ancient Rome. (In November 1793 a second Jacobin seal was adopted and the lady vanished, to be replaced by a very muscular Hercules, complete with a large club.) The liberty cap struck terror in the Orleanists in the 1830s and 1840s when it had become symbolic shorthand for a republic. It was treated as a somewhat ambiguous and embarrassing relic in 1848 for those who sought a democratic but not a social republic. There is no sign of a phrygian cap on the official seal of the Second Republic (see Plate 2 on p. xiii) which depicts a much more conservative, relaxed, seated female figure, wearing a halo made up of the sun's rays, holding the fasces and with a cock as an ornament on the carving of her chair. Her classical robe reveals almost nothing of her body. It is left to ears of corn to suggest the fruitfulness of the Republic. The postage stamps of the Republic showed a female adorned by ears of wheat.

The cap appears on more radical images such as la France Républicaine (see Plate 3 on p. xiv), where the lady confidently wears a phrygian cap, ornamented with a tricolour rosette and surmounted by a rampant Gallic cock. The tricolour ribbon round her neck holds a carpenter's level, then as now the most well known symbol of Freemasonry, which also represented equality to the revolutionaries. Her modest expression combined with complete mammary exposure owes much to images of the Virgin Mary and indicates the capacity of the republic to provide for its people. The liberty cap was a potent, if transient, symbol during the Paris Commune. Subsequently a republican government was so hostile to the emblem that in 1876 it successfully demanded the demolition of a large phrygian-capped statue erected in Dijon to celebrate the city's defence against the Prussians in October 1870. The less controversial symbols invented by the conservative tail-end of the Second Republic found favour again, both in France and in America, where the imagery of the official seal of the French Republic was later echoed in a better known Statue of Liberty.

The Gallic cock, regarded as a traditional symbol of the nation, also had a chequered history. Adopted by republicans as a populist image, he was liberally used in paintings, statues and elsewhere during the 1790s, but was ignominiously upstaged by the imperial eagle (back to classical antecedents). The cock was ignored by the Bourbons and reinstated by their cousin Louis-Philippe when he was made king in 1830. Although he was no longer specifically a republican cock, Marshal Soult had him replaced by a crown on military uniforms in the mid-1840s, with what consequences for the loyalty of the army in 1848 we do not know. We do know that after the February Revolution the republicans were quick to set unemployed embroiderers on to restoring him to naval and military uniforms. Louis-Napoleon found work for the same nimble fingers when the cock was again unpicked, this time in favour of the eagle. Only in the Third Republic was he allowed to resume a traditional 'popular' role, and he now crows, sometimes triumphantly, from France's rugby jerseys, among other places.

The human female form, both live and in effigy, was displayed to represent the 1789 Revolution, the First Republic and those virtues or goddesses deemed to epitomize the essential elements of both. There was nothing new in representing France as feminine, although the anti-feminism of Republic and Empire might, in retrospect, have given the image-makers pause for thought. Counter-revolutionaries often jeered at these allegories as 'Mariannes'. The name was simply one of the most commonly used girls' names at the time; a parallel in Britain of the 1990s might be Tracey. It signified at first merely the populist and probably rather vulgar connotations that the Right liked to attach to the Republic. The association of Marianne with a divinely inspired allegory of the Republic came later, in tandem with the elevation of the Christian Mary to divine status in the mid-nineteenth century. These later connotations proved more enduring, so that to observers at the end of the twentieth century, Marianne has become the timeless popular epitome of the Republic.

The revolutionary Marianne was always ambiguous. Top-hatted, tail-coated, middle-class citizens preferred fully dressed, mature, well-combed, calm female representations of the Republic in stone, bronze, or similar material. They would be adorned with a plethora of worthy, educational and highly moral symbols. Popular allegories of the Republic, such as those depicted on the Republican Calendar (see Plate 4 on p. xv) were more akin to our familiar page 3 beauties. This aggressively un-Christian new calendar, dating from 22 September 1792 when the republic had been declared, was adopted by the Convention in October 1793. The new months echoed the agricultural year beginning with *Vendémiaire*, the month of the wine harvest. Perhaps the lovely ladies were meant to reconcile the peasant to the three-week month, made up of ten *décadis*, each with new names of plants, animals and agricultural tools. The five remaining days in the year were to be given over to extra holidays (to make up a little for those lost week-ends). They were to be filled with festivals to celebrate republican qualities, talent (*génie*), industry, virtue, opinion and recompense. The calendar was used in official correspondence, often with old dates also indicated, until January 1806. (Fabre d'Eglantine, the calendar's inventor, was revealed as a financial whizz-kid swindler and guillotined in 1794.)

Wherever possible republican allegories would be live, young, well-rounded and semi-naked, with an obligatory phrygian cap. Statues or paintings were habitually encumbered with oversized suckling children, to represent the vitality of the Republic and presumably recalling images of the Virgin and Child. Honoré Daumier, the famous radical cartoonist who made Louis-Philippe into the immortal 'pear', honoured the Republic as an incredibly muscular earth-mother suckling two children with a third at her feet, whose own muscle-power and size suggest a more varied diet (see Plate 5 on p. xvi). The tricolour flag is clenched firmly and a laurel wreath recalls classical civic virtue. The uncluttered lines emphasize the uncompromising strength of this androgynous, awe-inspiring figure. (The painting, now in the Musée d'Orsay, was painted for a competition launched in March 1848 to find a figure for a medal to commemorate the 1848 Revolution. Daumier's sketch was placed eleventh out of twenty, but he never completed the final painting, nor was he paid the fee of 500 francs.)

There was a buoyant market in statuary to replace ubiquitous models of the guillotined king. They gradually became more warlike and by Year VIII the ladies had given way to columns, such as the Vendôme Column. Ladies re-emerged to symbolize the Republic in 1830 with the painting of Delacroix' famous bare-bosomed Liberty guiding the people (see Plate 6 on p. xvii) who may have represented an actual insurgent in the 1830 Revolution as well as being a symbol of the republic Delacroix had anticipated. She wears the phrygian cap, which the new Orleanist monarchy banned as threatening, and brandishes the flag of 1789, which the new monarchy adopted. With Notre Dame as a backcloth, the painting was too potent a recollection of popular revolution for Louis-Philippe to allow it to be displayed for long after its purchase by the State in 1831, and it spent all but a few months of the Orleanist monarchy in the basement of the Louvre.[11] (Delacroix subsequently undertook many official commemorative commissions in the Louve, Palais-Bourbon and Palais du Luxembourg for the regime.) In contrast to the curvaceous, banned Liberty, the enduring image of the Orleanist monarchy itself is male, but also a pear, thanks to Daumier. The Second Republic readopted the female allegory, as did the Third Republic, to distinguish itself from the man-on-horseback-pretending-to-be-Bonaparte image of Napoleon III.

Festivals and ceremonies were integral to the First Republic, offering publicity and entertainment, and filling the gap left by religious iconography and feast days. The fall of the Bastille was honoured annually and representations of the fortress, as well as pieces of its remains, were variously paraded and hawked. Plate 7 (on p. xvii) shows one such effigy being carried by four stout *sans-culottes* on 14 July 1792. The power of myth transcended the fact that there had been very few victims of tyranny in the Parisian fortress. Here the pall-bearers wear the costume of a militant patriot of 1792 – phrygian cap, red-and-white-and-blue striped pantaloons and sash, and a *carmagnole* top, whose name was the same as a famous revolutionary song. Busts representing liberty and other admirable qualities were carried, together with books to illustrate the importance of learning.[12]

Brightly coloured wood-block prints, the *Images d'Epinal*, were sold by hawkers and at fairs and did much to popularize whatever was the current vogue, here the Republic, later the Empire (see Plate 8 on p. xviii). The prints aimed to give value for money and to rival the pictures of saints. The one shown in Plate 8 was designed to celebrate the festival of the Supreme Being instituted by the Committee of Public Safety under Robespierre to replace catholicism root-and-branch. It almost brims over with symbolism: one buxom allegorical figure is flanked by a beehive, to indicate industry, and on the other side the results of labour, an overflowing horn of plenty (a somewhat ironical choice for a year of dearth). Her companion holds poles with both a tricolour flag and a phrygian cap and her left hand rests on a slab headed 'Rights of Man', which is ominously, but perhaps unintentionally, blank. At their feet is a plough, to reinforce the ideas of the Republic as the all-provider, and a grateful *sans-culotte* family. The scene is benevolently surveyed by the Egyptian eye, a rather chilling symbol of watchfulness. Both in 1830 and in 1848 the Orleanist monarchy and the Second Republic constructed their own festivals. The Orleanist regime revived the celebration of Bastille Day, but deliberately chose a midway position, requiring the Catholic Church to engage in religious celebrations of appropriate anniversaries, such as the fête day of the new monarch, in which the National Guard, brandishing tricolour flags, would parade in the church.

The republicans, outlawed after April 1834, and again in the early years of the Second Empire, used the funeral processions of leading adherents to rally supporters, a practice familiar to proscribed groups in our own day. In line with both Orleanist and republican tradition, the Second Republic held a funeral procession for those who died in the February Revolution, who were then buried at the foot of the July Column with the 1830 dead. The declaration of the Second Republic was celebrated with processions, fireworks and the illumination of public buildings.

One of the favourite ceremonies of the 1789 Revolution, adopted by the Republic, was the planting of a liberty tree, often a plane, usually surmounted by a phrygian cap. It was a continuation of the traditional planting of a sapling, or a Maypole, to celebrate the arrival of spring. The first liberty tree appears in the Rhône valley in May 1790 and in the next two years 60,000 were erected, not all with roots, some of them simple poles, all complete with traditional twined ribbons and revolutionary red caps. Plate 9 (see p. xix) illustrates a sapling of the early days of the First Republic being defended (presumably ineffectually) from the attacks of primitively armed marauding counter-revolutionary young 'brigands'. The decidedly heavy-handed recalling of the traditional fertility symbolism of the Maypole would have been at least as transparent in the 1790s as today. The practice was revived after the 1830 Revolution, sometimes as part of a display of popular anti-clericalism such as an attack on missionary crosses erected by touring evangelical priests during the Restoration. Prefects, mayors and National Guardsmen were often present at the tree-planting, although after the appointment of the conservative Périer ministry in March 1831, such official support for popular radicalism ended. A similar waning of official sanction for this popular ceremony occurred in 1848. Trees of liberty were vulnerable republican symbols. As regimes became more conservative, instructions were issued for trees to be felled, where this could be done discreetly, but many survived. Rarely do we know whether their longevity was due to republican affection, lethargy, or, as was recorded in one case during the Second Empire, beause the offending arboreal edifice was no sapling which would fall at a single blow, but had grown undisturbed and stoutly since the 1790s.

The National Guard was an essential part of such ceremonial/ carnival. The symbol of the 1789 Revolution in arms, the Guard had been formed in the early days of the Revolution both to defend revolutionary victories and to protect property. This ambiguous role persisted throughout the nineteenth century. The Guard was open to anyone who could afford the equipment and the time to drill. It included middle-class professionals, retired soldiers, artisans, wine-producers, and similar worthies. In 1814 the Bourbons retained the organization, but its association with the Revolution was such that Charles X dissolved it in 1827. Revived in 1830, honoured as an essential symbol of the new monarchy, in many areas it soon existed only on paper. However, in some towns, large and small, it became the nucleus of republican opposition, the democratic elections offering republicans, especially after 1834, their only opportunity to meet publicly with a common purpose. We shall encounter repeated incidents where the National Guard was on the side of radical critics, often fighting against the perceived evils of the economic policies of both Louis-Philippe and Louis-Napoleon. The radicalism of some National Guard battalions reached its peak during the Paris Commune of 1871 and this symbol of the revolutionary republic was finally dissolved by the Third Republic in 1876.

The images and ceremonies we have described were not always uniquely republican, nor were they uncontroversially adopted by republicans. Reference should also be made to popular songs, verses and plays which kept a republican idea alive, often in association with Bonapartist sentiments. This double ambiguity was also echoed in more formal written definitions of what the republic signified.

The Declaration of the Rights of Man of August 1789 is pivotal in any discussion of republicanism[13] today; bicentennial assessments of the Revolution were not complete without a reference to it, usually accompanied by an illustration of the document. There were several re-examinations of the previously somewhat disregarded text.[14] The Declaration was, of course, issued when the National Assembly was bent upon creating a constitutional monarchy, not a republic, although there was no reference to royal power in any of its 17 clauses. The repeated political upheaval of the revolutionary decades (1789–1814) was accompanied by constant constitution-writing. With each new constitution the Declaration of Rights was reworked, radically revised or eliminated. Most of these gradually lengthening declarations, like their constitutions, were subsequently forgotten. The 17-clause 1789 version of the Declaration headed the Constitution of 3 September 1791. It began with a general statement that the National Assembly, in the presence of the Supreme Being, recognized certain inalienable natural rights of the individual; liberty and equality; that social distinctions should based on the common good; that society should guarantee all men liberty, security for themselves and their property and the right to resist oppression; that sovereignty lay in the nation, which through its representatives made all law by which society should be regulated.

The 1791 Constitution lasted less than a year. The 1789 Declaration was even contested on grounds of gender,[15] but this was a challenge which most men and many women were delighted to ignore until feminists rediscovered it late in the twentieth century. The declaration of a republic in 1792 necessitated a new document and the Girondin and Jacobin factions in the new Assembly each produced rival versions. A Girondin draft constitution of February 1793 expanded the Declaration of Rights to 33 clauses but omitted the 1789 preamble which had explained why the Assembly thought a reminder of individual rights was needed.[16] The Girondin model emphasized the constitution as a 'social pact'; it abandoned the elitist franchise in favour of universal male suffrage and introduced a right of rebellion. Unlike the subsequent Jacobin model, which was also never implemented, although the Convention accepted it, the Girondin plan was soon forgotten. The Jacobin scheme,[17] which was much praised by republicans during the Orleanist monarchy, reverted to the 1789 preamble, except that the Declaration was proclaimed by 'the French people'. The Girondin decentralizing idea of allowing the primary electoral assemblies to discuss legislation was abandoned; sovereignty was to reside in an Assembly, which was to be elected by direct manhood suffrage. The 'social pact' disappeared, although the right of rebellion was retained.[18] This democratic constitution never came into operation and France was governed by a small committee of the Convention during the months of Jacobin dominance.

After Robespierre's overthrow his cautious enemies renamed the republic the Directory (1795–9) and published a constitution which was preceded by a Declaration of Rights and Duties.[19] The various Bonapartist constitutional laws of the Consulate (1799–1804) and Empire (1804–14) contained no statements on the rights of the citizen. The Restoration constitution (1814–30), despite its defiantly ultra-royalist proclamation of the divine right of the Bourbons to rule, included twelve clauses which encapsulated leading elements from the 1789 declaration.[20] Even Napoleon was obliged, after his escape from Elba and his reinstatement as emperor (1815), to reiterate all the promises made by the Bourbons.[21] In 1830 the Orleanist revision of the

Bourbon constitution (1830–48) began with a summary of the main principles of the 1789 declaration.[22]

The Second Republic (1848–52) was surprisingly negligent of historical precedent. The constitution-makers did not even attempt to equal the Orleanist declaration and certainly did not try to surpass it by copying the Jacobin declaration about which republicans had been so enthusiastic throughout the July Monarchy. In the constitution of November 1848 the 'duties' of citizens were summarized in clause 7, and the 'duties' of the republican government in clause 8, while subsequent clauses set out those rights which were to be guaranteed by the constitution.[23] The end result was a cautious and conservative statement, which included only restrained echoes of earlier declarations.

Napoleon III's imperial (1852–70) constitution of 15 January 1852 spoke of government and the President, but, like the constitutions of the First Empire, ignored the rights of the citizen.[24] The Third Republic (1870–1940) never included a declaration of rights within the various very practical and pragmatic laws by which it edged itself into permanency.[25] It was left to the preamble of the constitution of the Fourth Republic (1946–58) in 1946, repeated in the Fifth Republic in 1958, to reconstruct the idea of continuity with 1789. It affirmed: 'The French people solemnly proclaim their attachment to the Rights of Man and the principles of National Sovereignty as defined by the Declaration of 1789'.[26] Today the Declaration of 1789 is honoured, but all the other Declarations, except the Jacobin project of 1793 which Marxists liked, tend to be forgotten. In the nineteenth century the Declaration of 1789 was summarized in monarchist constitutions and left out of republican ones. It was, and is, important at the level of republican rhetoric, mythology and emotional commitment.

All would agree that the revolutionary principles of liberty, equality and fraternity are central to any definition of republicanism, with the proviso that they too were first enunciated during the constitutional monarchy. Superficially they might seem to require little explanation or qualification. In actuality the content and significance of each component of the triumvirate varied over time and republicans' arguments over these fundamental concepts became far more than a matter of semantics and fine-tuning. An analysis of what each meant, at different times, will be central to this book. What were the limits of liberty, both personal and political? Despite the claims of the Declaration of Rights, republicans created a new unfreedom with Jacobin concepts of republican virtue. During the nineteenth century republicans demanded freedom of expression, association and religion, but the more radical were inclined to be as intolerant as their Jacobin predecessors.

How did liberty and equality fare in the public sphere? During the First Republic some republicans favoured universal suffrage, but never for women. But commitment to representative institutions was more problematical. Rousseau had argued against representation. The legacy of the First Republic was diverse and divisive. Recourse to repressive political methods was a feature of the beleaguered governments of the First Republic, particularly the Jacobin period of rule by the Committee of Public Safety. It has even been argued that the Jacobin Terror was less a response to an emergency, than a vital stage in the evolution of the republic.

Many republicans served Napoleon as officials, army officers and as members of the various assemblies. In doing so did they become less republican, or were they convinced by the emperor's claims that he had completed the Revolution? In the Hundred Days in 1815 there was an even closer fusion between Bonapartism and the republicans.[27] During the Restoration and July Monarchy many retained sympathies with both republicanism and Bonapartism, although in 1848 Louis-Napoleon was rarely the beneficiary of such enthusiasm. In the Second Empire Louis-Napoleon tried to construct a parliamentary framework out of authoritarian beginnings, while restoring the plebiscitary corset invented by his great-uncle. At that time republicans denigrated plebiscites as fundamentally unfree. But since 1958 a Fifth French Republic has created a presidential plebiscitary regime so tolerable to the French that in 1993 a socialist president could cohabit with an Assembly containing only a tiny minority of socialists.

Parliamentary, representative government was not part of the republican tradition in the early nineteenth century. After 1830 the new republican movement began to favour a democratic franchise; democracy was envisaged as a instant solution to injustice and not specifically defined. The insurrectionary Blanqui was exceptional in his claim that a republic would need an interim period of dictatorship. The Second Republic taught republicans that the masses were not innately republican and that additional safeguards and preparation would be essential to ensure that democratic methods led to a republican regime.

Equality was just as controversial a principle. 1789 and the subsequent republic were, above all, an onslaught on privilege. The institutionalization of equality was deemed vital in the quest for a rational structure of society. Equality became a revolutionary principle and a republican slogan, ultimately signifying little more than the right of those who possessed military power to have their way. The equality of the individual (male only) was spelled out in the Codes of the Consulate and Empire, not the republic. But only the wealthy could effectively assert these claims.

Closely associated with equality and the most divisive element of the revolutionary trio was *fraternité*, which defies precise definition beyond such platitudes as 'a sympathetic awareness of the masses in politics'. It was seriously regarded by left-wingers, and was expressed in a variety of ways ranging from vague humanitarian, philanthropic sentiments to socialism and egalitarian communism. It found very practical expression when a generation of nineteenth-century republican doctors offered their services free to the poor and republicans ran evening classes in basic literacy. Fraternity took on a new meaning in the 1840s as socialist ideas developed.[28] Socialists were assumed to be republican. But all republicans did not become socialists and socialists had very diverse notions of the ideal state, even though they usually called it a republic. It must also be recalled that respect for liberty, equality and fraternity was not and is not confined to republicans.

Problems of definitions were part of the explanation of why the creation of a permanent republic presented so many difficulties to the French in the nineteenth century. Two final aspects remain, anti-clericalism and patriotism. Surely one uncontested element in republicanism is anti-clericalism, or put positively, the primacy of lay authority in the state?

Anti-clericalism was certainly important to republicans during the nineteenth century and is very much alive today. The institutional and economic framework of the Catholic Church was under profound attack from the early days of the 1789 Revolution. Those who supported the Revolution were all anti-clerical, whether they were constitutional monarchists or republicans. Many revolutionaries purchased the sequestrated church lands which were sold during the 1790s. Justifying their retention after 1814 necessarily involved a continuing commitment to anti-clericalism, especially during the Restoration's nationwide evangelical campaign to ask God's forgiveness for the Revolution. The cotton industry of Alsace was to a large extent located in former church property, much of it previously owned by religious orders. It was run by families, many of them Protestant, committed to 1789, who were liberal leaders in the 1820s, organizers of republican clubs in the 1830s and 40s and senior figures in the Second

Republic. They had, of course, confessional as well as ideological and economic reasons to be anti-clerical.

However, republicans were not alone in arguing for a lay state; the liberals who set up the July Monarchy were motivated in part by suspicion of the pro-clerical politics of Charles X (1824–30) and sustained in their take-over of power in 1830 by popular anti-clerical attitudes. In 1830–1 anti-clerical riots were encouraged by some officials of the July Monarchy,[29] although more conservative Orleanists quickly saw profit for themselves in an accommodation with the Church. However the Orleanists also began to create lay primary schools (Guizot Law, 1833) and lay training colleges for primary school teachers, which destroyed any chance of them acquiring the confidence of the Church.

The Church was so suspicious of the July Monarchy's initiatives in education that it greeted the Second Republic with relief, fielding candidates favourable to the Republic in the elections of April 1848. Such an alliance might seem totally inconsistent, but there were precedents. During the previous regime republicans and legitimists had sometimes cooperated to defeat Orleanists in elections and fear of their electoral deals caused Orleanist prefects like Achille Chaper in Dijon to lose sleep. The republicans of the Second Republic were not consistently anti-clerical. The Second Republic's major piece of legislation on education, the Falloux Law (1849), encouraged the expansion of schools run by religious orders, but it could be argued that this law was the work of very tepid 'republicans' running scared after the June Days.

In the 1860s a new generation of resolutely anti-clerical republicans emerged. The Ferry Laws completed the process of creating lay schools at all levels of education (1879–82) and in 1905 the separation of Church and state was finally decreed. This Third Republican legislation ensured the permanent marriage of republicanism and anti-clericalism, but such a monogamous relationship was far less identifiable earlier in the century. The honeymoon between republicans and the Church in 1848 was brief, but to define republicanism as simply 'anti-clerical' would be to ignore some interesting manoeuvrings and missed opportunities, such as the liberal catholic movement and its links with emergent socialism.

Anti-clericalism was central to the republican tradition and the anti-clerical institutional changes of the 1790s were never reversed. But they were also the most contentious and the biggest failure in the fight for men's (and women's) minds. The persecution of the Catholic Church was the most important single stimulus of opposition to the Revolution and the Republic in the 1790s, creating counter-revolutionary attitudes, and opposition to a republic as such, well beyond the nineteenth century. In 1796 the ultra-royalist writer Joseph de Maistre declared that the Revolution was satanic in inspiration. It was God's punishment on a sinful people.[30] The Church provided the confessional heart of opposition to the Revolution. It is unlikely that there would have been much of a counter-revolution, especially at a popular level, if there had only been the monarchy and nobles as foci.

Yet republicans were far from hostile to religion as such, certainly until the 1860s. A spiritual foundation for society and the state was considered to be as important as mass education. In trying to invent a new religion of the Supreme Being Robespierre had believed that faith in an omniscient spirituality was vital to man. Alexis de Tocqueville observed that, although at the time the revolutionaries appeared to be hostile to religion as such, in reality they were merely seeking to purge the political power which clerics had acquired.[31] Quinet, the great liberal intellectual writer of the mid-nineteenth century, believed that 1789 was above all spiritual in inspiration, a failed attempt to renew man's sense of his destiny.[32] The liberal historian Michelet, writing in the aftermath of the religious revival of the first half of the nineteenth century, went much further. For him a Christian god was central to the Revolution. Biblical imagery permeates his account of the 1790s. However he recognized the contradictions present in the period. 'The Revolution both continues Christianity and contradicts it. It is at once its heir and its adversary.'[33] Michelet's comments are pertinent in reminding us that, although republicans had not time for the hierarchy of Catholicism, they were not atheists.

Patriotism must be included in any republican 'catechism'. The rights of the citizen and nation were lauded in a First Republic desperate for men to fight for the Revolution at home and abroad. Simultaneously counter-revolutionaries were branded as traitors; émigrés in the Austrian Empire and elsewhere fought against France in the revolutionary wars.[34] Patriotism was firmly republican. The huge success of the revolutionary armies added a substantial Bonapartist and imperial slant, which reversed the original liberal impetus in favour of conquest and national glory, a taste which the defeats of 1814–15 did not obliterate.

The restored Bourbons, put back on the throne by France's enemies in ignominious circumstances, found it difficult to change this orientation. Although Charles X launched France's successful colonial expansion with the beginning of the conquest of Algeria in 1830, his enforced abdication meant that the Bourbons gained no credit for this African Empire. Republicans tried to maintain a monopoly of the patriotic high ground during the July Monarchy, but they were forced to share it with radical monarchists who in 1830/1 noisily demanded French intervention in revolts elsewhere. The leading radical daily was *Le National* and in the early 1830s many of the local radical/republican newspapers included 'patriot' in their names. However, many of those who criticized Louis-Philippe's governments for their lack of nationalist enterprise were radical monarchists rather than republicans.

The Second Republic proved disappointing in its ambiguous and modest support for revolution abroad and its decision to back the Papacy in its struggle with Mazzini and Garibaldi.[35] On the other hand, the Second Empire, hardly a left-wing republican regime, reasserted Bonapartist nationalism. But Louis-Napoleon's disasters in Mexico and limited successes in the Crimea and Italy served to discredit his nationalist image. An increasing number of his army officers were members of legitimist monarchist families. They were to be part of a right-wing nationalist movement under the Third Republic, when patriotism most definitely could no longer be defined exclusively as a liberal and liberating creed of the left.

While all of these elements constitute some of the main ingredients which republicans from the 1790s to the present day would recognize as aspects of the republican idea, it is important to put them into context. Concepts do not exercise an influence in isolation. In September 1792 a republic was less an ideal, or even an idea, than a response to invasion, at a time when the king was suspected of being in cahoots with the enemy. What is often forgotten by republican historians, and must be seen as in many ways the most important observation in any investigation of the ideas behind nineteenth-century republicanism, is that on 22 September 1792 the First Republic was set up in a dangerous and desperate emergency, when France was shaken by both civil war and foreign invasion. Ideals and theory were secondary to survival among educated middle-class republicans who undoubtedly placed great store on idealism in their speeches. In 1848 and again in 1870, when renewed attempts were made to create republican regimes, the circumstances were also those of crisis, political, economic, and in 1870, yet another Prussian invasion. At each juncture there was conflict between the urgent need for instant solutions of immediate problems and the conviction that a republic would be the final, perfect form of government for 'men full-grown'.

Republicans only got their chance to govern when times were out of joint and invariably quite inappropriate for the innovative institutional changes which they believed were needed. Like the enlightened writers who were their mentors, republicans were convinced that man and society could be perfected by education and institutional change. Because they tended to want radical reform, republicans were always a minority. Throughout the century many Frenchmen, most French-women and the governing elites of all of the major states of Europe bitterly rejected republican 'virtue' as dangerously disruptive. The legacy of the First Republic was bloody and contentious, as well as inspirational.

Revolution and republic were and are often treated as interchangeable, both as ideas and policies, and as the process by which change was effected. Any investigation of nineteenth-century republicanism which goes beyond polemic must distinguish both between revolution and republic and between policies and process. In the nineteenth century the republic and the 1789 Revolution were invariably treated as synonymous both by right-wing detractors and by republicans themselves who turned to the republican past in default of a republican present and in the wistful hope of a republican future. Obviously it would have been unthinkable in the nineteenth century to have claimed to be a republican and to have denied the legacy of 1789. But republicans were not alone in the nineteenth century in claiming to be heirs of 1789; liberal monarchists and Bonapartists demanded their share.

Commitment to the 1789 Revolution in its various subsequent manifestations tended to be as permanent as it was ambiguous. Ideological conviction, a career in government, the purchase of *biens nationaux*, some or all of these, would mark a man and his family and probably those they married through succeeding generations in the nineteenth century. A researcher in the national archives who asks for a personnel file of an individual prefect without the full Christian name risks being presented with a grandson, great-nephew or some other member of the dynasty. Far fewer families were specifically and continuously republican. Many had taken jobs with Napoleon. Many hoped initially that the compromise of 1814 would work. Between 1814 and 1870 the distinction between republicans and liberal monarchists was often very blurred. There were no separate republican groups until after the 1830 Revolution. Republicans of the July Monarchy (1830–48) had been liberal monarchists during the Restoration (1814–30). Many also retained Bonapartist sympathies. Left-wing monarchist opponents of the July Monarchy along with some more conservative Orleanists usually converted to the republic after February 1848. Others drew nearer to the republicans during the 1860s. It was a policy of opportunistic osmosis, seldom based on any real difference of principle. The individuals and families involved in this seepage habitually had a shared background of support for aspects of the 1789 Revolution.

In 1830 liberal monarchists considered themselves heirs of 1789, a claim loudly refuted by republicans. In the 1860s republicans began to ally with the same liberal monarchists in pursuit of parliamentary advantage and political reform.[36] Their alliance proved a fruitful basis for the compromise republic which succeeded in establishing itself after 1870. Once the Third Republic was secure, however, republican historians again asserted the uniqueness of the link between 1789 and the republic. After 1870 when there was no viable alternative to a republic, the claims of republicans to be the sole heirs of 1789 were understandable, but the history of nineteenth-century republicanism is more credible if one remembers that revolution and republic were not always identical.

If there was conflict over the inheritance of 1789 as a finished product, liberal monarchists were more than happy to leave republicans as undisputed heirs of revolution as a process. For them the Revolution was over and further violent change detestable. Republicans were ambivalent. After 1830, when an identifiable republican movement emerged, few republicans openly welcomed violent insurrection as a route to their ideal state. Indeed republican lawyers were inclined to be quite lyrical about their pacific intentions.[37] However, republican clubs always included the obligation to carry arms and undertake military training among their rules.[38]

Enthusiasm for the ideas and symbols of 1789 were major, if controversial, factors in nineteenth-century republicanism. In addition, and with even greater conflict, the definition of republican objectives became intertwined with projected solutions to the problems created by economic change. Popular republicanism had important social elements from the outset. Successive generations of peasants were committed to the revolutionary republic because feudal tenancies and the tithe had been abolished and because the sale of church lands enabled some to extend their holdings. Some, like Julien Sorel, believed that the revolutionary years had been a time of opportunity for ambitious lads. The inheritance was fraught with ambiguity. The revolutionaries had continued the old regime attack on communal property and had passed the Le Chapelier law which demanded that artisans carry a work-book. The revolutionary years saw the revival of detested indirect taxes. Yet in some regions popular enthusiasm for a revolutionary tradition, sometimes republican, often Bonapartist, persisted in the nineteenth century. It was usually displayed at times of economic crisis through sporadic violent rebellion against any established authority and the display of (sometimes homemade) republican or imperial symbols.

Artisan republicans, for not all republicans were bourgeois classicists, found themselves in a number of violent altercations with merchants and other proto-capitalists in defence of their way of life in these years. Somewhat ironically, since the 1789 Revolution had continued the onslaught on guilds and artisan independence, artisans believed, perhaps fortified by recollections of the Jacobin period of the First Republic, that revolutionary and republican ideas would protect them. Peasants tended to assume that radical and republican politicians were bound to sympathize with their intermittent violent complaints about the Forest Laws and other inroads into communal traditions in addition to their more frequent demonstrations about bread prices and indirect taxes. The confidence of artisans and peasants was not always well-founded.

As socialist ideas became associated with republicanism in the 1830s, the pressure to renounce revolution as a method grew, with the exception of a tiny number of extremists. Most socialists denounced violent confrontation. But the link with socialism made republicanism seem more threatening than ever to men of property, for a small number of socialists would have liked private property-owning to disappear and it was difficult to see how that could be achieved peacefully. Other socialists argued for an interventionist state to protect the victims of economic change, an almost equally revolution ary proposal to the elite.

Republicans did not create the three main revolutionary episodes in nineteenth-century France: the July Days in 1830 followed by subsequent sporadic unrest until 1834; the February Revolution and June Days in 1848, also succeeded by disturbances of various sorts until early 1852; finally the collapse of the Second Empire in September 1870 accompanied by urban conflict, culminating in the Paris Commune of March–May 1871. These violent upheavals were the product of a range of problems: social grievances resulting from short-term economic crisis in addition to the sócial problems already mentioned; political argument within the governing elite; military disaster in 1870; the subsequent panic of the *notables* when the coincidence of the political, social and economic crises made Paris, capital of the most centralized state in Europe and the fastest growing industrial nucleus in the country, volatile and hard to control. Although none of these periods of sustained political, social and economic uncertainty were republican in genesis, radical alterations in the political structure of the state were seen as solutions to the difficulties encountered. In nineteenth-century France a republic was considered the most radical solution and in 1848 and 1870 when those in charge panicked, republicans were left with the opportunity to govern.

While the idea of the republic is associated with the 1789 Declaration of the Rights of Man, images and notions of liberty, equality and fraternity, anti-clericalism and patriotism, this brief introduction indicates that the legacy, whether in memory, on paper or in stone or on canvas, was far from a republican monopoly. The republican inheritance of the 1790s was idealistic and moral; on that there is little dispute. There is broad agreement on certain components of republicanism, but even today the accord is tenuous, often illusory and exists more in the realms of mythology than political reality. In the nineteenth century attempts to agree on what the republic of the 1790s had meant, and the extent to which it could provide a blueprint for a new republic, stimulated more conflict than convergence, as the following chapters will show.

2   Historians and the Republic

Until the creation of the Fifth Republic in 1958 the republic always divided Frenchmen, those who welcomed 1789 honouring it, counter-revolutionaries detesting it. Its history became part catechism, part epic; for opponents a major factor in the decline of France and the French spirit; for the one, hagiography, for the other, demonology. This chapter will leave the demonologists on one side and concentrate on some of the more sympathetic writers, often also active politicians in the nineteenth century, who have tried to explain the significance of republicanism.

Since many republicans and Bonapartists were forcibly unemployed after Waterloo, apologist accounts of the revolutionary years soon began to appear. Still-ambitious redundant politicians were keen to place their own revolutionary careers in a good light. The popularity of historical writing of all kinds in these years provided a ready market. The Revolution was always portrayed as the progressive liberation, enlightenment and rational development of the human spirit, or as a recent work of literary criticism remarks, betraying late twentieth-century assumptions, 'theoretical fiction'.[1] Writers tended to describe the Revolution as an entity, running revolution and republic together. Descriptions of the 1789 Revolution also served as vehicles in which to display the inadequacies of the Restoration and to hint at acceptable alternatives to the Bourbons. The constitutional monarchy (1789–92) and the early phase of the First Republic (1792–3) were praised by those who found the counter-revolutionary aspirations of the ultra-royalists detestable. Titillating tales of gore and violence were perennial best-sellers. Between 1821 and 1828, 53 volumes of revolu-tionary memoirs were brought out by one publisher alone, who had originally planned a mere 12-volume collection.[2] The thirst for accounts of the Revolution became so pronounced that novelists such as Balzac and Hugo wrote fictionalized 'memoirs' of the period.

Towards the end of the Restoration the pace grew and more attention was focused on the Jacobin years (1793–4).[3] Writers like Thiers and Mignet,[4] when they were not writing for opposition newspapers, began to rescue Danton, Marat, Robespierre and the Convention from the pit of ignominy and total disgrace into which they had been cast by their detractors during the Directory, Consulate and Empire. The Terror was passed over quickly and regretfully, in contrast to the way in which the Directory and Napoleon had emphasized its horrors. The chroniclers stressed the patriotism of the men of the First Republic, who had reversed the initially disastrous war of 1792 and liberated French territory from the invading Prussians. Comparisons with 1814–15, the resented Peace of Paris and the occupation by Allied troops provided barely veiled criticism of the Bourbons. Thiers and Mignet summarized the Revolution as the triumph of the Third Estate over absolutism at a time when, in the 1820s, liberals were doing battle with ultra-royalist counter-revolutionaries. In 1828 even the communist Babeuf could be defended in print by his former fellow-conspirator, Buonarroti,[5] albeit via a Brussels publisher.

After the 1830 Revolution the victorious liberals, now the Orleanists and the ultra-royalists, now termed legitimists, were in accord that the July Revolution completed 1789. The Orleanists sighed with relief, the legitimists with elegant despair. The experience of 1830 stimulated many comparisons with the 1790s, especially among radicals rapidly disillusioned with the new Orleanist monarchy.[6] If speculation on a future republic was outlawed by prohibitive censorship in 1835, praise for past glories was the next best thing. Socialist historians like Etienne Cabet[7] depicted 1789 and 1830 as social as well as political revolutions. In their defence of the nobility, clergy and the crown and their criticism of the bourgeois beneficiaries of 1789, ultra-royalist anti-revolutionary commentators had already made this theme familiar.[8] Legitimists were venomous in their hatred and contempt for the bourgeois revolution which had robbed the nobility and Church of their lands and influence and executed the king. Socialists, in contrast, were delighted to see in the events of the 1790s the first major battle in the liberation of the poor. Cabet had hoped that 1830 would complete the process, but instead argued that it had been a mere confirmation of bourgeois power, a '*révolution escamotée*', smuggled away from the artisans who made it.[9] The republic he awaited would be the final liberation.

As well as comparing 1830 and 1789 in order to criticize the Orleanists, acounts of the 1790s became more analytical. Quinet[10] and Buchez and Roux began to write their versions,[11] the one eulogizing the poor, the other the role of elected assemblies. Quinet, a professor at the *Collège de France*, was pronouncedly anti-clerical, but argued that the Christian faith was central to the Revolution. Buchez was a republican and in the 1830s it had become the norm for republicans to highlight the democratic aspirations of the revolutionaries of the 1790s, hence his emphasis on the assemblies. Buchez did not neglect the poor or religion. He held Saint-Simonian and Christian beliefs and insisted that the Revolution was essentially both a class struggle and vitally important for Christians, which interpretation most members of the Catholic Church would have found contradictory, but socialists considered very satisfactory.

By the 1840s there was greater emphasis on the more contentious aspect of the 1790s, the Convention, the Terror and Robespierre. Between 1846 and the outbreak of the February Revolution four influential accounts of 1789 appeared, including the first volumes of the liberal, passionate and influential thesis of Michelet. For Michelet the Revolution was the apocalyptic liberation of an oppressed people from the tyranny of a grasping ruler.[12] Lamartine's romantic appraisal of the Girondins, which he explained was 'full of blood and tears, is full also of instruction for the people' was a popular success, despite its factual errors. Lamartine, a poet and member of the Chamber of Deputies, was also interested in the social inequalities of his own day.[13] The republican socialists Louis Blanc[14] and Esquiros,[15] even more profoundly and constructively concerned with contemporary socio economic change, told a more political story of the Revolution. Louis Blanc was already well established as an apologist for the Jacobin period of the Republic, but others introduced their readers to earlier, more moderate and therefore more palatable and respectable aspects of the Republic. By 1848 the First Republic, a negative and terrifying vision of Terror for nearly half a century, had been transformed by such accounts of the events of the Revolution into a democratic (in principle) and socially aware stage in the liberation of the French people.

The creation of a Second Republic and the rapid election of another Bonaparte to its presidency made nirvana seem far more complicated and remote. De la Hodde's investigation of secret societies and the republican party, published in 1850, supplied proof that there was a republican movement before 1848 with detailed lists of those involved in different events and organizations. It was well used by subsequent writers.[16] The disarray of the republicans themselves belied the neatness of de la Hodde's lists. The failures of 1848 became exercises in mutual recrimination when retold in exile. Those who recalled the disasters of the Second Republic during the Second Empire were, as always, failed politicians, anxious to justify their role in 1848,[17] as well as to show the continuity of 1848 with 1789. The need to explore, and where necessary, embroider, a republican tradition, was all the more marked because of the double failure of 1830 and the Second Republic and underscored by the resurrection of a Bonaparte. A second dictatorship in 50 years made it difficult to sustain the idea that the Revolution and subsequent republican tradition were a story of the liberation of the French people. The increasing intervention of the state in the lives of people also strained the claim that 1789 was a story of progress and liberty.

Socialist participants in the Second Republic also had problems in equating the reality of 1848 with their own theories. Louis Blanc, disappointed with the National Workshops of 1848 and appalled by the June Days, retreated into exile until 1870. In London he composed, not only an account of 1848 with himself centre-stage, but also a 12-volume history of the 1789 Revolution. Despite the events of 1848 Blanc continued to believe that the accession to power of the middle class in 1789 was an individualistic revolution which would eventually lead to the triumph of liberty and fraternity. The revolution he described was an affair of ideas, in which socio-economic factors were accidental circumstances. His account owed far more to Guizot than Marx.

Louis Blanc was not unique among socialists who rarely believed that revolution was a harbinger of the social reform they desired. Before Marx socialists were disinclined to link 1789, 1830 and 1848 causally with economic change. Although they generally argued that 1789 and 1830 were 'bourgeois' revolutions, they believed that the genesis of these upheavals, as well as that of 1848, was political conflict. All but Blanqui assumed that a socialist alternative to capitalism would be introduced peacefully, not through revolution. They were uncomfortably aware of social conflict between the bourgeoisie and the proletariat, but they were convinced that this should not be exploited by revolutionary means. For the early socialists class rivalries were a consequence of capitalism which had to be eliminated by institutional change and education.

Marx, on the other hand, assumed that all history was fundamentally predicated on class conflict. For him, 1789 was a middle-class revolt against aristocratic feudalism, 1830 the triumph of a financial bourgeoisie, while 1848 witnessed the success of a middling bourgeoisie. The June Days conveniently epitomized the first class-conscious rising of the proletariat.[18] It was naked class war, when the elite showed its true colours and destroyed all hope that 1848 would be a 'social' revolution. Along with Bloody Week at the end of the 1871 Paris Commune, the June Days became part of the martyrology of republicanism.

Marx and the liberal monarchist de Tocqueville[19] both have a share in the responsibility for this highly charged interpretation and both have exerted a dominant, if divergent, influence over subsequent writers and politicians. The view that the June Days heralded the demolition of a social republic and constituted a major battle in a class war was attractive to disappointed socialists like Marx, looking for scapegoats, and to frightened members of the elite like de Tocqueville, but it was not the whole story. It assumed that the National Workshops, whose closure provoked the June Days, were an attempt at major social innovation, an interpretation which would not have been shared by Louis Blanc and most contemporary socialists. However, it became part of a republican 'catechism' for later socialist historians. Marx had apparently discerned a rational pattern in what hitherto appeared to be unmitigated disaster and his interpretation, with its hope for the future, eventually took hold of the republican imagination, blending well with the equally apocalyptic qualities of Michelet and other liberals.

De Tocqueville's study of the origins of the 1789 Revolution[20] had an even greater influence than that of Marx. With the demise of a Marxist interpretation of the Revolution, he is receiving more acclaim than ever towards the end of the twentieth century.[21] A member of a legitimist family of *notables*, he disappointed his family by taking the oath to the Orleanist regime. From 1839 he was a liberal parliamentary critic of the July Monarchy, already praised for his 1835 study of American democracy. He was a member of the constitutional committee for the Second Republic and briefly Minister for Foreign Affairs in 1849. It was in his posthumously published memoirs that he expressed his loathing of what he saw as the selfish demands of the Parisian workers in June 1848.[22] Jailed momentarily at the coup d'état in 1851 and subsequently out of politics, he spent the rest of his life on his investigation into the Revolution, which was one of the most analytical to date.

De Tocqueville broke away from the tradition which had made the revolutionary years a romantic account of the liberation of an oppressed people from the enslavement of a monarch. He was more concerned with their oppression by the state. He set out to explain why it was that the reforming impetus of 1789 resulted in a centralized dictatorship, deeply conscious that a second republic had led to yet another dictatorship in his own time. He drew attention to the high degree of centralization of the pre-1789 monarchy itself. While agreeing that hostility to the Church had been a fundamental philosophical impetus to revolution, unlike earlier writers de Tocqueville emphasized the political and economic, rather than anti-religious, aspects of anti-clericalism. For him the revolutionary years had been above all an attempt to dismantle the enormous political and economic power of the aristocratically-led Catholic Church.

Although a fairly conservative liberal, de Tocqueville, in common with socialist writers like Cabet, viewed 1789 as the beginning of an essentially social revolution which ended in 1830. He believed the years between were years of constant conflict between a new France of the middle classes and the old France of the aristocracy. He considered that 1830 brought the victory of these middle classes and that further revolution in 1848 was the product of too narrow a concentration on the interests of a tiny political elite, a failure to listen to the demands of parliamentary reformers, of whom he was one of the more moderate. (De Tocqueville did not lack ambition.[23])

With the demise of the Second Empire in 1870, and the final creation of a stable republic, it became possible to write a credible account of republicanism for the first time. Third Republic historians of a conservative bent were keen to assert the credentials of their own brand of republicanism and distinguish the constitutional arrangements of their republic from those of the liberal Empire of 1870, which in reality they closely resembled. For them republicanism was quintessentially democratic and non-revolutionary. The republican tradition and movement of the nineteenth century, they argued, had been thwarted by repeated revolution. The prolific Third Republic historian, lawyer and former Second Empire bureaucrat, Thureau-Dangin, had a notable influence upon conservative successors, for he said what they wanted to hear.[24] Writing in 1874, when monarchists still had expectations of the restoration of some sort of royalty, he was anxious to lecture contemporary monarchists on unity and republicans on the folly of 'that fatal and sterile circle of revolutions'.[25]

Georges Weill and Chernov, the most influential Third Republic historians of nineteenth-century republicanism, judging by their presence in footnotes, especially those of Anglo-Saxon sceptics of the Marxist tradition, shared Thureau-Dangin's scorn of revolution. Weill's account of the republican movement from 1814 to 1870 was first published in 1900 and several times reprinted, most recently in 1987.[26] In this influential work the moderate Third Republic was seen as the culmination of a democratic process which began in 1789 and a single republican movement which was in existence from 1814 to 1870. His is a history of high politics. His republicans are serious, sincere, always motivated by political considerations of the highest order, or rather they ought to have been. Weill has rather a schoolmasterly, didactic tone. He is frequently at odds with the actual republicans of earlier years. He had no time for insurrection and conspiracy. For him republicanism meant the triumph of democracy; revolution was its enemy, not its agent. He wrote a history of men, events and of ideas; economic and social trends are absent from his text and so little considered that they are not even dismissed as irrelevant. When he refers in passing to 'workers' and 'peasants' they are shadowy and insubstantial wraiths.

From the comparative security of the *lycée* Carnot in the 1890s, Weill stated that the cause of democracy was never advanced by insurrection. The 1830 Revolution itself had been such a blow to monarchy and the republican movement grew so rapidly in the following years that its success would have been assured, Weill claimed, had it not been dragged down by association with insurrection and the apologists of Robespierre. Instead republicans persisted in their faith in revolutionary means, refusing to acknowledge that a secure republic needed the sanction of, and respect for, the law. In line with his anti-insurrectionary inclinations, Weill ends his study in 1870, omitting all mention of the Paris Commune.[27] His interpretation has always pleased liberal, non- or anti-socialist and anti-Marxist historians, but it gives an incomplete impression of its subject.

Chernov's studies of the republicans from the July Monarchy to the Second Empire, published between 1901 and 1906, never achieved the acclaim, or the number of editions of those of Weill, but they are often quoted.[28] Chernov claimed that, as a constitutional lawyer, he was trying not to write an abstract philosophical treatise, but to trace the actual strategies employed by republicans in these years. For both Weill and Chernov pre-1870 republicanism had to fit into their democratic, but otherwise rather conservative view of post-1870 republicanism. For both writers the First Republic was a warning, not a model for the future. Their occasional references to 'the Mountain' are made in the condemnatory tone of an Orleanist official. For both of them the poor were a powerful, but basically passive force, about whom almost nothing had to be said and whose needs were satisfied by the creation of parliamentary democracy. Chervov's exploration of social questions did not go beyond a summary of the ideas of various socialist writers. Neither wasted much ink on the means by which a republic eventually emerged; both assumed that words counted for much more than fighting. Both designate the republicans as a 'party', yet spend much of their time describing the divisions and differences between them. The liberal historical tradition which they epitomized proved very durable. In 1931 Perreux[29] relied heavily on Chernov and both writers are a notable source for revisionists today.

A very different approach to the origins of the republic took off with preparations for the centenary of 1789. In 1881 a committee was set up to organize a fitting remembrance; in 1887 the periodical *La Révolution Française* was started. This was edited by Aulard, who a year earlier, in 1886, had launched a course on the history of the Revolution at the Sorbonne, jointly financed by Paris and the central government. In 1891 a Chair in the history of the Revolution was inaugurated at the Sorbonne. The government convened an historical commission to collect and publish documents on the Revolution, the fruits of whose labours, still used by present-day researchers of the Revolution, give a clear indication of *fin-de-siècle* orthodoxy. The way in which the surviving official records of the revolutionary republic of the 1790s were prepared and presented in bound volumes gives an overwhelming impression of a centralized, bureaucratic Jacobin state.[30] To a remarkable extent the archivist created a view of the Revolution which acted as a straitjacket for subsequent historians.

In 1901 Aulard brought out his study of the political history of the Revolution, which was very expressive of a radical–socialist view, with a distinct partiality for Danton. Jaurès, whose doctoral thesis was examined by Aulard, put the socialist case, which he believed complemented that of Aulard. Rival schools of revolutionary orthodoxy grew up. Mathiez, who ran the *Société des Etudes Robespierristes* and edited the *Annales Historiques de la Révolution Française* completed his predictably Robespierrist account of 1789. He stressed the role of the poor, compared the experiences of France in the First World War with those of the 1790s, and like the bulk of his contemporaries believed that 1789 was the first of a series of revolutions which reached a crescendo in the Bolshevik Revolution in Russia. His belief that the Communists were the fitting heirs to the Jacobins was not shaken until 1933.[31]

Since the early years of the twentieth century, when the Third Republic had proved its durability by surviving longer than any other post-revolutionary regime, French historians, with the exception of right-wingers, generally shared two other assumptions about republicanism. First, that after the collapse of the First Republic the restoration of a permanent republican regime had only been a matter of time. Secondly, most believed that this ideal republic would be an anti-clerical, centralized state which they thought was in a 'Jacobin' tradition, modelled on aspects of the First Republic. But the dominant creed, because it was assumed that only then would perfection be attained, was socialist. The republic would become a proletarian state and ultimately, a classless society. The republican orthodoxy of the Third Republic was unchangingly a compound of Jacobin–Marxist millenarianism until after the Second World War.

The first of these presuppositions, that France was predestined to be a republic, produced some startling interpretations of evidence, which lay undetected for long periods. The leading historian of his generation, Seignobos, totally ignored reality in claiming that the majority in the Constituent Assembly of 1848 were actually republicans in the mould of *Le National*, when they were opportunist legitimist and Orleanist post-revolution converts.[32] When the Second Republic collapsed historians looked for traitors and martyrs instead of accepting that there was little support for a republic at any time in 1848. Thus the history of the Second Republic, in the hands of Third Republic historians, became a cacophony of error, deception and missed opportunity. The failure of 1848 had denied France's natural destiny to become a republic. A similar sense of disappointment occurred after the collapse of the Third Republic itself in 1940, with left- and right-wing politicians blaming each other.

The impact of Marxist–socialist thinking on the nature of the Revolution and the Republic and the relationship between them was considerable and intensely reassuring. Political and socio-economic change were rolled up together inseparably. The contributions of pre-Marx socialists to republicanism tended to be undervalued or dismissed by those who shared Marx's view that reformist socialists like Buchez and Louis Blanc delayed the achievement of the desired goal and that utopians like Cabet were out of touch with reality. Both the positive and negative contributions of the early socialists were often distorted or ignored. The repeated revolutions of the nineteenth century were not mistakes, failures, but part of a logical, rational theory of economic development. 1789 was portrayed as a bourgeois revolution, not as the early socialists, and indeed Marx himself, had described it, as the triumph of wealthy non-nobles of all kinds, but as the beginning of the dominance of an entrepreneurial bourgeoisie. The Jacobin Republic became quintessentially a bourgeois regime, 1830 a bourgeois revolution because it brought to power an entrepreneurial middle class, and not because, as the early socialists had thought, it had failed to shift power from the traditional landowning, professional bourgeoisie.[33] Marx's analyses of 1830, 1848 and 1871 were accepted unquestioningly. The success of the Bolsheviks in Russia in 1917 and after appeared to be the final proof both of Marx's theory of capitalism and of the interrelationship between political revolution and socio-economic change.

In this 'grand design' of history revolutions were the accelerator of change and social classes the motor. The nobility were on the descent, the bourgeoisie ascendant and from 1848 the proletariat was beginning to claim its inheritance. Divisions within social classes and social groups which did not fit the Marxist theory of change were cast aside. Significant aspects of popular protest, such as peasant attempts to fight against the Forest Laws and artisan initiatives like the creation of mutual-aid and other societies, tended to be ignored. Thus historical presentations of the 1789 Revolution and republicanism, whether socialist or Marxist or both, were inclined to be anachronistic, presenting a messianic, determinist, stylized and often unrealistic appraisal of urban nineteenth-century republicanism, particularly for the years down to 1871[34] when artisanal, agrarian economic structures actually remained dominant in France. Meanwhile the impeccable empirical research of the same Third Republic socialist historians was beginning to produce a far less apocalyptic and more nuanced impression of social change.[35]

The probing of Marxist republican orthodoxy began with news of the purges in Stalinist Russia and for the French with the disastrous collapse of the Third Republic in 1940. The interpretation of history as an unbroken web of progress towards the socialist republic was no longer sustainable. The exposure of the nakedness of Marxist republicanism, begun in the early 1950s by the questioning and lucid hypotheses of Alfred Cobban[36] and taken up by his research students and others in Britain and America, is too familiar to need repeating here.[37] Empirical analyses of social groups did not uphold Marxist messianism. Neither the revolutionaries of 1789 nor the Jacobin republicans of 1793 were merchant capitalists, but members of the traditional middle classes. Although Cobban's thesis was regarded by the French as an attack on the significance of the Revolution as such and his works were not translated into French for more than a generation, the idea that socio-economic change did not dictate the political agenda of 1789 began to attract the attention of historians in France. From the late 1950s doctoral theses on different French regions revealed the lack of 'class' consensus, and demonstrated the significance of social groups whom the Marxists had ignored and the need to look at social change over long periods of time. More recently historians have begun to re-emphasize the political issues of the late eighteenth century.

Revisionists began to question whether there really was a close connection between the growth of capitalism and the 1789 Revolution. They adopted the Napoleonic term *notables* to describe the post-revolutionary elite, which they have shown was not entirely bourgeois, and certainly not an entrepreneurial bourgeoisie, as Marxists believed, but an amalgam of nobles and bourgeois.[38] Revisionists suggested that the dominance of *notables* had little to do with 1789, but was related to long-term socio-economic change, on which the 1789 Revolution had only a modest impact. The survival of noble power well into the nineteenth century has been noted.[39] In the effort to dismantle Marxism it should be remembered that the revolutionary years did benefit a traditional bourgeois elite of landowners and professional men, especially lawyers and civil servants, both with *biens nationaux* and with improved career prospects. Investigations of the 'bourgeois' revolution of 1830 support the views of early socialists, that 1830 confirmed the power of this elite,[40] a dominance reinforced, rather than reduced, by revolution in 1848,[41] the establishment of a Bonapartist Second Empire and the creation of the Third Republic.

If revolution did not directly produce a new elite, but simply confirmed its prestige, neither was revolution itself necessarily the product of capitalism. The June Days[42] and the Paris Commune of 1871[43] have been dismissed from their Marxist pinnacle as quintessentially revolts of a modern proletariat. From the 1960s historians have observed the growth of republican attitudes during the nineteenth century not only as a consequence of enlightened modernity in industrializing areas like Paris, where the notion of republicanism as a modernizing socialist force might have some relevance, but as a feature of traditional artisan industry and some of the poorest regions of southern France.[44] All would concur that French republicanism was a direct product of 1789, but in recent years historians have paid more attention to popular protest, endemic throughout, but especially marked in the periodic economic depressions (chiefly 1816–18, 1827–32, 1845–8, but minor episodes also in 1839 and the late 1860s). Historians have identified a popular radicalism which was inspired by a variety of issues; protests against changes in artisan industries which reduced the independence of craftsmen; complaints about the erosion of communal agrarian institutions by poorer peasants; the frustration of more independent peasants who tried to produce for the market and became indebted to moneylenders; attempts to preserve local political traditions against the advance of centralization. Popular unrest was at least as much anachronistic as modernizing in its inspiration.[45]

Peasant discontent with the downgrading of communal rights, intensified by the 1789 Revolution and rampant in the Forest Laws of 1827, plus complaints about taxes on wine and grain, all contributed a background of popular unrest which reached peaks in the years of harvest failure, but was always present. The emergence of an area of peasant radicalism in southern France during the Second Republic, and the permanent survival of such attitudes into substantial pockets of communist voters in the twentieth century, seemed to accord ill with Marx's dismissal of the peasant as a political drone. In a series of articles published first in the 1940s and then brought together as a book in 1976,[46] Soboul analysed the significance of issues such as the survival of communal rights and the elimination of fallow in the radicalization of the rural community. The theme was deployed by others who drew quite unMarxist conclusions from detailed regional investigations. Vigier was a pioneer with his account of the Alpine region,[47] Agulhon made an exhaustive study of the Var.[48] Focusing on a remote and poor area, Agulhon noted the link between traditional forms of sociability and local autonomy with an enthusiasm for the gains of 1789 among the peasantry. He identified a strong municipal popular political tradition and explained radicalism partly in terms of slightly better-off peasants producing for a volatile market and consequently in debt to moneylenders and partly as a protest by the poor against the 'modernization' of the rural economy, which reduced the role of rural industry and undermined communal traditions and with them the domestic economy of the poor. Corbin's fascinating and valuable study of the Limousin explored similar issues.[49]

Whether peasant or artisan activists were archaic or modernizing and whether they can be called republicans attracted the attention of American historians of France. Aminzade examined the basis of radicalism within the artisan community in Toulouse.[50] Merriman has investigated the response of urban communities to the 'agony' of the republic,[51] while Stewart-McDougall has shown the degree to which the radicalism of the artisans of Lyon in the Second Republic, while influenced by socialists, was intrinsically traditional.[52] The degree to which worker organizations such as mutual-aid societies were traditionally or socialist-inspired has created a lively debate.[53] Some historians were convinced that peasant radicals were identifiably republican,[54] while others denied it.[55]

The rebellion of 1851–2 against Louis-Napoleon's coup proved an interesting case study. The rebellion was denigrated as a mere *jacquerie*, or traditional peasant revolt, by Second Empire commentators and ignored by Third Republic historians. Zola's view of rural republicanism as primarily the opportunistic attempt to settle old scores and family quarrels[56] retains an appeal which can be sustained by archival evidence. Eugène Weber[57] has agreed that 'republican' sentiment was usually little more than local rivalries, with almost no connection with national politics. He insists that peasants pursued only traditional goals, motivated by economic and personal grievances. In December 1851, with radical republican 'democ-soc' (to indicate their support for radical social reforms as well as democracy) *notables* to provide leadership and interpretation, the peasants were mere tools to be manipulated for national issues irrelevant to them. Margadant,[58] on the other hand, taking up the themes raised by Agulhon, insisted that the two dozen southern departments which resisted the coup were inspired by republican concerns and were affected by socialist ideas, which they expressed in traditional forms of protest.

If account is taken, not just of the events of the Second Republic, but of developments since 1789 as a whole, popular republicanism can be seen as both archaic and modern. Peasant disturbances were a continual feature of rural society and those writers who stress the 'archaic' or traditional nature of complaints present a very persuasive case. However, 1789 had a decisive impact on French society and what is sometimes overlooked by those who try to choose between 'archaism' and 'modernity' is that this impact was far from uniform. The Revolution created opportunities for those with liquid assets, and this applied equally to the well-off peasant, artisan, lawyer and any owner of *biens nationaux*. The Revolution also vastly extended expectations among the disaffected, the poorer peasants and artisans in particular. 1789 heralded a period of political disturbance of unprecedented length in modern times. As Jones[59] has shown, those who took part in repeated peasant protests in the Massif Central in these years believed that they were 'modernizers', fighting either to protect the gains of 89 or to complete that revolution.

The most important issues were peasant landownership and the lessening of the tax burden, but the implications of revolutionary rhetoric varied according to the economic position of the individual. Those who formed the republican elite in the Second Republic tended to belong to the better-off element in the local community, those who took part in popular demonstrations were poorer. Did they have the same goals? Agulhon and others answer 'yes', Weber does not ask the question, but assumes that almost coincidentally on occasions they did. It is not an easy problem to address since the information which has survived tends to provide evidence only about the democ-soc elite. Weber begins to approach the situation when he comments on the variety of punishments accorded by the courts to the democ-soc rebels of 1851. The elite got much lighter sentences than did the poor.

Did a section of the rural community use the language of 1789 to justify a protest which was in reality as much a protest against the Revolution as a reiteration of traditional or archaic complaints? Many of those who took part in rural unrest throughout the first half of the nineteenth century were, by the nature of their complaints, hostile to the 'modernizers' of 1789, anxious to defend communal rights against the inroads of the revolutionaries of the 1790s and all subsequent legislators, whatever their political affiliation. In simple, but realistic terms, as recorded by Balzac throughout his *Comédie Humaine*, the fat cats profited from all revolutions, the poorer peasant did not. Ironically, the repeated protests of the losers actually furthered the cause of the better-off. The idea that bourgeois republicans and peasant and artisan rioters were in accord was a fiction of romantic liberal and Marxist historiography. Successive republics, from 1792 onwards, were no more sympathetic to the protests of peasants struggling to retain communal institutions and artisans fighting against proto-capitalist merchants, than more overtly conservative systems. Edmonds, in his study of Lyon, concludes, regretfully, that the Terror in Lyon helped to bring together power and traditional property by destroying the clubs, and thus overwhelming the new aspirants who had run the city in 1792–3.[60]

Marxist historians were patriots before they were socialists and feared that the dismissal of the Marxist superstructure would belittle the 1789 Revolution and the republican tradition, especially by removing the international significance of the French example.[61] While conceding, to some degree, that the Revolution and the Republic were not the product of an enterpreneurial bourgeoisie,[62] and claiming, with some justice, that they had never suggested that such a group, alone, had made 1789 or triumphed in the First Republic, that revisionists had attacked a straw man, Marxists defended the long-term significance of the events of the Revolution. The bicentenary of the Revolution led to a re-emphasis of political issues. Historians returned to a republicanism reminiscent of that of Georges Weill, and it is no accident that his venerable account was reissued in the late 1980s. De Tocqueville now gets far more attention than Marx, although the latter is still praised, not as a theorist but as an acute observer.[63] The doyen of this generation of revolutionary historians, Furet, in a study of the left and the Revolution in the middle of the nineteenth century, focused on the contributions of Quinet and Michelet[64] to explain how the revolutionary years were seen from a nineteenth-century perspective. A similar route was taken in an extensive collection of conference papers edited by Furet and Mona Ozouf[65] and two simultaneously appearing Furet compilations.[66] Anglo-American historians have returned to the writings of the *philosophes* to explain the origins of 1789.[67]

Historians no longer write of a republican 'party' or 'movement' in the nineteenth century and Marxist determinism is dead. Absorption with the Jacobin origins of republicanism has given way to an interest in much earlier European antecedents and in the immediate predecessors of the Jacobins, the period of constitutional monarchy (1789–92) and the Girondin phase of the Republic. In 1982 Nicolet wrote of the republican 'idea'.[68] A classical scholar himself, he observed the legacy of ancient Greece and Rome in the ideas, imagery and symbolism of the men of the First Republic. For Nicolet the Republic was a political and a philosophical entity. He referred his readers to parliamentary debates and newspapers. There are no bread prices, strikes, not even a passing comment about the Forest Laws. However, unlike Weill, with whom his account has similarities, his description of nineteenth-century republicanism before the Third Republic was very brief. It is no accident that Nicolet ended his story with 1924, when the creation of the radical–socialist alliance under Herriot seemed, in his view, to have brought the Republic full circle.

In recent times 1789 and 1792, the years of the constitutional monarchy and the 'Girondin' republic, have attracted renewed interest as historians have sought an image of the republic that is neither Jacobin nor Marxist. The long-forgotten *Idéologues* of the Directory are recognized. We are now asked to be aware of *La République du Centre*.[69] Perhaps the years of the constitutional monarchy (1814–48) may come into their own as a period peopled with those (with the exception of the ultras), who saw themselves as heirs of the early years of the Revolution of 1789. Recent investigations of the July Monarchy do something to rescue these years from the ignominious contempt of the socialists,[70] although French historians remain unconvinced that a monarchy could ever be the heir to the revolutionary tradition.[71] The history of the Second Republic is also beginning to sound more convincing. Recent investigation has led to a more nuanced approach[72] as the republic is beginning to emerge from the shackles of dogma and illusion. It is now portrayed as an 'apprenticeship', in which a new electorate and inexperienced politicians began to learn how to create a democracy.[73] The whole century after the original Revolution has been described as a constant conflict between opposing principles until, after the Commune of 1871, 'The French Revolution was coming into port'.[74]

The development of the Fifth Republic and the institutions of the European Community keep the issue of republicanism very much alive. A series of seminars between 1985 and 1988, published in 1992, and involving some of the leading researchers in the field,[75] offered a discussion not only of past republics, but also of prognoses for the future. The republic, it is suggested at the outset, can be seen as a political model, in the same way as absolute monarchy. The presidential, state-centred Fifth Republic is contrasted with the individualistic, parliament-dominated Third Republic, which appears to be a golden age for some of these essayists. Paradise being irretrievable, they suggest that the republic should be interpreted as a political form which adapts to circumstance, perhaps in the form of a wax model or computer disc. However, the reader should beware! It is clear that for the contributors the Gaullist Republic presents a more than transient 'model' of a republic, against which the 'idea' can be measured. A Marxist–socialist republicanism has given way to a Gaullist vision. There is the suggestion that the spiritual antecedent of the Fifth Republic was the Girondin-phase of the First Republic. The satirical weekly *Le Canard Enchaîné* always preferred to compare de Gaulle's presidency with Louis XIV's France. It might be more valid to see the Republic of the 1990s as the heir of the Napoleonic Empire, or perhaps of the liberalized Second Empire of Louis-Napoleon.

The French debate on the European Community was revealing of 1990s attitudes to the republic. The Maastricht referendum in September 1992 offered some interesting illustrations. Apparently the French see the Republic as parliamentary, but as democracy enhanced both by the election of the president and the use of referenda, two approaches as much respected by republicans in the 1990s as they were detested by republicans in the 1860s. The Mitterand view of Maastricht stressed that French sovereignty would not be sacrificed in the Community. Proportionality, by further developing the decentralizing strategies pursued by France since 1969, will add to, not dilute, the rights of the French. The Maastricht referendum, in which a mere 51 per cent of the French voted for the Treaty, revealed a country in which party divisions, previously the bread-and-butter of the Republic, were irrelevant, with some major figures in the main parties opposing Maastricht, while the leaders of all these parties backed the President's request for ratification. The centralized Jacobin, parliamentary republic has given way to a presidential, televised spectacle; Gaullist, but Bonapartist too, with barely a trace of the left-wing parties.

The political developments and historical investigations of the late twentieth century have on the one hand discredited the Soviet Russian version of socialism and on the other disproved the immediate relevance of a Marxist analysis of capitalism. In doing so the European communist states have proved vulnerable to the revolutionary determination of an educated minority when backed by mass protest at a time of economic crisis. Is this an ironical reversal of Marx's predictions, illustrating the failure of socialism and the viability of capitalism? It might be comforting for a Western capitalist to make this assumption. However, the international capitalist edifice, crowned by democracy and papered over by international relief and policing agencies, seems even less secure in the 1990s, when threatened by nationalist demands and harassed by the threat of ecological disasters, than it did in the late nineteenth century. In complacently rejecting Marxist theory, it is important to appreciate the significance of economic factors as a background to political upheaval, and the continuing failure of humankind to find a framework in which to co-exist harmoniously. Capitalism seems no more secure an economic system now than it did to Marx. The ideals of the Declaration of Rights and the early socialists are more relevant and more neglected than ever.

3 The Legacy of the First Republic and the Napoleonic Empire

The French Revolution from its inception challenged privilege, demanding that 'rights' be justified by more than tradition and purchase, whether they be the rights of the Church or of the aristocracy. It might seem that the logical sequel to this attack on privilege would be the elimination of the monarchy, the source of much of the power within society and the state. The calling of the Estates-General in 1789 was surrounded by ambiguity; Louis XVI and his advisers envisaged a transient gathering to help resolve a financial crisis, while many of those elected saw the opportunity to create a representative system of government such as had been discussed in various quarters in France during the century. In just over three years from the calling of the Estates General of May 1789, the king was replaced by a republic. Why was a republic declared? Why, subsequently, did it prove impossible to establish a settled form of government? Why did a military dictatorship emerge and what was the relationship between the republican and the imperial experiences?

At the outset the Revolution was not republican; its failure led to the declaration of a republic. The two privileged Orders or Estates, the Church and the nobility, along with the more privileged members of the Third Estate, essentially the wealthy middle classes, had been in constant conflict with the king over the limits of royal authority long before 1789. The constitutional monarchy projected by Malouet, Mounier and others in the early months of the Revolution was not unrealistic in principle.[1] True, some members of the National Assembly were barely monarchist from the outset. The king was at least equally reluctant to accept the role assigned to him by the

Assembly and forced upon him by episodes of mass violence in the capital and elsewhere. There was no question that Louis XVI detested the work of the constitution-makers. His flight to Varennes in June 1791 ensured that his signature on the September 1791 constitution was a matter of compulsion not compromise. But the route to resistance or counter-revolution seemed unclear and littered with contradictory advice.[2]

At first the king had few allies. There was very little enthusiasm for unrestrained royal authority. The constitution could have worked, by leaving a relatively friendless king with little authority. In September 1791 France remained a monarchy, but the constitution stated unequivocally that sovereignty belonged to the whole nation, that power was to be exercised by the principle of representation and delegated to an elected National Assembly and a king. The king was to be called 'king of the French people' and, on his accession, was to take an oath of loyalty to the nation and to the constitution.[3] He appointed his own ministers, but the National Assembly had sole power to make law and could not be dissolved by the king. A leading French authority recently described the king under this arrangement as 'the president of a republic calling itself a monarchy'.[4]

The emergence of a counter-revolutionary movement exploded this constitutional fiction and promoted the declaration of a republic. It is unlikely that a counter-revolution would have made much headway if it had relied exclusively on monarchist passions. The most important single issue which created a counter-revolution was the attack launched by the National Assembly on the Church. The revolutionaries were no accidental anti-clerics. They were determined to dismantle the First Order, the most wealthy and privileged corporation in the state, whose economic dominance was hedged around with religious beliefs and formalized in ways the rationalizing legislators of 1789 found repugnant and socially corrosive. After abolishing the tithe, a special tax collected by the Church to finance its activities, the revolutionaries confiscated all church property, an irreparable social, economic, financial and political loss, for the ancien regime Church had been the largest single landowner in France. All clergy were obliged to take an oath of allegiance to the state, thus challenging the authority of senior clerics in France and in Rome. The Civil Constitution of the Clergy (1790) provided for clerical salaries to be paid by the state. The revolutionaries hoped that the political, social and economic influence of the First Order in pre-revolutionary society had been swept away.

Instead the attack on the Church stimulated widespread resistance and criticism of the revolution. A counter-revolution was born at both mass and elite levels. Few questioned the initial attack on the wealth of the highly privileged senior bishops, who were sons of the most powerful noble families, but the bulk of parish priests were not rich and were from very ordinary, often peasant backgrounds.[5] One of the few ladders of social betterment for ambitious sons of peasants was destroyed. When the land of the Church was sequestrated, so was its ability to fulfil all the social functions it had previously undertaken, albeit often badly and with much justified criticism. Revolutionary anti-clericals dismantled the embryonic social services which the Church had provided, such as poor relief, hospitals, the organization of wet-nurses, what little basic schooling existed, as well as providing many jobs for the lay population. Almost no substitute organizations were created. Cash from the sale of church lands was far less than had been anticipated. It was not that revolutionaries lacked the will, but that the war consumed revenue and brought inflation.[6] In addition many people, even those who were not particularly religious, saw the attack on the Church as an attempt by an interfering state to destroy the basic landmarks of their social existence, including ceremonies of birth, marriage and death.[7] The clergy did not hesitate to exploit these worries. Popular resistance led to civil war, particularly in the west, which dragged on throughout the 1790s, diverting the energy and income of successive revolutionary governments. Anti-clerical policies thus became the crucial issue which created opposition to the revolution.

The Church reacted by allying its cause to that of the king which ensured that the revolutionaries would not only have to struggle against civil war but would also have to become republicans. Most bishops were members of very wealthy and prestigious noble families. Like other nobles, they responded to the demands of the revolutionaries by scheming against the Assembly and ultimately by emigrating.[8] They found succour among neighbouring monarchies, which then expressed belligerent support for the beleaguered royal family, Church and aristocracy. This helped to cement revolutionary and republican sentiments, especially when the revolutionaries declared war on Austria, one of the hosts of the *émigrés*, in April 1792.

In agreement over anti-clericalism, the educated middle-class leaders of revolution in the National and later the Legislative Assemblies were divided in their approach to their political objectives. The more radical were prepared to manipulate contemporary popular unrest, itself a product of both political and economic factors. From the outset the process of revolutionary change had been a compound of brain and brawn. Men educated in the rather contradictory philosophical concepts of the Enlightenment struggled to assert their own views and to maintain an ascendancy over peasant and artisan communities with their own different and compelling interests. From the capture of the Bastille onwards, the latter became increasingly aware of their power to influence political decisions.

The onslaught on privilege which the Assembly launched from the night of August 4th onwards proved contagious. Sieyès had asserted that the Third Estate was the real French nation. He intended merely to include the educated middle classes in a new equation of power. During the night of August 4th, the National Assembly, on behalf of the Second Order, renounced feudal rights, which could not have been welcomed by the many members of the wealthy Third Estate themselves who had bought the right to levy a variety of dues on tenants in addition to rents. This was only the beginning. All privileged corporations, which included those of the Third Estate itself, came under fire. Repeated popular unrest by groups of peasants and artisans threatened the attempt to reach an equilibrium. Most of the middle-class members of the National Assembly had meant the principle of equality to destroy the privileges which distinguished between them and the first two Orders, not to give the poor equal status with themselves. To preserve their own authority in the constitutional arrangements of September 1791, the majority in the Assembly distinguished between 'active' and 'passive' citizens, only the former of whom, men of property who paid tax equivalent to three days' labour, could vote, while limiting candidature to an even more elite group of taxpayers. These decisions were the occasion of bitter dispute in the Assembly, including Robespierre and Marat, who were fiercely opposed to the distinctions.

The apparent pursuit of equality allied with popular unrest helped to turn a political and constitutional argument into an uncontrollably violent social revolution. Equality stopped even pretending to be egalitarian and became a new species of privilege. Revolution and republic became virulently anti-noble as well as anti-clerical. From the summer of 1792 the lands of *émigrés* (many of whom were noble) who fled France in protest at the Revolution were confiscated and sold. Nobles were denied the rights of citizens.

Popular demonstrations, encouraged by more radical politicians, began to have more impact than votes, particularly after the declaration of war in 1792. The unpreparedness of the army, consequent military setbacks within France as well as on her borders and the rapidly diminishing grasp of the Legislative Assembly, led to the declaration in July of *'la patrie en danger'*. The rival Girondin (Brissotin) and Jacobin factions in the Assembly vied to control upheavals both in the provinces and in Paris. The former summoned provincial National Guard units to the capital. They hoped to reassert their own credibility, badly shaken as the war they had declared served to intensify rather than eliminate counter-revolution and proved to be not at all the glorious crusade to liberate the peoples of Europe they had expected.

It was no longer a question of whether the king should go, but when. The monarchy had been catastrophically discredited by its association with counter-revolutionary groups at home and abroad. Conversely, the attack on the Church guaranteed that counter-revolution would have a popular, if internally very divided base. The case for the removal of Louis XVI, still tenuous after his flight in the summer of 1791, was made self-evident by war at home and abroad.[9] As an ambivalent and indecisive pivot for opponents of the Revolution, the king was both an embarrassment and a potential danger.

In August 1792 popular unrest in Paris, culminating in an attack on the Tuileries, pushed the Revolution into overdrive. The day of 10 August 1792, when a revolutionary commune was declared in Paris, was the most murderous of the revolutionary *journées* to date, with nearly 400 killed or wounded. The king was arrested and suspended by the Legislative Assembly. A republic existed in fact, but a republic which was palpably the product of chaos and near anarchy. A new constituent assembly was summoned, a National Convention, its name recalling the American republican model.[10] But the form of the republic could not be a matter for cool compromise. Verdun fell to the advancing Prussians on 2 September 1792 and the disintegrating French army seemed unlikely to offer significant resistance. Serious food shortages and internal divisions in France threatened to leave her an easy prey. Counter-revolutionary movements, especially in the south, met sharp resistance from Jacobin clubs. Indicative of the panic, confusion and desperation of the times were the week-long massacres of prisoners suspected of disloyalty to France in early September in Paris and in other towns. Roughly half of those on remand in the capital (1400) were summarily killed, 75 per cent of whom were not even political prisoners.[11] It was in this anarchic atmosphere that the Convention was elected.

The Convention was heralded by its partisans and subsequent

sympathizers as France's first democratic Assembly. The elections were held in two stages; first a democratic vote in primary assemblies, which merely selected the candidates for the Convention, and for which barely a tenth of the 7 million men enfranchised turned out. Secondary assemblies then elected the actual members. Each electoral college was composed of between 300 and 600 men of 25 and over. The secondary assemblies were dominated by middle-class civil servants, professionals and property-owners, those who had been the 'active' citizens in the previous constitution. They elected their own kind; over a third held public office, many had served in the earlier assemblies.[12]

Confidence began to return. In less than three weeks French armies began to push back the Prussians. A day later, on September 21st, the Convention finally decided to declare France a republic. The first republican constitution provoked even more argument than did that of 1791. The Girondin proposal of February 1793 was followed by a Jacobin one which was adopted in June. The Jacobin constitution consecrated the right of rebellion. Provision was made for annual direct democratic elections. The elected Convention, at war with itself and in conflict with the Paris Commune, was obliged to delegate power to a small number of committees to facilitate decision-making in difficult and dangerous times. Decisions about the conduct of war within France and outside her borders, the provision and pricing of food to alleviate the threat of mass starvation, were taken by the twelve-man Committee of Public Safety. Perhaps because the emergencies that were faced were so genuine, the republican leaders tried to dispense with everything from the past. They sought to justify what might otherwise be seen as arbitrary decisions by the elaboration of a republican, idealist philosophy. The new start was made tangible and ever-present by the institution of a complete new republican calendar. A religion of the Supreme Being replaced the rebellious Catholic church.

The concentration of power in the hands of a small group, an apparent contradiction of the principle of the sovereignty of the people, was explained in varying, and rather contradictory ways. Marat and St Just invoked the emergency situation. The concept of the republic was associated with dictatorship in a classical sense, involving the transient elevation of a 'saviour of the nation'. Robespierre's dominance was thus justified, as was that of Napoleon in 1799. On the other hand comparisons were made in a negative sense with the classical world; a prolonged dictatorship in a republic was condemned as despotism. In such terms was Robespierre's deposition urged. To others, the extreme policies of the Committee were tolerable as a necessary stage in the natural history of the republic. A concept of republican virtue was invoked, of which the committee and the ascendant Jacobin clubs claimed a monopoly. A republic born of confusion and necessity was lauded as the rule of virtue and the just. The Republic was interpreted as a platonic ideal by Robespierre in a range of exhortatory speeches. In his last address to the Convention, 26 July 1794 (8 Thermidor Year II) he summed up his concept of republican morality and puritanism.

> The French Revolution is the first ever to be founded on the theory of the rights of humanity and the principles of justice. Other revolutions were concerned solely with personal ambition; ours is founded on justice.[13]

Robespierre himself seemed genuinely to uphold such beliefs. For others the Revolution was indeed an opportunity to pursue personal ambition, masked by altruistic claims and achieved by the unprecedented persecution of opponents. The rule of justice and virtue led to the escalation of Terror directed arbitrarily and summarily against anyone suspected of being an enemy of the Republic and executed by the Jacobin clubs, at the height of which Robespierre himself was overthrown.

To what extent was this oligarchical, threatening and unpredictable Jacobin phase of the Republic, which will always be associated with the most extreme manifestations of the Terror, shaped by the war and internal crises? To what extent was this an 'inevitable' stage in revolution comparable with similar phenomena discernible in twentieth-century revolutions? These questions preoccupied later commentators. The Jacobin episode, more than any other period of the First Republic, shaped attitudes to republicanism and revolution for many years. The Jacobin experience ensured that property-owners would shun democratic institutions, even though the ballot box played a minimal role in the activities of the Jacobins. The violence and upheaval of these years meant that a republic would be feared by the better-off in the nineteenth century.

If the memory of the Committee of Public Safety, the Sections and *sans-culotte* influence appalled men of property in the nineteenth century, the Thermidorians, as those who overthrew Robespierre on 10 Thermidor were called, were despised. Both accusations were somewhat unjust. There is no doubt that the Thermidorians were not simply trying to save their own skins. Robespierre's overthrow was followed by the dismantling of the Convention and the promulgation of yet another republican constitution, that of 5 Fructidor Year III (22 August 1795). Indirect elections were restored. Primary electoral colleges of all adult males with a permanent residence selected members of the secondary assemblies. The constitution set out in detail the necessary property qualifications for electors, who had to own property equal in value to between 150 and 200 work-days. There were thus only 30,000 real voters, half the number enfranchised by the 1791 constitution. They selected the judges and administrators in their localities as well as members for the two legislative assemblies. Legislative power was split between the Council of 500 which proposed legislation and the Council of the Elders which voted on it. Executive power was to be separately exercised by a Directory of five men elected by the legislative assembly, the lower house selecting the candidates, the upper house voting on them.[14] The more conservative republican politicians now in control genuinely tried to create a stable republic which would avoid the dangers of both democracy and dictatorship.

The Directory was given an unofficial ideological justification by an assortment of moderate republicans who came to be called *idéologues*. The focus of the group was the *Académie des sciences morales et politiques*, started in 1795, which included Volney, Sieyès and Destutt de Tracy. The *idéologues* were men who had not prospered during the Convention and not unnaturally were partisans of the limited representative government of the Directory. Their reward tended to be official posts of an academic nature. An early honeymoon with Bonapartism came to an abrupt end when Napoleon disbanded the *Académie*.[15]

The Revolution and subsequent republic were concerned with social as well as political issues. The Declaration of Rights of 1789 sanctified private property, the confiscation of church and *émigré* lands notwithstanding. Those who were deprived of venal office were compensated. Pressure from the poor who suffered during a period of scarcity and high food prices during the 1790s obliged the Jacobins to try to set a ceiling on food prices and for some the 'maximum' represented an attack on private property.

The Directory effectively asserted the dominance of a property-owning middle class, who were more concerned with their economic and social security than with political representation. Their views were challenged by the egalitarian heir of the *enragés*, Babeuf, and stridently expressed in his newspaper, *Tribune*, and in the secret associations, the *Panthéon* and *The Secret Directory of Public Safety*, in 1796. Babeuf sought to overthrow the Directory by revolution, and to restore the Jacobin constitution of 1793 with the addition of total economic equality, arguing that political equality without economic would simply be a source of discord and perpetual conflict. His associates, the Equals, as they called themselves, established agents in each of the twelve *arrondissements* of Paris to prepare for a seizure of power. Babeuf was known to favour a brief interim dictatorship. If political democracy was delayed, economic equality was to be introduced without delay. *Emigré* property would be divided among the poor, who would be housed in their vacant mansions. All goods in the state pawnshops were to be redeemed without payment. A free community of goods and labour would then be created.

However, the main and most enthusiastic agent of the Equals was also a police spy and on 21 Floréal Year IV, the leaders were rounded up; 59 men were arrested, of whom 47 were brought to trial. Babeuf made no secret of his views: 'Private property is the source of all the calamities upon this earth.'[16] 'We look to common property, or the community of goods.'[17] Babeuf's rejection of private ownership, his argument that individual men could only demand the use of the land, was one that was to become familiar a couple of generations later, but it was totally unacceptable to his contemporaries. He was executed along with Darthé and his ideas were pushed out of sight by the *notables* who had done well out of buying former church and *émigré* lands and intended to keep them. But Babeuf had proposed a new social agenda for republicanism, which was a spectre which haunted property-owners throughout the nineteenth century.

The challenge posed by Babeuf, although quickly dismantled, was but one de-stabilizing episode in the short-lived Directory. The problems of persistent internal upheaval and the demands of foreign war made settled constitutional government difficult. Fear of a royalist resurgence and the personal ambition of individuals like Sieyès, prompted the Directors to rely on the army. Napoleon, one of the most successful generals, and certainly the best publicist, was not unwilling to take advantage of the desire of the Directors to undermine the elected assemblies. The coup of 19 Brumaire, 10 November 1799, constituted their military overthrow and their replacement by three consuls – Napoleon, Sieyès and Roger-Ducos. The Directory always suffered from a bad press, reviled in modern times by Marxist historians as the 'bourgeois' republic. Napoleon claimed credit for its achievements, especially economic recovery and the establishment of viable financial and administrative institutions.[18]

The Republic survived the Brumaire coup only in name. To the

Anglo-Saxon mind there is always a certain inconsistency in calling a military dictatorship a republic. For those imbued in classical tradition there was no inherent contradiction between the two. The history of the previous five years of the Directory itself illustrated how far the republic had moved from its early striving for representative institutions. In this respect it was entirely logical to call the constitution of December 1799 republican. The constitution explained eloquently how electoral lists were to be compiled, but this was in inverse proportion to the significance of both the elections and the resulting assemblies. Elections were made even more indirect than under the Directory. All adult males were to select a tenth of their numbers from whom local officials could be chosen. A tenth of the local list of names was then used to select a departmental list from which departmental administrators and candidates for national appointments were to be chosen. If the Directory had shown by its creation of a tiny electorate how insignificant the revered principle of representation had become, the Consulate finally buried the sovereignty of the people under a plethora of three powerless assemblies.

There was to be a Legislative Assembly, a Tribunate and a Senate, all of which had the shadow of a legislative role.[19] Senators were to be named for life by the existing senate, from lists selected by the other assemblies and the first consul. This assembly, consisting of Napoleon's most loyal servants, was later, ironically, to organize his deposition. All legislation was to be proposed by the government, communicated to the Tribunate and decreed by the legislative body. The elected 100-member Tribunate could discuss legislation proposed by the government. When its debates became too lively, it was halved, divided into mere sectional groups and finally abolished in 1807. The legislative body of 300 members listened to three Tribunate delegates explain why they supported a piece of legislation and then voted on it, with no discussion. After the abolition of the Tribunate, the legislative body was allowed to debate, but it was such an insignificant shadow of the revolutionary assemblies of the 1790s that its discussions were of no account. The separation of powers, so dear to the revolutionaries in the early 1790s, existed only as a bureaucratic fudge to separate those elected from the exercise of power.[20] The republic moved about as far away from the electoral principle, while retaining the form, as it was possible to go. The lack of genuine consultation was underlined by the use of a plebiscite to confirm national acceptability of this coup.

Real power lay with three consuls, initially named for ten years, effectively by themselves. From the outset it was the first consul,

Napoleon, who was in control, appointing ministers, members of the council of state, judges, and so on. The plebiscite which was held to give democratic sanction to these arrangements was accompanied by a proclamation issued in the name of the three consuls. They claimed:

> The constitution is based on genuine representative principles, on the sacred rights of property, equality and liberty.The institutions they have created will be strong and stable, in order to guarantee the rights of citizens and the needs of the state. Citizens, the revolution is set in the principles on which it was first based; the revolution is over.[21]

Subsequent modifications were issued as *senatus-consulte* and confirmed by plebiscites, including that of May 1804 which declared 'The government of the republic is placed in the hands of an Emperor.'[22] Having affirmed that Napoleon was the chosen 'emperor of the French people' the rest of this lengthy document, which shuffled the existing cardboard cut-out institutions, spoke of 'the Empire'. The Republic was quietly forgotten between constitutional clauses. From 1802 Napoleon's saint day, August 15th, became a public holiday. The republican festivals of July 14th and 1 Vendémaire, celebrated for the sake of appearances until 1804, were quietly interred. In 1806 the republican calendar was abolished along with the fashion for revolutionary first names.

The abortive and powerless assemblies of the Empire were a hollow echo of the political liberalism of the 1790s. Napoleon's reported judgement can have done little to encourage the survival of a representative spirit: 'In the Tribunate are a dozen or so metaphysicians only fit for the garbage heap. They are vermin on my clothes. I am a soldier, a son of the Revolution. I will not tolerate being insulted like a king.'[23] How could the Bonapartist military dictatorship be squared with the earlier aspirations for political liberty and constitutional government?

How was it that men were prepared to abandon ideals of representation and elected parliaments for which they had struggled in the early 1790s? Even more difficult to explain was why they were willing then and later to find the Republic and the Empire compatible institutions. Many must have been relieved to read a proclamation stating that the Revolution *was* over. Cynically one might discern the answer in the proclamation of the consuls of 1799 when 'property' is listed as the first 'sacred right'. One can argue that from the fall of

Robespierre property-owners were primarily in search of security. In such terms the proclamation was reassuring. Stability and security were more basic needs than representative government. The individual was promised personal security, much was made of the arbitrary nature of the Terror of the early 1790s. By 1799 it appeared that only the army could provide tangible guarantees. Despite the promises, the Consulate and Empire survived in an atmosphere of perpetual emergency. The concept of the nation at arms, under threat, with life always out of a regular pattern, with a large proportion of the adult male population fighting abroad, was ever present.

Later Napoleon tried to claim that the arbitrary character of his regime had been forced on him by jealous and bellicose foreign enemies. In his memoirs written a few years later in exile on St Helena, Napoleon continued to embroider this exercise in deception, assuring his readers of his own liberal intentions, which had been thwarted by the jealousy and belligerence of France's foreign enemies. His great-nephew Louis-Napoleon was to elaborate this lie when he wrote:

> The Emperor Napoleon has contributed more than anyone else to hasten the reign of liberty by preserving the moral influence of the Revolution and diminishing the fear which it inspired. Without the Consulate and Empire the Revolution would have been merely a great drama, leaving grand recollections but few practical results.[24]

The great-nephew may have deceived himself about his uncle's constitutional intentions, but contemporaries surely were fully aware that in this respect the republic of the Consulate was a deception. However, we have seen that by 1799 elections and representation had become tarnished ideals. To what extent did the Napoleonic Republic/Empire offer adequate compensations?

The army provided massive military conquests, which satisfied the greed of some of Napoleon's followers, could be portrayed as a patriotic legitimation of the Revolution and, while triumphant, paid for themselves. The more the Republic was successfully exported, the more justified seemed a military regime at home. The repeated military engagements from 1792 to 1815 were always depicted as the product of foreign, rather than French, aggression. Napoleon could be vaunted as a brilliant general and the saviour of the Revolution. Patriotism was always upheld as a precious ideal by revolutionaries and the need to recruit men to the colours made it all the more necessary to encourage men to honour the nation. The impressive list of conquests achieved under the leadership of Napoleon, giving France an unsurpassed European Empire, must surely offer the most convincing, if cynical explanation why Frenchmen were prepared to envisage the Empire as the ultimate triumph of the Republic.

Curiously, in at least two senses, the Napoleonic era encapsulated much of the Republic. Firstly, the rationalizing institutional reforms launched in the early 1790s were finally completed during the Consulate. Ironically, the final form was even more rigidly centralized than the ancien regime had been, as de Tocqueville was to note half a century later. Secondly, Napoleon retained in office many former republicans, as well as attracting back a high proportion of monarchist servants.

The Empire provided jobs; perhaps it was better to be a paid *fonctionnaire* than an unpaid legislator. Some revolutionaries would not serve Napoleon, but many did, underlining the comforting official claim that the Revolution was indeed 'over'. Napoleon stressed continuity with the Revolution; 240 out of the 300 men in the new Legislative Body were taken straight from the assemblies of the Directory. Only 21 had never sat in a revolutionary assembly. All had been active supporters of the Revolution. Only 26 members of the new Tribunate had never sat in a revolutionary assembly and 69 were plucked from Directorial assemblies, 5 from an earlier one.[25] Two-thirds of the old members of the Convention who had voted the death of the king accepted jobs from Napoleon.[26] Over half of the prefects appointed under the new legislation on local government in 1800 had been members of the Revolutionary assemblies.[27]

Recent research on the elites of the Revolution and the Empire illustrates the compromise reached. If the Republic had initially hoped to destroy privilege, making all men 'citizens', abolishing aristocracy and trying, at its best (and worst), to base government on 'justice and virtue', the Consulate finally abandoned the attempt. Instead of a new ruling elite of the worthy, a coalition of complacent republicans and former ancien regime men emerged. There was a pronounced and growing level of continuity between Napoleonic and Bourbon officials. Roughly a third of Napoleon's men had served Louis XVI.[28] Nearly a half of all noble families, 174 out of 370, rallied to Napoleon, although it should be noted that this included only 23 out of 147 of the most senior court families.[29]

The revolutionaries had launched an ambitious programme to modernize and rationalize French institutions. Napoleon claimed that the years of the Consulate and Empire witnessed the completion of this process. To what extent does this help to explain the intertwining of the Republic with Napoleon? The abolition of privilege and its replacement by decentralized elections for the appointment of officials had seemed to be the answer to ancien regime centralization. However, the scale of the task, combined with the enormous drain of foreign and civil war, helped to render administration incoherent, bankrupt and often non-existent.[30] The revolutionaries were forced to centralize. Attachment to provincial autonomy became a luxury of counter-revolutionaries (whose less overtly 'royalist' predecessors had opposed the centralizing policies of successive Bourbon kings[31]). The Jacobin state invoked and developed centralized agencies to assert its control. Although the Directory retained the principle of locally elected officials, in effect the republic had moved irrevocably towards a centralized, highly bureaucratic form.

The Directory regenerated the process of rationalization, but it was under Napoleon that the foundations of the modern French state were completed. He took every opportunity to claim all the credit for this achievement, but leading architects were former ancien regime bureaucratic *notables*, such as Lebrun and Gaudin.[32] The codification of French law, launched by the revolutionaries, was completed. A centralized judiciary replaced the revolutionary attempt to provide for elected judges and the summary 'justice' of the Terror. The urgent need for efficient government in a time of war meant a return to centralization with the designation of Paris-appointed prefects to the revolutionary departments.

Decisions were orchestrated by a council of state, reminiscent of the ancien regime royal council, whose members were appointed by the consuls. This council was the pinnacle of an increasingly centralized administrative framework. It served partly as a body of administrative experts, partly as a training ground for future bureaucrats. It drafted legislation, under the direction of the consuls. During the Empire it became accepted practice for young men who sought employment as prefects, to train as *auditeurs* in the council. Their subsequent experience on special missions to specific departments and in other capacities, prepared them for a prefectoral role. Financial, educational and other reforms were similarly centralized. The new structures provided the most enduring evidence that the Consulate was a continuation of the Republic and that Napoleon was the heir to the Revolution. In this very tangible sense it could be claimed that the Revolution and Republic lived on in the Empire.

The Republic initiated the process by which France developed its present state structure. Thus in a vital respect, the settled modern institutional framework of the state, it can be seen that the Consulate, and even the Empire, could lay claim to be heirs to the Republic. The projects which produced the institutions through which France still functions were initiated in the early years of the Republic, matured during the Directory,[33] but owed their completion to the succeeding regime. There is no doubt that the coup of Brumaire wrought fundamental changes in these institutions, resulting in more centralized and hierarchical structures than the revolutionaries had intended when they began to transform the varied and sometimes conflicting administrative and judicial bodies of ancien regime France.[34] It was under the dictatorship of Napoleon that the Republic finally came to terms with the ancien regime it had tried to eradicate, both in the shape of the modern French state and in the personnel of those who administered it.

A second distinct feature of the Republic was the attempt to create a defined and written constitutional framework. The republicans of the 1790s cherished the notion of the sovereignty of the people and experimented with a variety of forms by which the will of the nation might be represented. The assemblies of the Consulate and Empire provided no more than a flimsy veil to an undisguised military dictatorship, despite the efforts of Napoleon and his self-appointed heir to pretend otherwise. His 'elected' assemblies were mere parodies of representation. The plebiscites he introduced echo, albeit in a distorted form, a concept of representation which together with the activities of the Committee of Public Safety, heralds totalitarian 'representative' constructs of the twentieth century.

The republicans of the First Republic had treasured the theory of individual liberty, enshrined in the Declaration of the Rights of Man. The Consulate and Empire were no more considerate of these ideals than the Convention, but also limited both freedom of association and expression at the behest of Napoleon. But at least Napoleon did not resort to the self-righteous claims of republican virtue expressed during the Convention.

Napoleon never faced substantial internal opposition. The turmoil of the decade of revolution reconciled men of property to a dictatorship. The few attempts to unseat the emperor were modest, ideologically confused and easily defeated. There was no serious republican challenge to his military dictatorship, likewise no concerted assault by monarchists, despite the fact that the coup of Brumaire was justified on the grounds that a monarchist attempt was imminent. Indeed the few onslaughts on Bonapartism which occurred tended to be the work of a mixture of republican and monarchist no-hopers. Typical were the two attempts of Malet, a republican general. In 1808, while in Paris, accused of running illegal gambling casinos to lighten and enrichen his Italian tour of duty, Malet and a small group of republicans determined to effect a coup while Napoleon was busy in Spain. The conspiracy discovered, the danger was so slight that Malet was easily able to escape from his consequent imprisonment to plot again. This time he used the opportunity of Napoleon's absence in Russia to announce the emperor's death in the military campaign and once more to attempt a coup. Several leading officials were fooled before Malet was rearrested. His second attempt was a curious mix of republican and monarchist ambitions. Two of his early-morning (he was arrested by 10 a.m.) provisional government of 1812 were members of the royalist *chevaliers de la foi*.[35]

This aristocratic secret organization, the *chevaliers de la foi*, formed in 1810, had a considerable following in the south, but little effective contact with the exiled royal family while the Empire seemed secure. Negotiations for a Bourbon restoration received some impetus following the disastrous invasion of Russia. Bourbon agents, constantly beavering away throughout the Empire, began to find listeners. The Pretender promised to respect the revolutionary administrative, judicial and land settlements, and the law codes and offered to bring the increasingly costly and damaging war to an end.

With setbacks in Spain and the enormity of the Russian invasion, a cost-benefit analysis of France's great patriotic war was increasingly unfavourable. In 1813 there were revolts against conscription. The human costs of the war were beginning to have an impact on morale. From 1805 until the end of the Empire the death toll among officers was 15,000, with another 35,000 injured. An indication of the significance of this figure was the rate at which new officers could be trained. Saint-Cyr, the main academy, produced only 4000 new officers in these years, despite strenuous efforts.[36] In total the casualty figures for the 22 years of constant campaigning equalled those of the First World War, roughly 1.5 million dead. The economic consequences of the war were equally disastrous. The population of Paris fell by nearly 50 per cent. France lost colonial possessions and trading routes, was cut off from the world economy and concentrated wealth on an ultimately abortive attempt at European domination. Cities such as Bordeaux, which became a target for the Wellington invasion plan, viewed the persistence of the war and the Empire as serious impediments to their economic revival. But there was very little active support for a monarchy. Even in Bordeaux, a city of 70,000, the royalists were only able to muster an army of 800 in the spring of 1814 to support the return of the king, and then only when the imperial prefect and most of the garrison had already left. There was a royalist riot in Marseille in mid-April, but the Vendée, the traditional royalist stronghold, failed to move.

Despite military defeat, Napoleon retained considerable support within the army, particularly in the east. There were tax riots, especially against the *droits réunis*, which de-stabilized the fragile monarchy. Clearly the elimination of the Empire in 1814 owed nothing to republican critics and very little to the efforts of the resurgent monarchists. The Empire was destroyed by military defeat, the invasion of France and the entry of foreign armies into Paris. Heartily sick of war and convinced that the emperor alone was the obstacle to peace, Napoleon's enemies were determined to remove him from the throne, but the island of Elba proved an insecure exile. Why his replacement was the Bourbon claimant is the subject matter of the next chapter. But Napoleon's escape and his subsequent Hundred Day rule is a not insignificant postscript to any consideration of the republican and Bonapartist tradition.

Napoleon's escape from Elba and his return to France was a piece of pure individual opportunism. His decision was determined by pro-pinquity and the intelligence he received concerning army hostility to Bourbon military demobilization. He landed near Cannes with just over 1000 followers on 1 March 1815. The Bourbon regime melted away, the royal brothers once more went into exile, many of their officials simply renewing their loyalty to the emperor. There was no armed resistance. By March 20th Napoleon was in Paris.

The acclamation he received and his return to power, even though short-lived, had important consequences, both for the relationship of republican and Bonapartist ideas and for the future of the Second Bourbon Restoration which followed Napoleon's second defeat. It is widely held that the Hundred Days did much to transform Bonapartism from military dictatorship into a popular movement. Men flocked back to Napoleon out of free will, not compulsion. The return helped to fuse attitudes which had previously existed separately, if not entirely antagonistically. The Hundred Days served to merge republican, especially Jacobin, sentiments with Bonapartist sympathies and to engage the support of liberals, previously suspicious of Napoleon.

A key individual was Benjamin Constant. Constant, along with

Mme de Stael, had always been quintessentially an eloquent apologist of the moderate Directory. In his theoretical writings he defended liberal, elitist, parliamentary government. He never became reconciled to the Empire and at first energetically attacked its revival. In May 1815 he published his *Principes de Politique* in which he declared in clear and simple brevity for 'the liberty of the individual, press freedom, elimination of arbitrary elements in government and respect for the rights of all men'.[37] Constant makes it clear that what he has to say is equally relevant to a monarchy, or an empire. He did not oppose an hereditary head of state, but argued for the separation of royal and executive power. He accepted that the king should appoint the government, but as a neutral arbiter, selecting men acceptable to the majority in the Assembly. Napoleon is specifically approved as head of state because he has declared that he will govern with an elected assembly and respect liberal principles.[38] Constant was swept into the council of state and engaged to prepare the *Acte Additionnel aux Constitutions de l'Empire*, as Napoleon entitled it, in an attempt to pretend that the Restoration had not occurred. Napoleon was obliged at least to equal the liberal tenets of the Constitutional Charter of 1814. He went further. The preamble claimed:

> In all the fifteen years since we were called upon by the will of the French people to govern the State, we have tried, always profiting from experience, to develop a constitutional system according to the needs and wishes of the nation. ... Our ultimate aim was the creation of a great European federation, which we believed to be in tune with the spirit of the age and with the progress of civilization. In the hope of achieving this on as large a scale with the greatest possible hope of stability, we postponed the publication of a certain amount of internal legislation, particularly that designed to protect the liberty of the individual. ... With all of this in mind, we now propose to develop representative institutions.[39]

The belligerence of foreign powers, he claimed, had prevented him from setting up a fully representative regime earlier. The document which followed was more liberal than the 1814 Charter which Louis XVIII had issued, for national sovereignty, not the will of the ruler, was stressed as its legitimation. Revolutionary, rather than classical, terminology was employed. 'Representatives of the People' were to be elected. The typical Bonapartist plebiscite held to confirm the new arrangements attracted only a minority of voters; 1.5 million in favour,

4802 against. Elections were held immediately for the new Chamber, with the participation of only 33,000 of the 69,000 enfranchised voters. Liberals dominated the new assembly, controlling 500 of the 629 seats. Only 80 Bonapartists were chosen. Napoleon had hoped for an obedient assembly, but found himself in partnership with an extremely argumentative one. The 'Additional Act' would probably have been forgotten had Waterloo been won instead of lost, on the strength of Napoleon's first encounter with an assembly which talked back at him.

Napoleon's 'liberalism' was unconvincing as a statement of political intent, but in other respects the merging of republican and Bonapartist personnel and policies was very significant. The liberals of the subsequent Bourbon regime were to hold both Bonapartist and republican sympathies, perceiving desirable and familiar elements of both in the revolutionary tradition they honoured. This alliance of Bonapartists and revolutionaries, formalized in the creation of the federations to defend the revived emperor, is often depicted as a new departure.[40] Thureau-Dangin noted that the episode created an 'unnatural, but subsequently permanent alliance of Bonapartists and liberals'. He argued that the anti-monarchist attitudes of the left during the Second Restoration owed much to the events of the Hundred Days. The Hundred Days meant that the left would no longer be loyal to the Bourbons, although they were never openly revolutionary.[41] The Hundred Days helped to create the notion of a liberal Empire, which Napoleon himself was to embroider in his memoirs written on St Helena.

The tumultuous years 1789–1814 left a large section of the population, both within the elite and among the less well-off, committed to the Revolution either because they remained attached to the ideals of liberty and equality, despite the many blind alleys of this quarter-century, because they believed the new institutional framework honoured these precepts to some degree, because they had benefited by securing land, employment, had been obliged to fight for their country, or any mixture of these. It was unlikely that anyone sharing any of these experiences would again accept the notion of an hereditary monarchy sanctified by a Christian deity. However, the revolutionary years pointed to no clear political alternative. The constitutional monarchy had been virtually stillborn, aspirations for a democratic republic had led to a variety of divisive oligarchical experiments, the Empire, despite Napoleon's attempts to gain the support of both revolutionaries and those who had served the old monarchy, was ultimately disastrous. Yet in 1814 all except the political framework of the previous regime was retained. To a considerable degree Louis XVIII was a republican/imperial monarch, although unlike his cousin who became king in 1830, he chose not to brag about it.

4 · Conspirators and Parliamentarians: Republicans 1814–1830

In 1814 France's future form of government was determined by an unholy alliance of the Great Powers who defeated Napoleon and the emperor's former officials, some of whom had been republican in the 1790s. Why it was that a republic was not contemplated? To what extent was the opposition to the restored Bourbon monarchy which developed subsequently republican in character?

Guizot observed that in 1814 republicans 'had no set of beliefs . . . they had lived through the Revolution with its promises, excesses, defeat, and were fearful. The defeat of Napoleon, in whom they had believed, left them in total disarray'.[1] The most ambitious republicans had served the emperor; republican and Bonapartist ideas had become inextricably fused and in 1814 both were associated with defeat, invasion and the presence of an army of occupation. Republican traditions were confused, bloody and dictatorial. No incontrovertible link could be forged with concepts of individual liberty, political freedom or parliamentary government. Republicanism could not offer an alternative set of social and economic beliefs. Those who had worked with revolutionary or Napoleonic governments thought of themselves as professional politicians and administrators and had job continuity as their major preoccupation in 1814. It was in their career interests to be royalists. It was Lafayette, not the royalists, who demanded Napoleon's abdication after Waterloo.

If it was expedient for former Bonapartists and republicans to forget their past, supporters of the restored Bourbons were even more anxious to obliterate all reference to the revolutionary years. In his study of

60

republicanism Weill began with the premiss that a republic was not even considered in 1814: 'La république pour les classes élevées, c'était le jacobinisme, c'était le guillotine, c'était 1793'.[2] Few have ever disputed this claim.[3] Republican notions were about as acceptable to Bourbon supporters as were communist ones to McCarthyites in America after the Second World War. Anyone who had been in state service during the previous quarter-century was likely to be condemned indiscriminately as 'revolutionary', 'republican' or 'Jacobin' by Restoration officials, especially after the Hundred Days, whatever his actual political affiliation. The royalists and especially the ultra-royalists of the Bourbon Restoration (1814–30) tried to pretend that the First Republic had never existed. The history of the Revolution was not taught in schools. Restoration royalists were anti-revolutionary; some were more positive and asserted a counter-revolutionary alternative.[4] For those sympathetic to the restored Bourbons, whether ultra-royalist or no, the Republic signified a regime hostile to their preferences in far more than politics. The First Republic was a regime, not only without a king, but one which guillotined the man regarded by them, not just as temporal ruler, but as appointed by God to govern. A republic was anti-God, quintessentially anti-Christ.[5]

The decision to make France a monarchy in 1814 was principally the work of her enemies. In 1813 when Napoleon made it clear he would not agree to rule a reduced Empire and sign a negotiated peace, Britain, Russia, Prussia and Austria had finally signed an alliance at Chaumont and committed themselves to his overthrow. The defeat of the Empire and the invasion of France in 1814, repeated in 1815 after Napoleon's escape from Elba, meant that France's enemies would dictate not only her borders, but also the broad outline of her political structure. The Allies took the opportunity to snatch away the huge empire the French had acquired during the wars, smother any remnants of radical revolutionary ideology by dividing up 'liberated' territory among themselves and eliminate the Bonaparte dynasty. There was Allied agreement that France should become a monarchy. However, the alliance of France's enemies was opportunistic and the British were rather less proscriptive in their ideas on what was a desirable political system than the others. The decision to restore the old dynasty was pragmatic not ideological, and far from a foregone conclusion.

A Bourbon counter-revolutionary movement had existed in Europe from the arrival of the first *émigrés* in the Austrian Empire in 1789. Throughout the war years France's enemies had regarded the exiled royalists as a useful, if exasperating and expensive, potential fifth column. The future Louis XVIII was subsidized by the British government at the rate of £20,000 a year from 1796. The Orleans family, the younger and often rival branch of the Bourbon clan, were also financed. Momentarily in 1814 Louis-Philippe, duke of Orleans, was considered for the throne, but he maintained a loyalty to the Bourbon claimant which was uncharacteristic for his family. Alexander I of Russia dallied with the idea of Bernadotte, former revolutionary and imperial marshal, crown prince and ruler of Sweden since 1810, who had deserted Napoleon and in 1814 commanded one of the Allied armies. Metternich thought very briefly of Marie-Louise, wife of Napoleon's young son. On balance, the Bourbons seemed the best prospect for the future peace of Europe, although even the Russian emperor was hesitant to restore them a second time after Waterloo.

The military defeat of Napoleon in 1814 and again after the Hundred Days discredited both the Republic and the Empire as governing systems for the French. Napoleon's troops remained eager to defend him but by March 1814 his military position was untenable and his marshals, led by Marmont, urged the acceptance of an armistice. The Allies made it clear when they occupied Paris in April 1814 that they would not negotiate with Napoleon or his relatives. The British, chief paymasters and leaders in the Allied coalition,[6] were determined that the Bourbons should not be restored as absolute rulers. A constitutional settlement would be in tune with British attitudes and would make the change of regime tolerable to Napoleon's governing elite. The Allies had no ambitions to topple any but Napoleon and his family. Indeed it was important to retain the support of Napoleon's officials in order to maintain continuity and avoid civil war in France.

Having made the basic decision in favour of a Bourbon monarchy, the Allies left it to the French to establish the details. The Napoleonic Senate was urged to form a provisional government which five senators duly joined. On April 2nd they announced the deposition of their former employer, who accepted their decision on the 6th. A constitutional commission was created, including senators. The craftiest of the emperor's former servants, Talleyrand, managed to manoeuvre himself into a leading role.

Thus the constitutional arrangements for Napoleon's replacement were made, not by monarchists, but by the emperor's own servants.[7] The commission took the constitution of 1791 as its model. They invited the late king's brother to become 'king of the French people'. Their constitution of April 6th provided for a bicameral legislature, an independent judiciary, an amnesty for political opinions, freedom of the press and religion and promised that the revolutionary land settlement would be permanent.[8] On April 14th the Senate gave provisional authority to the comte d'Artois, the intransigently ultra-royalist brother of the new king and on May 2nd they pledged homage to Louis XVIII.

There were disappointments in store for the kingmakers. The new king ignored their plan. A new constitutional commission of nine senators, nine members of the legislative body and three royal nominees produced a revised constitution, which effectively was the work of the three men nominated by the king. Most offensive was the preamble to the new constitution, which talked of the constitution as '*octroyée*', a grant of royal grace and favour in continuity with ancien regime royal charters. It was indeed entitled a '*Charte Constitutionnel*'. The king was to be 'king of France', called to the throne by 'divine providence', not the French people.[9] The new constitution was discussed by no elected assembly, it was a royal diktat.

The preamble and title aside, the Charter was in reality a compromise document, setting up a bicameral constitutional system, with a Chamber of Deputies elected by a lucky 90,000 adult males who paid an annual tax bill of at least 300 francs a year. All legislation was to be submitted for their approval, and although they had no direct voice in the selection of ministers, in practice government policy had to coincide with the parliamentary majority if it was to work. The Bourbon Restoration was a constitutional, if not a parliamentary regime. Catholicism was restored as the state religion, but freedom of conscience and freedom of speech were promised. The revolutionary land settlement was guaranteed and all of the revolutionary and imperial administrative, legal, judicial, financial and educational institutions were maintained. Napoleonic titles were to be recognized. Effectively this was the Empire, with a Bourbon replacing a Bonaparte, plus somewhat British-style (though not British-made) constitutional additions. To reward them for their complaisance, the Peace of Paris, although it reduced the French to their 1792 borders, minus a number of colonies, imposed neither indemnity nor army of occupation.

The former imperial *notables* who might have resented a Restoration were satisfied by the political settlement, relieved by the decision to guarantee *biens nationaux* in the constitution and above all delighted at the small number of destitutions. The attitude of the king himself and of his advisers does much to explain the ease with which the First Restoration was accepted. Louis XVIII recognized the need both to retain the benefits of the institutional modernization and centralization of the two previous decades and to employ experienced bureaucrats. There was thus a high level of continuity of personnel at the First Restoration. The royal payroll included 76 per cent of Napoleon's men; 45 of Napoleon's 87 prefects along with many other officials were retained. Of the new prefects, 29 per cent had worked under the Empire. In total two-thirds of the new prefects, who held a key administrative role, had served Napoleon in the same capacity. The new 149-strong Chamber of Peers included 103 senators and marshals of the Empire. Indeed only 37 senators were left out. Similar continuity was respected within the judiciary.

This atmosphere of conciliation was reversed by Napoleon's escape, dramatic 100-day rule, final defeat at Waterloo and the subsequent reaction of ultra-royalists. Perhaps the harmony had been an illusion, and would not have survived. It was obvious that a restoration of the old monarchy, albeit in tandem with the revolutionary institutions and a written constitution, would invoke hostility and suspicion among those who had served the Republic and Empire, even if they kept their old jobs. The king may have received Napoleonic nobles at court, but senior old noble families scorned and spurned them. There were some worrying signs for the Napoleonic elite. The proportion of noble prefects doubled to almost 65 per cent during the First Restoration.[10] *Emigrés* and ultra-royalists who had high expectations of a restoration were equally frustrated by their limited career opportunities in 1814. However, the willingness of the new 'royalist' officials to revert to Napoleon in the Hundred Days meant that the Second Restoration was accompanied by bitterness and violence, a White Terror, in which extremist monarchists exacted vengeance on the Hundred-Day turncoats.

The experience of the Hundred Days was crucial in the revival, and to some extent the transformation, of republicanism. It contributed to the fusion of republican and Bonapartist loyalties. The experience of living under a restored monarchy, especially the attitude and pronouncements of the king's brother, the comte d'Artois, had revived old anti-clerical and anti-noble attitudes, making Napoleon's promises on his return to abolish 'feudal' titles and expel the returned *émigrés* attractive. A third of Napoleon's old nobles rallied to him, and his less honoured former servants were even more enthusiastic.[11] Ironically, popular Bonapartism was greatly enhanced in the aftermath of defeat. The Hundred Days helped further to modify the military and dictatorial reality of Bonapartism, forging unprecedented alliances among liberals, traditional Bonapartists and republicans and linking them with popular sentiments. Out of patriotism, pragmatism, or because they believed Napoleon could be held to the liberalism of the Additional Act, some formerly unrepentant republicans rallied to Napoleon in 1815. The myth of revolutionary, even liberal Bonapartism, had begun to roll.

The amount of support for the emperor in 1815 should not be overestimated. Brittany and the Vendée rose against him and many other areas including Flanders, Artois, Normandy, Languedoc and Provence refused to back him. Promises of support in 1815 were as likely to be anti-Bourbon and patriotic as pro-Napoleon. Some Bonapartists were actually hostile because they disliked the Additional Act. In the six weeks before the battle of Waterloo a federative movement began spontaneously, reminiscent of that of 1789–91. Napoleon hesitated to engage with the *fédérés* at first, in view of the radicalism of the *fédéré* movement during the early 1790s. Indeed 13 of the federations of 1815 federations of 1815 were led by regicide members of the Convention, many of them former Jacobins, seven of whom had gone on to serve Napoleon, while six had been out of politics completely since the Terror.[12] Leading radical Jacobins in the Sarthe, Goyet and Bazin, joined Napoleon for the first time in 1815, organizing federations in Le Mans and Paris.[13] In the western departments the leaders were old Girondins. They claimed that they were trying to rediscover the revolutionary unity of 1789. It was a fragile alliance. The first federative pact was signed on April 29th by students, clerks and apprentices in the five Breton departments with the full support of Napoleon's agent, but was never pronouncedly Bonapartist and Napoleon's main supporters in the region did not join. Their proclamation in defence of liberty and the Revolution and determination to form mobile columns to defend France was reprinted in the *Moniteur*. On May 7th a Lyon federation emerged, headed by Jars, the Hundred-Day mayor, backed by Napoleon's commissioner with a committee of 40, all of whom were officials or national guardsmen. The Lyon group was the work of local Bonapartists and became the model for other federations, which were officially directed and patriotically inspired. Their successful launch depended on local circumstances; where royalism was strong, as in the Vendée, so was enthusiasm for the federations.

The urgent need to defend Paris brought 12,000 men into its federations by May 12th, most of them armed, including artisans from Saint Antoine and Saint Marceau, as well as former Napoleonic soldiers. In other places the members were never armed. Patriotism was the most powerful single motor. In Dijon the Austrian occupation in 1814 brought republicans and Bonapartists together as never before. Some Dijon *fédérés* had been Austrian prisoners of war. Some federations only wanted to defend their own village. Some were very political. Some faded quickly after Waterloo; others only got up steam afterwards, to fight not the Allies, but the ultras.[14] What was significant was the fusion of republican and Bonapartist sentiment, the numbers involved and the social mix of adherents. Thiers calculated 20,000 in the Breton association alone. Lyon and Strasbourg stood at 4000, with 3000 in Nancy, while Paris attracted 25,000 signatories to the Pact.[15] The federations were not the national guard under another name; they were often rivals and drawn from more modest middle-class, artisan, sometimes as in the Gard (Protestant) peasant backgrounds. Many were students, some teachers. They were often referred to in Brittany as '*jeunes gens*'. Their leaders were more wealthy, often lawyers, merchants, officials, sometimes nobles. Where membership lists permit identification, in Dijon, Rennes, Grenoble and in western France, it is apparent that *fédérés* were the nucleus of left-wing opposition to the Restoration.[16]

Persecution during the White Terror cemented the bond of republicans and Bonapartists. Left-wing sentiments began to take shape in reaction to a perceived counter-revolution. The violent response of the ultra-royalists in 1815 was a significant trigger in turning the quiescent scepticism of former republicans and Bonapartists into active criticism of the monarchy. Ultras had been disappointed with the First Restoration, both ideologically and personally. The failure of Napoleon's Hundred-Day return gave them the chance to exact the vengeance they sought. All ultras abhorred the Revolution, but their responses varied.[17] Some were anti-revolutionary, others postulated a counter-revolutionary solution to the fait accompli of the 1790s, some nourished a mix of anti- and counter-revolutionary responses. The anti-revolutionaries were 'super' monarchists. They cherished a romanticized, idealized and totally unhistoric view of the ancien regime. They believed, with unhistoric fervour, that ancien regime France had been harmoniously ruled by king, Church and nobles. If such a trinity had ever combined to rule, which is more than doubtful, that age was long past. The ultras, many of whom had spent the entire revolutionary period in exile, appeared unaware that their view of history, and the potential for its resurrection, was anachronistic. They expected that the restored monarch, trailing clouds of divine right glory, as if his brother had never been executed in 1793, would share their faith in romantic mythology.

Other ultras were counter-revolutionary, holding the views of their leading thinkers, de Bonald[18] and de Maistre,[19] that the Revolution had happened because all had not been well with the ancien regime. Thus they did not want a return to 1789 but a specifically *counter-revolution*. Ultras had a lot to say about constitutions in the heady days of the *chambre introuvable*. It is not entirely clear whether the implementation of a constitutional charter was seen as part of an alternative, monarchist revolution, or whether it was part of the armoury of anti-revolution. Some argued that the various charters issued by ancien regime kings were a pre-1789 constitution. Whereas the anti-revolutionaries were more royalist than Louis XVIII, the counter-revolutionaries were sometimes less royalist. They sought local autonomy and limitations on the power of Paris, which, given the centralization of France, meant limitations on the power of the king. There were discernible echoes of the protests of *notables* before 1789, of the *parlements* and local estates who had argued that the Crown had been trying to undermine the traditional rights and privileges of the aristocracy and the Church to accentuate the absolutism of the king.

The ultras were disappointed with their new king. Louis assumed that he ruled a centralized state, that prefects appointed from Paris would do his bidding. The ultras anticipated that the restoration of the monarchy would bring a dilution of Napoleonic centralization and restore regional, traditional, provincial liberties, quite forgetting that the ancien regime monarchy itself had been a highly centralized state. They resented the retention of the new revolutionary and Napoleonic institutions by which France was now governed. Napoleon's escape gave them the opportunity to be heard and to act. The White Terror of 1815 was the work of the ultras, trying to teach both the Bonapartists and Louis XVIII a lesson. The terrorists were led in the south by the duc d'Angoulême, son of Artois. Much of the support for ultra ideas came from the more catholic Midi and the West and a number of sympathizers spent the Hundred Days with Angoulême in Spain, rather than in Ghent with the king. In many respects the anarchic revenge of the White Terror in the south in 1815–16 was the expression of this determination to resurrect the old provinces as autonomous units.

But even more, the White Terror was a punishment for the Bonapartists and those republicans who had joined in federations to defend the revived Empire of 1815. Terrorist violence and total lawlessness were confined to Provence and eastern Languedoc. Elsewhere the White Terror involved harassment and the removal of Hundred-Day men from office. Royalist officials were usually in collusion with the Terror. In the catholic Midi only the Protestants had returned to Napoleon in 1815; catholic monarchists had formed secret armies which began to exact their vengeance after Waterloo. Assassinations and arbitrary imprisonments followed. In Marseille on June 24th 50 were killed, 200 injured and houses were burned down. The lawlessness spread through the Rhône valley, and the departing commander of the Toulon garrison was murdered in Avignon on July 24th.

In Toulouse the local *verdets* wore the green *cocarde* of the comte d'Artois, champion of the ultra-royalists. The moderate royalist commander of the Toulouse National Guard appointed from Paris was murdered when he tried to merge the *verdets* with the Guard. There was wild talk of setting up an autonomous southern kingdom of 'Occitania'. It was a religious civil war too, whose echoes went back to the sixteenth century. In Langedoc 37 Protestants, who had done well out of the revolutionary years, were murdered; 2500, including notable industrialists, fled. The Austrian occupation of the Var, Bouches-du-Rhône and Gard brought the wave of revenge to an end.[20]

There was no White Terror in Brittany. The Breton federations had been anti-*chouan*, but disciplined and orderly. No royalists had been put to the sword and the federations collapsed after Waterloo. In eastern and north-eastern France the ubiquity of the federations, plus the presence of foreign troops, meant that violent Terror was inconceivable. But destitutions, house searches, arrests and police surveillance were common in areas where federations had existed. Participation in a federation might mark an individual for persecution. Hernoux, mayor of Dijon in the Hundred Days and a *fédéré* leader, was one of many to lose his job and be imprisoned after Napoleon's fall.

The White Terror, bloody or not, ensured that lines of conflict were drawn. New laws were rushed through to permit the arrest of those suspected of plotting; there was legislation against seditious literature and special courts (*cours prévotales*) were set up to facilitate the speedy trial of those accused. In the event 6000 were sentenced, mostly not very severely, and only 250 of them by the special courts. However, there were dramatic and unpopular death sentences, notably the condemnation and execution of general Ney by the Chamber of Peers. In total 17 generals and officers were sent to trial by the military courts. The arrest of 37 others was ordered, although some were allowed to escape into exile. The Chamber was made hereditary, 94 new peers were created, and 29 peers who had reverted to Napoleon were deprived of their titles. Sweeping purges of the turncoat officials followed. Between 25 and 33 per cent were dismissed at all levels in the provinces as well as in Paris. The new monarchy thus discarded many of the most energetic and experienced officials and the White Terror ensured that such men could never safely be regarded as part of the status quo of a restored monarchy.

It can be no accident that victims of the White Terror were often leaders of the liberal opposition in the 1820s and the 1830 Revolution. Hernoux was to be the main liberal politician in his department. In Metz, de Merville, secretary-general of the prefecture in the Hundred Days, was to lead the opposition to the new monarchy during his subsequent prolonged period of unemployment. Former Napoleonic officials dismissed in 1815, often lawyers by profession, made up the inner core of an opposition, which may not have been wholly created by the White Terror, but was certainly identified and united by that experience. It would be simplistic perhaps to suppose that resentment at the injustices of the White Terror and disappointed ambition alone helped to create this opposition, but it was significant that active, influential men were deprived of their official posts and were in a position to become articulate foci for discontent.

Some of those who helped to create centres of opposition were predominantly Bonapartist[21] in their sympathies. Former imperial officers, retired on half-pay and left by the Restoration with little to do except lead the National Guard battalions and talk about past adventures until the disbandment of the Guard in 1827, provided a nucleus for the glorification of the former regime.[22] After Napoleon's defeat, the reaction of the government, particularly bitter because so many officers and men rejoined Napoleon during the Hundred Days, was to retire as many as possible of the members of his army and to efface imperial military traditions. The number of officers was reduced by 14,000 and the army cut to 324,000 men. A number of the commanders of the imperial army were arraigned as traitors and shot.[23] Imperial regiments were replaced by infantry regiments recruited and organized according to departments and the structure of cavalry and artillery units was deliberately altered to try to counter Bonapartist traditions. *Emigrés* were promoted.

Chaos and a possible Bonapartist backlash were only averted by the appointment of Gouvion St Cyr, one of Napoleon's marshals and a known liberal, as Minister of War in 1817.[24] Many former Bonapartist officers were then reintegrated. A surprising 75 per cent of officers were

Napoleonic veterans as late as 1824, mostly men from very modest backgrounds promoted from the ranks. Military reformers tried to replace Bonapartist enthusiasms with a monarchist, aristocratic, anti-bourgeois, anti-civilian ethos.[25] They were not entirely successful. An elitist and a popular Bonapartist legend was nurtured by frustration and inactivity.

The memory of the foreign policy successes of the emperor was a decisive factor in a continuing enthusiasm for the imperial years, particularly, if rather contradictorily, in the eastern departments which were invaded twice during the wars, in 1792–3 and in the campaigns of 1814–15. In the Côte-d'Or some cantons were implacably anti-monarchist from the time of the first invasion. The new monarchy, not the old Empire, was associated from the beginning with defeat and occupation, even though the occupation was actually beneficial for the economy of the area.[26]

The peace settlement of 1815 created tensions absent in that of 1814. To ensure the security of Europe, the final defeat of France was accompanied by an Allied occupation of all or part of 61 departments by, at the outset, 1,200,000 soldiers, which had to be funded by the French to the tune of 250 million francs a year and had to be endured until a substantial indemnity of 700 million francs had been paid. France was reduced to her 1789 borders. It can be no accident that the left-wing opposition to the Bourbons which developed was particularly pronounced in the occupied departments, which bore the cost and humiliation of occupation.

However, the twice-restored king was circumspect and did his best to defuse the tense situation of 1815. Advisers such as Fouché, who had served Napoleon, urged continued conciliation to avoid civil war, at a time when, he asserted (undoubtedly with mixed motives) in October 1815, only ten departments could be counted as royalist.[27] The first parliament elected after the second restoration was nicknamed the *chambre introuvable*, because 90 per cent of its members were resolutely ultra. Convinced that the ultras were dangerously divisive, Louis dissolved the assembly. Its successor contained only 90 ultras among its 238 members. In the Chamber of Peers a centre-right bloc of constitutional royalists and former imperial nobles emerged which contributed to stability.[28] The first crisis was thus defused by the realism of the king and his immediate advisers. Subsequently, the ultras were never more than a noisy minority within the royalists, but partisans of the revolutionary years were always aware of them as total enemies.

Left-wing critics of the restored Bourbons did not fit into precise ideological categories, an inevitable consequence of the varied experiences of the previous quarter-century. They were united by a pronounced patriotism and outspoken support for 1789, both ideological and economic, for many had bought *biens nationaux* in the 1790s. It would be quite misleading to talk of defined republican, Bonapartist or liberal groups in Restoration France. Critics might well have both republican and Bonapartist sympathies and be associated with liberal affiliations in the 1820s. There were many critics of the Bourbons within the existing political elite and among the disenfranchised middle class, but there is also evidence, in Paris and the departments, of more artisan participation than has often been acknowledged in the past.

In addition to the disgruntled politicians and veterans, there was a new generation. Family tradition ensured that republicanism would not die; there were the heirs of the old republicans, including the Cavaignacs and Carnot, whose father had been a regicide. But there were many others, men concerned, not just with the need to speak up for the 1789 Revolution, but to take cognizance of the social impact of industrial change, writers influenced by the writings of Saint-Simon and the ideas of Babeuf as popularized by Buonarroti in 1828.[29] It has been suggested that these young men represented the opposition of a whole educated, mainly middle-class generation.[30] There appears to be a cohort, basically those born 1792–1803, who, children of Romanticism, believed that with them the world was born anew. They held to 'Truth' as an absolute and generally adopted a high moral tone. It was a generation which had experienced first-hand, not the traumas of the Revolution, but the fall of the Empire. They were the first generation educated in the *lycées* and the new imperial faculties. It is quite noticeable that whole groups of young men in the various secret voluntary associations of the 1820s had attended the same *lycées* and fascinating 'ven' diagrams can be drawn to show their overlapping interests.[31] Most influential were those who clustered around Victor Cousin at the *École Normale*. Cousin was lecturer in philosophy at the Sorbonne from 1815, when he was only 23, and his rather securalist philosophy was popular with the young and regarded as dangerously revolutionary by the new monarchist *notables*. He went back to the ideals of the original 1789 Revolution. He began his first lecture:

It is to those of you whose age is close to mine that I dare to speak at this moment; to you who will form the emerging generation; to you, the sole support, the last hope of our dear and unfortunate country. Gentlemen, you passionately love the fatherland; if you wish to save it, espouse our noble doctrines.[32]

The persecution of the faculties and individual professors by the government added to the charisma of personalities and generational conflict. One of Cousin's students was Dubois, who helped launch, and was the main editor of, the *Globe*. Another key figure was Bazard, a founder of the *charbonnerie*. The young thought of the *charbonnerie* as their organization, regarding the older members as interlopers. Subsequently, many lost faith in the power of the sword and moved on to the pen, as prolific journalists.

The transition between Empire and Restoration seems to have been significant in generational definition. The way in which the Empire was depicted as a time of hope and the birth of an open society, the Restoration as a closing of doors of opportunity to the young, was immortalized in the characterization of Julien Sorel in *Le Rouge et le Noir*, which was first published in November 1830.[33] With defeat in 1814–15 and the return of the old monarchy, the new educational system seemed to be both betrayed and a betrayal. The young students expected more than the future seemed to offer. Their teachers in the *lycées* hastened to swear loyalty to the monarchy, introduce religious teaching and to change the names of their institutions to *collèges royaux*. This did not stop them welcoming the return of Napoleon in 1815. Between 1815 and 1822 there were major incidents in 16 of the 38 *collèges*.

Unrest became endemic within higher education also. In 1815 the medical schools were unable to reopen because of the scale of rioting against the monarchy and in 1816 the *Ecole Polytechnique* was closed and purged. In 1819 the doyen of the liberals, Royer-Collard, Cousin's patron, resigned when the law faculty in Paris was closed and in 1822 the *Ecole Normale* was shut and Cousin's lectures banned until 1828.[34] History was an equally inflammatory subject. Guizot, professor of history at the Sorbonne since 1812, inspired men like Destutt de Tracy, the Fabre brothers and Marrast with his lectures on representative government. This was hardly a neutral subject in Restoration France, and Guizot lost his appointment in the council of state in the aftermath of the murder of the duc de Berri and subsequently was deprived of his university post. University unrest spread to Grenoble, Montpellier, Toulouse and Poitiers.[35] It should be noted that the 'trouble-makers' were not the 'generation of 1820' but their professors.

Senior members of the faculties were outraged at the censorship of the spoken word. The written word also came under fire and its defence became a potent focus for opposition to the Bourbons. Censorship rankled, even though it was less stringent than during the Empire. There had been a huge expansion in the number of books in print and twice as many publishers in 1825 as in 1813.[36] One subject in vogue was history, with a fivefold increase in historical works between 1812 and 1825. Some, but by no means all, historical works were disguised criticism of the regime. The history of the First Republic, entirely neglected in schools, became a best-seller.[37] The Convention became a cult. Another historical comparison which came readily to the pens of government critics was the perceived similarity between Louis XVIII and Charles X and Charles II and James II of England.

In his eloquent presentation of a generational thesis of opposition, Alan Spitzer singles out the *Globe*. The *Globe* was founded by two members of the *charbonnerie*, Leroux and Dubois;[38] its brief was to provide a synthesis of new thinking on science, literature and philosophy. Dubois was the dominant influence and many of its contributors were *normaliens* and ex-*carbonaros*. Dubois espoused the high ground of liberalism, demanding tolerance even for the Jesuits. The paper had a clutch of academics who had been dismissed for their liberalism on its staff who did not belong to the young age cohort. The Saint-Simonian *Producteur* with Bazard and Buchez as contributors was another circle of young journalists which had equally close links with the *charbonnerie*.

But criticism of the regime in books, journals and newspapers extended far beyond two publications and one generation. During the Restoration the left-of-centre press was particularly important because of its unparalleled popularity. In 1826 the Parisian daily papers which would have considered themselves to the left of politics had 50,000 subscribers, their rivals only 15,000. The *Constitutionnel* was the most popular with 20,000 subscribers. Casimir Périer was both a stockholder and a contributor. Thiers wrote for it. The *Constitutionnel* was a respected and influential paper, particularly within the business community; founded in 1815, despite its initial criticism of the Empire, the paper showed considerable sympathy for Bonapartism.[39] In 1828 the *Journal des Débats* had the second largest circulation, 11,000, after the *Constitutionnel*. Chateaubriand was one of its founders, but it took a firmly anti-Villèle stance from 1824 when Chateaubriand was dismissed from the government. Guizot, Royer-Collard and Salvandy were among its writers. In 1827 the *Journal* was one of the founders of the Society for the Freedom of the Press and was one of the staunchest backers of *Aide-toi* (*Aide-toi, le ciel t'aidera*, a pressure group founded by liberal voters and deputies to fight governmental electoral corruption). The *Courrier*, with only 6000 subscribers, barely covered its running costs and had little impact on the business world. However it attracted some of the most notable liberal writers and some whose views veered towards the Republic. Their correspondents included Guizot and Barrot and its senior editors were de Broglie and Benjamin Constant. The *Journal de Commerce*, as its name implies, was designed as a businessmen's paper. It was both liberal and anti-clerical, but had only 2500 subscribers in 1828. The *Gazette des Tribunaux*, founded in 1825 to serve the liberal legal community, had 3000 subscribers.

Four new papers founded in 1829, two of which were overtly republican, two liberal, epitomized the growing polarization of politics. The *Jeune France*, started in June, with Marrast as editor, took an idealistic republican stance. The *Tribune des Départements*, also begun in June and run by the Fabre brothers, moved from faith in *Aide-toi*, to a theoretical 'patriotic' republicanism. The *Temps* (October 1829) was owned by 74 liberal deputies, including Périer. Guizot, de Broglie, Lafayette and Dupont de l'Eure provided articles for its anti-Polignac programme. The *National* was the only Orleanist newcomer. It was financed by Laffitte and Baron Louis and its three main editors were Thiers, Mignet and Carrel. Among the many periodicals probably the most distinguished was the *Revue Française*, which devoted its monthly editions to literary and historical themes. Its writers included three dismissed professors, Cousin, Jouffroy and Guizot. Carrel, Thiers, Duvergier de Hauranne and Rémusat also provided articles. The liberal press was far from unanimous in its interpretation of contemporary politics, but from August 1829 opposition to Polignac provided the missing cement.[40]

Total subscription figures were very low by modern standards, but it should be remembered that an annual subscription would cost between 72 and 80 francs. However, the Parisian press was buttressed by a network of cheaper local papers. Circulation figures do not give a true picture of readership, since cafés and *cabinets de lectures* subscribed and through them one copy of a paper might reach several hundred readers.[41] In times of crisis papers were read aloud in the street. Restrictive press laws[42] and consequent trials in the 1820s gave a boost to the left, creating yet another cause around which they could unite and seek popular support, especially when acquittals were far more likely than condemnation.

Editors of local papers were usually the organizers of the local left-wing secret group in the early 20s and a few years later they were helping to run electoral committees for the liberals. They would store, advertise and circulate petitions; against indirect taxes on wine in 1828–9, for the abolition of the *loi septennale*, in favour of elected local councils and to resist the payment of direct taxes not sanctioned by parliament in 1829–30. About 500 signed this last petition in the Nord, 200 in the Bas-Rhin.[43] Liberal deputies usually headed the lists. At the end of 1829 when the liberal paper in Dijon joined in, inspired by Hernoux, the deputy, they informed their readers that the movement was already well established in Brittany, Lorraine, Champagne, Paris and Rouen.[44] Prefectoral attempts to prosecute the liberal paper in Boulogne because it published the terms of the association and urged all liberal men and women to unite against the government, '*cette nouvelle tête de Méduse*', failed to secure a conviction.[45]

What were these highly educated sons of the bourgeoisie complaining about? Their grievances were not, of course, confined to France. The *Globe* addressed itself to Europe. There was a malaise among the young which was Europewide. It has been attributed to an excess of educated men[46] by historians of Prussia as well as of France. In reality promotion prospects had never been better, but in the last few years the top jobs in education had been snaffled by the clergy. By 1827, 66 of the 88 professors of philosophy at the *collèges royaux* were priests appointed to try to alter the previously liberal tone.

Venality of office, a major target of the revolutionaries in 1789, had crept back during the Empire and blossomed as a canker during the Restoration. The legal profession flourished as the beleaguered Bourbons embarked on more and more prosecutions for political offences, but reorganization of the profession in 1822 extended the period of probation for young lawyers. The medical profession was also at odds with the regime. During the war years a new category of *officier de santé* had been introduced. After a much shorter spell of training than doctors, these men were in demand on the battlefield. But in peacetime it soon became apparent that there were too many medically qualified men around. Doctors complained of being undercut by the *officiers*, the Bourbon regime treated their complaints as treasonable. Young doctors complained that their seniors refused to retire and thus denied them promotion.[47] The medical faculties were accused of being hotbeds of Bonapartism. In 1822 when there were rumblings that the first lecture of the session was too preoccupied with religion, the medical faculty was closed and reorganized and all the most talented men, who also happened to be the fiercest critics of the government, were excluded.

The young often perceived themselves to be at war not just with the Bourbons, but with the entire older generation, Bonapartist as well. They believed, like every group of young adults, that they had nothing to learn from the old and everything to teach them. The young certainly dominated secret organizations and government persecution must have solidified their identification as a group. But their leaders, within the universities and elsewhere, were of the older generation.

Criticism of the Restoration was expressed partly through conspiracies and secret societies, partly in newspapers and in the Chamber of Deputies, often by many of the same people. Conspiracy was ubiquitous on both the extreme right and left of politics. The left organized itself through secret conspiracy, not just because Article 291 of the Penal Code demanded that publicly organized groups of more than 20 members secure official sanction, but also because the right was similarly organized and secrecy was considered vital to combat secrecy; perhaps because secret societies preserved intimacy and identity in an age when the political community was growing and becoming anonymous. A major target of the left were the *Chevaliers de la Foi*, which had been the centre of clerico-monarchist secret manoeuvrings since 1810. Founded by comte Ferdinand de Bertier as an antimasonic secret society, it had worked somewhat ineffectually for a Bourbon restoration. From 1815 it was specifically ultra-royalist, headed by the comte d'Artois who was heir to the throne, and contained many priests. Opponents spoke of it as a secret government, opposed to the king.[48] A number of its members also belonged to the *Congrégation*, which appeared to be a public, philanthropic catholic association, but its Jesuit connections did not reassure the left-wingers, who always associated it with the *Chevaliers*. Another target of suspicion was that of the repeated evangelical missions, which although also public were specifically anti-1789, and added to this pervasive and powerful underground.

Left-wing conspiratorial formations developed in opposition to those of the ultras. They were most successful in areas with a radical revolutionary tradition, which usually also tied in with areas where the federations had been active in 1815. Their growth was frequently provoked by continued persecution. In 1816 Joseph Rey,[49] a radical lawyer in Grenoble, founded *L'Union*. In May 1816 he tried to institute a republican coup in the town with perhaps as many as 4000 retired Napoleonic veterans and others. Six were killed in the skirmishes and

25 were subsequently tried and executed. In June 1817 Bonapartist sentiments were expressed and the *tricolore* was flown in Lyon during artisan riots over the collapse of the silk trade and the high price of basic foods. As in Grenoble, government repression was severe. Sent to investigate, General Marmont came to the conclusion that the commander of the Lyon garrison, General Canuel, had fabricated the conspiracy; prisoners were released, officials dismissed. Canuel was later accused of participating in an ultra conspiracy against Louis XVIII. In 1818 a Paris branch of the Grenoble *Union* was set up including Lafayette,[50] drawn in by Rey's friend, Destutt de Tracy, Manuel, Corcelles, Merilhou and the generals Thiard and Corbineau.[51] In total fewer than 30 students became members, including Bazard. In 1819, when the *abbé* Grégoire was denied his seat in the Chamber after he had been elected in Grenoble with the help of the *Union*, the society became more pronouncedly radical.

The *Chevaliers de la Liberté* were formed in Saumur to combat the machinations of the ultra *Chevaliers*, after members of the latter, who were students in the local military school, prevented Benjamin Constant attending a banquet organized by his constituents. The nucleus of members were men who had lost their jobs at the Second Restoration, including former *fédérés*, old soldiers and some students of the military college itself. Rumours that *biens nationaux* might be reclaimed by their former owners attracted small landowners to the organization which spread in all the five departments of the *Vendée*. They were linked both to a *comité directeur* in Paris and to groups in Grenoble, Lyon and other eastern towns. In February 1822 the Dijon chief prosecutor sent the *garde des sceaux* full details of the local branch of their *chevaliers de la liberté* and of their efforts to gain support within the garrison.[52] Their aim was the overthrow of the regime. Later they combined with the *charbonnerie* and commentators do not always distinguish between the two.

All of these secret societies were specifically insurrectionary and the early 1820s witnessed a small number of minor conspiracies against the regime, usually originating among junior army officers.[53] Rumours abounded, amply expanded by spies who needed a good story for their bread-and-butter. In 1820 came the *conspiration* or *complot de l'est*, in which apparently there was to be a major rising in the garrisons of eastern France, starting with Alsace, to proclaim Napoleon Emperor, and just to make sure, to murder the duc d'Angoulême. The organizers were Lafayette, Voyer d'Argenson, Laffitte and Gévaudon. The duc d'Angoulême himself was sent on a tour of the east to rally support and met a frosty reception in Dijon, Lyon, Grenoble and Besançon, where the *tricolore* was flown and groups of retired Bonapartist soldiers muttered darkly. He finished his tour in Strasbourg, Metz and Nancy and must have wondered just how many friends he had in high places. But the departments which were supposed to rise, such as the Doubs, remained totally tranquil.[54]

The *Amis de la Verité* Masonic lodge in Paris, founded by young radicals such as Buchez, Bazard, Flottard and Joubert probably in 1818, was Bonapartist and consciously political, attracting some lawyers but mainly law and medical students – their oldest member was 28. At the time of their recognition by the Grand Orient (the Establishment epi-centre of Masonry), their meetings were attracting up to 1000 people, although their membership lists showed only 45. They organized a procession in protest at the law of the double vote in 1820 in which one of their number was killed. Subsequently many took part in a planned military rising in Paris, dressed as National Guardsmen. Prosecution followed. Buchez, Bazard and Joubert fled to Naples, from where Buchez and Joubert returned with the idea of the *charbonnerie*.[55] The *Amis* became a *charbonnerie* group and the idea quickly spread.

The *charbonnerie* was a secret organization, divided into tiny cells of 20 or less. Symbolism and rites similar to those of Freemasonry were used. In the Italian *carbonari*, a man joined as an apprentice and was only gradually initiated into the secrets of the group. He would be introduced to the members blindfolded, carrying leaves and earth, symbolically to build a fire and cook. He had to declare that he was bringing faith, hope and charity to all '*bons cousins charbonniers*'. Only then was he allowed to enter the *vendita* or meeting place proper. He was questioned about his moral values and his willingness to give to the poor. A certain amount of larking about took place; he was sent outside to the forest, tripped up repeatedly and ordered to walk through a fire which represented the flame of charity. Finally he had to kneel, place his hands on a hatchet and swear to keep the secrets of the movement. His blindfolds were then removed; he was threatened with death if he revealed these secrets and ordered to repeat the initiation oath. He was then an apprentice. Their sacred code was 'faith, hope and charity' and they signalled to fellow apprentices by pressing their middle finger onto the right thumb. The apprentice could become a Master; here emphasis was placed on the idea of Jesus Christ as the Grand Master of the Universe. Initiation consisted of a mock trial of Jesus. The passwords changed to 'fern and nettle' and the sacred words 'honour, virtue and probity'. The master was told that Jesus was the first *carbonaro*.

There were between seven and nine grades of membership, but there are no written records of procedures beyond the first two. In some lodges Masters were told that their aim was to destroy tyrannical governments.[56] In France the groups were hierarchically arranged, so that only one man from each *vente* (literally a stack of felled timber, presumably with which actual charcoal burners worked) knew the members of the superior one, up to a *vente suprême* located in Paris. At its height the *charbonnerie* had about 60,000 members in 60 departments, a majority in the east,[57] with strongholds in Metz, Nancy, Strasbourg, Mulhouse, Neufbrisach, Belfort and further south in Marseille and particularly in Lyon. The Dijon group, which included Etienne Cabet, consisted of 12 *ventes*.[58] They established friendly relations with the artillery regiment stationed in Auxonne. In the Franche-Comté the *charbonnerie* developed out of traditional fraternal artisan organizations, the *Bons Cousins or Charbonniers*, and had no links with the Italians.

The *ventes* were armed.[59] Each member had to supply a gun and 25 rounds of ammunition. The stated aims were vaguely, not specifically, subversive, stressing the brotherhood and equality of man, and they attracted young idealists as well as republicans and Bonapartists unreconciled to the new regime. Many had been *fédérés* in 1815; seven out of the twelve groups in Dijon were led by former *fédérés*.[60] The units were usually led by former Napoleonic officers and officials, but also attracted a new generation, too young to have known the Revolution, mainly young soldiers and students of law and medicine,[61] such as Trélat (later a republican), Leroux (a future socialist), the radical journalist Cauchois-Lemaire and Augustin Thierry (former secretary of Saint-Simon). The *vente* in Dijon also included some artisans and clerks. Liberal *notables* were deeply involved, both financially and as members. Mauguin, future deputy for Dijon and a well-known Paris lawyer, was both a member of the *vente suprême* in Paris and associated with the Dijon group.[62] Lafayette, Voyer d'Argenson, de Corcelles, Beauséjour, J. Koechlin, de Schonen, Fabvier, Merilhou, Dupont and Barthe were all members.[63] Soldiers might join civilian units, or form special military ones. In the army the *haute vente* was called a *legion*, the *ventes centrales* were *cohortes*, the *ventes particulières* were *centuries* and the smallest basic group a *manipule*.

The *charbonnerie* quickly linked up with the *Chevaliers* in the west and grew rapidly in the south and east. Sometimes both names were used; in 1822 the government prosecutor in Dijon sent the statutes of the local *Chevaliers* to Paris, which were similar to those of the *charbonnerie*, although the names of members mentioned were different. Members promised to uphold the Charter, if necessary with their lives, and had to provide themselves with a weapon. They were grouped in tens; their watchwords were *liberté* and *patrie*. The prosecutor was convinced that it was a wholly subversive organization. It was led by a number of Napoleonic officers who had been forced to retire at the Restoration, including Silvestre, Nanteuil and Anthony, and attracted young people and members of the local garrison.[64]

Other secret left-wing groups were set up with a variety of names. In Chaumont, Haute-Marne, *L'Ordre et l'Amitié* began in 1818. Its members took an oath to love and defend Napoleon but, as was often the case, its small size and informal structure kept it safe from prosecution. Typically, its focus was the local opposition newspaper, *Courrier de la Haute-Marne*, whose editor Cousot printed their small pamphlets anonymously. Members paid a subscription of 15 centîmes a month. The society was composed of artisans, including a baker, a small merchant and a minor civil servant, and its treasurer was Barotte, a trainee printer from Dijon.[65] In 1823 the ringleader Cousot was finally successfully convicted, the nagging of the prosecutor overcoming the reluctance of the jury.[66] The jury were probably correct to regard a 3000 franc fine excessive, for such groups were often as much concerned with sociability as insurrection. In December 1822 the local firemen in Lons-le-Saulnier set up a *Bons Cousins Charbonniers*, but the prosecutor concluded that this was just an excuse to hold an annual banquet and get drunk,[67] so he left them alone.

In eastern France the *charbonnerie* was the basis for an attempt to use the army against the regime in December 1821. Junior officers in the Belfort garrison were to raise the *tricolore*, march on Colmar and proclaim a provisional government, comprising Lafayette, Corcelles (*père*), Voyer d'Argenson, Dupont de l'Eure and Koechlin, all local liberal *notables*, several of whom had provided money for the scheme.[68] There were to be similar risings in Marseille and Saumur. The commanding general in Saumur got wind of the plan, but seemed unimpressed. On 18–19 December 1821 some of the Saumur conspirators were killed fighting a fire in the garrison and details of the conspiracy were found on their bodies, leading to the arrest of 30 junior officers. The Belfort rising, coordinated by Joubert and Bazard, was postponed. But the Neuf-Brisach garrison became nervous when the rising was delayed and in Belfort suspicions were aroused. On hearing of secret meetings at a local inn, the colonel of the regiment ordered the arrest of those involved.[69] Some fled to neighbouring Baden and Switzerland. In Colmar 44 men were put on trial, but the charges were imprecise. Six officers and one lawyer were sentenced to death for plotting against the security of the state and four others, including Jacques Koechlin, mayor of Mulhouse during the Hundred Days, received prison sentences. The government prosecutor complained that the jury had been bribed to acquit the accused,[70] but Restoration juries seldom took political charges seriously, especially when no obvious harm had been done.

A plot to spring the prisoners led to another abortive rising. Colonel Caron, a Bonapartist retired on half-pay at the Restoration,[71] who had recently been acquitted of trying to organize a conspiracy in Paris in 1820, was set up by members of the Colmar garrison who were government spies. He led 90 soldiers, with some officers disguised as soldiers, from Colmar to Nancy, chanting '*Vive Napoleon II*'. As they were preparing to pitch camp for the night, Caron was arrested by some of his own men and taken back to Colmar. He was sentenced to death by a military court and shot.[72] His associate, Roger, was given 20 years by a civil court, but released after two years because of loud protests from liberals like General Foy that the two men had been led on by the soldiers.[73]

In February 1822 General Berton, another Napoleonic officer retired on half-pay, led a rising on Thouars, helped by a disaffected section of the National Guard. A hundred or so of them marched on Saumur, but overnight his support dwindled and next day 43 were arrested. Berton was later caught and sentenced to death with five associates. A further rising was planned within the army by junior officers, including Sergeant-Major Bories and sergeants Goubin, Raoulx and Pommier, who had joined the Masonic lodge *Amis de la Verité* and were involved with the *charbonnerie* while stationed with the forty-fifth regiment in Paris in 1821. When they were moved to la Rochelle in January 1822 the news of their extra-curricular activities had already reached their commanding officer and General Despinois, the commander of the Twelfth Military Division who was already investigating the case of General Berton. All four were arrested and accused of plotting, and with the exception of Bories made full confessions. Their conspiracy trial, in August and September 1822 in Paris, became a major tourist attraction. They were condemned to death by the military court; attempts to contrive their escape failed and they were executed on 21 September 1822.[74] Bories died stoically and they all became martyrs of the left.

There were a multitude of plots, but none got off the drawing board. Partly this was because of the activities of police spies. Conspiracies and secret societies were habitually open secrets and the government employed both police agents and independent spies, who often acted as double agents. The director of the Phoenix Insurance Company in Dijon was a member of the local *charbonnerie* and was paid 25,000 francs by the prefect for his double-dealing.

Those who joined secret societies sometimes had an ambivalent attitude to violent revolution. Conspirators were idealists and insurrectionary in thought rather than deed. It has been suggested that the soldiers involved were motivated as much by the boredom of provincial garrison life as by Bonapartist or republican memories.[75] Contemporary reports by senior officers of affrays between the garrison and the local population, fights in cafés, seduced wives and other misbehaviour give sustenance to such an interpretation. Stendhal's novel describing the life of Lucien Leuwen, the son of a wealthy banker garrisoned in Nancy, and his dalliance with republicanism and local ladies, gave wider publicity to the problems of peace-time soldiering.[76] *Notables* seem to have regarded participation in and control of insurrectionary plots and the *charbonnerie* itself as a sort of insurance policy, to maintain their leadership of radical opinion, while not disassociating themselves entirely from the legal political game. One is sometimes tempted to wonder whether the rather feeble conspiracies of the period were not attempts by the agents to raise their income, as they were paid entirely by results. Spying was perhaps many times more lucrative than selling insurance.

The *charbonnerie* was an outlet for discontent, frustration and idealism, but it did not propose an alternative to the restored monarchy. It never became more than a matter of patriotic, democratic, humanitarian and vaguely republican sentiments, a philosophical rather than a directly subversive training, despite the plots. Members were largely Bonapartist until Napoleon's death; their Bonapartism was primarily nationalist in inspiration. There was a republican flavour too;[77] the republican element was idealistic, theoretical and humanitarian, deliberately turning its back on the memory of dictatorship and the Jacobin Terror. Members later branched out in various radical directions. Leroux and Buchez adopted Saint-Simonist ideas, Cabet republican and utopian socialist, others, like Blanqui, became revolutionary republicans. Yet others, like Dupont de l'Eure and Montalivet, were Orleanists. The *charbonnerie* was primarily a movement of young men from comfortably-off families, although lists of members of secret groups frequently mention a predominance of artisans and lower middle-class occupations and soldier members were NCOs, presumably from the same sort of background.

The *charbonnerie*'s closest spiritual, organizational and personal links were with Freemasonry. Many Freemasons became members, the ideas of the two groups were similar and the rites and ceremonies closely related. Many Masons supported the Belfort conspiracy.[78] Both Masons and the *charbonnerie* earned a papal condemnation in 1821. There was, in some eastern departments, a close correlation between the leading members of local lodges and liberals who came to power after the revolution of 1830.[79] Mauguin, a leading radical *avocat* and political activist, who played a role in the July Days in Paris, was a Mason, as indeed was Lafayette. Dr Turck was a local Mason in the Vosges who joined the *charbonnerie* and became a republican in the July Monarchy.[80] The correlation was so common as to make its absence surprising. Many Masons were involved in radical politics, but the Masonic lodges were not themselves instruments of dissent. Only ultras believed that Masonry itself was subversive. Many lodges of Free-masons gained official authorization during the Restoration and Grand Masters were careful to ensure that their rites were not offensive to the king, while Decazes played a leading role in their reorganization. Active political opposition was organized through other chan-nels.[81]

During 1822 interest in conspiracy and in the *charbonnerie* was fading. In May 1823 officials in Dijon were still worried that the local *charbonnerie* units, under Cabet and Hernoux, were planning to link the groups in Dijon, Dôle, Besançon, Lyon, Grenoble and other parts of the east with men from the neighbouring garrisons in a major revolt, but nothing came of it, beyond a spate of unexplained fires.[82] Typical of other *ventes*, the members in Dijon developed new interests. Why? Failed and stillborn conspiracies must have been disillusioning and the punishments of the courts fairly numbing. But there were more positive reasons. Firstly, in 1822 the government intervened in an internal Spanish dispute over succession to the throne. Troops were sent to Spain. A number of *charbonnerie ventes* depended on support from soldiers, especially NCOs, who were temporarily removed from the scene. Some members of the French *charbonnerie* fought on the side of the Spanish liberals. Secondly, government intervention in elections became so crass that the defence of the electoral system became an issue of sufficient magnitude to merit the full attention of critics of the regime. Finally, the vague humanitarianism of the *charbonnerie* began to take a more precise form with the development of Saint-Simonian doctrines and groups, particularly after the death of Saint-Simon in 1825.

Saint-Simon's own political affiliation was ambiguous. In his book *L'Industrie* published in 1817, he stressed the need for the development of a new form of society, to match contemporary industrial change, in which those in control of the economy would have a major role in the direction of the state. He had hoped that the French Revolution would lead in that direction and in his disappointment rejected both Napoleon and the liberals. For a time he put his faith in the restored monarchy, but in his later years transferred his loyalty to a purified, simple Christianity, which he described in his last book, published shortly before his death in 1825.[83] Saint-Simon's followers became increasingly critical of existing industrial society and convinced of the need for radical social reform. They formed a distinct group, adopting the religious ideas of Saint-Simon's later years. They attracted altruistic, idealistic supporters from the middle class, especially among a number of newly qualified doctors who were to emerge as an influential element of later republicanism.

Other members of the *charbonnerie* concentrated their energies on the defence of the 1814 constitution and the electoral system. Left-wing criticism began to focus on legal means and tactics, the twin fulcrums of which were the Chamber of Deputies and the press. Critics became merged into what historians have described as a liberal group,[84] although at the time there was no formal unity or organization, in an age when political parties were regarded as divisive and almost treasonable. Left-leaning critics of the Restoration were known as Independents or *doctrinaires*, because they defended the 1814 constitution as a 'doctrine' and an electorate 'independent' of government influence. They were committed to the moderate gains of 1789 and anxious to dispel any connection between themselves and violent aspects of the Revolution. Men such as Guizot and Royer-Collard consciously associated themselves with the years of constitutional monarchy during the 1789 Revolution, praising both representative and open government.[85] They admired the British system. A number, including Duvergier de Hauranne, Royer-Collard, the duc de Broglie, Charles de Rémusat and Madame de Stael, visited Britain as guests of Whig politicians, attending election meetings and the House of Commons (which proved a rather disillusioning experience). On his return in 1826 Duvergier de Hauranne eagerly described to the readers of the *Globe* the glories of free speech exemplified in the British press, circulating libraries and the Commons.[86]

Some commentators identify *doctrinaires* as the more moderate element, who were consciously grooming themselves for political power and include men like Guizot and de Broglie in this category. The Independents were more radical and naturally 'children of opposition', including Constant, Lafayette, Manuel, Sebastiani and Foy. In their ideas and tactics there was little to separate them.[87] Later, in the 1820s they were usually called simply liberals, or 'left' and 'centre-left' in analyses of the composition of parliament. They were very divided among themselves and aspired to no coherent doctrine, despite their name (which was given with a note of irony, perhaps).[88]

Liberals were influential in the Decazes government from 1818 and, typically, were outspoken and enthusiastic defenders of the constitution of 1814 against the diatribes of the ultras. They called themselves constitutionalists and insisted that they were suspicious of the arbitrariness of both absolutism and revolution. They considered themselves politically conservative and rejected the labels 'left' or 'centre-left'. They welcomed the distinction made in the 1791 constitution between 'active' and 'passive' citizens. They admired representative institutions, under the control of a wealthy 'independent' minority. 'Independence' was measured by a high tax qualification for voters. They did not demand full parliamentary government. They were inclined to praise 'the sovereignty of the people', by which they meant the sovereignty of reason and justice. They argued that political rights should be limited to all educated and reasonable men. On the other hand they thought that personal liberty was a democratic right. They spoke up for freedom of association and actively worked for press freedom; many wrote for the liberal newspapers. They sometimes, for instance in Alsace, were what later became classically liberal, calling for freedom of trade, but many manufacturers sought a more, rather than a less protectionist commercial policy. They favoured less, not more, government.

Liberalism was thus very eclectic, embracing a wide variety of political loyalties, including men who later became Orleanist, like Rémusat, others who were Bonapartist, like Prévost-Paradol, and republicans, such as Jules Simon and Vacherot.[89] The leading thinker was Benjamin Constant who, like many, had supported Napoleon in the Hundred Days. Constant left for Britain at the Second Restoration, returning in September 1816. He successively edited the liberal papers *Mercure* and *Minervre*,[90] becoming the focus for liberal views in the

Chamber of Deputies as deputy for the Sarthe. But many royalists, except extreme ultras, shared some liberal views, particularly on the need to maintain an elected assembly. A typical 'conservative liberal' was Chateaubriand, who in *De la Monarchie selon la Charte* accepted the material achievements of 1789, including the land settlement, and concepts of individual freedom, especially press liberty and a parliamentary system, but could not stomach the moral content of the Revolution, above all the attack on the Church.[91] Most royalists were aware that, despite revolutionary and Bonapartist antecedents and professional disappointments, liberals were not revolutionaries, although involvement in the *charbonnerie* might have stretched their credulity.

The ultras' reaction to the murder of the duc de Berri, Louis XVIII's brother's heir, in 1820 and the growing influence of Artois, particularly after the appointment of the Villèle government in 1822, accentuated the fears of the liberals. The ultras claimed that the murder was a liberal plot. The emotional backlash, although less violent than in the White Terror, allowed the ultra minority to trim the constitution. The franchise was restricted, giving the quarter most wealthy a second vote. Thereafter less than 25,000 voters elected 165 deputies in special departmental electoral colleges; they then joined the rest of the electorate to choose the remaining 265 members. This was a specifically ultra measure and well understood by the political community. The richest voters were always landowners because the *cens* or franchise was based on tax payments. The *foncière*, or land tax, was by far the most onerous of the four direct taxes on which the *cens* was based, the next largest, the *patente*, being a commercial or industrial tax which was calculated, not on profits (the French long resisted a true income tax), but on the value of the property in which the business was conducted. It was assumed that France's richest landowners were bound to be monarchists, probably ultra-royalist, and a second vote for such men would ensure a complaisant Chamber of Deputies for the foreseeable future.

The liberals were incensed by the law of the double vote and particularly so when the 1824 election left them with only about 40 seats out of 430. Apart from the *chambre introuvable*, it was the most royalist assembly during the entire Restoration, including a mere 29 liberals elected in the *arrondissement* constituencies and 9 in the double vote departmental electoral colleges. Antagonism was all the more profound because immediately after this election parliament passed a *loi septennale*, which changed the system of election. In future the assembly would no longer be re-elected in fifths each year, but in its entirety every seven years. Liberal anger reached a peak when the new chamber also decided that the new law would apply retrospectively to the parliament then in session.

The accession of Artois as Charles X in 1824 confirmed the fears of the left. Ultra influence over government policy on sensitive issues became irresistible. Religion was an especially explosive item and the new king's ceremonial coronation at Rheims cathedral contrasted with the simple, constitutional arrangements of 1814. Left-wing critics were far from being anti-religious but they were alarmed by the perceptible increase in the educational, social and political influence of the Catholic Church in these years. The activities of the *Missions de la France* were condemned in the Chamber by liberal deputies as inflammatory and illegal.[92] The high point of each of their nationwide evangelical campaigns was a passionate service in which the forgiveness of the Almighty was sought for the sins of the Revolution. Equally pertinent was the increased presence of the Church in education. Liberals likewise deplored the appointment of Mgr de Fraysinnous as Grand Master of the University of Paris, the bureaucratic heart of the state system of secondary education, in 1822.

The ultras' greatest triumph was the law against sacrilege orchestrated by the 100 *chevaliers de la foi* in the 1824 Chamber.[93] Although never enforced, the law helped to confirm left-wing suspicions and unite parliamentary liberals on an anti-clerical platform. The Church seemed to be gaining ground, not just in the religious demesne, which was not much resented, but also in re-establishing a powerful influence over society. Worst of all, for those of liberal sympathies, was the increasingly close relationship between the Church and politics, epitomized by the presence of ultras in senior posts within the Church hierarchy, including Mgr de Quelen, archbishop of Paris and Cardinal Rohan-Chabot, archbishop of Besançon. Official demands for clerical support in elections became more pronounced after the accession of Charles X. The fusion of liberal and anti-clerical sentiments was thus reinforced.

Biens nationaux were another divisive issue which was exacerbated by ultra legislative successes. Ownership of former church and *émigré* lands was confirmed in the constitution. Unsold *émigré* land, mostly woodland, was returned to its former owners in 1815. *Emigrés* never lost hope and still sought compensation for land which they had lost. In 1825 the royalist assembly agreed to float a state loan and pay compensation. The loan was regarded with a mixture of resentment and suspicion by the new owners of *biens nationaux*, who argued that the legislation called into question the legitimacy of their own titles to property.

Most inflammatory and inept of all the ultra strategies was the prolonged attack on the electoral system so treasured by the liberals. Before 1827 there was no recognized system for checking electoral lists and prefects had virtually invented lists which they thought would win elections.[94] The number of qualified voters fell from 110,000 in 1817 to 96,525 in 1820 and finally to 79,138 in 1829. In the department of the Ain there were 617 voters in 1820, 485 in 1828. The elimination of those qualified to stand as candidates was even more dramatic; in 1820 there were 18,561 *éligibles*, in 1828, 14,548, a loss of nearly one-quarter.[95] In the same period the population rose by about 3.5 million and there was no sudden impoverishment of the wealthy to correspond to the shrinking electoral lists. Neither do tax changes account for the embarrassing disappearance of inconvenient voters. Prefects simply excluded them by negligence, fraudulence and ham-fisted deception.[96]

Since electoral colleges were mostly small and local *notables* formed a tight group interrelated by friendship, family, marriage and professional ties, a small number of the very wealthy usually controlled the choice of deputy. What is astonishing, given the size of the electorate and its wealth (and therefore assumed conservatism), plus the irresistible attraction of central government patronage, was that after 1824 increasing numbers of electoral colleges refused to rubber-stamp approved ministerial candidates. In 1829 there was a total of 169 voters in the relatively poor department of the Vosges, in the three constituencies of which, according to the detailed calculations of the prefect, 93 were '*gauche*', 43 were '*flottant*' and only 33 were reliably '*droit*', even though the prefect had done all he could ·to threaten officials who were voters to 'think of the conditions under which they had accepted their official post' and similar warnings.[97]

The left had been at war with prefects for much of the Restoration but in 1827 new rules for the revision of electoral lists offered them the chance to take prefects to court. Two organizations advised voters: the *Société des Amis de la Liberté de la Presse* urged them to ensure that their names appeared on the electoral lists,[98] while lawyers and journalists, including the editors of the *Globe*, adopted a more formal and thoroughly legalistic approach. The offices of the *Globe* were used as headquarters[99] from where, under the chairmanship of Guizot in Paris, they organized committees in the capital and in the provinces, aptly named *Aide-toi, le ciel t'aidera*,[100] to ensure that all of those entitled to appear in the electoral lists did so. Guizot's presidency in 1827 was nominal, because of his wife's death. The Paris group met and selected a steering committee of 20 and then disbanded, to circumvent the law. The committee included Guizot (elected to the Chamber in 1830 thanks to *Aide-toi*), Barrot, Barthe, Damiron, Desclozeaux, Desloges, Dubois, Duchatel, Duvergier de Hauranne, Joubert, Lerminier, Marchais, Paravey, Remusat, Renouard, Sautelet and Vitet. The Parisian *Aide-toi* had no more than 100 members in 1827 and local groups were encouraged to stay small to remain within the law. They included liberals and some republicans such as Bienvilliers, Carnot, Bastide and Thomas.[101] Many of those who set out to organize local committees had been *fédérés* and had been active in the old *charbonnerie*.[102] Goyet, an old Jacobin, more recently a *fédéré*, and his *Propagateur de la Sarthe* had helped to secure the election of four liberal deputies, including Lafayette and Constant.[103] Five out of seven of the Rennes committee were old *fédérés*.[104] Hernoux was a key figure in the Côte-d'Or's committee and was elected to the Chamber for Dijon in 1829.

Aide-toi, as its name indicates, tried to encourage individuals to 'help themselves', to sharpen their awareness that local prefects, acting on the orders of the Minister of the Interior, were deliberately and fraudulently subverting the franchise, by including on the voting register individuals whose political preferences were pleasing to the government, and excluding known liberals whose tax payments would have qualified them to vote. Until liberal pressure helped to regularize the revision of electoral lists in 1827,[105] their renewal was at the discretion of prefects, which left room for a range of tricks to be perpetrated on those potential liberal voters, who had neither the time nor the acumen to furnish the necessary proof that they paid the 300 francs in direct taxes required to be a voter.

Aide-toi circulated brief, informative simple pamphlets, instruction manuals on how to prevent disenfranchisement, and 80,000 copies of their first *Manuel de l'électeur* were printed. *Aide-toi* also published pamphlets explaining how a prefect ought to conduct an election. These very practical and instructive leaflets were written in a calm, clear style and the writers stressed that everything they proposed was within the law, and was indeed designed to enable others to uphold the law.[106] They explained to prospective electors how to take legal action if they were incorrectly left off the lists, or if the election was irregularly conducted. The number of such actions mushroomed. After the 1827 election 22 prefects were accused of improper electoral practice and 10 were found guilty in varying degrees. The committees worked with local liberal newspapers and both groups were ready when Villèle opted for a general election in November 1827. They proposed candidates and organized complaints about prefectoral malpractice.

As a direct consequence of their campaign, electoral lists grew, in some departments by as much as 40 per cent in 1827. Many *Aide-toi* supporters were lawyers, which helped to ensure the success of the numerous resulting court cases. Within a short time there were *Aide-toi* committees in over 60 departments, not only monitoring the electoral procedures of increasingly nervous officials, but also conducting vigorous and triumphant campaigns on behalf of liberal candidates. Liberals had been increasingly successful in by-elections since 1824. In the first general election under the new system in 1827 the liberals, at 180, were equal in numbers to the royalists, with 60–80 ultras holding the balance. The *Aide-toi* had succeeded. Villèle resigned.

The king responded constitutionally and in the accepted tradition of the Restoration appointed a compromise government, led by Martignac with the liberal leader Royer-Collard as president of the Chamber of Deputies. Martignac did not hesitate to approach issues which were of concern to the liberals. There were lengthy debates and enquiries into the economic crisis,[107] which did nothing to improve poor trade, increasing rates of bankruptcy in depressed industries, or to solve the problems of the wine-producers or the food shortages. Bourbon officials argued that the liberals profited from this multifaceted depression to attack the regime. In reality the entrepreneurial and landowning elites (often one and the same) were appalled by the growing level of urban and rural popular violence and, although they blamed the government's commercial policy for the crisis, liberals were in conflict with each other, as well as with the government, when it came to solutions. Wine-producers hit out at tariffs and indirect taxes, silkweavers were also hostile to tariffs, but coal, iron and wool producers thought protectionism did not go far enough, while cotton manufacturers were divided among themselves. The industrial recession and the problems of agriculture exposed both the divisions among liberals and their fear of revolution, but Charles X did not have the wisdom to profit from the situation. Instead, the government's very public failure to propose solutions intensified opposition.[108]

Martignac also tried to appeal to the liberals by banning the Jesuits and introducing legislation to make local councils elected instead of centrally nominated bodies. The bill to make local councils elective, an issue dear to both ultras and liberals, albeit for different reasons, was hotly debated for three months from the opening of the 1829 session. Martignac, in line with the wishes of the ultras, proposed that the electorate be confined to the 25 per cent most wealthy parliamentary electors, in order, it was claimed, to exclude extraneous national political issues from matters of purely local concern. The liberals opposed the enfranchisement of only the double-vote electors. Indeed some, such as Reinach, deputy in the Haut-Rhin, were pressing for the abolition of the double-vote law itself, while others, including André, also deputy for the Haut-Rhin, argued that voting rights in general should be given to a wider section of the population.[109] Benjamin Constant drew the government's attention to the fact that over half the existing voters who exercised a second vote did not vote for government candidates; less wealthy members of the *classe intermédiare* were more reliable royalists.[110] Instead of pursuing a solution, the king withdrew the local council proposal in a summary fashion,[111] it having served no purpose except to focus opposition.

Martignac resigned. If he had followed accepted convention, Charles should have appointed a left-of-centre government, especially as the liberals had won most of the by-elections since November 1827. But the ultras argued that the liberals' criticism of Martignac's efforts indicated that they were indeed revolutionaries. In August 1829 the king made the unprecedented appointment of a group of ultra ministers totally unacceptable to the Chamber, including Charles's close friend the prince de Polignac as Minister of Foreign Affairs. Polignac, a former *émigré* and diplomat with no parliamentary or governmental experience, was promoted to the presidency of the council of ministers in November. Such a choice could only render France even more ungovernable, especially when it was accompanied by the creation of 76 new and tractable peers to stack the Upper House. Liberals argued, through their newspapers and electoral committees, that the appointment of an ultra government was a challenge to parliament, virtually a coup d'état.[112] The parliamentary session was postponed until March 1830, which intensified their suspicions. *Aide-toi* organized banquets for liberal deputies and petitions refusing to pay taxes not voted by the Chamber.[113]

In his opening address to parliament in 1830, the king attacked his critics and called for unity behind his government. Instead the liberal majority successfully proposed an unprecedented motion of no confidence in the government, while insisting on their loyalty to the crown. The motion was passed by 221 votes. On March 19th Charles announced the dissolution of the Chamber of Deputies, the first occasion since his brother had disposed of the *chambre introuvable* in 1816.[114] In May the Chamber was formally dissolved and new elections called for June and July.

Aide-toi printed a new series of informative pamphlets as soon as it became clear that there was to be an election.[115] The government could not match the network of communication and propaganda which was provided by the liberal press with Polignac and clerical electioneering as its main targets. The 221 liberal deputies became popular heroes, fêted by supporters in innumerable and well-attended banquets.[116] Government candidates faced a well-organized opposition whose enthusiasm and unity had been strengthened by recent events. In traditional liberal areas prefects could give no expectation of reversing the results of 1827.

The elections were held on June 23rd in the *arrondissement* colleges and on July 3rd in the departmental constituencies. Voting was delayed in 20 departments where disputes over the electoral list had not been settled by the time of the election. Of the 428 elected, 270 were liberals, including 202 of the fêted 221. Only 145 convinced 'royalists' were chosen. (See Map 1, Appendix Three). Despite all the manipulation of electoral laws, lists and processes, Charles's personal political preferences were unacceptable to the tiny, very rich elite. This is all the more staggering when account is taken of the enormous number of deputies who were 'place-men', holding official paid posts, while in parliament. In 1828, of the 1500 men who had sat in parliament during the Restoration, 1200 came into this category. At no time was the proportion of *fonctionnaire* deputies less than 40 per cent. Even this did nothing to guarantee ministerial security.

By mid-July 1830 the challenge to the Polignac government was incontrovertible. It was still open to the king to appoint ministers in tune with the parliamentary majority. To claim, as did the ultras, that this would have turned the world upside down in terrifying revolution, was nonsense. The liberals wanted constitutional government, admittedly a government in their own image. The personal intervention of the king in the elections made the crisis an acute constitutional one, seen by Charles as a matter of principle, not of mere personalities. He viewed the verdict of the electorate, as he had done the vote of the 221 deputies, as an attack on the authority of the ruler. His final response on July 25th was to use the personal legislative power allowed to the king in an emergency to dispense with existing laws and issue decrees or ordinances. These Four Ordinances of St Cloud were the immediate catalyst of revolution.

The Four Ordinances accused the liberals of subversion. Were they revolutionaries, were they republican? The king had tied his future so completely to Polignac's government that it was virtually impossible to rail against the one and remain loyal to the other. The liberals needed little enough invitation to criticize Charles given his championship of the ultras. The liberals were totally anti-ultra. Were they also anti-monarchist? The support which many had given to the *charbonnerie* might indicate an affirmative answer.

The *Aide-toi* committees were almost pompously and insultingly legal and legalistic but some of the organizers, especially in the provinces, were former republicans and Bonapartists, who had retained much of their earlier radicalism and were delighted that the blatant cheating of royalist officials provided them with an opportunity to criticize the regime. However, the majority was very cautious. Many would have been appalled at any suggestion that they were consorting with republicans. *Aide-toi* also secured the support of moderate royalists, themselves suspicious of the clericalism of the ultras, particularly of the Polignac government of 1829. Only an extreme ultra could have depicted *Aide-toi* as hostile to the Bourbon Restoration as such. For the liberals the political crisis of 1830 was limited and specific, turning on the issue of ministerial responsibility, not the redundancy of the monarchy.

No distinct republican philosophy developed among the critics of the Restoration, indeed the word was always used very vaguely, as if definition was superfluous. Duvergier de Hauranne, Restoration liberal and July Monarchy suffrage reformer, employed the terms liberal and republican interchangeably. For him a republican was simply someone who believed in parliamentary government.[117] For some radicals republicanism was essentially an ideal incorporating concepts of national independence and democracy. For others it involved a rather romanticized notion of fraternity. Social issues began to have an appeal in the late 1820s, as the deleterious effects of structural change in industry began to be visible.

Bonapartism and republicanism were blended together and leavened with a healthy regard for the practical and finally emerged as a vaguely liberal sentiment. The military glories were remembered, the economic disasters put on one side. The constitutional promises of the Hundred Days were recalled, the reality of dictatorship forgotten. A number of the politicians who took a lead in the July Days, notably the lawyer, Mauguin, had loyalties both to the Empire and to the Republic, but ultimately plumped for neither. By 1830 the Empire was a romantic memory for many former soldiers, revered, but with no expectation of a rebirth. After Napoleon's death, the most emphatic dampener was surely the absence of a suitable candidate. 'L'Aiglon', Napoleon's son, was in his teens, but was both sickly and had been raised in Vienna in an anti-French atmosphere. At this stage the subsequent successful contender, Louis-Napoleon, Napoleon's great-nephew, deferred to l'Aiglon's claims and was employing his talents elsewhere. Popular Bonapartism there was; the prefect of the Haut-Rhin commented in 1829 that over 300 portraits of Napoleon had been sold in just one canton in the previous fortnight, but the fact that this recently appointed individual had been prefect in the Cantal during the White Terror and had been instrumental in the arrest of General Ney might have contributed to a stiffening of local attitudes.[118] There was a veritable rash of Bonapartist iconography selling in the Luneville and Colmar markets that summer.[119] But in 1830 romantic Bonapartism was harmless mythology.

An Orleanist alternative was under discussion on the eve of the July Revolution, proposed by Louis-Philippe's banker, Jacques Laffitte, and publicized in *Le National* and by a rash of historical works which far from innocently compared seventeenth-century England and early nineteenth-century France. However, beneath their opposition to Polignac, critics were deeply divided on an acceptable alternative to Charles X and preferred to retain him rather than risk upheaval. For many Charles was indecisive and anachronistic, rather than Machiavellian or malign.

While the final decision to issue decree laws dissolving the new parliament before it had met, reducing the electorate by 75 per cent, and closing the liberal newspapers, was an inflammatory ultra challenge, the liberals must accept some responsibility for contributing to the polarization of politics. They were committed to 1789 as diluted in the 1814 Charter. But they acted as legalistic and rather timid schoolmasters, not insurgents. The revolutionary fighters were not the wealthy politicians but artisans, at odds with the government over economic problems, but also concerned over political questions and themselves alert to the gains and expectations of the 1789 Revolution. It is tempting to assume that the *décorés de juillet* had been *fédérés* and in the *charbonnerie*, but it is only a guess. Nor can we say that the insurgents were any more republican than the timid liberal politicians, who would probably have given in to the Ordinances if a Parisian revolt had not gone out of control.

5   Revolution and Popular Unrest: Republicans 1830–1835

The 1830 Revolution, the 'Three Glorious Days' as it was called with relief at its brevity and relative mildness, was not a republican revolution.[1] Nor was it a Bonapartist revolt, a bourgeois revolution, as the disillusioned republicans and socialists labelled it, not even an Orleanist coup, even though the duke of Orleans was made king immediately afterwards. The Revolution was the product of the coincidence of a political conflict between the king and the liberals in the Chamber of Deputies and an economic recession which had started in 1827. The political crisis was partly a continuation of the 1789 revolutionary conflict over where power lay. During the Restoration a tolerable compromise had been reached by which the king selected ministers who would be acceptable to the Chamber of Deputies. After the liberal victories in the 1830 election Charles X decided that article 14 of the 1814 Constitution, which allowed him to issue decree laws in an emergency, could be used to scotch the liberals, by now a 'revolutionary' threat in his mind. The Four Ordinances of St Cloud, signed on July 25th, ordered the liberal newspapers to cease publication, dissolved the new assembly, reduced the electorate to the quarter most rich, and called new elections.

The ordinances were condemned as illegal in a protest issued by 44 liberal journalists when they appeared in *Le Moniteur* next day, but the editors were not united. The most republican of the papers, the *Tribune*, declined to appear, in deference to the ordinances, as did the two largest, *Le Constitutionnel* and the *Journal de Débats*. The defiant papers were those with a preference for Orleanism: the *National*, the *Globe*, and the *Temps*. The liberal members of the Chamber of Deputies, about 80

95

of whom were in Paris, were even more divided and reluctant to defy the government. The king lost control of Paris and his throne because the political crisis became intertwined with the economic one.

Since the onset of the depression there had been constant marches and demonstrations in central Paris by artisans complaining about shortage of work and food and the soaring price of basic foods. On Monday July 26th, a good day for a riot because it was a holiday, they were joined by their neighbours, the perpetually disgruntled print workers, on the streets as a direct consequence of the Four Ordinances. The artisan quarters on the right bank were cheek-by-jowl with the newspaper offices, government buildings, and the elegant residences of the deputies. The central districts were a volatile mix at any time. In July 1830, although Charles complained that the liberals wanted to overthrow him, he made no provision for military or police reinforcements to ensure that his predictably explosive ordinances were enforced. This was probably an even greater error than the ordinances themselves. The crowds of protesters grew, barricades were erected, and the small number of troops available lost heart as colleagues deserted behind the barricades and the National Guard, dissolved by Charles in 1827, appeared and took control.

The liberal deputies continued to hesitate through the three days of street fighting in which about 2000 people were killed. It was left to the journalists, particularly at the *National*, to join with a few of the more daring deputies to stage a takeover at the *hôtel de ville* on July 29th. On the 30th Thiers of the *National* placarded Paris with posters recommending Louis-Philippe, duke of Orleans, as a replacement for Charles. The self-appointed provisional administration of the *hôtel de ville* included a proportion whose personal views were sympathetic to republicanism, including Lafayette, Mauguin, de Schonen and Audry de Puyravaeau. However, they knew that they were few and, perhaps partly to excuse their willingness to compromise, they deferred to the apparent fears of the more conservative that foreign invasion might result if a republic were declared and the Peace of Paris so blatantly breached, or that civil war might result, if a republic were attempted. In retrospect both arguments against a republic, which were tediously repeated at the time, seem flimsy rationalizations. There would have been very little support for a republic in 1830, certainly not enough to cause civil war.

Thus, led by Lafayette, the radicals accepted the tentative and timid compromise of some of the liberal members of the Chamber of Deputies, and agreed to appoint Louis-Philippe as a king 'surrounded by republican institutions', including the restored National Guard and the *tricolore* flag of the Revolution. The phrase 'republican institutions' was used initially with no hint of irony, but there was no agreement on what they were to be. Such a phrase, like the companion epithet, 'citizen king', reminded the deputies that the change of regime would never have occurred without a violent artisan insurrection. 1830 was from the start, as Cabet asserted, a *'révolution escamotée'*.

A specific republican movement emerged after the July Days. In the next four years networks of opposition societies, of an increasingly republican nature, sprang up in France, challenged by Orleanist persecution and finally smothered by repressive legislation in 1834–5. Here we shall consider the origins of this movement, its scope and impact in the early 1830s. Three circumstances helped to shape the republicanism of these years: the frustrated ambitions, and perhaps also ideals, of a number of liberals dissatisfied with the outcome of the 1830 Revolution; the economic crisis, exacerbated by the July Days, which led to intensified popular effervescence, laced with disappointment at the failure of the new regime to address economic grievances; finally, the impact of long-term economic and social change, which was beginning to stimulate socialist ideas among the bourgeoisie and to some degree among artisans.

At the outset the creation of an Orleanist monarch, appointed by parliament, was not unattractive to those with republican sympathies. Duvergier de Hauranne, Restoration liberal and July Monarchy political reformer, commented in the conclusion to his 10-volume history of parliamentary government:

> Between the republic, which was inconceivable, and the legitimate monarchy, which no longer existed, what better than a parliamentary monarchy, a veritable republic with an hereditary presidency, which properly understood and faithfully executed, would guarantee government by the people and give the opportunity for further political and social reform.[2]

However, the more conservative liberals preferred to think of Louis-Philippe as next in line to the throne (which he wasn't – quite) and their unwillingness to defer to other more radical liberals and use the opportunity of the July Days first to organize a popular vote to confirm the monarch of their choice and then to embark on a programme of liberal reform, ensured a lively political debate.

The events of the early 1790s meant that every nineteenth-century revolution in France was followed by the mushrooming of political clubs whose leaders consciously imitated their historic mentors. 1830 was no exception. The number of societies formed was small, partly because those Restoration liberal *notables* now in the saddle sporting Orleanist colours made a determined assault on popular unrest and tried, with at least as much energy as their 'illiberal' predecessors, to enforce article 291 of the Penal Code.[3] The clubs which emerged caused particular apprehension to the new elite, partly because the power of the Orleanists themselves was born of revolution, in part because the clubs flaunted a self-proclaimed Jacobin inheritance both in their structure and in their ideas, and because some clubs attracted artisan and peasant support as the economic depression deepened; finally because some of the new Orleanist officials joined the clubs and a number preferred to resign from government service when bullied by Casimir Périer rather than give up their membership.

At the time of the Revolution the main opposition political organization was *Aide-toi, le ciel t'aidera*. Before 1830 its mission had been to promote constitutional government by protecting the electoral system. After the July Days many of its members secured government jobs, like Guizot, and resigned from *Aide-toi*. Those who remained did so either because they had failed in their quest for an official appointment, or because they had hoped that the Revolution would bring liberal reforms to the existing electoral system. *Aide-toi* broadened its goals to include a larger electorate, economic and fiscal reform and universal education. It also continued to act as an electoral pressure group, but now for candidates ranging from the *mouvement*, radical candidates critical of Orleanist governments such as Hernoux, to the small number of avowedly republican candidates, including Cabet. Local committees vetted parliamentary candidates and were vigorous agents in national, local and National Guard elections. They continued their leaflet campaign, now aimed at the conservative *résistance*, as Périer's brand of Orleanism came to be called, since he urged resistance to change, and 30,000 of their pamphlets were issued in 1832. *Aide-toi* remained legal, legalistic, a source of information and measured criticism of the unwillingness of conservative Orleanists to consider gradual reform. It always consisted of an educated elite, even though it wanted to extend the boundaries of the electoral community. Members of *Aide-toi* were prosperous, many were lawyers or professional men. In 1832, when Garnier-Pagès launched a membership drive in the provinces, the initial subscription was 5 francs with an annual fee of 12 francs.[4] Some of those who were supporters of *Aide-toi* were to become republicans within a short time. But *Aide-toi* was a vehicle for the development of parliamentary institutions, not for the creation of a republic.

The *Amis du Peuple*, which was set up on 30 July 1830 as a public society with no limit on numbers, in flagrant defiance of the Code, was very different. It immediately condemned the new regime for its failure to call a constituent assembly after the Revolution. The *Amis du Peuple* commented drily that the assembled deputies spent less time rewriting the constitution than the previous parliament had devoted to discussing river fishing. Indeed, they claimed, the text of the revised constitution was not even read before the assembly voted on it.[5] They held large, noisy public meetings in a riding stable; but their placards challenging the legality of the Chamber of Deputies led to the arrest and imprisonment of their president Hubert, Thierry, their treasurer, and David, their printer.[6] The society, which had only 150 members on its books, was forced to adopt a clandestine structure, meeting in a building owned by the Freemasons. Their leaders were implicated in the riots which followed the judicial decision merely to imprison the ex-ministers of Charles X when they had been found guilty of causing the Revolution. As a result 19 members were arrested, including Godefrey Cavaignac, Guinard and Trélat, and later acquitted. They formed a battalion to help the Belgians in 1831 and were at the centre of most of the Parisian popular demonstrations in the first two years of the regime. The *Amis* liked to present themselves as 'Jacobins'. Raspail, when he became president, urged consideration of social and educational problems and tried to get associates to finance the education of poor families in the capital. The *Amis* also kept in touch with provincial groups and numerous autonomous radical clubs were founded, particularly in eastern France. An attempt to deny the right of association and to condemn the leaders of the *Amis* as patrons of an illegal organization was dismissed by the assize court in Paris in December 1832.[7]

The *Société des Droits de l'Homme* was founded at the same time. It was less active than the *Amis* until after the June insurrection of 1832, when the *Amis* were forced to close and the *Droits de l'Homme* took over as the main republican club, absorbing *Amis* enclaves. Then the *Droits de l'Homme* applied itself to recruitment and some measure of standardization and centralization. In Paris alone it had 750 members when the two societies merged. It seems to have been very structured and rather a bureaucratic society, to judge by the lists of rules and members uncovered by prefects. There was a central committee of 11 directors, with 12 commissioners for each *arrondissement* of Paris and 48 for each *quartier*, who had the responsibility for the organization of the sections. Each section had a separate name and could claim to be an independent club, to evade the law. Sections were given names such as Robespierre, St Just and Babeuf. In April 1833 the leaders of one section were arrested and the whole society was declared illegal by the courts, but the decision seems to have had little immediate impact. The *Droits de l'Homme* made a positive effort to establish provincial clubs and correspond with them. In the autumn of 1833 Garnier-Pagès and other leaders visited regional republican clubs to encourage them to link up with Paris and a number modelled themselves on Parisian sections, while retaining their autonomy. In November 1833 Cavaignac was the president, Vignerte vice-president, and the committee included Berrier-Fontaine, d'Argenson, Guinard, Lebon, Kersausie, Audry de Puyraveau, Beaumont, Desjardins and Tito. Later de Ludre replaced Vignerte and Delente and Recurt joined the committee. At its height it had about 3000 members in Paris alone.[8]

In addition to these two main clubs, there were other sometimes short-lived organizations set up to publicize such issues as national defence, press freedom and universal education. Radicalism was strongly linked with patriotism and a *National Association* to protect France should the Allies try to restore Charles X found vociferous, if ephemeral support, in the spring of 1831 among those who genuinely feared a Prussian invasion but also wanted it to be known that they were uncomfortable under the increasingly conservative regime. The association had 1500 supporters, 'from all social classes' in Metz alone.[9]

The *Association polytechnique* was founded after the July Days by former students of the college who had tended the wounded during the fighting. It was presided over by the duc de Choiseul-Praslin, himself an engineer, and counted two deputies, Victor de Tracy and Larabit, among its members along with Auguste Comte and Vauvilliers, an *inspecteur des ponts et chaussées*. There were plenty of volunteers among graduate *polytechniciens* to give classes. Some were Saint-Simonian in their sympathies and the original rather Establishment society was transformed in June 1831. Its successor was the *Association pour l'instruction gratuite du peuple*. It was headed by Alexandre de Laborde with Dupont de l'Eure as vice-president. Shortly afterwards a general meeting was held and Dupont de l'Eure took over; Cormenin came in as vice-president. Its secretary was Lechevallier and the committee included Barrot, Lafayette, Garnier-Pagès, Laffitte, Arago, Cabet,

Mauguin, Salverte, Voyer d'Argenson, Audry de Puyraveau, Granvelle, de Lasteyrie, Teste, Recurt, Berrier-Fontaine, Dolley and Marchais, who represented an impressive and significant move to the left, although not as far as the *Amis*.[10] Parisian members, men and women, were grouped in *cohortes*, subdivided into *centuries* and *décuries* and they paid a weekly subscription of 25 centîmes, or 13 francs per annum. Outside the capital, where its appeal was limited to the larger towns, it was organized by commune. The central committee in Paris was re-elected twice a year. Total membership reached 3000 by the end of 1833, including 60 members of parliament.

The *Fondateur* was its devoted publicist between October 1832 and March 1833, when it was succeeded by Cabet's *Populaire*. With such a leadership, it was increasingly republican in spirit, but because of its direct involvement with the Parisian poor, issues of social, rather than political, reform were emphasized. In 1833 2500 people were enrolled in its 54 classes. The broad basic general knowledge taught was reinforced by simple, cheap booklets. By November the society had grown by over 50 per cent and its range of courses was still increasing. The scope of the organization had broadened; doctors and lawyers offered their services free and the society also offered a job-hunting facility. In 1833 Cabet became general-secretary and editor of *Le Fondateur*. Curiously, although sympathetic, Cabet never joined the parent organization, the *Société des Droits de l'Homme* itself. When Lechevallier was forced to flee to England after the unrest of 5 and 6 June 1832 the society collapsed, to be resurrected on 13 January 1833 under the title *Association pour l'instruction libre et gratuite du peuple* with Cabet as the secretary and Arago as vice-president and it was now indisputably republican.[11]

There were associations with related aims in provincial France. For instance in November 1830 the Saint-Simonian doctor, Guépin, founded the *Société Industrielle de Nantes* which, in addition to many other philanthropic initiatives, ran evening classes and in 1832 secured a grant of 6000 francs from the government for an apprenticeship scheme. Guépin even got 2000 francs from the duke of Orleans. Generous donations allowed the society to acquire its own building, with a library, space to run a clinic and money to launch a mutual-aid fund.[12] Orleanist enthusiasm quickly waned, as it did with the Parisian society. Typical of the all-embracing nature of many regional societies was another of Guépin's ventures, of which he was elected president. In January 1833 he announced the formation of the *Réunion de l'Ouest* and organized meetings of delegates from the six neighbouring departments. The new society was divided into three sections, the Sciences, Industry and Arts. Guépin himself drew up the science report. He urged free evening classes in a wide range of subjects, suffrage reform and opportunities for women. The 50 delegates who assembled at the first meeting saw themselves as the intellectual hub of western France; some were keen to be a political pressure group, an indication of the all-embracing scope of provincial clubs.

The *Association de la presse*, or *Association pour la liberté de la presse*, which was started in Lyon under the leadership of Cormenin, took up the theme of its namesake during the Restoration. It was devoted to combating the increasingly rigorous censorship imposed by successive Orleanist governments (press freedom never materialized).[13] This was an expensive activity, since its first duty was to pay a 6000 franc fine levied on the *Tribune*. In the summer of 1833 it changed its name to *Association républicaine pour la défense de la liberté de la presse patriotique et de la liberté individuelle*, indicating a hardening of attitudes typical of the time. By the end of 1833 its help was sought so frequently that five committees had been created. The *comité d'enquête* investigated prefectoral contraventions of the press laws. It was headed by Cabet and also included Marrast and Guinard. The *comité de défense* offered practical help to accused journalists and was presided over by Joly with Dupont and Marie. The *comité de sécours, prisons et des finances* organized subscriptions and other financial help for those accused and for political prisoners in general. There was also a *comité de législation*, headed by Lafayette with Carrel and Garnier-Pagès. The overseeing *comité central de la presse* had as its presidents Audry de Puyraveau, d'Argenson and Cavaignac.[14] Many provincial offshoots developed.

In Paris these different societies were separate, but with overlapping membership lists and close links. In provincial towns there was often only one club, usually with several sections.[15] A lively example was the Republican Circle in Dijon, which corresponded with both the *Amis* and the *Droits de l'Homme* in Paris.[16] It generated and encouraged other groups, corresponding with and sending representatives to societies in Beaune, Semur, Nuits and St Jean. The perceptive Orleanist prefect, Achille Chaper,[17] remarked drily that its members liked to pretend that the ramifications of the organization were nationwide and that the future lay with them. The excitement and mystery was very attractive to villagers.[18] In Nantes the local club was the *Cercle National*, which by November 1833 was affiliated to the *Droits de l'Homme* in Paris. As was habitual with such groups, its twice-weekly meetings were held informally in local cafés, making it difficult for the prefect to prove that it was formally constituted.

Republican clubs recruited best in eastern France with large clubs in Metz, Strasbourg, Epinal, Colmar and Nancy. Further south they were active in Franche-Comté and Burgundy, with energetic and substantial clubs in Besançon, Arbois, Dijon, Châlons, Beaune, Seurre, Grenoble and Lyon. The Lyon club was in close correspondence with societies in St Etienne (organized by Caussidière) and Grenoble, where Garnier-Pagès was the deputy and the National Guard constituted a republican stronghold. Branches were added in Vienne and Villefranche. All were subdivided into small sections: 18 in Besançon in early 1834, over 60 in Dijon, with 40 tiny groups in surrounding communes. In contrast there was little republican enthusiasm in northern France or in the west, with the auspicious exceptions of Rennes, Nantes and Poitiers. Clubs and newspapers were more plentiful in the Midi, not in Bordeaux, but in Toulouse, Montauban, Auch, ⸱ Bayonne, Perpignan, Montpellier, Hérault, Marseille, Aix and Var. There were a few notable examples in the Centre: Trélat edited the *Patriote* in the Puy-de-Dôme and there were clubs in Clermont-Ferrand and Moulin.[19]

What sort of people became members? There were some *notables*, landowners and industrialists, who had been in the liberal opposition to Charles X. Identifiable leaders rapidly emerged, including a handful of older generation liberals from the Restoration, especially Voyer d'Argenson and a small number of younger deputies, in particular Garnier-Pagès. Most were young, particularly in the *Amis* and *Droits de l'Homme*. The leaders of the *Amis* included Cavaignac, Blanqui, Buchez, Trélat and Raspail: the heir of a republican of the 1790s, an insurgent, a writer and two doctors. Members of parliament included Cabet, de Ludre, Lafayette, Lamarque, Audry de Puyraveau, Laboissière and Dupont de l'Eure.[20] Among journalists the outstanding figures were Marrast, editor of *Le Tribune des départements*, and Carrel, editor of *Le National*. Nearly all arrived at republicanism via *Aide-toi*, the *charbonnerie* and a family or personal commitment to the broad outlines of the 1789 Revolution.

Their followers included law and medical students, young clerks, shop assistants, artisans and some peasants. There was usually a high proportion of established lawyers, not infrequently including members of the judiciary. The Dijon president was a *notaire* and Demontry, the departmental organizer of the *Amis* and *Droits de l'Homme*, was also a lawyer.[21] The government prosecutor and his deputy in Dijon were in cahoots to such a degree that prosecution was impossible.[22] Doctors were always prominent, the roll-call is extensive: Raspail, Trélat, Turck (Vosges), Guépin (Nantes) and many more. Journalists usually

founded the clubs; in Besançon the president was the editor of the
Patriote; Gerbaut, the editor of the *Sentinelle*, was a leading republican in
the Vosges.[23] National Guard officers were always present; in Dijon all
the committee members were officers. Even in smaller communes like
Arbois, the enthusiasm of the Guard meant that they would not fight
for 'law and order' during popular demonstrations.[24] Republican clubs
also sought out soldiers, and did well among junior non-commissioned
artillery officers. The Dijon battalion had to be transferred because
Demay, decorated for his contribution to the July Days, but later
dismissed from the army for his republicanism, converted too many
soldiers.[25] In Strasbourg 30 of the 100 members of the republican
society were officers in the 49th regiment and many students from the
Ecole Militaire enrolled in early 1834.[26]

Socially then, the clubs had an appeal similar to that of Restoration
formations like the *charbonnerie* and *Aide-toi*. It appears that an even
higher proportion of July Monarchy clubs were artisan, with some
peasant backing too. In 1834 the majority of members of the Parisian
Droits de l'Homme were artisans. The membership list for one section
showed 80 per cent artisans and 4 per cent students and intellectuals.
The sections often met at the members' workplace and there was a
definite attempt to group members on a trade basis.[27] Other clubs, and
not exclusively those in Paris and Lyon, positively encouraged the less
well-off. The *Société Patriotique et Populaire* in Metz, led by local *notables*
like Bouchotte, the mayor, included and encouraged young cabinet-
makers and stone-cutters and other artisans who constituted a high
proportion of their large membership. Meetings habitually were 200-
strong.[28] The Strasbourg club was similar; the 500–600 tobacco
workers, constantly at odds with the government, had been enrolled.[29]
The club in Nantes attracted artisans, including tailors and wigmakers,
as well as soldiers and lawyers. Interest was not confined to urban
workers. The liveliest club of all, Arbois, a small rural commune, ready
to declare a republic at any time, was composed of wine-producers,
weavers, plasterers, carpenters and other tradesmen.[30] Being a
member would allow a man to cock a snook at the mayor or local
landowner.[31] The republicans of Lyon did not turn the silkweavers into
revolutionaries, but they did try to enlist worker support with a
membership fee of only 50 centîmes a month. The republican club in
Metz offered cheaper membership only in March 1834, reducing its
annual subscription from 10 to 2 francs. But although artisans were
welcome, the destitute and needy poor were not.[32] The reduction of fees
to attract artisans was common at that moment and perhaps was

intended to cement an alliance with men who feared that new legislation would make their trade associations illegal.

Republican clubs all adopted a semi-secret structure, a simplified version of that of the Freemasons and the *charbonnerie*. The Dijon club was divided into *centuries* and *décaries*, each with about 18 members. In 1834, when the prefect had the names of members of 39 of the 67 sections, total membership in the Côte-d'Or may have been 1000.[33] In early 1834 mass meetings became more common and were sometimes held in the open air on the outskirts of the commune. The description of such a gathering in a later period given by Zola in *La Fortune des Rougon* is reminiscent of prefectoral reports of 1834. Presumably with legislation before parliament caution and secrecy seemed less relevant. In Châlons the *Droits de l'Homme* had 1500 members and regularly held meetings of 400–500 in those weeks.[34] The parent group in Paris claimed a total membership of 4000 in 1833. Obviously these figures were at best approximations, because detailed membership lists like those acquired by Chaper, prefect in Dijon, and the prefect of the Bas-Rhin in Strasbourg were comparatively rare. Some prefects supplied wildly exaggerated totals. Nonetheless, it seems that the *Droits de l'Homme* grew rapidly during 1833, attracting much larger numbers of students and artisans than the *Amis* had done, and ten times as many members.[35] If any of these estimates have substance, Guizot's claim in a speech to the Chamber demanding a ban on republican clubs in April 1833, that the *Droits de l'Homme* totalled 3000 members, was a serious underestimation.

What did it signify to be a republican? Was there a distinct republican ideology or mentality in these years? Some republicans were former liberals disappointed with the choice of Louis-Philippe in 1830, and/or disgruntled because they had failed to secure office. It was not uncommon for an individual to pass from liberalism in 1830 to the *mouvement* and on to republicanism. Cabet, a former member of the *charbonnerie* and of *Aide-toi*, took part in the July Days in Paris, was made *procureur-général* in Corsica, was fired by Périer, joined the *mouvement* group and was soon deputy for Dijon.[36] His popular history of the 'people's' Revolution of 1830 published in 1831 was extended to two volumes in 1833 as his scorn for the Orleanists grew.[37] While recognizing that a republic would not have commanded majority support in 1830, Cabet regretted that a Constituent Assembly had not been called.[38] The book was prosecuted five times and Cabet quickly became the leading republican publicist.[39]

In a pamphlet to celebrate the successful launch of his own

newspaper *Le Populaire*, Cabet defended his philosophy. Enemies always associated the First Republic with the Terror and dictatorship, but Cabet reminded his readers that these enemies had run their own White Terror in 1815–16[40] and dictatorship had been a response to wartime emergencies. He recalled the Latin meaning of republic: government based on the sovereignty of the people. This should be organized in a constitution and laws made by and for the nation. This constitution should guarantee man's natural rights to liberty, equality and security for his person and his property. The freedoms he cherished included freedom of religion, of association, of the press, and the abolition of monopolies and other constraints on economic freedom. All citizens should be equal in both rights and obligations in all respects, personal and political.

In order to achieve such equality, Cabet demanded that the state should provide free education and medical care for the poor and ensure that there was no lack of fairly rewarded employment. To make political liberty meaningful, Cabet demanded a salary for deputies. An elected national assembly should be pre-eminent and an executive elected for a strictly limited period. He wanted greater local autonomy and increased independence for the judiciary. Army officers should be elected by the soldiers in the same way that officers for the National Guard were chosen. Cabet's ideas were shared by many, although not all, republicans.

In 1832 the *Droits de l'Homme* published a pamphlet in the form of a catechism which began:

Q. What is the Republic?
A. The Republic is a state, whatever its form of government, where law is the expression of the general will. All legitimate governments, in which public interest is predominant, are republican.

Q. What is a republican?
A. It is someone who puts public interest before private, seeks equal rights, justice for all, and does all the good for others that he hopes they will do for him.[41]

Most of the republicans of the early 1830s were idealists. A republic meant above all the rule of virtue, the end of corruption. Carrel wrote in his paper *Le National*, 'on dit que nous n'avons pas assez de vertus pour vivre en république; je réponds que nous n'avons peut-être plus assez de vices pour vivre en monarchie'.[42] Republicans thought of themselves as patriots, hence the choice of name for many of their local papers, their championship of the National Associations in 1831 and their support for revolutions in the Italian states, Belgium and Poland.

The republicans believed that they were the true heirs of the 1789 Revolution. They praised concepts of the sovereignty of the people, urging a broad electorate, although they were not precisely democratic. Apparently their goal was a parliamentary, not merely constitutional, government with the executive occupying a relatively minor role. Distancing themselves philosophically from the Orleanists was in some respects only a matter of degree. The Orleanists also claimed to be parliamentarians and heirs of 1789. In September 1830 Guizot chose an allegorical representation of the session of the National Assembly of 23 June 1789 representing 'Liberty, the Nation, the Republic' to ornament the Chamber of Deputies.[43]

Republicans were apparently equally enthusiastic parliamentarians, but whereas Guizot shunned the images of 1793 when he selected episodes to illustrate the history of parliaments for the new *Musée historique* at Versailles,[44] the Convention was central to republican thinking. But their actual pronouncements were generalized and their enthusiasm for the Jacobin republic ambiguous. All identified with the political concepts of the early 1790s, but they could not agree on a precise model. Some looked back to the Constituent Assembly, the younger generation were more inclined to honour the Convention, others were more specifically Robespierrist and their failure to agree caused many arguments in the early 1830s. Groups subdivided, not just to circumvent the Penal Code, but because leaders squabbled. In Marseille, Lyon, almost anywhere republicans massed in substantial numbers, they quarrelled. The Rousseauist and idealist catechism printed by the *Droits de l'Homme* was insulting the 'Girondins' by the time it reached page 9.

Buonarroti taught a younger generation of republicans to love the Jacobin constitution of 1793 in his description of Babeuf's Conspiracy of the Equals of 1796. One of the participants who escaped the guillotine, Buonarroti published his account, he claimed, to fulfil a long-cherished promise to his former associates.[45] The book was well received in France where it was reissued in 1830. It might be compared to Mao's *Little Red Book*, except that there is more evidence that Buonarroti was read and not merely carried. Buonarroti was able to settle in Paris after the 1830 Revolution, thanks to the amnesty for earlier political condemnations granted by the new régime,[46] as the septuagenarian guru of a new generation of republicans. International status followed; an English translation appeared in 1836, the work of a leading Chartist, which compared Babeuf's ideas with those of Robert Owen.[47] Buonarroti held court among the younger republicans in Paris until his death in 1837. A crowd of 1500 mourners followed his coffin.[48]

Buonarroti presented Jacobinism as a democratic and an egalitarian revolution[49] and laid the ground-rules for a new kind of republicanism. He paid no attention to the Girondins, who had been central to many Restoration interpretations. He was, predictably, very hostile to the Directory. Buonarroti had been an eager supporter of the Jacobin Republic and undertook a number of diplomatic missions on its behalf.[50] In his book the Jacobin Constitution of 1793, never implemented because of the demands of war and the subsequent overthrow of Robespierre on 9th Thermidor 1794, was reprinted in full as a blueprint for a future fully democratic republic. Not only the Jacobins, but also Babeuf, became martyrs for the post-imperial generation of republicans, largely as a result of Buonarroti's well-timed book.[51] Until its publication with accompanying documents concerning Babeuf's trial, Babeuf had been disregarded by the large number of writers of all political persuasions who competed for an eager market in their attempts to explain the 1789 Revolution. Buonarroti revered him. He ignored the not-inconsiderable differences between the Jacobins and Babeuf and passed over the violence of the Terror in terms of vague, generalized regret.[52]

Babeuf had made a number of assumptions which, via Buonarroti, were attractive to the conspirators of later generations. Buonarroti turned the Jacobin Constitution into a romantic democractic ideal. The arbitrary, violent aspects of the Jacobin era were subsumed in praise for their democratic constitutional plans. True, Babeuf had also assumed that a period of dictatorship would follow his egalitarian revolution, but he had been confident that it would be transient. Democratic ideals were thus postulated by Buonarroti as the main feature of true Jacobinism. Ironically, since Babeuf's economic thinking would have been anathema to many Jacobins in the 1790s (Robespierre never questioned the survival and value of private property as such), it was Buonarroti who did much to mould his supporters' concept of Jacobinism. Jacobinism was changed from demonology to agreeable mythology.

Buonarroti was eagerly followed by the younger generation of republicans. One of his followers, Laponneraye, published two editions of Robespierre's speeches, the first was a two-volume edition in 1832, then a three-volume collection 10 years later.[53] The *Droits de l'Homme* reprinted the Jacobin Declaration of the Rights of Man, which had been included in Buonarroti's defence of Babeuf, among its rules[54] and local clubs like that in Lyon swore allegiance to it. The veteran republican Voyer d'Argenson defended the Jacobin Declaration in the Chamber of Deputies in January 1834 during debates on legislation which muzzled the emergent republican movement.[55] However, the actual Jacobin period was not renowned either for its respect for individual rights or for democratic consultation. Idealist republicans might read the 1793 constitution; others would remember, or be told about, the less agreeable aspect of Jacobin Terror and dictatorship. Charles Teste, a collaborator of Buonarroti and d'Argenson, explained that the republic of the future would involve a short period of dictatorship.[56]

In the early 1830s republicanism always had a contradictory image. Republicans themselves were far from confident that a nascent republic would be sufficiently acceptable to the majority to risk being democratic from the outset. Nor were republicans in accord about how a republic could be established. Some were motivated by idealism and believed that people could be educated to live within a republic. The final speech for the defence in the numerous republican trials of the early 1830s invariably presented an idyllic vision of a utopian republic of peace. Cavaignac, president of the *Amis du Peuple*, described such a republic in his trial in December 1832:

> The first condition would be to preserve France as a unitary state, in which the people would be sovereign and the masses would be adequately provided for . . . we don't want to destroy, but to build on the broad and solid foundations of the sovereignty of the people and the rights of all.[57]

Others welcomed the thrill of insurrection. Republicans were no longer hesitant to declare that force might be needed in creating a republic. The Declaration of Rights of the *Droits de l'Homme* echoed the Jacobin constitution of 1793 when it declared: 'When a government violates the rights of the people, the people has a sacred right and indispensable duty to rebel.'[58] The 1830 Revolution itself seemed to prove that insurrection could be justified and that a modest amount of force could topple a regime. Republicans never forgot that lesson, but they did not all relish it.

Bonapartist affiliations were not entirely forgotten. Some of the older generation who had worked for Napoleon and the Hundred Days and had been dismissed from government jobs by Périer in March 1831 after a brief return to employment under Louis-Philippe, reinforced the alliance. Raspail, one of the philanthropic republican doctors of the younger generation, who was president of the *Amis* and a leader of the *Droits de l'Homme*, always had a romantic admiration for Napoleon.[59] Guépin, a doctor in Nantes, a recent convert to republicanism via Saint-Simon, and who was president of the republican club, provided a wax model of Napoleon for the celebration of the July Days in 1833. The republican boss in the Saône-et-Loire, the lawyer Menaud, wrote a book in which he claimed that Napoleon had prophesied that France would become a republic again. The absence of a Bonapartist candidate encouraged sympathizers to favour a republican alternative.

What were the immediate objectives of republicans? All talked of the development of the 1789 Revolution, particularly in view of their disillusion with the 'tame' revolution of 1830. There was considerable disappointment with the minor scale of electoral reform after the July Days. The 300 franc franchise was reduced to 200 francs and a small number of 100 franc taxpayers were given the vote if they were members of academies, or could be considered *capacités*, distinguished in some laudable manner. The tax qualification for parliamentary candidates was halved to 500 francs. In 1831 municipal councils became elective and in 1833 so did all local councils. But in order to have a sufficient minimum number of voters, especially for municipal elections and in poorer departments, the actual voting qualification often fell to 80 francs or below. Republicans were among those radical critics who argued that there was thus no logic in retaining a 200 franc minimum for any elections. National Guard officers were elected democratically. The frequency with which republicans were chosen as officers in the Guard was enough reason for Orleanists to disregard demands for franchise reform.

The debate on parliamentary reform in Britain fuelled further criticism of the elitist taxpayers' system which France retained, even though the 1832 Act in Britain was not noticeably more liberal than that of the July Monarchy. In 1833–4 *Aide-toi* and *Droits de l'Homme* together launched a franchise reform campaign. Republicans went further and urged political democracy, but in non-specific terms. The Arbois club petitioned the Chamber of Deputies to enfranchise all taxpayers. The Dijon society praised the sovereignty of the people. But a democratic programme, which all republicans did not welcome anyway, was not uniquely, or even intrinsically, republican. Napoleon had used plebiscites and as early as 1815 some legitimists had speculated on the conservative potential of a mass electorate.

In common with the *mouvement* deputies, republicans demanded that office-holders should be excluded from the Chamber of Deputies. In 1830 the liberals had insisted that deputies who accepted a public appointment should seek a renewed mandate from their constituents, but this became a mere formality and in no way guaranteed a deputy's independence. Republicans also sought payment for deputies and the abolition of the 500 franc tax qualification for parliamentary candidates.[60]

Republicans did not confine themselves to political issues. They addressed themselves to the problems of the poor in a more direct manner than other radical formations. Buonarroti offered them a radical agenda. His hero, Babeuf, a former feudal lawyer, had argued in 1796 that political revolution would never progress until social revolution, involving the equal division of all property, had been achieved. Babeuf had been guillotined and more modest objectives were pursued by the later generation, although communist schemes were not abandoned. The Saint-Simonists urged social reform, from an altruistic, 'do-gooder' middle-class perspective. The republicans, some of whom were Saint-Simonists for a time in the late twenties and early thirties, proposed and disagreed over a social programme. About all they could really agree on was universal free education. Babouvist communism had little impact at this juncture.[61] It is not easy to judge whether the Robespierrist Declaration of Rights was any more than a talisman. Recognizing the sanctity of private ownership, the Declaration stated that society owed succour and employment to the poor. This had a particular relevance during the years of economic depression 1827–32, when some republicans took a philanthropic stance, while others began to formulate a variety of socialist solutions.

In a pamphlet of September 1830 the *Amis* launched a cry which Cabet, Louis Blanc and others were to make familiar, that the July Days had been the work of artisans and that they should rightfully gain both economically and politically from the Revolution. Nearly a year later, in a pamphlet to celebrate the July Days, Trélat railed at the 'spectre of the July Revolution' taken over by 'greedy lawyers, who had never suffered and knew nothing of the problems of the people'.[62] Cabet was to talk about a '*révolution escamotée*'.[63] The Revolution was followed by an intensification of the economic crisis. Lack of confidence aggravated the commercial and industrial depression and the 1830 harvest was no better than that of 1829. Artisan and peasant unrest escalated throughout France, partly to put pressure on the new regime to help, later because of disappointment that the Orleanists were even less sympathetic to the poor than the Polignac government had been. Grain and tax riots and industrial disputes multiplied. At the end of July 1830 the *Amis de Peuple* demanded the abolition of the *droits réunis* on wine in their first pamphlet. This was distributed by pedlars as communes in wine-producing areas were under siege for up to a week from crowds who attacked the tax offices, burned the registers and chased the officials out of town.[64]

Parisian printers expressed Luddite fury that new machines would make them redundant.[65] In the capital growing crowds of unemployed workers of all kinds criticized the inaction of the Orleanists repeatedly during the remaining months of 1830 and for the following two years. Strikes became common, especially in luxury trades such as tailoring.[66] Lack of work and high food prices were central to their complaints. However, there is little direct evidence that those involved in popular unrest thought that a republic would offer them more. The sacking of the church of St Germain l'Auxerrois in February 1831, the felling of missionary crosses and other incidents throughout France in the first two years of the regime, are an indication of popular anti-clericalism. Enthusiasm for the erection of Trees of Liberty might be taken to suggest patriotic sentiments, but those suffering the direct impact of the economic crisis were largely taken up with the issues of food and work. Apart from the tree-planting, Bonapartist emblems and songs which recalled the military glory of that period seemed to have almost as much appeal as republican imagery. But was this sort of sentimental Bonapartism any more than cheap ornaments for the walls of ghastly lodgings and amusement for artisan drinking clubs?

In these years when even modest technological change might put machines beyond the pocket of master craftsmen, when the cotton factory industry of Mulhouse first found too much work for handloom weavers and then left them unemployed when weaving machines were introduced into factories, when the expansion of rural industry robbed the traditional urban masters' organizations of control of prices, and when repeated short-term commercial and industrial crises along with harvest failure meant that survival depended on municipal or private charity, artisans increasingly struggled to set up self-help groups in the shape of mutual-aid societies. In the eighteenth century the traditional artisan *confréries* and *compagnonnages* provided basic sick pay for members and helped to protect wages and conditions of work. The *compagnonnages* also ran houses where journeymen could lodge as they

moved around the country during their training. The *confréries* had a
religious base, the *compagnonnages* involved rituals and secret symbols
not unlike Masonry.[67] The Le Chapelier Law of 1791 and subsequent
legislation undermined both.

New forms of artisan mutual-aid protection began to develop. In
1809 there were 28 *sociétés de secours mutuels* in Paris with a total
membership of 2520. This had grown to 79 societies in 1818, and 128 in
1821 with a membership of over 10,000. By 1840 there were 232 with
over 16,000 adherents. They were artisanal, small and almost
exclusively male. The entrance fee was between 10 and 30 francs, with
monthly premiums of between 1 and 2 francs. They provided sickness
benefit of up to 2 francs, halved after 90 days, and medical care. Old
age pensions, where offered, were usually about 150 francs a year, and
burial costs were covered. They were very solemn bureaucratic
organizations, but even so often had difficulties paying all they
promised, especially pensions. With such a high membership fee only
prosperous artisans could join, and it is not surprising that there were
few women's groups. Even though they covered only perhaps one-tenth
of the working population of the capital at any one time they served as
an example of worker self-help. Although they were non-political, the
July Monarchy in particular worried about their radical potential.[68] In
1832, at the height of government persecution of political societies, the
number of mutual-aid groups in Paris fell from 201 to 131 and
membership slumped.[69]

Elsewhere aspects of mutualism were less neutral than they appear
to have been in the capital. In Lyon there were mutual-aid societies
which simply provided social insurance. But in 1827 the *Society of
Surveillance and Mutual Indication* was formed by Pierre Charnier and 80
master silkweavers to strive for the 'moral regeneration of the *fabrique*'
(the silk industry) and to recover the independence of the weavers. By
March 1833 there were 1200 members,[70] by 1834 there were 3000,
nearly 40 per cent of all master weavers. The society was divided into
small lodges, subdivided into smaller cells. Until 1833 only married
masters could join. The entry fee was 5 francs with a monthly fee of 1
franc. The society was a mutual-aid society, like those of Paris, but it
was also the spearhead for the fight against the silk merchants. The
society was entirely secret, and even its normal mutual-aid functions
could appear threatening to a nervous government. In April 1834 5000
weavers, *canuts*, attended the funeral of a member.[71] The journeymen in
silk also formed an association in 1831, the *Society of Ferrandiniers* (the
name relates to a type of silk cloth), which by 1834 had 600 members

and was a cross between the masters' group, with which it had close relations, and *compagnonnages*, which were active in Lyon, but not in the silk industry.

In Paris police reports constantly stressed the attempts of the *Amis du Peuple* and to a lesser degree the Saint-Simonians to engage the support of the unemployed. But the republicans appeared primarily concerned with political disputes and the rescue of their beleaguered newspapers.[72] Later the *Droits de l'Homme* demanded the abolition of both the wine tax and the equally detested salt tax,[73] both of which had been removed during the 1789 Revolution and later revived because of the revenue they raised. In a trial in 1832 Cavaignac denied that republicans were trying to overturn society:

> The worker should not be exploited by the capitalist; he should not be totally dependent on his wages; there should be a public banking system, the chance of education . . . the right of association . . . Work should be the basis of political rights, not property, because society lives by its work, not its ownership of property.[74]

But pious though the sentiments might be, it all remained very non-specific and could have had only very limited appeal to artisans who were forming their own mutual-aid societies to try to protect themselves.

Aside from their emphasis on tax reform, republicans seemed unaware of the really poor, especially in the countryside. They showed no concern at all for the question of communal land and access to common forest land, which was probably the biggest single issue for the rural poor. The revolutionaries of the 1790s had accelerated the decline of common rights; reduced access and the sale of forests led to further erosion, notably the Forest Code of 1827. Protests at the erosion of common rights were not infrequent. In February 1832 in Remiremont, Vosges, a crowd of up to 400 miserably failed to challenge the new code.[75] When the republicans claimed to care for the poor, they seem to have forgotten such people. But however little the republicans offered, it was more than the Orleanists did. In November 1833 when the *Droits de l'Homme* underwent a shake-up to try to resolve differences, their social programme was noticeably more extensive. They urged the accumulation of 'social capital' by the government for loans to individuals, reminiscent of Louis Blanc's later much publicized scheme. They demanded centralized distribution of goods, in advance of Cabet's ambitious programme. It is unsurprising therefore that wine-producers and artisans joined republican clubs, which attacked the hostile Orleanist centralized state and gave the less privileged a sense of identity.

Economic and social reforms were part of a republican future, but very impressionistically sketched. The first manifesto of the *Amis* committed the society to the defence of the interests of the lower classes and improvements in their moral and physical condition. In 1834 the *Patriote* in the Saône-et-Loire claimed that a republic would be a 'social ladder' for 'the most humble of day-labourers'.[76] Republicans were humanitarian, philanthropic, but rarely egalitarian, beyond the vaguest aphorisms. Few were Babouvist; many were educated property-owners and feared any threat to the existing social order. Most republicans in these years imagined that a republic would be a centralized, benevolent state. The poor would be grateful members of this new world.

The economic crisis of 1827–32 and the broader problems of artisans in industries like printing, tailoring and silk experiencing challenges to traditional structures, and of peasants vainly combating the onslaught of a modernizing centralized state on communal institutions, form the background to the republican movement of the early 1830s. Interaction between the suffering poor and republicans was far less than Orleanists feared. The republicans were divided on social questions. At this stage they offered no serious alternative to the traditional palliatives offered by the Orleanists. In 1833 the *Droits de l'Homme* took up the increasingly popular notion that the unpredictable economic depressions and crippling competition of capitalism could be eliminated by setting up associations of workers, with capital provided by the government. But, as always, they insisted that democracy was a prerequisite for other changes.[77] Artisans were more preoccupied with technical innovations and structural changes such as the growth of 'putting out' in the tailoring trades which was increasing the employment of cheaper women's labour and forcing journeymen to join the new *confection*, or 'ready-made' firms, thus robbing them of both income and independence. Proto-capitalism and the introduction of machines seemed progressive to some republicans. They were beginning to be aware that industrial change and urban growth were producing a volatile situation, but very few understood the problems or saw the grievances of artisans as a route to a second republic.

Individual republicans made practical, personal and immediate contributions to alleviate the contemporary social crisis. Trélat, Raspail, Guépin and other doctors were moved by the miserable state of the poor to work among them, offering free health care. The contribution of one individual could be substantial. Guépin, like many, was a member of the *charbonnerie* and later, while a medical student in Paris, became involved with the Saint-Simonians. He became an eye specialist in Nantes, where he joined the liberal opposition to Polignac and took a leading role in fighting against the prefect during the July Days in 1830. Disappointed with the lack of reform after the Revolution, in November 1839 Guépin founded the *Société Industrielle de Nantes* to provide help for unemployed workers, mainly in road construction, to offer a range of social services and to launch a mutual-aid fund. Plans to provide retirement pensions for workers were included. Guépin himself ran the clinic. He became a republican around 1832 when he lost faith in the willingness of the new regime to help the poor.[78] In 1832 he helped to set up a short-lived tailors' cooperative.

Thus we can see that republican ideology was maturing in the early 1830s, but as it did so republicans found themselves in conflict over both political and social questions. Were they more in accord on short-term objectives, methods and tactics? First, they wanted to inform. They were eager to highlight the inadequacies of the Orleanist regime and to explain the virtues and desirability of a republic. Publicity was vital. The societies were crucial to their organization, but survived only by endless subdivision and subterfuge. In April 1831 with a law against *attroupements*, unlawful public meetings, Périer tried to ban big gatherings. In December 1832 the *Amis du Peuple* was accused of running a society in contravention of the Civil Code. In his defence speech Cavaignac argued that the right of association was a basic, natural human right. The jury agreed with him and all the accused were acquitted.

Republicans used both newspapers and short, cheap pamphlets as propaganda as never before. Newspapers were central to the creation and sustenance of republican clubs, both in Paris and in about 50 regional centres. The republicans were able to build on the success of the liberal press in the Restoration. The *Tribune des départements* rejoiced in the designation 'republican' on 31 July 1830, while the *National* gave measured support. Periodicals like Cavaignac's *Paris Révolutionnaire* seemed to fascinate an intellectual audience which enjoyed a flirtation with a slightly 'dangerous' political concept. In June 1833 Cabet started the newspaper which was to make his name well known in artisan circles, *Le Populaire*. It began as a Sunday paper. It was unique in being partly owned and written by artisans themselves (shares in the paper were sold to groups of workers). In less than two months its circulation had reached 12,000. At 10 francs for an annual subscription, it was much cheaper than any rival. At the time newspapers were sold only by subscription; the *Populaire* was also distributed by 24 public hawkers on the street-corners of Paris near the old Rue Jean-Jacques Rousseau in the Latin Quarter where it was printed and in the nearby artisan districts. Cabet also tried to encourage peasant readership. Within a few weeks the radical society for the freedom of the press which helped to circulate the small republican pamphlets of the Friends of the People, had combined with local republican clubs to organize 70 subscription groups and reading circles in the provinces. Previously such activities had been reserved for the better-off middle-class reader.

Within a couple of months Cabet was planning to bring out a second weekly edition. One edition was printed on Saturday, for distribution in Paris on Sunday. The second would appear on Wednesday and Thursday, in time to reach the provinces by Sunday. There would be special articles on agricultural topics in this second edition. On the Sunday after the first seven numbers had been published, these copies were bound as a pamphlet, *La République du Populaire*.[79] Cabet stressed the need for gradual improvements in conditions for working people. The paper's outspoken defence of the rights of workers to form unions led to inevitable prosecution in January 1834 and the disappearance of the paper. Condemned, Cabet found himself with the most punitive sentence ever imposed, two years jail, a fine of 4400 francs and four years subsequent civil death. He preferred exile and spent the next five years in England.

In the provinces there was a flowering of opposition newspapers, mainly left-wing, but there were a number of legitimist *Gazettes* too, subsidized by wealthy sympathizers. A politicized local press was a very new development; during the Restoration there were a much smaller number of local papers and their political affiliations were almost imperceptible. The left-wing local press flourished in the eastern and south-eastern departments after the July Days. The papers launched membership drives for the clubs. The *Patriote* in Besançon, in its first edition, praised *Aide-toi* and kept the membership lists of the society in its offices. The *Patriote* in Dijon conducted successful publicity for the *Amis*. In the Vosges the society found a sympathetic agent in the *Sentinelle* and its editors, Gerbaut and Mathieu, the latter a convinced disciple of Buonarroti.[80] Although subscription rates were high, it should be remembered that the popular *cabinets de lecture* would take a range of papers. Even so newspaper reading was principally a middle-class activity. Only in Lyon was there an artisan paper to rival *Le Populaire*.

The radical papers were tolerated at first after the July Revolution, and the Laffitte government in November raised the hopes of those who wanted liberal reforms that these might be achieved. But the appointment of the *résistance* Périer administration of March 1831 led to persecution and prosecution. The jury system and the presence of a number of radicals within the judiciary ensured there were few convictions. The trial always offered one of the best means of publicity and a record of the trial and the glorious acquittal would inevitably be published in pamphlet-form. In 1832 when Gerbaut of Epinal was accused for the third time of insult to government and monarch and again acquitted, the government prosecutor complained that the newspaper's habit of printing the names and addresses of the jurors exposed them to the ridicule of their neighbours if they voted for a conviction. On this occasion only three did so. However, defence costs progressively weakened such papers. In June 1832 the *Tribune des départements* was facing its 52nd trial in less than two years.

While a subscription, even to a local paper, was expensive, pamphlets were cheap. The *Amis* specialized in short, simple leaflets, clearly designed for a less well-educated market. In Epinal the local club was so poor that leaflets were written by hand.[81] Pamphlets were sold in the countryside by hawkers, *crieurs publics*, who would sell anything that was easy to carry. They were a useful way to reach country people, who were accustomed to buy a wide range of items from them, from ribbons to the work of the *bibliothèque bleue*.[82]

Another traditional form of publicity in this period when large-scale societies were banned . was to hold banquets to honour leading sympathetic politicians, who would be invited to give speeches. The republicans exploited this medium with great success. One held in Dijon in December 1833 in favour of electoral reform was attended by 600 diners, including mayors from nearby communes.[83] After the meal there would be reform speeches by politicians such as Garnier-Pagès or Cormenin. Another popular conscious-raising exercise was to collect for a politically correct cause. The republicans organized repeated subscriptions, including one for the Poles, defeated in their struggle for freedom from Russian control, and many small ones to help distressed newspapers.

Publicity and banquets were one side of republicanism. Some republicans wanted to seize power. There was always an insurrectionary strand, which could never be entirely ignored, partly because the revolutionary tradition of the 1790s legitimized the violent overthrow of regimes and more tangibly because National Guard battalions were usually sympathetic to popular unrest. The sections of the *Amis* and *Droits de l'Homme* were supposed to be armed. Members in Dijon, Beaune and elsewhere were instructed to provide themselves with a gun and ammunition, and this must have been fairly easy for National Guardsmen and soldier members. Clubs were ordered to drill and hold target practices; the Arbois club even claimed that such exercises were not subversive.

In his account of Babeuf's conspiracy, Buonarroti urged republicans to take the opportunity of popular disaffection during an economic crisis to seize power, as Babeuf had tried to do in 1796. There is no doubt that the economic crisis helped to sustain republican agitation and government apprehension alike. The Laffitte government of November 1830 was sometimes ambivalent and hesitated to crush popular unrest and found ready support from some of the newly appointed local officials especially those out of office since the Hundred Days. Casimir Périer, in office from March 1831, took a firm line, combining the dismissal of those public servants compromised, especially in the recent anti-clerical riots which followed the memorial service for the duc de Berri in the church of St Germain l'Auxerrois, with thorough investigation and repression. A new membership drive by republican clubs in March 1832 brought the immediate response from the government: 'The first responsibility of the administration is to maintain public order, by offering those political groups which threaten it an invincible resistance.'[84] Governments were constantly afraid that political criticism and economic grievance could be welded into popular insurrection.

The most worrying episode was in Lyon in November 1831. The silk industry, the dominant trade in the city, was at the centre. Silk was produced in small independent workshops and over 50,000 workers, 25 per cent of the working population of the city, were involved. It was a growth industry during the Restoration, but suffered setbacks during the depression of 1827–32. But beneath the expansion, there was proto-capitalist economic change which led to serious social conflict. The weavers were in repeated deadlock with silk merchants. The increase of rural industry outside the control of the master-weavers' organizations allowed merchants to buy woven silk cheaper, ignoring the traditional, but often neglected, concept of a *tarif*, or negotiated fixed price. The development of the Jacquard loom on which the more expensive, fashionable patterned silks were woven, obliged weavers to borrow capital from merchants to buy the new larger, more complex loom and acquire more spacious properties with higher ceilings in which it could be installed.

After the 1830 Revolution the silk trade suffered further setbacks, but in 1831 a new prefect, Dumolard, acceded to the demands of the weavers, the *canuts*, to try to negotiate a set price for silk. Informed of the disapproval of his Parisian bosses, Dumolard retracted. Silkweavers, disappointed at the decision of the prefect not to intervene in their long-running dispute with merchants over rates of pay, and with, as was the norm in such conflicts, the National Guard of central Lyon, which had many weaver members, on their side, drove the local garrison out of town. Tartly informed by Paris that the government's policy was to remain 'neutral', the prefect lost both Lyon and his job.[85] The government was at pains to emphasize that the silkweavers were not politically motivated.[86] The weavers were certainly disillusioned with the ineptness and double-dealing of the local agent of central government politics, Dumolard, and after the army had returned to the city with reinforcements could have had little faith in the support of local politicians, like Prunelle, the mayor and deputy. The events of Lyon in November 1831 showed once more the potential which popular unrest could offer republicans, if they could make use of it.[87]

In a pamphlet headed 'Le Guerre Civile', the *Amis du Peuple* revealed their incomprehension. They referred to the weavers as '*ouvriers*', which would not have pleased them, and made sympathetic noises about poverty. About the only thing the republicans really seem to have understood about *la Grande Fabrique*, was the slogan of the *canuts*, '*Vivre libre en travaillant, ou mourir en combattant*'.[88] The rising in Lyon was the most dramatic of many popular disturbances in these years. It was certainly not republican, but it offered a vigorous display of the social orientation of the Orleanists, that they would not shrink from using the army to enforce the rights of the better-off. It is true that the government quickly voted an additional 18 million francs to help the unemployed,[89] but, given the timing, this must have looked like conscience-money.

The next major popular disturbance was in Paris in the summer of 1832 at the height of the cholera outbreak, and was political and directly linked to the *Amis*. There was pressure from rank and file members of the *Amis*, after the death of Périer, for an armed uprising, though the leaders resisted. There was even an expectation that the parliamentary opposition, some 130-strong, might be sympathetic. On June 5th, the funeral of the radical hero, General Lamarque, another cholera victim, provided the occasion for what was described by Louis Blanc as the first truly republican insurrection since 1815.[90] The flying of the red flag, the sight of a revolutionary phyrgian bonnet and rumours that the *hôtel de ville* had fallen to insurgents, provoked troops to open fire as the funeral speeches for Lamarque were in progress. Barricades went up in the traditional central artisan districts behind the *hôtel de ville*. But the republican leaders urged caution and on June 6th left the artisans to a hopeless fight with the National Guard. A total of 800 were killed or wounded. Paris was put in a state of siege, the arrested were charged; seven were condemned to death (commuted to deportation), four to deportation. None were the leaders of the *Amis du Peuple* who earlier had appeared to encourage the demonstration.

When the economy began to recover in the summer of 1832, both popular unrest and support for republican papers and clubs declined, which was fortunate for the Orleanists whose lawcourts remained persistently liberal. In December 1832 the government failed in its attempt to prosecute the *Amis du Peuple* for contravention of the Code. But in 1833 there was a wave of industrial unrest as workers tried to improve rates of pay reduced during the depression. The *Droits de l'Homme* and the revived *Association républicaine pour la défense de la liberté de la presse patriotique et de la liberté individuelle* made concerted attempts to recruit, sometimes with little success.[91] However, a banquet planned to honour Garnier-Pagès in Lyon already had 6000 subscribers when the prefect nervously banned it.

The republicans had targeted Lyon, but at first totally misread the situation by presenting themselves as partisans of modernization. They misunderstood the structure of the silk industry and antagonized weavers by favouring industrial 'freedom', when weavers were anxious precisely to restrict the 'freedom' of merchants to pay the lowest rate possible for woven silk. Republicans were slow to appreciate the complexities of the industry. The *Droits de l'Homme* made approaches and some converts among the weavers toward the end of 1833, but their propaganda was very general and did not attempt to address the issues which worried local people. A recruiting pamphlet, 'To the People. People suffer because they do not govern themselves' promised that all would be well if the poor had the vote. On economic issues all it could say was: 'Agriculture and industry will thrive if the salt, wheat and tobacco duties are removed . . . along with the *droits réunis*.'[92] The abolition of all controls was just what the *canuts* did not want. Such insensitive propaganda was more likely to attract the merchants (*fabricants*) rather than the masters and journeymen. Some Lyon republicans were unsympathetic to the weavers and in general the republican movement was more concerned with internecine local political rivalries, defining themselves as 'Girondin' and 'Jacobin' and reliving the personal and ideological conflicts of the 1790s. More in tune with the problems of industrial change the Saint-Simonists, established in the city since 1831 and active in the local press, also hoped to find converts.

Faced with the renewed efforts of the tiny republican movement, the Orleanists seemed to be running before the wind of three myths, largely of their own imaginings. Ministers were convinced that the Lyon silkweavers were a threat to the regime; that they had been won over to republicanism and that a nationwide conspiracy was to be launched by both groups with Lyon as the focus in the spring of 1834. A three-pronged attack was launched; to stop the circulation of republican pamphlets, to close the clubs, and to force their newspapers out of business. In February 1834 hawkers were forced to apply to the prefect to ply their wares, which permit could be revoked at any time. Legislation was brought before parliament to force all societies to disband, whatever their size.

At the beginning of 1834 weavers of Lyon were once again in dispute with the merchants over the price to be paid for woven silk. The weavers were also aware that the proposed new legislation on associations would force their Mutual Duty and Ferrandinier societies to close. A strike was called once more. On February 14th all 25,000 looms in Lyon came to an agreed standstill, under the same provocative black banners as 1831 but there was no quick military victory this time. The society lacked strike funds and weavers were forced back to their looms within a week.[93] The strike leaders were committed for trial.

Silkweavers were primarily concerned with the survival and prosperity of their families and their trade. They believed that successive Orleanist governments had waged war against them. Weavers were deeply resentful both of the tariff policy of the regime and of the official proclamation of laissez-faire, which protected the employer by using troops against strikers, but banned coalitions of workers. But memories of the First Republic in Lyon did not encourage weavers to expect much from republicans. It had been the silk merchants who had found the Girondins to their taste in the early 1790s.[94] The February strike was a trade dispute. However, the imminence of the new legislation made a strict separation of economic and political motivation impossible. All societies, political and trade, expected to be forced to disband.

Agitation in Lyon persisted because of the inflammatory decision to hold the trial of the strike leaders at the precise time when the bill to outlaw all associations was before Parliament. Artisans feared that *compagnonnages*, as well as the *Mutuellistes*, would be forced to disband by the new legislation, despite denials by the government. The law, introduced into the Assembly by Barthe, Minister of Justice and a former member of the *charbonnerie*, secured a majority of 246 to 154 in the Chamber of Deputies on April 10th. All societies, whatever their size or nature, were obliged to seek prefectoral sanction. The penalty for belonging to an illegal organization was increased from a fine to one year's imprisonment and a 1000 franc fine. Whoever owned the property where an illegal meeting was held was equally liable.

The postponed trial of strike leaders opened on April 9th in an atmosphere which the local administration had allowed to become overcharged. Onlookers threw stones, the troops on duty around the *palais de justice* opened fire. Barricades were erected in defence and by April 15th 300 were dead. The artillery were used to blast the central weaving districts with little discrimination. The newer outlying Croix Rousse weaving district had been carefully isolated by fortifications built since the last rising and was attacked separately. Most of the casualties among the troops were due to their inexperience in inner-city guerrilla tactics. Between 3000 and 6000 artisans felt that they had been left with no choice but to take arms against the professional army and the merchants in the Croix Rousse National Guard. Of those arrested 37 per cent were weavers, mainly journeymen. The rest were mostly from other trades. A mere 15 per cent were in either a political or even a workers' association. Of the 100 arrested and sent for trial on charges of conspiracy against the government, 39 were republicans. Of these 8 were eventually tried.[95] The ferocity of the government's response meant that the official line had to be maintained that unrest in Lyons was part of a long-discussed plot republicans had boasted about since the beginning of the year.[96]

In reality, anxiety about the proposed legislation and how to oppose it contributed much to stirring up a divided republican movement, no longer buttressed by popular unrest as the short-term economic recession faded. Police informers convinced the government that a major republican rising throughout eastern and south-eastern France was planned to coincide with riots in Lyon.[97] Informers made their contribution by inventing or even creating conspiracies. The regular perambulations of the radical journalist Mathieu and other delegates to visit the different clubs were recorded by the various prefects, presumably to prove to their masters that a total ban on all societies was needed.

A full-blown republican conspiracy theory had been inflated in 1833–4 by nervous officials and spies. One such spy, Mascarène, a member of a local regiment, persuaded Mathieu to set up a new society in order to substantiate his claim that Mathieu was the focal point of a vast conspiracy.[98] It is hard to believe that anyone was taken in by Mascarène, so self-evidently spy and conspirator combined. His commander, General Hulot, had requested his transfer to North Africa a few months earlier, precisely for these reasons. If the government wanted a conspiracy badly enough to accept a poorly invented one, the republicans were also remarkably gullible. In February 1834 Mathieu moved between Nancy and Châlons whipping up support and weapons for a concerted rising, threatening anyone prepared to listen that a republic would soon be declared. His companion was Mascarène. How could Mathieu have failed to notice that his most active supporter was a double-agent? Mascarène's commanding officer gave him permission to go, apparently hoping that if Mascarène met with some success in subverting part of the regiment stationed in Lyon, government repression would be justified.[99]

Junior officers, lowly paid, bored and with little hope of promotion, had been keen, if inept, conspirators in the 1820s. The republican clubs of the early 1830s offered similar enticements: companionship, drink and the thrill of defying authority. One of Mascarène's victims was Clement Thomas, a 25-year-old junior officer stationed in Luneville, an associate of the *Droits de l'Homme* under the patronage of leading radicals such as de Ludre. A scheme was put into his head, not unlike one of the abortive conspiracies of the 1820s. He was to march the three Luneville regiments to Nancy, link up with that garrison and then attack the capital. There were many disgruntled junior officers in these regiments, following recent reorganization. Thomas enlisted the support of two colleagues, Bernard and Tricotel, during meetings in local cafés. The news of fighting in Lyon encouraged them. Tricotel went ahead to Nancy. On April 16th the conspirators met again in a local café, but when they returned to their quarters ready for action they found that the plot was discovered. They were arrested. Mascarène denied that he had fabricated their plot when they were all finally brought to trial a year later, but the evidence of the unfortunate and naïve trio does not bear out his claims.[100] There were a few other isolated incidents, including the declaration of a republic by the Arbois club.[101]

In Paris republican leaders were unprepared for action when the news of the Lyon rioting broke. The government ordered the arrest of 500 militants and banned the publication of the *Tribune*. A small rising did take place, although the leaders tried to prevent it, considering the time quite inauspicious. On April 13th barricades went up in the artisan districts, but the next day the attempt was repressed with unnecessary bloodshed in the massacre of the rue Transnonain.[102]

The attempted 'risings' all had a common motive, resistance to the new legislation, but they were not synchronized to be a takeover of power. The government continued to insist that there had been a conspiracy, despite all evidence to the contrary. The official web of suspicion, lies and intrigue had to be sustained. The government ordered the arrest of 2000 so-called leaders, 164 of whom were finally tried, not by the wilfully independent assize court, but by the Chamber of Peers in May 1835. During their year in prison, the accused were depicted as victims. There was never any evidence of a great conspiracy and most of those arrested were released without accusation. But those accused failed to disport themselves as martyrs; they argued amongst themselves and some refused to go to court. The adventurer republican Fieschi's bloody attempt to kill Louis-Philippe at the end of July 1835 during which 18 were killed and 22 wounded deprived them of all popular sympathy, even though he had no connection with them.

After over six months of hearings, in January 1836 sentences were passed. Trélat was fined 10,000 francs and sentenced to three years' jail for his defence speech in which he denied the right of the court to try him. Some republican editors were sentenced for articles such as one in the Besançon *Patriote*, which had proclaimed, in capitals, on 3 March 1834 that 'insurrection is a public duty'.[103] The comments of the young soldiers under questioning indicate extreme naïveté. One said his mother would never have allowed him to be a republican; another that drink, not conspiracy, was his undoing. Mascarène was acquitted.[104] Leading republicans, including Cavaignac and Cabet, avoided trial by sailing to England. After all the fuss, the convicted were released in 1837 and in 1840 the exiles were allowed to return to France. The relatively light sentences and the long delay in trying the *accusés d'avril*, as they were called, may be contrasted with the death sentences instantly executed by the Restoration regime for similar 'offences'. But one might also contrast the large numbers killed in Lyon and the dead in Paris in 1834 with the absence of similar victims among the *charbonnerie*.

While the trial was being organized the legislation against the clubs had been put into effect. A large number of the members left and some of the radical clubs disappeared, partly pushed to the wall by financial problems. Only in towns where republicanism had been particularly strong is there evidence of groups continuing to meet. In July 1834 the Dijon club, reduced mainly to its artisan members, had debts of 14,000 francs.[105] Often former republican clubs re-emerged under non-political guises. The Dijon club bounced back as a music society; the prefect had to give it authorization, having long complained of a dearth of local interest in music.[106] A year later, Demay, one of the old republican leaders, was running a bookshop and a literary salon in Dijon, shielded by the support of leading members in the local judiciary. In Strasbourg the club continued to meet at its usual café as a 'patriotic circle' and was successfully acquitted on a sedition charge. In Châlons the club became a *société de bienfaisance* in 1835 and a branch of *Jeune Europe* was also started with a subscription of 50 cents a month.[107] But many of the smaller groups folded.

Laws against the radical press, urged on by the Fieschi attempt on the king, reached the statute book in September 1835 and were to remain in force, with brief intervals, until 1881.[108] The initial caution money paid by an editor was raised, new press 'crimes' were introduced, but most important, press cases were no longer to be tried by juries. Those indicted of insult to the king risked a fine of 50,000 francs and a year in jail. Newspapers could no longer publish the details of a trial. The word 'republic' could not be used.[109] The terms of the September Laws were comprehensive and draconian, but almost superfluous. The worst scourge of the Orleanists, the *Tribune*, had folded in May 1835, following 111 prosecutions and 20 condemnations, totalling 49 years jail for the editor and fines of 150,000 francs. The *Réformateur*, relentlessly pursued, closed in October 1835. Carrel's *National* and the monthly *Journal du Peuple* survived, but were forced to adopt a more concealed scorn of the regime. Daumier, the republican caricaturist whose moving representation of the Transnonain shootings brought anger at the lack of humanity of the Orleanists, was forced to turn his attention to the equally fruitful unveiling of the superficiality, pomposity and self-seeking of contemporary society.

The new laws attacked a defeated enemy in the provinces. The repeated prosecutions since 1830 of both the radical left and right, had already forced most papers out of business. Mathieu's *Sentinelle des*

Vosges disappeared in 1833, the editor of the Besançon *Patriote*, accused of conspiring in April 1834, was sentenced to 20 years hard labour, and exposed as an embezzler who had lived in Besançon under a false name. The paper was finished. The Dijon *Patriote*, acquitted on a charge of sedition in April 1834, survived until the new law, but with increasing difficulty; its sales fell catastrophically from 470 to 354, 30 of which were actually given away. In the Puy-de-Dôme the *Patriote* survived the new laws; in Lyon the *Glaneuse* was almost bankrupt in January 1834 and closed down in March when its editor was jailed. Only the *Echo de la Fabrique*, out of a handful of earlier opposition newspapers, was still publishing.

Since March 1831 successive Orleanist governments had been unrelentingly repressive. Casimir Périer had laboured to purge his administration of the many *mouvement* sympathizers who had gained jobs after the July Days and to create a stable, professional and politically conservative body of officials. The magistrature was another matter, and government critics, who were sufficiently independent to block convictions of legitimists as well as republicans, remained in key positions in a number of towns, including Dijon and Besançon. Republican sympathizers also survived in municipal councils and, even more visibly, among the elected officers of the National Guard. Some battalions, like that of Strasbourg, were disbanded for this reason.[110]

Identifiable and assertive republican societies and newspapers were the product of conservative Orleanist *résistance*, an unwillingness to tolerate dissent and countenance gradual change. Some leading politicians, energetic local *notables* and outstanding journalists were involved in the movement. The fact of a continuing and worsening economic recession and more long-term disharmony within the agricultural and industrial economies created popular unrest which was both a backdrop for the clubs and afforded the possibility of mass support. However, those who called themselves republicans could not agree on an agenda or whether it was in their brief to try to act as a vanguard insurrectionary party or an embryonic workers' education organization and medical service. Republicans were in conflict on the inheritance of the 1789 Revolution and on how to develop its legacy. Republicans were fatally divided over both message and medium. There was some superficial accord on a 'Jacobin' republic, but little definition. There was no agreement on how a republic could be created. In theory republicans believed in insurrection, but in June 1832 and April 1834 the societies drew back from popular movements.

In the early 1830s republicans were thrown into disarray by a second revolution, within the economy. Their worst cleavages were yet to emerge. How should republicans react to the social and economic problems of industrial change? In the years to 1835 the question was as yet embryonic but increasingly debated. In the following years some republicans turned to a variety of socialist theories and tried to blend them with republicanism. Others rejected socialism and concentrated on political reform. A few continued to believe in insurrection and assumed that discontented workers would be natural allies.

6   The Republic Outlawed: Insurrection and Reform 1835–1848

Between the September laws of 1835, which muzzled the republican press, and the February Revolution of 1848, those who continued to hold out against Orleanism were divided and marginalized, by their own actions as much as by government manoeuvres. Three main strands of radical opposition – insurrectionary, reformist and socialist – can be discerned for the purposes of the historian's urge to tidy up the past (individuals might, of course, be a mixture of these). A tiny minority maintained the belief that a republic could emerge from a popular rising; the remainder were irresolute. Should energy be consolidated around an attempt to develop parliamentary institutions, in which case electoral and suffrage reform had priority, or did the visible social problems of an industrializing society dictate that social reform should dominate the agenda? If so, should this be piecemeal, radical, revolutionary or utopian? All republicans were certainly not socialist, socialists tended to favour a republic, but as a means, not as an end in itself. The two issues of electoral and social reform came to dominate debates among a quarrelsome and largely middle-class minority, few of whose adherents believed that the creation of a republic was possible or likely, and certainly not at the beginning of 1848.

After 1835 only a tiny minority continued to believe that a republic was a practical immediate possibility. Since legal means of persuasion were denied them, emphasis became concentrated on direct violent action. Insurrection remained the strategy of those who believed that not just a republic, but a socialist republic, was an achievable, immediate goal.[1] These militants, themselves wracked by internecine

129

rivalries, were dominated by Auguste Blanqui, who almost alone argued for an immediate revolution. 'When one demolishes the old world, the new is awaiting discovery in its ruins; one final hammer blow and it is triumphantly displayed'.[2]

The 1790s and 1830 itself justified confidence in insurrection as the means to bring about change. Buonarroti's account of the 1796 Conspiracy of the Equals offered a blueprint for insurrection which never ceased to convince a new generation of insurgents. Buonarroti held to Babeuf's belief that a tiny minority of trained and determined civil insurgents could overthrow a government and thus gain control of the centralized state. His revolutionary model was the secret society, split into small cells, where only one member was known to the next group in the hierarchical chain of command, a concept based loosely on the structure of Freemasonry. Babeuf and later insurgents had total confidence that artisans and also soldiers would instinctively and instantly identify with their revolution, particularly in a time of devastating economic recession, because his revolution was meant to secure economic and political equality simultaneously.[3]

Babeuf's rejection of private ownership which appalled his bourgeois contemporaries, his argument that individual men could only demand the use, not the permanent possession, of land, had an appeal to a new idealistic generation in the 1820s. Cabet and others began to echo some of Babeuf's ideas, though often they were far less radical than the man whom some early socialists acknowledged, with varying degrees of accuracy, as their mentor. Babeuf feared that the economic resources of his society were circumscribed to such a degree that even his reorganization would be an equalization of poverty. The early socialists, children of an age of economic growth, assumed an expanding economy and expected that any moves towards equalization could fill everyone's belly. It might therefore be said that the ideological link between Babeuf and those who came later was sentimental rather than real. It has been argued, persuasively, that the identification of the socialist Louis Blanc with Babeuf was mistaken, that Babeuf was more a *sans-culotte* than a precursor of socialism.[4] However, Blanqui's notions in particular were very close to those of Buonarroti's version of Babeuf. Babouvism was thus one of the strands in the insurrectionary and socialist theories which developed in the 1830s, although, with the exception of Blanqui, most socialists, it should be noted, were not insurrectionaries.

Babouvist ideas were transformed from paper into action by a minute group in which the leading figure was Auguste Blanqui, who was the classic conspirator.[5] He was nick-named '*l'enfermé*' because over half of his adult life, about 34 years in all, was spent in jail. He never lost the conviction that a tiny, conspiratorial revolutionary group could bring down the corrupt system of the July Monarchy and its successors and create a socialist republic. Unlike many early socialists, his published writings were fairly sparse. He is remembered as an activist, an insurgent.

Blanqui's republicanism was in part a family tradition. His father, a teacher in Tuscany, had been a Girondin sympathizer in the Convention, incarcerated by the Jacobins, and later a Napoleonic prefect. Auguste and his equally brilliant elder brother Adolphe attended the elitist *lycée* Charlemagne. Both joined the *charbonnerie*, along with many of their generation. Auguste went on to study law, write a little for the *Globe* and take part in political demonstrations during Charles X's reign. He was rewarded with the *croix de juillet*, for his otherwise anonymous role during the 1830 Revolution, but was soon at odds with the July Monarchy and attempting to stir up further revolution. His brother, ironically, became a pillar of the Orleanist Establishment; he was appointed professor at the Conservatoire and Director of the School of Commerce.

A leading student activist in the republican *Amis du Peuple*, in July 1831 Blanqui was arrested together with Raspail,[6] Trélat and other leaders of the society and charged with violations of the press laws. Their trial, which opened in December, offered Blanqui the opportunity to enlarge on his socialist republicanism in a speech which subsequently appeared as a pamphlet.[7] When asked by the president of the court to state his profession, Blanqui, who lived in the artisan district of St Antoine, replied '*prolétaire*' (worker). 'That is not a profession' was the response; to which Blanqui replied, 'How can that be? It is the profession of 30 million French people, who survive by their work and are deprived of all political rights'. Blanqui's job description was solemnly entered into the records of the trial. 'I am accused of having told 30 million French people, all proletarians like me, that they have the right to live. . . . the Minister of Justice seeks to unleash your vengeance against what he presents to you as a threat to you and your property . . . Thus today I stand, not before judges but enemies.' Accused of encouraging the poor to rise up against the rich, Blanqui claimed it was the rich who oppressed the poor. The poor paid most in taxes, duty was charged on imported grain, which protected the rich farmer, but made the bread of the poor expensive. High tariffs on foreign iron made tools costly, while reciprocal action by foreign governments denied French wine an export market. A whole range of indirect taxes added to the misery of the poor.

Blanqui proceeded to detail the beneficiaries of such revenue; the extensive progeny of the new king, the compost-heap of sinecurists and hangers-on, the privileged electorate perhaps, but never the poor. The solution was first, universal suffrage, so that laws could be enacted for the benefit of all. What was needed for a viable republic, Blanqui argued, was not merely the implementation of the Jacobin Constitution, which many regarded as a scarecrow spectre, but social equality.[8] Blanqui thus firmly established himself as both a socialist and a democrat and was one of the first to define the concept of class conflict. The jury were appalled. They acquitted all of the accused after a mere 15 minutes discussion, but declared Blanqui guilty of stirring up class hatred in his defence speech. He was fined 200 francs and sentenced to a year's imprisonment, very little of which he served, due to repeated bouts of ill health, including cholera. (Jails seem to have had a very free-and-easy approach or perhaps were afraid that sick inmates would spread infection.)

In 1834 Auguste launched the *Réformateur* and became editor of the *Libérateur*, a periodical which was to be devoted to republicanism and social reform. The latter, designed to sell at 2 sous an issue under the banner '*Unité, Egalité, Fraternité*', did not get beyond the first issue. In the first number Blanqui made it clear that social reform mattered more to him than a republic, which was merely the tool by which a just society might be best obtained. He was prepared to abandon a republic if it did not live up to his expectations.

There is no evidence that Blanqui took part in the unrest which accompanied the debate on the law on associations of 1834, although some commentators include his name among participants. Blanqui argued that the laws of 1834 were such an affront to liberty that they gave the individual the right to rebel.[9] Following the demise of the *Société des Droits de l'Homme* in 1834, which was forced to disband by the new legislation, the *Société des Familles* was created phoenix-like by Hadot-Desages, the democrat printer. Anxious to recruit members, its name recalled Saint-Simonian terminology, which continued to exercise an appeal among radicals, despite the wayward conduct of L'Enfantin and his disciples. The *Familles* adopted a similar military and Masonic structure to that of the defunct *Droits de l'Homme*. Social issues were stressed, but there was no special emphasis on republicanism, in the hope of encouraging a broad spectrum of sympathy. Blanqui became a leading member, along with Barbès, Bernard and Eugène

Lamieussons. Barbès (1809–1870),[10] a wealthy Creole from Carcassonne, where his father was a doctor, via Guadeloupe, studied law, joined the *Droits de l'Homme* and was one of the defenders of the 'conspirators' of 1834. He shared a house with Blanqui. His political loyalties were made clear in a pamphlet he wrote in 1837 attacking the great disparities of wealth in contemporary society, which earned him a month in jail.[11] Bernard, a printer, a republican democrat and contributor to *Revue Républicaine*, who had been associated with the Saint-Simonians and in 1833 had encouraged printworkers to form an association and strike, had become close friends with Barbès during the trial of the 'conspirators' of April 1834.[12] The centre of the society was the 'family', a group of 6–10 members; between five and six families formed a section, two or three sections a *quartier* and at the centre was a committee. No minutes of meetings were to be kept and members had to promise to be willing to fight for a social revolution.

By the end of 1835 the society was gaining new members at the rate of 200 a month, but the Fieschi shootings caused setbacks, even though the would-be assassin of the king had no contact with the *Familles*. By the summer of 1836 there were about 1200 members, mostly young, and predominantly artisans, *negoçiants* and students, with some junior army officers and National Guardsmen. The Paris society was in touch with a club in Lyon and attempted to infiltrate the regiments stationed in the capital, to such a degree that the latter were moved to North Africa. Ironically, military backing seems to have been much less than that secured by earlier clubs, which had been anxious to stress more of an evolutionary ethos. Provincial links appear to have been few, in contrast to the network of relationships in the early 1830s, even though a number of the local clubs in Strasbourg and elsewhere survived the 1834 legislation. In June 1836 the Strasbourg republican club held a fund-raising banquet to help those jailed for political offences in the capital and raised 350 francs.[13] In 1839 the society had 200 members, including 23 municipal councillors. In 1839, 144 of the 204 men included in the prefect's list of republicans in the Strasbourg club were either artisans or involved in wholesale or retail trade, but it is not possible to gauge how prosperous or otherwise were the brewers who occupy so prominent a place on the list.[14]

The *Familles* and its successor the *Saisons* were military, revolutionary formations committed to seize power at the first possible opportunity. The middle-class leaders concentrated on amassing weapons and ammunition, publishing a few clandestine pamphlets and meeting their artisan supporters in tiny groups. Their main secret paper up to July

1838 was the *Moniteur républicain*, later the *Homme Libre*, whose editors were arrested shortly before the rising of May 1839. The leaders of both societies were committed to a new *jacquerie*, in the words of the government prosecutor in 1839. They wanted radical social revolution, arguing that workers were the sole producers of wealth and should therefore be the only beneficiaries.[15] Unlike earlier republican clubs, the *Familles* evinced no interest in the education or social welfare of the poor, or in the conversion of the middle class to gradual and peaceful change.

Secret societies were always riddled with informers. A store of the *Familles'* weapons and ammunition together with membership lists was found by the Parisian police. Barbès and Blanqui were arrested, Blanqui dramatically swallowing some of the lists. The *Procès de Poudres*, the 'Gunpowder' Trial, opened in October 1836. All denied the charge of conspiracy but four were condemned, including Blanqui, together with Beaufort, Robier and Robert. Blanqui was sentenced to two years imprisonment, a fine of 3000 francs and two years subsequent police surveillance. Barbès spent a year in jail. Once more, despite the seriousness of the charge, in May 1837 all were soon at liberty, following a general amnesty for political prisoners announced to celebrate the marriage of the duke of Orleans.

The organizers of the *Familles* rapidly regrouped in 1837 as the *Saisons*, the Society of the Seasons. Its structure was hierarchical but somewhat more labyrinthine than its predecessor. The basic unit was the 'week' *(semaine)*, consisting of six men plus 'Sunday' *(dimanche)*, the leader. Four weeks naturally made up a 'month', whose leader, *juillet*, would only know the four leaders of the 'weeks'. The total membership of the three 'months' made a 'season' *(saison)*, led by *printemps*, who would only know the three *juillets*. Four 'seasons' constituted a year led by an *agent révolutionnaire*. No written membership lists were to be kept (the Family ones perhaps proved rather indigestible), but initiation ceremonies followed earlier models and acolytes took an oath to the republic: 'In the name of the Republic, I swear eternal hatred to all kings, aristocrats and all oppressors of humanity'.[16]

The monthly subscription was a modest 50 centîmes, much lower than that for earlier societies, and the hat was passed around at meetings to meet the cost of weapons. Funds did not come easily and towards the end no membership fees were levied. There was no attempt to secure support within the army, because it was judged too risky. Like the *Familles*, there were few provincial links, apart from Lyon. A high proportion of members were artisans and some *Seasons* were composed entirely from men in one trade. Although this was unusual at the time, it was probably spontaneous, rather than a response to direction from the leadership.

Tailors were the largest single element, as they were in a strike movement a year later. Their participation was a direct consequence of structural changes in tailoring which were undermining the artisanal character of the industry and destroying the independence and prosperity of the journeymen. The master tailors were increasingly 'putting-out' less skilled jobs to women at lower rates and journeymen were being obliged to work for 'merchant-tailors' who had opened large workshops producing for the new ready-made, off-the-peg trade. The journeymen seized on any available means to express their disgust at the inroads of capitalist enterprise into their craft. The *Seasons* was but one tactic. By the beginning of 1838 the *Seasons* were a 900-strong organization, according to the Parisian police. Among the leaders were Barbès, Martin Bernard, Quignot, Notré and Meillard, with Blanqui as the undisputed senior figure. Like the *Familles*, the society met in small groups on Sunday afternoons in a variety of spots, mainly cafés. They took care to be inconspicuous, unlike the flagrantly public 'secret' clubs of the early 1830s.

The *Seasons*, like its predecessor, was conceived by Blanqui as a vanguard insurrectionary movement. Gone were the evolutionary pious hopes of the republicans of the early 1830s, who had expected that through evening classes and health care the disadvantaged would gain the enlightenment to seek a gradual move towards a republic. Blanqui wanted the same ultimate goal, but by more direct means. Unlike more moderate republicans, he also assumed that the disadvantaged were already republican and that once a rising had been launched by his vanguard party, the masses would join them on the streets. He believed that revolution was brought about by the direction and leadership of 'professional' revolutionaries, that the mass of the population was only awaiting a signal to rise and that the centralized state could be taken over rapidly.

The speed with which the regime had been changed in 1830 convinced many, including the Orleanist victors, of the fragility of political systems and of the volatility, tractability and revolutionary potential of the masses. All that was needed was a nucleus of convinced, armed and determined conspirators and a sufficiently de-stabilized situation in the capital. Meanwhile, like the *Familles*, the *Seasons* concentrated on stockpiling weapons. From time to time during 1838 individuals were arrested carrying quantities of cartridges, sometimes more were discovered in their homes and in July 1838 three men who had been jailed after the Gunpowder trial were arrested as they worked on a batch of cartridges. Subsequently a veritable arsenal was uncovered.

Painstaking plans were laid for a rising on Sunday 12 May 1839, at 2.30 p.m. A Sunday, being a holiday, was the best day if popular support was to be hoped for. The coincidence of an economic recession with a prolonged ministerial crisis may have convinced Blanqui that circumstances were similar to those of July 1830. News of Chartist activities in England contributed to a belief that change was possible. Additionally, a major horserace meeting on that day meant that few National Guardsmen would be available for duty. Finally, Blanqui was afraid that he would lose control of the *Seasons* unless a major strike was attempted. The Prefecture of Police and the main bridges were to be seized, enabling the plotters to hold the right bank of the Seine from the Marais to Montmartre. A proclamation prepared for the occasion announced a people's republic:

> The hour of doom has struck for our oppressors. People arise! Your enemies will disappear like dust in a storm. Strike! Exterminate the base henchmen and willing accomplices of our tyrants! Forward! Long live the Republic![17]

The rising was to be led by Blanqui, Barbès, Martin-Bernard and Dubosc, the editor of the *Journal du Peuple*. Their proclamation also included the names of Voyer d'Argenson, Lamennais and Laponneraye, very well-known radicals, but who were not actually involved in the *Seasons*. Following the successful overthrow of the Orleanist regime a provisional government was to be set up composed of Blanqui, Barbès and Martin Bernard.

Only the main leaders knew of the project. In the previous weeks stocks of powder had been built up; some said 3000 cartridges, some 12,000. Weapons were to be seized by raids on armourers' shops once the rising was under way. The main body of men were called to assemble as if for a regular review, starting in various cafés in the rue St Denis, rue St Martin and surrounding streets. Assaults began on key installations. Barbès himself led a column of 600 men to the *palais de justice* where he urged the troops on duty to join him. A refusal led to fighting. The guard-post at the *palais* succumbed, but the troops at the prefecture opposite resisted and reinforcements were brought in. Meanwhile Blanqui took the nearby *hôtel de ville*, but was soon in combat with the municipal guard for control. Men were sent to take control of the *mairies* of other Paris districts. Barricades went up in the artisan quarters of St Denis and St Martin and in the Temple area. Armourers' shops were sacked by the rebels. However they were met by fierce resistance from the troops, who by 11 p.m. had re-established control.[18] On the following day only a few isolated barricades remained in the Marais area near the *hôtel de ville*.

Who took part? About 66 rebels were killed, or died from their wounds, including 5 women, and 28 on the government side. All the main leaders were speedily incarcerated and charged.[19] Within 24 hours nearly 300 arrests had been made, the final total reaching almost 700. Many were speedily released, leaving just under 300 to be called for trial. Nearly 87 per cent were workers, mainly artisans. The rest were middle class. The social profile of the participants was very similar to the crowd in June 1848, but rather different from the membership of the republican societies of the early 1830s when even in Paris only 66 per cent of the Society of the Rights of Man were artisan and the majority of provincial associates were middle class. The luxury trades of central Paris predominated as usual. The largest single element were textile workers (39), closely followed by workers in the high quality metallurgical trades (37) and cabinet-makers (31), all of whom, like the 28 building workers and 26 leather workers, suffered in the recurring economic recessions of these years. They were young, the average age being 27, since married men with families would be actively discouraged from risking what earning potential they had. Most were not Parisian by birth: 64.5 per cent were outsiders, but mostly from neighbouring departments.

The trial of 22 of the conspirators by the supreme court of appeal, the *Cour des Pairs*, opened with unprecedented speed on 27 June.[20] (Those rounded up after the events of April 1834 had languished in jail for over a year before their trial.) The accusing magistrate cited records of the association to prove its treasonable nature, which had been found in Barbès' lodgings and which, it was alleged, were in Barbès' handwriting. Barbès's recent pamphlet against poverty was presented as evidence and reprinted in the proceedings of the trial; there was nothing in it which was an incitement to rebel. Although there was no evidence that the conspirators were connected with other subversive movements, it was claimed that statements in their papers implied support for Fieschi's bloodthirsty attempt on the king's life. It was also alleged that Meunier, who had tried to assassinate Louis-Philippe in December 1836, was a member of the *Familles*.[21] The prosecuting magistrate insisted that the society was totally committed to the overthrow of the Orleanist regime, the creation of a republic and the redistribution of the wealth of France among the poor.

Barbès was sentenced to death, although this was later commuted to forced labour for life. Bernard was deported. Blanqui himself was finally arrested in October. His attempt to take arsenic while awaiting trial was foiled and his trial, along with the final 30 remaining conspirators, opened in January 1840. He refused to address the court and offered no defence, apart from an uncharacteristically brief statement that the republicans had not intended to be barbaric. His death sentence was commuted to deportation following an appeal by his long-suffering wife to Louis-Philippe.[22]

Why did the rising fail? Unlike 1830 it was an organized movement, planned and timed like a bank robbery. The precedent of the July Days was misleading; 1830 was not a premeditated revolution. In 1839 there were recognized and accepted self-chosen leaders; but there were too many who expected to exercise supreme command. In many respects the planning was meticulous; ammunition had been amassed and secreted at strategic points, the location of barricades was not left to chance. Lists of key points, *mairies*, armourers' shops and so on had been compiled. Arrangements had been made for the care of the injured. But the ammunition available was insufficient and inadequate supplies of arms were secured by raids on armourers.

The rising did not attract a spontaneous mass following as Blanqui had predicted. Later Barbès was to criticize Blanqui for hesitation. Above all, unlike 1830, the elite rallied instantly to the regime. The 1839 political crisis was a mere ministerial hiccup compared with both 1830 and 1848. The National Guard did not don its uniform on the rebel side as it had done in 1830, even though there was considerable republican sympathy in the surviving units, especially in the provinces. In contrast to 1830 the municipal guard took an active part in combating the insurrection, as did the regular troops. Indeed the radical paper, the *National*, later suggested that the rising was engineered by *agents provocateurs*, police agents who in time-honoured fashion had joined the *Seasons* to incite its members to precipitous suicide. It was indeed a curious coincidence that the prolonged ministerial crisis subsided immediately with the appointment of the duc de Dalmatie and a government to the taste of the king, as Lamartine had predicted it would if a real threat emerged.[23]

It would not be unrealistic to suggest that Blanqui's faith in a popular rising was based on supreme ignorance of the artisan community and an arrogant and self-destructive messianism. Members of the educated middle class like Blanqui might try to convince artisans that they should work for a radically different socio-economic and political order, but their success rate was very low. Only at times of profound economic malaise did the incidence and coincidence of popular unrest and insurrectionary activity develop, and then only briefly. In periods of economic crisis reports from local officials bristle with accounts of riots over grain supplies and prices, and in opposition to the destruction of communal rights, especially with regard to forests and with tales of artisan demonstrations and strikes, usually well laced with commentaries on the demon drink. But outside the periods of specific crisis, such as 1827–32, 1845–8 and on a minor note, 1839 itself, gendarmerie, prefectoral and other official reports usually confine their comments on public order to the monosyllabic '*néant*', nothing to report.

In 1840 the republican publicist Thoré was still claiming that 7 million out of 8 million of the 'active' (artisan) population and their wives and families were potential revolutionaries because of the poverty of their lives.[24] Orleanist courts responded to such threats rather more than did the poor, who were mostly quiescent. Louis-Philippe survived more assassination squads than the most bloodthirsty Mafia chief and the failure of each attempt served to discredit the cause of violent revolution.

Blanqui was to spend the remaining years of the constitutional monarchy in prison, starting with Mont St Michel. His main associates, including Barbès and Martin Bernard, were also incarcerated for the same period. Blanqui continued to believe in the efficacy of a vanguard revolutionary party reinforced by a mass rising of the working class, even though neither historical nor recent experience gave credence to his ideas. The left-wing newspapers were out of sympathy with the May rising and a *Nouvelles Saisons* attracted only 60 followers and created no public stir other than a routine presence to accompany the funeral procession of Garnier-Pagès. Interestingly Albert, the rather anonymous working man who was to be a member of the provisional government in 1848, was a prominent participant.[25]

The insurrectionary route to socialism was overtaken, for a time, by a variety of other plans. Conspiracy gave way to preoccupation with a conflicting range of socialist models for a reformed society and to more modest plans for gradual change within the parliamentary system of the limited monarchy. However Blanqui was to remain a hero of the revolutionary tradition until his death.[26] He participated in three other failed conspiracies; in May 1848 and twice in 1870. He was to become an international star when Lenin recognized a debt of gratitude to Blanqui in developing his own theory of the 'vanguard' party. The success of the Bolshevik Revolution seemed at last to prove the insurrectionary techniques of Babeuf and Blanqui correct, at least for socialists. From the 1920s onwards the two insurgents were subjected to almost more historical investigation in Russian than in French. It is still easy to dismiss insurgency in times of peace and tranquillity, less so when poverty seems ubiquitous. In 1868 Blanqui wrote 'A revolutionary must always be prepared to struggle and fight to the death'.[27] A few months before his own death, somewhat disappointed with the Third Republic, he wrote to a friend: 'Each time I took part in an insurrection I felt it the most sacred and important thing I could do. My worst fear is that in times to come people will no longer be driven to rise, whether out of lethargy or opportunism'.[28]

Secret cabals of revolutionary plotters seemed as much a threat to the nineteenth-century centralized state as they have apparently proved their efficacy in the Eastern Europe of our own times. Today the combination of intimacy and ubiquity encourages news reporters to present the view that a determined minority can carry out a popular revolution, preferably live in front of the camera. In the 1830s the memory of the failure of successive regimes to control popular insurrection in the 1790s, and in 1830 itself, left governments genuinely, and justifiably, nervous of revolutionary agitators.

After 1835, and even more decisively after the disastrous failure of Blanqui's two societies, faith in insurrectionary tactics declined. Conspiracy gave way to more modest plans for gradual change within the parliamentary system of the limited monarchy.[29] As in the late 1820s the main opposition leaders were parliamentarians and left-wing journalists. However, the circumstances were very different. In 1830 the liberals held a resounding majority in the Restoration Chamber of Deputies, whereas throughout the 1840s those who sought change were in a minority. In the late 1820s governments had become progressively weaker, as the king had tried to ignore the wishes of the parliamentary majority. The opposite was the case in Orleanist France, where the fragile and transient governing coalitions of the 1830s gave way to a Guizot-led cabinet which survived from tentative beginnings in 1840 to the Revolution of February 1848, with increasing confidence, especially in the elections of 1846. In such circumstances it was unrealistic to expect a governing conservative majority, however disparate, to reform itself.[30]

After the hounding of the republicans in 1834–5 suffrage reform was discussed from time to time, but did not re-emerge as a serious issue until 1839, when fragile governments, Blanqui's conspiracy and a minor economic recession with resulting popular unrest seemed to offer a chance of success. A petition campaign, organized by the radical papers, especially *Le National*, upwards of 30 local papers and moderate left-wing deputies including Laffitte, Arago, Dupont de l'Eure and Martin (de Strasbourg), was launched, which secured more than 188,000 signatures for an electoral reform which would have made all National Guardsmen voters. Since the National Guard was open to anyone who could equip himself with rifle and uniform, this was a radical proposal. In January 1840 Parisian National Guardsmen, in defiance of their senior officers, marched through the capital to the homes of the four deputies, to thank them for organizing the petition. The Chamber of Deputies was predictably unmoved, even though *Le National* pointed out, in May 1840, that the petition was signed by 45 presidents or *juges* in *tribunaux*, 2 *lieutenants-généraux*, 4 *maréchaux de camp*, 37 members of departmental general councils and 8 members of the *Institut*. In presenting the petition to parliament Arago alarmed his listeners by his demand for government action on the economic depression to prevent workers being attracted by 'certain dangerous doctrines'. They were equally disturbed when he associated the campaign for electoral reform with fulsome praise for the Convention. Thiers, leader of the centre-left and dependent on the left for the survival of his government from March to October 1840, nonetheless roundly condemned any plan for the introduction of universal suffrage.'To interpret national sovereignty as votes for all is the most false and dangerous proposal for any society.'

When reform was circumvented and ignored in the Chamber, the campaign to extend the franchise was taken out to the people.To a certain extent the Chartist movement in Britain was an inspiration to the reformers. The Chartists were also demanding universal manhood suffrage and the abolition of property qualifications for members of parliament. Since societies were forbidden, banquets, previously used to honour a deputy, were held by subscription, usually 4 francs, at the end of which a number of speeches and toasts would favour the theme of reform.[31] Such banquets were far from populist, often a substantial proportion of the diners were local *notables*, including mayors and other dignitaries. Prefects often remarked with displeasure on such a large official presence, but were equally convinced that the dinners were harmless, convivial occasions.

Almost a hundred reform committees existed, in every department. As one might expect, they were strongest in the east, but also in Normandy and the Loire valley. Only in Brittany and the south-west were people fairly indifferent. In Nantes Dr Guépin spoke up for electoral reform and backed the strikes of local workers for better wages and conditions which were taking place at the same time.

Vigorous reform committees were in place in Lyon, Grenoble, Strasbourg and Metz. In addition there were committees in Lille, Marseille, Clermont, Mâcon, Honfleur, Vesoul and Guéret. On June 1st a banquet for 490 was held in the tenth *arrondissment* of Paris; on July 1st a communist banquet, not part of the campaign, was held in Belleville. The celebration of Bastille Day was a special event that year. The cremated remains of those who had fallen in the 1830 Revolution, disinterred from temporary burial where they had fallen at the Louvre and other areas of conflict, were to be laid to rest at the new *colonne de juillet* at the Bastille. A commemorative banquet planned in the artisan district of Saint-Antoine was banned by the government. Rémusat, in issuing the ban, said that he was less afraid of unrest than criticism from '*gens tranquilles*' should he let it go ahead.[32] Banquets were held in Rouen, Marseille, Poitiers and Chagny, apparently to the terror of local legitimists. On August 31st a banquet at Châtillon was several thousand strong and patriotic speeches in favour of war with Britain accompanied the usual reformist material. Indeed the question of reform was closely associated with the government's pacific diplomatic manoeuvrings with Britain. On October 15th an attempt on the life of the king by Darmès discredited the reformers, whose campaign was said to have encouraged the assassin.

In October 1840 came a new government, dominated by Guizot, the leader of 25–30 *doctrinaires*, an intelligent and capable group who were influential beyond their small numerical strength. This new administration seemed no more likely to survive than any in the previous ten years. Of the 459 members of the Chamber of Deputies 300 could be considered conservatives. This central group were roughly divided into a left centre, which answered to Thiers, a right centre which supported any government to the taste of the king, and 15–20 men who were known as the 'Third Party', who reckoned themselves independent of all party influences. Guizot seems to have dreamt of moulding a Chamber of Deputies with two main parties, as in Britain. His 'loyal' opposition was the 'dynastic' left, led by Odilon Barrot.[33] The extremes of left and right, republicans and legitimists, were each about 25 deputies. In theory Guizot's government (actually led by Soult for tactical reasons until 1847) should have appealed to all conservatives, but since the Molé government which it replaced had depended on the same group and Molé and Guizot were longstanding enemies, the future of the new government was not bright.[34] When parliamentary reform was broached, as it was repeatedly in subsequent sessions of parliament, Guizot took the evasive line which became infuriatingly standard during the next seven years, saying that it was a subject which should not be neglected, but that the July Monarchy was still too young a regime to attempt radical political change; 200-franc electors, he claimed, represented the interests of the less wealthy quite adequately.[35]

The left could not agree on a reform programme. The non-revolutionary left was not only small, it was very divided. The *gauche dynastique* believed in moderate political reform within the monarchist system and were represented by parliamentarians such as Barrot and Thiers. They shaded into men who wanted increasing levels of participation in parliament, culminating in those who had confidence in universal male suffrage. Their views were best represented until the early 1840s by *Le National*, edited by Armand Marrast. Until his death in 1841 the main figure was Garnier-Pagès,[36] deputy for the Isère from 1831, who rejected insurrection and socialism, pinning his hopes on press freedom, social reform and, from 1840, universal suffrage. Further to the left were men who linked parliamentary with social reform. From 1843 they were most aggressively represented by Ledru-Rollin's new paper, *La Réforme*. A section of this group were socialists, of a variety of persuasions. Socialist ideas, which absorbed much of the energy of reforming republicans, were even more divisive. However, there is no doubt that electoral reform or the pursuit of *Icarie* or the *Organization of Work* seemed to many more practicable than insurrection as a technique of opposition. Only about half a dozen would have called themselves republican. The term generally used for the most extreme was 'radical', borrowed from English politics.

The leader of the most radical critics of the monarchy was Ledru-Rollin.[37] Son and grandson of leading scientists, Ledru-Rollin trained as a lawyer and was immediately involved in republican politics, writing on behalf of those shot in the rue Transnonain in 1834 and defending those accused in the so-called conspiracy of the same year. Significantly he was elected to the Chamber in 1841 to replace Garnier-Pagès; he advocated a more radical programme than did his predecessor. On the eve of his election for the Sarthe, he spoke of the need for democracy and republican institutions. Guizot brought a prosecution against him, in which most of the notable figures on the left spoke in his defence, including Berryer, Marrast, Barrot, Arago and Marie. In 1843 he was one of the founders and main financial backers of *La Réforme*, which quickly became the leading showpiece for those who demanded more than mere parliamentary reform within a monarchist context. *La Réforme*, under its editors, first Godefroy Cavaignac, then Flocon, constantly stressed the need for radical social legislation as well as universal manhood suffrage. In his contributions to the paper Louis Blanc demanded a progressive system of direct taxation, free and obligatory primary education and greater state involvement in the economy. In a *'Manifeste aux Travailleurs'*, *La Réforme* urged working people, Chartist-style, to sign petitions in favour of universal suffrage as the first step in the programme. Along with Ledru-Rollin were a mere handful of extreme radicals, including Arago, Hippolyte Carnot, Garnier-Pagès, brother of the republican leader of the 1830s, and Marie. All except Garnier-Pagès, who was a merchant, were lawyers.

Since opposition was muted and divided within parliament, those who disagreed with the king were forced to operate outside the Chambers to get a hearing. The movement for suffrage extension and reform attracted both Barrot's *Gauche Dynastique* (many of whom were the old *mouvement*) and moderate middle-class republicans, in a programme designed to modify, not revolutionize, the monarchy. The campaigners were divided in their objectives. Some were more concerned with electoral reform to 'purify' the existing system, to end government intervention, particularly by banning the packing of parliament by yes-men who held official posts. Criticism of the high proportion of office-holders in the Chamber was common before the 1830 Revolution, although at that time the deputies were no catspaws of the king. After the July Days the liberal victors put through legislation which obliged a deputy to submit himself for re-election if he received an official position while in parliament. The resulting by-election was never more than an acclamation for the deputy, a recognition that many voters prized their deputy's official role, as a route to jobs and cash for themselves and the department. Placemen were regarded as an advantage by many local notables, not as a manifestation of corruption.

The most radical reformers urged suffrage revision, the extension of the right to vote. After the 1830 revolution the franchise had been widened modestly. The majority within the *pays légal* did not quarrel with a suffrage based on some sort of criterion of wealth, which was widely equated with worth and independence. The right to vote was determined by wealth, expressed in the sum paid annually in direct taxes, giving an electorate of 166,000 rising to a quarter of a million by the mid-1840s. The *foncière*, or land tax, was the most substantial contributor to this total, so not surprisingly, the bulk of voters were landowners, except in the largest towns. The *patente*, or tax on industrial or commercial property, was very light in comparison. Wealthy forge-owners and cotton magnates often qualified as voters on land, rather than industrial, tax. This tendency was enhanced by the nature of direct taxation, which was a tax on the value of property, not on income.

Proposals for a broader-based electorate expressed during the July Monarchy were rejected without serious debate, even though local elections enfranchised 2 million, without obvious danger to the political fabric.[38] Thus, although the existence of a constitution was an advantage envied by foreign liberals and copied abroad in 1848, both the ambiguity and the inflexibility of the document put the Charter at the centre of the political conflicts which destroyed both nineteenth-century French monarchies.

More compelling in the agenda of parliamentary reform was the need to rethink constituency boundaries to reflect urban growth and population movements. The over-representation of less-populated rural areas and the under-representation of towns was constantly stressed, with statistics which were logical, emphasizing the demographic drift to the north and east, first observed by Dupin in the 1820s and which became gradually more pronounced.[39] There was no mechanism to adjust constituency boundaries to conform to demographic changes, merely to include those who qualified by tax payments. Constituencies were very small and the size of electorates very varied. The poorest, least populated departments were increasingly visibly over-represented as urban industrial development became more and more concentrated in Paris and the north and east. In the department of the Nord there was one voter for every 152 people in 1837; in the *chef-lieu*, Lille, the figure was one for 51. To the chagrin of the left-wing opposition their success in the larger cities was drowned in France as a whole. In 1846 a majority of votes went to opposition candidates in the largest cities, including Paris, Lille, Marseille, Nantes and Bordeaux,[40] but Guizot's majority was strengthened in the rural seats. Deputies represented tiny minorities of the nation. In 1846, 84 per cent were elected with less than 400 votes, 152 with less than 200. The real concern of the reformers was plain. Greater representation for the growing cities and a reduction in seats for rural areas with falling numbers would be entirely to the advantage of the reformers themselves. It was therefore contrary to the interests of the majority in the Assembly to listen and act, so they did neither.

Reformers stressed the elitist and unrepresentative character of the Orleanist parliament. The Chamber was certainly an elite. A tax payment of 500 francs a year was an essential prerequisite for a candidate, which would presuppose an income of 2500 francs a year. The potential pool of candidates was about 50,000. Most were wealthy landowners. Few doctors would qualify, very few teachers – a *lycée* teacher would be lucky to have an income of 1500 francs. Over 100 deputies paid between 500 and 800 francs in tax and only 30 paid over 5000 francs. The more left-wing tended to be in the lower income group, but some of the richest were among the most radical MPs. Hartmann, a radical Alsatian deputy, one of the leading cotton magnates, paid a tax roll of 8000 francs, ran a salon in Paris and organized the left-wing backbench deputies. Deputies received no salary and the cost of maintaining a house in Paris as well as property in a constituency was high. They were a closely linked group, with a fast-developing dynastic tradition and much intermarriage; five Périers were deputies in the nineteenth century. Republicans argued for the abolition of the tax qualification for candidates and the introduction of salaries for deputies.

Guizot's hold on power was not strengthened by the election he called in 1842, specifically to try to improve his position. Antagonistically puritanical in his public life (his salon partner the *princesse* de Lieven was a different matter), he was constantly forced to compromise his principles to preserve his government, which did not improve the opposition's opinion of his ministers, or of the existing parliamentary system. In 1845 his theoretical majority of 60 slumped to 8. In 1846 Guizot was re-elected with a secure majority, 291 to 168 opponents, for the first time, but his hold on power was entirely dependent on rural constituencies and, the opposition alleged, placemen who, as always, occupied 40 per cent of the seats. In 1842, 12 out of the 14 deputies elected in the Seine were left-wing critics, including two republicans, Marie and Carnot. This was a shock to the government, for previously between four and six had been conservatives. In 1846, 9000 out of 14,000 Parisian votes went to opponents of Guizot.[41] The radical vote in major urban conurbations, the left argued, indicated the urgent need for parliamentary reform. Even within the conservative ranks support for reform emerged after the 1846 election, among a small group of up to 40 progressive conservatives, including the duc de Morny, a wealthy property-owner, connected perhaps intimately with Talleyrand, the marquis de Castellane, married to Talleyrand's great-niece and a member of an old noble family which had supported Napoleon and the Restoration, Adolphe Blanqui, brother of the conspirator, and Emile de Girardin, the journalist.[42] While the progressives would not openly defy Guizot, they were critical of his constant stalling, not only over parliamentary reform, but particularly over economic reforms to boost growth.

Reform bills were a regular feature of these years. They tended to do better than the divisions among Guizot's opponents might indicate. In 1842 a reform bill introduced by Ducos was defeated by 234 votes to 193. Both dynastic opposition and republican leaders were convinced that Guizot's hold on power could not be shaken without suffrage reform. After the 1846 election reform legislation was again introduced in the Assembly. Duvergier de Hauranne was a notable moderate and a persuasive advocate.[43] Thiers and Barrot, also speaking as reforming Orleanists, were joined by republican reformers including Ledru-Rollin, Garnier-Pagès and Marie. In 1847 Duvergier de Hauranne's electoral reform bill recommended a reduction in the *cens* to 100 francs. This was dismissed by 252 votes to 154 in the Chamber of Deputies. Rémusat's more modest bill for parliamentary reform would have made the holding of certain public offices incompatible with membership of the Chamber. This would have taken away the seats of the existing conservative deputies. The bill went down more narrowly, 219 to 170. Some only voted with Guizot because his promise to consider reform sounded more convincing than usual. The strength of feeling for reform can be gauged by comparing these votes with support for the traditional address from the throne opening the session, which had a majority of 243 to 130. Guizot's majorities over amendments to the reform bills slumped to 43, then to 37.[44] But, despite the narrowness of some of these votes, it was unrealistic to expect Guizot to abdicate power when the existing electorate had just strengthened his position, so the frustrated reformers once more launched an extra-parliamentary programme in May 1847.

An appeal beyond the elitist confines of parliament was likely to attract more support than in 1840. France was in the midst of the most severe economic recession since that of the early 1830s. All branches of the economy were affected. Railway mania in the early 1840s had given way to a severe financial downturn from 1845, when it was realized that the construction of a rail network would be prolonged and that profits would not be as swift and substantial as was first anticipated. The collapse in the value of railway shares catapulted financial markets throughout Europe into recession, taking industry with them. A predictable sharp rise in unemployment and underemployment followed, with consequent social unrest, particularly in the larger and more industrial cities, especially Paris. As in the early 30s, this was unfortunately and coincidentally accompanied by harvest failures. Potato blight in 1845 and subsequent years devastated the crop, the staple food of the poor in northern Europe. Wheat and other grains also did badly in adverse climatic conditions. Food prices rocketed and supplies were uncertain and scarce. Both in towns of all sizes, and in rural communities where many families depended on a combination of agricultural and artisanal pursuits, undernourishment and worse became acute between 1845 and 1848. As usual the government was blamed for its commercial policies, which kept cheap grain out, although in fact no one had any to sell. Age-old complaints against indirect taxes on wine and salt re-emerged, as did grievances about the deliberate rundown of the communal system, especially forest rights. Traditional short-term remedies, private and municipal charity, were attempted. In Nantes, where unemployment was high,[45] the republican philanthropist Dr Guépin was elected to the municipal council in 1846 and helped to set up nine charity workshops.

Popular unrest increased as the economic crisis worsened. Paris was particularly vulnerable. It continued to be by far the largest city and the fastest growing, in terms both of population and industry. In 1831 its population was 861,436; by 1846 it had grown to 1,277,064.[46] In some respects the central twelve *arrondissements* were little changed with a large artisan community crowded into twisting narrow streets and concentrating on the production of luxury goods, metalwork, furniture, textiles, and so on. The traditional artisanate had been joined in recent years by railway workers at Batignolles, the employees at the gare d'Orléans, gangs of building workers hard at work on plans for urban development which were to be completed during the Second Empire and finally, in the more distant suburbs there were the beginnings of factory development at La Villette, Aubervilliers, Pantin, Belleville and Charonne. Paris was expanding. There were new districts under construction from the *octroi* barrier to the line of forts started by Thiers in 1840, in which fields alternated with streets. Beyond these were the suburbs.

In the early 1830s Saint-Simonian and rather vague altruistic republican sentiments had some limited and temporary attractions for artisans concerned about basic survival for themselves and their families. The campaign for electoral reform also channelled some aspects of worker grievances. The political system was portrayed as culprit and saviour in a number of reform speeches, although the cost of a ticket to the reform banquets would have been well beyond the means of workers, even in times of economic plenty. In July 1847 Dr Guépin in Nantes presided over a banquet to commemorate the 1830 revolution. In his speech he spoke of the need for cooperation between workers and the middle classes. But he scorned the banquet campaign itself, preferring a more comprehensive *cahier de doléances* on the lines of 1789 which would include social reform as well.

The aim of the banquet campaign of 1847–8 was to press the case for a wider franchise, although the precise details of how wide were left unsettled, there being a considerable measure of disagreement among reformers.[47] The banqueteers of the 1840s were far from unanimous. Odilon Barrot, one of the leaders and heroes of the movement, who spoke at eight banquets, deplored the failure of Orleanism to base itself firmly on what he described as '*la classe moyenne*', clinging to a very narrow elite franchise. The Orleanists, he claimed, acted not from principle, but from fear of further revolution, like that which had created the regime itself.[48] Banquets represented an appeal to a wider audience than parliament but reformers such as Duvergier de Hauranne, Barrot and Léon de Maleville had little taste for popular action beyond law-abiding and bourgeois banquets and even the more radical organizers like Carnot and Garnier-Pagès were content with the elitist style of proceedings.

The banquet campaign for electoral reform began and ended in Paris. As in the days of *Aide-toi*, the campaign for suffrage reform was spearheaded by committees which had worked for opposition candidates in the recent elections, notably that of the Seine. Chivvied along by the republican publisher, Pagnerre, reformers were encouraged to adopt a traditional format: a petition plus banquets to put pressure on parliament. Some of the more moderate left-wingers, including Thiers, Dufaure and Rémusat, refused to join the campaign, considering that an appeal outside parliament was illegal. Indeed only a minority of the deputies who had voted for reform took part in banquets. The reformers took counsel from Cobden, then on a visit to Paris, on the organization of his successful extra-parliamentary endeavours in Britain. To begin with, the banquets were organized and dominated by the *gauche dynastique* anxious for modest suffrage reforms which might give them a better chance of ousting Guizot. Initially Odilon Barrot was the most sought-after speaker. The first banquet, at Château-Rouge in Paris on 9 July 1847, was a sell-out, with over 1200 subscribers. Guest speakers expressed generalized support for moderate reform; it was hard to go further since there was never any agreement on how radical the changes should be.[49] Current political practice was declared corrupt in important respects. There were also speeches in favour of social reform in the light of the misery experienced by workers in the depression.

Only a limited number of departments had the will, means or personnel to run their own banquets. Those towns with an opposition newspaper or deputy imitated Paris. The Central Committee of the Seine provided advice to local groups and names of suitable national figures who could be asked to speak. Banquets were presided over by local notables – the opposition deputy was always a central figure. The mayor, as in Saint-Quentin, might take the chair; the president of the Chamber of Commerce, as in Saintes and Saint-Jean-d'Angély, might make one of the speeches. Members of local departmental councils were prominent; it should be recalled that 16 departmental councils had voted for electoral reform in their annual meeting that year. All 16, including Aisne, Côte-d'Or, Moselle, Nord, Oise, Haut-Rhin, Saône-et-Loire, Seine and Vosges, subsequently held reform banquets.

A toast to the 'king of the French people' was taken before the speeches. Some banquets were moderate, some almost exclusively republican, although the most left-wing elements around Ledru-Rollin and *La Réforme* initially refused to cooperate with monarchist organizers or to take any interest. By the beginning of November 22 banquets had been held. A banquet planned for Lille on November 7th attracted over 700 subscribers. Ledru-Rollin was persuaded to speak, to the chagrin of Barrot and others who deplored his emphasis on workers' rights and social reform. Angered at his presence, the moderates withdrew. Ledru-Rollin was warmly applauded when he spoke of the need for democratic republican and social reform: 'I say that those who pay the taxes of blood and sweat and silver have the right to participate in the government which disposes of all these riches'.[50] He ended with a toast to 'the improvement in the condition of the working class'.[51] The involvement of Ledru-Rollin signified an escalation of the campaign. Toasts to the 'right to work' were made in Valence, presided over by Léo de Sieyès and Castries, chaired by Léon de Maleville.[52]

It was clear, however, when the artisan paper *L'Atelier* organized a meeting of the various reform groups in 1846 that *La Réforme* was nearer to Marie than the more socially radical Louis Blanc.[53] Victor Considérant, socialist editor of *Démocratie Pacifique* and member of the departmental general council of the Seine, assured those who attended the banquet in Montargis on November 22nd that reform was urgent to avoid serious conflict. None of the various bourgeois factions had close relations with artisan groups and the *gauche dynastique* and other elements seeking very modest reform Thiers- or Barrot-style, assumed that bourgeois radicals would, when pressed, settle for a minimum political programme and leave social reform, over which there was much dispute, on one side. The parameters of political reform were just as fudged and ambiguous. Ledru-Rollin made no secret of his championship of universal male suffrage, nor of his affinity with republicanism. Would the former necessarily involve the overthrow of Louis-Philippe and the creation of a republic? Radicals of a jacobin bent had no doubt of this, but others were far from convinced, especially as such a strategy was unlikely to be achieved by reform, discussion and peaceful means. Thus radicals were not only few in number, with almost no appeal outside Paris and the larger towns, they were often far more at war with each other than with the Orleanist regime.

After the Lille banquet, Ledru-Rollin, his newspaper *La Réforme* and his associates, competed with the original monarchist moderates for control of a reform movement which thus became very divided and with no clear message. On November 21st Ledru-Rollin took part in a second radical banquet, this time in Dijon, a city known for its left-wing preferences; the republican Mauguin and the republican socialist Etienne Cabet had both served as deputies for Dijon during the July Monarchy. As many as 1300 radicals attended and listened to speeches by Arago, Louis Blanc, Ledru-Rollin and others. Universal suffrage, the sovereignty of the people and the Convention were all toasted in terms which disturbed more moderate reformers. On the 26th it was the turn of Lyon and a banquet with a more moderate tone and an even larger attendance, 1600. On December 19th at Châlons-sur-Saône Ledru-Rollin offered an indisputably republican mouthful of a toast 'To the unity of the French Revolution, to the indivisibility of the Constituent Assembly, the Legislative Assembly and the Convention'.[54] The pace of the campaign quickened as it grew near to the end of December when parliament would reassemble; 14 moderate banquets were well attended in different areas, despite the colder weather. The Rouen banquet held on Christmas Day urged campaign unity.

Duvergier de Hauranne stressed the need for reform to purify the electoral system so that national, rather than individual and local interests, predominated.

The banquet campaign did not seem to cause undue alarm within the government even though some 70 banquets were held between July 1847 and February 1848[55] in which 100 members of the Chamber of Deputies[56] and more than 22,000 subscribers participated. They were geographically concentrated in 28 departments in the Nord, the Paris, Saône and Rhône regions,[57] areas where the *charbonnerie*, *Aide-toi* and the republican clubs did well. Some banquet organizers encountered obstruction, but not prohibition, despite the pronounced popular unrest of these months provoked by the economic crisis. Journalists were prosecuted for their radical reports of banquets, officials were castigated for their participation.

Assuming that perhaps four times as many people heard the speeches as subscribed to the banquet, the campaign, while the largest of its kind in the years of the constitutional monarchy, did not force Guizot's hand. The government seemed to assume that the king's popularity would preserve him and them, an assumption which was echoed in the speech from the throne on the opening of parliament on December 28th when Louis-Philippe criticized the *passions ennemies et aveugles* which were stimulating unrest. The deputies who supported the banquet campaign defended the legality of their actions in the debate on the speech, although the peers seemed more interested in reform than the lower house. The Chamber of Deputies turned to financial matters. The often-quoted (especially by its author) speech of de Tocqueville on January 27th was exceptional. Tocqueville, a liberal theorist, already well known for his study of America and his criticism of the Orleanist regime,[58] gave a very depressing riposte to the optimistic speech from the throne a month earlier. 'The wind of revolution is in the air' he declared. The government had completely failed to take any account of the serious social problems and there was an atmosphere of moral decay in public life itself. The spirit of the government, he proclaimed, 'is dragging us to the abyss'. His colleagues dismissed his warnings, observing that Tocqueville was always a prophet of doom,[59] and embarked on a lengthy debate on foreign affairs.

It was not until February 7th that the Chamber of Deputies returned to its debate on the speech from the throne. The government was now sufficiently worried by the banquets to consider a total ban and it was suggested that legislation dating back to 1790 could be used for this purpose. Curious, observed Duvergier de Hauranne, one of the main supporters of reform in the Chamber, why then had the repressive legislation of 1834 been introduced? He launched into his favourite theme, the corruption of the existing system, quoting Guizot's words of 1820, criticizing the Restoration: 'representative government has become a façade behind which despicable cabals and private ambitions masquaraded as public interest.'

The debate developed into a discussion on the right to hold public meetings. Speakers, including Odilon Barrot, made repeated references to their disappointment with the changes effected in 1830. The large attendance at banquets was, suggested Barrot, a fair indication of the strength of public feeling; the refusal of the government to pay attention left it prey to more violent means. Ledru-Rollin quoted the Declaration of the Rights of 1793, which defended the right of assembly, in his view, a natural right of man. However, a conservative amendment to the speech from the throne, demanding a debate on the whole issue of parliamentary reform and that the government introduce a 'wise and moderate' bill of its own, was rejected by 222 votes to 189.[60] In mid-February the traditional address to the speech from the throne was supported by 241 to 3.

Outside parliament the subject was not dead. On February 9th Ledru-Rollin threatened to revive the idea of a strike of taxpayers which had been mooted shortly before the 1830 Revolution. A number of banquets were held during the weeks when the speech from the throne was under review, including a revolutionary communist one in Limoges. It reflected the idiosyncratic ideas of the organizer, the utopian Théodore Bac, but government circles were alarmed that Bac was trying to agitate the local workforce. A predominantly republican banquet planned for the Latin Quarter of Paris in mid-January was threatened with a government ban and postponed on the orders of the police to February 22nd. The banquet was planned by the officers of the 12th legion of the National Guard, one of the most radical legions, being·in part recruited in the workers' district of Saint-Marcel. To make the occasion more acceptable to the authorities the price of a ticket was raised from 3 to 6 francs, attendance was restricted to qualified voters and the locale was shifted, the Saint-Marcel area being considered too volatile. Ledru-Rollin was scheduled to be one of the chief speakers, but withdrew when 80 other deputies declared that they would not attend if he did. Finally the organizers were ordered to cancel the banquet when La Réforme announced that it would be preceded by a march of the unemployed. On February 21st the Chamber of Deputies was forced to return to the subject by pressure from the reform group within its doors. Barrot urged a full debate, but the Minister of the Interior, Duchâtel, continued to muzzle any discussion, arguing that the ban on the Paris banquet had to be maintained because of the threat of the accompanying mass demonstration.

Other factors ensured that the cancelled banquet was now bound to be used as a vehicle for advertising broader, and in some ways more pressing, problems. The social impact of the prolonged economic crisis contributed far more to de-stabilizing Louis-Philippe's France than the banquet campaign. A second republic would never have emerged from a cancelled banquet, had it not been for the severe economic depression of these years. Before the February Revolution, 1848, a republic was not even on the agenda of republicans. Uncompromising republicans were a tiny fringe, some middle-class lawyers and journalists, some modest businessmen and some artisans.

Since 1834–5 there had been no overt republican organizations, the sole remaining nuclei being the Parisian radical papers with Daumier discreetly caricaturing the king from the rear,[61] a few isolated clubs and, ironically, within the establishment, the National Guard, whose elected officers were nearly always republican. But the Guard counted for little, and where it seemed markedly truculent and disposed towards active criticism, was quickly forced to disband. The Second Republic was the product of economic crisis and Orleanist panic, an abdication rather than a seizure of power; a scenario very reminiscent of 1830. However, it should be noted that, although the banquet campaign alone would never have led to a republic, it was frequently the leaders of the campaign who, in Paris and especially in the provinces, took control once Louis-Philippe had been removed.

7 Socialist Utopians and Reformers before 1848

Socialism was a major formative influence in the new republicanism which developed after the 1830 Revolution. This chapter assesses the positive and negative contributions of socialist ideas to republicanism before the Revolution of 1848. Pierre Leroux in 1832 was the first person in France to use the term 'socialism'. In the 30s and 40s the debate on the evils of advancing industrialization and urbanization became 'the social question' and a paramount preoccupation for thinkers, politicians, journalists and novelists. In the 1830s and 40s some socialists assumed that a form of republican framework would be appropriate for their dreams, some republicans likewise imagined that social reform would be an intrinsic component of a republic, but others were afraid that socialism was a threat rather than an asset to their ideal republic.

In adding new dimensions to republicanism, socialism therefore created new divisions. In 1840 Thoré divided the 'democrat party' as he called it ('republican' would have been provocative – Thoré was prosecuted for this pamphlet anyway) into four groups. There were middle-class electoral reformers around Marrast, back from exile and editing *Le National*. Secondly, there were communist elements among artisans in Paris, Lyon and Rouen. Then there were insurrectionaries. Finally, and this was the point of the pamphlet, there were the Young Democrats, under his leadership, he claimed, who wanted to unite workers and the bourgeoisie to bring about reform.[1] The groups were far more fluid than Thoré admitted. Socialist ideas, which included communist and nascent anarchist aspects, were very varied, both in methodology and objectives, and far more limited in their appeal than Thoré and Orleanist official reactions might have led one to think.

155

Socialism was an amalgam of responses to the Enlightenment, the 1789 Revolution and above all economic change.[2] In these years most socialist theories and populists were middle-class. Some wrote mainly to frighten or persuade their own kind, some for working people. They wrote to warn that modernization, political and economic, was creating economic misery and threatening social collapse. They deplored the way in which recent economic changes had led to class divisions and conflict between the 'idle' and the 'proletariat'. The latter term was used to mean anyone who worked for a living, therefore the vast majority of the population; later 'idle' was more specifically defined as the 'bourgeoisie' and included anyone living on profits gained from the labour of others, either on the land, or in industry and commerce. They blamed gross disparities of wealth on capitalism, which they sometimes defined as the exploitation of worker by employer or sometimes as more generalized oppression of the poor by the rich through taxation, a situation often related causally to 1789. Socialists were inclined to believe that the elimination of social conflict and the improvement of the material condition of the proletariat could best be achieved by some sort of republican regime, but were far more divided on political solutions than subsequent and dominant Marxist analyses indicated. Only since the Second World War when Marxist ideological domination of socialism began to be questioned, have realistic appraisals of pre-Marxist socialist contributions to social and political issues been possible.

There were almost as many socialist solutions to contemporary problems as there were theorists. Early socialists were moralists rather than politicians, seeking a new moral social framework at least as much as an economic or a political system. In tune with the thinkers of the Enlightenment and the revolutionaries of the 1790s, they stressed the importance of education to civilize and control man's selfish and exploitative instincts. Religion was equally vital; not that of the catholic hierarchy, but a primitive Christianity. Religion was part of the idea of class struggle, with Jesus the first *sansculotte*, representing the interests of the suffering workers. The emphasis of early socialists on popular religion was important in securing support at a time when a rapid increase in literacy (in 1829 45 per cent of army recruits were literate compared with 63 per cent in 1848) meant that the less well-off were attracted to the idea of Jesus as the Christ of the poor.[3]

The French Revolution had a decisive influence on the development of socialist ideas.[4] The attack on privilege, manifest in the abolition of feudalism, of nobility itself, of the manifold privileges, including the ownership of land by the Catholic Church and the elimination of the monarchy, was seen less than half a century later as a crucial egalitarian groundwork for a 'social' or 'socialist' state. Some socialists, especially Louis Blanc, who believed that the centralized state should have an important role in the creation of a socialist society, revered the Jacobin period of the First Republic. Article 21 of the Jacobin Constitution of 1793 seemed particularly relevant: '*Les secours publics sont une dette sacrée. La société doit la subsistance aux citoyens malheureux, soit en leur procurant du travail, soit en assurant les moyens d'exister à ceux qui sont hors d'état de travailler.*' Babeuf, as interpreted by Buonarroti, was a model for some socialists; Proudhon referred to his account of the 1796 conspiracy as 'our Bible'. Babeuf has often been heralded as the first communist, although he did not attack private ownership as such. He hoped, if his revolution had succeeded, either to redistribute all land equally (14 acres for each household) or to introduce a progressive tax.

The theories of the early socialists were solutions to the problems middle-class observers thought had been created by the relatively modest technical and structural changes in the predominant artisan trades, to the social problems of urbanization and to a small extent as a response to the development of factory industry. Early socialists were primarily concerned with the preservation of artisan structures to fight proto-capitalism, or the creation of a harmonious, non-competitive modern system. They sought ways in which the middle classes and the proletariat could cooperate peacefully. Babeuf's call to revolution, the echoes of which have already been considered, found few enthusiasts. Although socialists disagreed about how to counteract the evils of 'competition' or capitalism as they saw it, there was a broad consensus that the solution lay in substituting some sort of 'association' to protect the individual. That 'association' might be one of workers in a producer cooperative, of workers financed by a bank, by the state, or of an innovative commune, a model village, involving the establishment of an alternative lifestyle or of unions of workers.

The specific contributions of leading socialists will be assessed comparatively. The main figures will be examined more or less in the chronological order in which their writings were published, simply because, although there are some obvious links between certain of them, socialists were more inclined to emphasize their differences than what they held in common. The impact of the socialists on the educated elite whom they hoped to convert and on the proletariat, the victims with whom they thought they empathized, will be investigated. In recent years historians have disagreed with some vigour over the relationship between socialists and workers,[5] over the extent to which worker organizations and thinking were influenced by socialist theory or were conditioned much more by traditional norms and institutions like *compagnonnages*. There can be no doubt that the theorists did not always understand the problems they agonized over in the way in which their 'proletariat' understood them.

It is certain that artisans, peasants and the large number of families who depended on both agrarian and industrial occupations, would have found the blanket term 'proletariat' inappropriate, probably as offensive as ethnic groups find the various labels attached to them in the twentieth century. Unfortunately for the historian, it was only the literate worker who was prepared to accept bourgeois models, who contributed to newspapers, had his poems and memoirs published, and is therefore accessible.[6] Socialists were primarily interested in the problems of literate urban artisans, tailors, printers, silkweavers and the like, and showed little appreciation of the fact that one of the major structural changes in early nineteenth-century industry was the enormous expansion of rural industry. Nor were socialists very aware of the problems which the attack on the communal system by better-off proto-capitalist peasant farmers and other tenants had on the bulk of those who depended on agriculture for their livelihood. The rural poor were fairly invisible to socialist commentators. Socialists, for all their praise for artisan cooperatives, were often as much modernizers as the capitalists they deplored. Their brief was to sanitize modernization and turn the 'proletariat' into well-behaved imitations of the middle classes. This chapter will try to assess what they sought, how far they secured 'proletarian' sanction and to what degree they alienated or pleased a 'bourgeois' audience. It may be objected that, given the available evidence, the questions posed are unanswerable, or that the answers are negative. It is our contention that the negative and hostile responses encountered by socialists were of overwhelming importance to mid-nineteenth-century republicanism.

It is customary to begin with Saint-Simon, which may seem odd because he was no socialist, but he launched a 'doctrine' which was an important springboard for most socialists.[7] Saint-Simon (1760–1825), a member of a high-ranking noble family, had welcomed the 1789 Revolution, renounced his title, made a huge fortune from *biens nationaux* which he subsequently lost, and took a clerical job from which, in comparative poverty, he emerged as a social theorist. In 1819 he ran a newspaper, *L'Organisateur*, and in 1821 published the first volume of *Système industriel*, swiftly followed by a *Catéchisme des*

Industriels.[8] A scientific age, he claimed, merited a scientific and positive approach to government. He postulated that economic change, being both qualitative and quantative, necessitated a completely reshaped society. Saint-Simon's theories tried to take account of the ideas of the Enlightenment, the social impact of the French Revolution and the potential consequences of industrialism. Old landed and military elites had to be replaced by those in possession of the new wealth from commerce and industry. He wanted more than a rational social framework; he was specifically concerned with the problems of social inequality and poverty. At the end of his life he also concluded that a new form of purified Christianity, returning to the basic principles of Christ's disciples, was vital as a moral superstructure.[9]

Saint-Simon argued that 1789 had begun the process of adjustment of government and society necessary for the modern world, but although the privileges of the nobles had been checked and the bourgeoisie had secured a role in the state, more changes were needed if further revolution and upheaval were to be averted. The *industriels*, he claimed, should have control and the most wealthy of them should determine the budget and policy. Among *industriels* Saint-Simon included not just industrialists, but anyone who contributed to the wealth of the nation by working, from artisan and farmer to forge-owner. He divided France into two classes: *industriels*, the productive majority of the nation, and the *classe oisive*, the wealthy idle, noble and bourgeois.[10] This idea of class was not new, but perhaps its expression by a renegade member of one of the most senior noble families gave Saint-Simon's account a certain piquancy. Saint-Simon wrote fast and frequently changed his mind; it is easy to find contradictions in his thought. He did not develop a single, coherent blueprint for the future. In many ways the moral framework he envisaged for the new industrial age was democratic, but he was convinced that the new rich should govern.

After his death in 1825 his followers, led by Rodrigues, Halévy, Duvergier and Bailly, agreed to publicize his ideas, but the movement was soon taken over by the republican Bazard and Enfantin. For a year until 1826 they ran a weekly paper, *Le Producteur*. In 1828 Bazard organized a series of lectures describing their ideas which were published,[11] providing a description of 'class' divisions in society and a clear account of Saint-Simon's demands for a rational social order. The Saint-Simonians won converts among young men who were to be influential in later years, including Carnot, a leading politician in 1848, and Michel Chevalier, of the free trade treaty of 1860. In 1830 Leroux dedicated his paper *Le Globe* to their doctrines. Saint-Simonianism was clearly a springboard for modern socialism. Saint-Simonians opposed hereditary right and had as a watchword '*A chacun selon sa capacité, à chaque capacité suivant ses oeuvres*'; the first pleased socialists, the second was too elitist for their taste. Increasingly under the control of Enfantin, self-proclaimed 'Father', the 'Family' as the group called themselves, began to move in other directions which were to prove self-destructive.

Meanwhile, small earnest philanthropic groups of Saint-Simonians were in evidence in major French cities in the early 1830s, light-years away from the self-obsessed posturings of Enfantin. They were generally composed of high-minded, educated idealists, often former *carbonaro*, who were anxious about the problems of impoverished workers, and particularly concerned that the economic deprivation of the artisans did not turn them into insurgents. They were not all wealthy, but were generally comfortably-off philanthropists.

Typical was Dr Guépin in Nantes. Guépin subscribed to the *Globe* in the early 1830s and maintained his links with former fellow students working elsewhere in France. Guépin, influenced by Saint-Simonian ideas, organized work for the unemployed in the economic crisis years and worker cooperatives – not to mention evening classes. In early 1833 a group of Saint-Simonians were sent from Lyon by a friend of Guépin's. The doctor helped them to produce a publicity leaflet to explain their mission to help deprived workers. The dockworkers whom they hoped to convert were unreceptive; there were instances of stone-throwing and other insults. The workers were unimpressed by the Saint-Simonian costume of white trousers, blue tunic and red waistcoat, buttoned at the back, to remind members of man's interdependence. The local priests quickly convinced the stevedores that the Saint-Simonians, bourgeois to a man, were government agents sent to persuade them to give up their faith and declare a republic. Rumours went around that they had been sent to cut wages, while the prefect thought they were stirring up the workers to demand higher wages. The Saint-Simonians were banned from seeking converts, or even wearing their costume. Guépin protected them and paid their bills, still convinced that they were a good thing, although the behaviour of the group and Enfantin's peculiarities were beginning to worry him.

Saint-Simonianism fizzled out as a mainstream movement. The outlandish costumes, customs and 'communal' adultery of the 'Family', in which wealthy ladies abandoned their husbands for Enfantin, not to mention his expedition to Egypt, stretched the credulity of essentially puritanical followers like Guépin. The idealism and philanthrophy of such men turned towards the specifically socialist proposals of Fourier and Cabet and in the direction of overtly republican politics.

Fourier, like Saint-Simon, was essentially concerned with the organization of industrial society and the material welfare of the individual. Unlike Saint-Simon, he did not expect a centralized state to initiate reform and he deplored Saint-Simonian schemes. Fourier (1772–1837) was the son of a prosperous merchant of Besançon who, reluctantly, was obliged to follow the same calling throughout his life. Fourier is often described as the heir to Babeuf and the first 'collectivist',[12] but this is to make Fourier into more of a Fourierist than he was. He thought that people worked better in voluntary associations, but allowed participants to keep their private property rights within his communes.[13] Efficient organization was the answer and Fourier's basic scheme was straightforward: a model village with large, communal workshops and living quarters, a pleasant environment and attractive and rewarding occupations for each individual. Unfortunately for his followers, Fourier was a fantasizer with words and his philosophical and psychological justification of his schemes was sometimes bizarrely expressed in terminology which ultimately had meaning only for him. Saint-Simon, of course, left the fantasies to his disciples; Fourier's disciples worked hard to smooth away their master's wilder imaginings.

In a scheme somewhat like that of Robert Owen, Fourier saw the future in *phalanges*, model autonomous communities. He first described his *harmonien*, his new man, in 1808, but his best known work was not published until 1829.[14] His ideal *phalange* was a group of 1600–2000 committed to social improvement, but not to social or financial equality. Some members might donate property, which would then be communally owned; others would retain both their private property and the right to pass it to their heirs. Those who initially contributed only their labour could later buy shares. The *phalange* was a profit-sharing combine. Within the community all would work, not at a single trade, but at a variety of jobs each day. Fourier believed that the individual could only concentrate on one activity for about an hour. Therefore a number of different goods would be produced in a large workshop, so that men and women (he was not dismissive of female talent) should be able to move easily and happily between jobs. Everyone would be guaranteed a basic living wage. The surplus profit made by the group would be divided on the basis of 5/12 according to labour performed, 4/12 to capital invested, and 3/12 according to talent displayed. Such a split, he argued, would accommodate man's competitive urges in a positive, manageable form. The *phalange* would be run by its members as a direct democracy, although Fourier was not particularly interested in working out the details of this aspect of his scheme. The community would meet in full assembly to distribute income and to elect its officers and directors. This Rousseauesque direct democracy would be reinforced by a strong emphasis on education and culture to enlighten and uplift members. Each *phalange* would have an opera house within the *phalanstère*, or communal buildings.

The rationale behind Fourier's theory was not economic, but moral. He was searching for social harmony.[15] This could only be realized, he argued, if man's psychology was understood. Man was driven by twelve passions (many may never have been aware that they possessed such a large number) and within a properly-run *phalange* these would be harnessed to the best advantage of the individual and the community. Fourier set an ideal size of around 1600 for the community because he thought this would give the best blend of these passions. When the reader encounters Fourier's account of regulative, alternating and composite passions, it is tempting to conclude that the canonical hour of concentration is past! Fourier's criticism of capitalism as chicanery and fraud is readily comprehensible, even to the unsympathetic, but when he embarks upon a 'Synoptical Table of the Characteristics of Civilized Commerce' and enumerates 36 elements, he is apt to lose a few readers, even though the elements included familiar items such as bankruptcy, piracy and smuggling.[16] For all his hostility to capitalism, Fourier looked to the wealthy to set up *phalanges*. His ideal community was to be based on human will and consent, never upon force or revolution, which Fourier feared and detested. Like most socialists, there was no space in his arrangements for the unwashed, unmotivated poor.

Fourier's theories were known in Britain. There were brief translations of his ideas into English.[17] In the early 1830s he acquired a small group of followers and a paper, *Le Phalanstère*, founded in 1832, but his notions were always a minority taste. Not surprisingly, given the detail of his theories rather than the broad outline, Fourier complained constantly of being misunderstood, even in his last work.[18] After Fourier's death his ideas were taken up by Victor Considérant, an eager publicist, who was much keener than Fourier on political democracy within the *phalange*[19] and did much to secure a wider audience for the ideas of his master.[20] Some novelists popularized the concepts; Zola describes a *phalanstère* in *Le Travail*, while Sue documents an actual experiment in *Les misères des enfants trouvés*. A number of philanthropic industrialists took up the theme, although their ideas tended to be nearer to those of Owen, an important cotton manufacturer in Lanarkshire,[21] than Fourier. André Godin built a model industrial village, the Familistery of Guise. Godin (1817–88) was attracted to Fourier's ideas, but the workers' community he founded was specifically philanthropic and paternalistic and more long-lasting than most of the *phalanges*.[22]

A *phalange* was founded at Condé-sur-Vesgre (Rambouillet) in 1832, which was supported by Saint-Simonians such as Dr Guépin, who was a friend of the landowner who donated the property for the experiment. By 1840 there were 16 such experiments in the United States of America, although by 1855 all had folded. Fourier's influence should not be judged by the transitory nature of the communities. The decentralized, self-help aspects they upheld had a continuing appeal to the dominant artisanal element in French industry and to those republicans who did not want an increasingly powerful, centralized, bureaucratic state. Later in the nineteenth century anarchists like Bakunin hailed Fourier as their inspiration, which Fourier might not have regarded as a compliment.

Buchez (1796–1865) tried to bring Saint-Simonian, democratic and Christian traditions to a practical synthesis in the development of cooperativism. He was not simply a political and social theorist and historian; he had close links with working people; he helped to set up worker-cooperatives and to start the first worker-run newspaper.[23] Buchez was both a republican and a socialist. His preferred republic was democratic and parliamentary, but he did not want state-run socialism. He did not believe in revolutionary tactics. He looked for practical solutions, created by working people themselves, with some initial financial assistance and a sympathetic, non-interventionist government.

Buchez's origins were more humble than many socialists; his father, a partisan of the Revolution, was a minor official in the collection of the *octroi* in Paris from the time of the Directory who died not long after his dismissal at the Second Restoration. At first Buchez was similarly employed, but after his father's rapid decline and death, he decided to study medicine. He helped to found the *Amis de la Verité* and the *charbonnerie* and was arrested but finally acquitted after the Alsace conspiracy of 1822. In 1825, convinced that violent insurrection would achieve nothing, he joined the Saint-Simonians shortly before Saint-Simon's death. He was attracted by Saint-Simon's concern for the poor, his desire to trace out a new social order and the role for religion which he sketched within society. In 1826 he was writing for *Le Producteur*, particularly on medical questions. In 1827 he and Trélat founded the *Journal des Progrès des sciences et institutions médicales*. At the end of 1829 he left the sect (Bazard remained a member until 1831), convinced that those who remained were mistaken and he and the handful who left were the true philosophical heirs of Saint-Simon.

Buchez took part in the 1830 Revolution, helped to start the *Amis du Peuple*, but was largely preoccupied with journalism. He founded the *Européen*, which ran, with a break, from December 1831 to 1838. When it was forced to close, unable to raise the necessary caution-money, there were 34 contributors. Articles were unsigned, expressing the consensus view of the *Ecole buchezienne*; they ranged from solutions to the ills of France's socio-economic system to political theory. There was sympathy for *L'Avenir*, when that liberal catholic paper was forced to close. The title of the periodical indicated long-term aspirations for European cooperation, but Buchez was also profoundly nationalist and believed that France had an outstanding role in Europe. In 1847, he and Jules Bastide founded the *Revue Nationale*. A great part of his time was devoted to historical writing, and his reputation as a historian was made by his *Introduction à la science de l'histoire* in 1833, where he showed himself a fan of Condorcet and a believer in a theory of progress and the ability of science to predict. His *Histoire parlementaire de la Révolution Française* (1834–9), which he wrote with J.-C. Roux-Lavergne, contained 40 volumes. He also gave lectures to groups of Parisian artisans, whom he always referred to as the labouring aristocracy.

Buchez started from, and returned to, the belief that Christianity had to be the focus of society and was one of the keys to the problem of how to reshape society peacefully to make it fairer for working people. He also argued that the scientific study and understanding of the past was crucial to the emergence of a more equitable society in his own time. He believed that there was a Christian pattern in the past. He was one of the first historians to interpret the French Revolution as a class struggle between the bourgeoisie and the people. The Jacobins were his defenders of democratic, working class interests. He also argued, and this was perhaps the most controversial of his views in the 1830s, that Catholics ought to see the Revolution as a beneficial force. The Jacobins, he said, appreciated the value of religion to society, but made the mistake of rejecting Christianity. He had no time for Babeuf, who rejected religion in its entirety.

Buchez was very preoccupied with the problem of the status of working people. Like others he believed in the value of education and universal suffrage. But he argued that the whole system of entrepreneurial capitalism had to be replaced; entrepreneurs were mere parasites. His long-term solution was that all producers should own the means of production. In the meantime the state should organize a bank to lend funds to groups of artisans, and laws banning associations of workers should be repealed. He developed a plan for worker cooperatives, to be run and owned by workers themselves, with only a negligible role for the state when absolutely necessary. His ideas were unusual in that they had practical results. Influenced by him, a group of artisans founded the most successful workers' paper of its day, *L'Atelier*. In 1834 he helped to found a jewellers' cooperative in Paris which lasted until 1873, with a maximum of 17 members at any one time.

Other socialists, as they came to study the proletariat, became aware that a fruitful form of worker association, given the fact that some workers were not independent artisans with the resources to form producer combines, would be unions of workers to combat reductions in rates of pay, to fight lay-offs, organize strikes and generally provide a united front against persecution by employers, *conseils des prudhommes* and the state. Traditional journeymen's *compagnonnages* and other associations had offered some protection, but the problems encountered in the first half of the nineteenth century were different both in kind and in scale. Artisans devised their own solutions, sometimes rooted in the defence or development of existing traditional artisan institutions.[24] Printers in Paris and silkweavers in Lyon used new mutual-aid associations to protect themselves.

The response of successive Orleanist governments was consistently unsympathetic to anything potentially disruptive and 'political' and did much to make socialist diatribes about the wealthy more credible. Independent artisans were treated as criminals or rebels. Governments openly and forcefully sided with the wealthiest property-owner. The right of association was totally eliminated in the spring of 1834. Mutual-aid societies were tolerated only where innocuous and apolitical. Some socialists continued to argue that combinations of workers could be used to sustain and defend the proletariat. Flora Tristan pressed the case that the existing mutual-aid societies were only a start since each was small and included only the most prosperous artisans. Workers had to make the effort to create much bigger, more demanding, organizations. A union could protect workers, even against the hostility of the state, if it included enough workers, from as large a range of trades as possible.[25] In 1845 the *Compagnie des industries unies* was formed by a combination of artisans, republicans and socialists. The aim was to form associations in all trades to combine together for mutual benefit in both production and the market-place, although there was some disagreement over whether the target should be a single or multiple associations for each trade. Schemes that were more modest in scope were more likely to succeed, but shortage of capital was always a drawback.

Strikes, a rare occurrence in these years, were invariably met by detachments of troops. Those workers who organized strikes tended to be not employees, such as cotton operatives in Alsace, among whom women and children proliferated and who were submissive, but independent artisans like the *canuts*, who struck not over 'wage' rates, but to try to press for the reinstatement of traditional negotiated rates of renumeration. Worker organizations never had the resources to sustain more than a brief strike, even without the added aggravation of the Orleanist boot and bayonet. Thus, although a tiny minority of the more prosperous and therefore resilient artisans might protect themselves against the vagaries of economic fluctuations by banding together in mutual-aid societies, 'politically-motivated' unions and strikes were rare and uniformly disastrous. Indeed 'association' was palpably no answer to constantly recurring cyclical depressions like those of 1827–32, 1839 and the mid-40s, for these were disasters which neither governments, the wealthy merchant, the employer and certainly not the artisan could resolve or control.

The socialist who seemed to make most sense to working people and who inspired the largest worker organization during the July Monarchy, was Etienne Cabet. Cabet, like Buchez, had direct and close contacts with artisans, especially printworkers. Like Buchez he believed that artisans could, by peaceful means and organization, create better conditions and new structures for themselves. For much of his life he hoped that this could be done in cooperation and harmony with the bourgeoisie. Again like Buchez, Cabet also believed that a revitalized primitive Christianity was central to the development of sharing, instead of destructively competitive, attitudes. Lamennais was also reaching a wide audience on a similar theme. His books linking social and Christian issues, including *Paroles d'un Croyant* (1834) and *Livre du Peuple* (1837), were well-received. Like the socialist pamphlets, a cheap edition of the latter was sold by public hawkers and 10,000 copies were sold within a few days of publication.[26]

Etienne Cabet (1788–1856) reached utopian republican socialism via Orleanism. He was the son of a comfortably-off Dijonnais master cooper who gave his son the best education he could afford at the local *lycée*, and enabled him to qualify as an *avocat*. Sharing his father's sympathy for the 1789 Revolution, Etienne joined the *Fédération Bourguignonne* in the Hundred Days, which marked him as a revolutionary Bonapartist. During the White Terror Cabet defended local Bonapartists, whose leaders like Etienne Hernoux, mayor of Dijon in the Hundred Days, were thrown into jail. Cabet became known at Lafayette's Parisian salon, where he met Laffitte and Dupont de l'Eure. He joined the *charbonnerie* in Paris and became a member of the *vente centrale* and the *vente suprême*, but fell out with the organization.[27] His own political views remained fairly moderate. In 1827 he wrote on the need for political change in an Orleanist vein, justifying the Terror and the Convention on the grounds of necessity. He formed part of the liberal electoral organization *Aide-toi, le ciel t'aidera*.

Until 1834 Cabet's views were typical of many liberal monarchists turned moderate republican, such as Dupont de l'Eure, except that Cabet was more specifically and practically humanitarian. However unlike other republicans who concerned themselves with the condition of the workers, such as Blanqui, Cabet never recommended class war and revolution. During his spell in exile in London he got to know Robert Owen and his writing and became a communist. During this time he first wrote historical works to explain to ordinary people the basis of philosophy, morals and politics. He wrote popular accounts of universal history, a history of the English people, a parallel survey of the French nation and a history of the French Revolution. Appalled by repeated political and social discord, he concluded that social inequality was at its root. A society based on the principle of equality was the answer. He wrote *Histoire populaire de la Révolution Française*[28] in which he claimed that the Jacobins, now far more in favour with him than in his earlier writings, might have developed a communist state, had not Robespierre been assassinated.

In 1839 the so-called 'conspirators' of 1834 were pardoned and Cabet quickly returned to Paris. In March 1841 *Le Populaire* was reborn, followed by other communist papers, and equally soon doing battle with the lawcourts again, although Cabet's gradualist communism made successful prosecution difficult. The term communist was used in early nineteenth-century France very loosely, to embrace a wide range of radical ideas, but was primarily ideologically a development of revolutionary Babouvism. Cabet defended communism from assumptions that it was invariably insurrectionary and threatening. The idea of *communauté*, he soothed his readers, was both a doctrine and a philosophical system, including morals, religion, education, social organization and politics. It was intensely moral, committed to combating vice and crime with the weapons of reason and education.[29]

Political action and education were the tools with which Cabet proposed to remodel society. A democratic political system was a vital prerequisite. Cabet's *Voyage en Icarie* was first published in 1840 in two volumes and reprinted five times up to 1848. Cabet presented his ideal society not as a theoretical construct or as a polemic, but in a form familiar to contemporaries, as a traveller's tale. The distant island of Icarie is seen through the eyes of a young English lord, Carisdall, as, perhaps, part of his 'improving' Grand Tour. The book is presented as a 'translation from English'. It is written in simple language and would have been comprehensible to those with limited education and leisure. Icarie dispensed with the social evils of early nineteenth-century capitalism which obsessed novelists and social and economic commentators at that time, by simply eliminating all economic competition. Icarie's economy was entirely self-contained: any foreign trade would be conducted by the community and domestic commerce would disappear. Icarie did away with all buying and selling. There was no money – everyone contributed to the economy and in equal measure drew from it.

In *Voyage en Icarie* Cabet tried to outline his programme for an egalitarian, democratic state which would fulfil the promises of 1789. He believed that *Icarie* would show how social equality could work. In addition to a common education system, Cabet's plan provided for standard housing, furnishings, clothing and food. Equal demands would be made on people in the work situation. He recognized that this would involve major restructuring of the economy, applying the rational and intelligent principles of 'community'. All land and industry would be communally owned. All work would be communal, but his was not an anachronistic plea for a romanticized artisan golden age. Work would be done in huge workshops with the most advanced equipment.[30] Machines would be used wherever possible to increase production and to do dangerous and unpleasant tasks. Men would be able to concentrate on developing better and better machines and work would become short, easy and agreeable. Land would be farmed communally and its produce divided among the members of the community.

Cabet defended his notion of 'community' from the charge that it was too utopian and that it would mean merely equal misery for all. He argued that it would give immediate benefits to the poor, without robbing the rich. The potential for industrial growth would be harnessed in the process. The community's economy would be self-sufficient, satisfying its entire requirements and no more. All goods would be stored in enormous warehouses and equally distributed among all citizens and workers. Everyone would be equally provided with food, clothing and housing, according to their needs, on the sole condition that each should perform a fair and equal amount of work. There would be no more poverty, wealth or servants. No one would be either exploited or an exploiter. Thus there would be no more jealousy or hatred; few idlers, drunks or thieves. Education and material comfort would eventually eliminate all crime and evil-doing. There would be no further need for criminal law, courts, police, prisons, scaffolds, and so forth. The family would be the source of total happiness. Marriage would be pure pleasure, freed from dowries and with divorce, rarely needed, but on demand. Women would be both equal and revered. The object of the community would be to provide first what was essential, then what was useful and finally what was pure pleasure, limited only by reason, the law and the need to provide equally for all.

Icarie was a perfect representative democratic republic. The elected legislative assembly of 2000 was supreme. It was in permanent session, 50 per cent renewed each year. All members of the community were citizens, electors and eligible for election, both to the legislative and the primary electoral assemblies. The primary assemblies themselves played a leading role in day-to-day government, a feature reminiscent of the Girondin and Jacobin projected constitutions of 1793. All citizens voted on legislation through these assemblies. The Legislative Assembly elected the Executive, renewed by halves each year.[31] The executive, consisting of a president and a committee of 15, merely implemented legislation. All public officials were be elected for a limited period. But Icarie was no liberal republic. By 1840 the individualism of the 1789 Declaration of Rights was abhorrent to Cabet. He argued that the idea of 'liberty' was 'a mistake, a sin, a grave evil'.[32] The rights of the community took complete precedence over the demands of the individual. Freedom of the press was unknown in Icarie, which sported one official newspaper.

Cabet described all major aspects of social organization, from the types of housing, furniture and food, to the system of education of Icarie with a thoroughness unparallelled by any other contemporary socialist. Mothercraft was taught to pregnant women. A newspaper for mothers advised on issues such as breastfeeding. Up to 5 years of age children were reared by both parents among children of their own age. From 5 to 18 formal education took over. All children rose at 5 a.m. (a perfect society indeed!). They were at school by 8.30. Teaching emphasized the natural sciences; Latin and Greek did not appear. At 18 came professional education for all, male and female. All occupations commanded equal respect. A seven-hour day was the norm in summer, six hours in winter. Women performed their own domestic work until 8.30, followed by their regular job (perfect for whom?). Men and women worked together in large workshops.[33]

Religion was the cornerstone of the philosophic and moral system in Icarie. There were no ceremonies or hierarchies. Icarie had no established or formal religion; its guiding principles were to love others as oneself and 'Do as you would be done by'. Cabet writes about 'Divinity', not a specific god. Icariens were taught about the various world religions and left to make up their own minds whether they wanted to adhere to a particular one.[34]

Cabet argued that France could become an Icarie; not by revolution, which he totally rejected, but by persuasion and education. An enlightened minority would inform, persuade and convince the rest over a couple of generations.[35] In the meantime, once the general principle of community was accepted, a democratic government would improve the condition of working people. In this transitory phase private property would remain – state ownership would grow through gifts of land. Cabet saw himself as a gradualist, a reformer, a moderate. He was prepared to give his backing to all reforming groups, including both socialist and parliamentary reformers.

Cabet's ideas have been described as Voltarian,[36] although the direct democracy of Icarie is more reminiscent of Rousseau. His utopianism was entirely bound up with an Enlightenment-inspired confidence in the pre-eminent influence of reason developed through education. He believed that even the rich would come to understand the superiority of his community and freely give up their private property. He had no time for revolution and it has been suggested that his influence among artisans had a calming impact in 1848. He argued that most revolutions were counter-productive, either strengthening the status quo or allowing a self-interested dictator to take over.[37]

Although he was very critical of the 1789 Revolution, he approved of the ideas on association which developed in its Jacobin phase, which he thought was an embryonic revolution of the people.[38]

By 1846 Cabet's low-price artisan newspaper *Le Populaire*, with a circulation of 4500, was outselling all other radical papers and each copy probably had about 25 readers. *L'Atelier*, a wholly artisan-produced paper, sold a mere 1000, a minority of which were read by workers. *Le Populaire* was written in simple language, as was Cabet's widely circulated annual *Almanach*. Three-quarters of *Le Populaire's* shareholders were artisans. In the 1840s Cabet quickly became the acknowledged leader of the first large-scale specifically workers' movement, *Le Société pour fonder l'Icarie* (the Icarians), which was rather ironical, for Cabet had originally hoped for cooperation between workers and the middle classes. By 1844 there were about 100,000 Icarians[39] Paris and Lyon were the two main centres, with groups in 78 departments. Most supporters were workers, the bulk of them traditional artisans; only about 4 per cent were middle class. Icarianism had a particular appeal to cabinet-makers, textile-workers, shoemakers; trades in which the craftsmen felt their skills were being undermined by the development of machines. Of the 22 cities where there were subscribers to *Le Populaire*, only 3 were modern industrial centres. There were neither mass meetings nor sophisticated bureaucracy; Icarianism spread by word of mouth and a vast stream of publications. Cabet went far beyond statements of generalized appeals for the liberation of the proletariat. For instance, a detailed survey of working practices appeared in *Le Populaire* over three months in 1842.

Cabet turned increasingly to overtly Christian statements. Christian imagery was present in *Voyage en Icarie*; he likened the way in which the idea of community would be preached to the aristocracy to Jesus's approach to converting people.[40] Religion replaced the idea of class struggle, with Jesus representing the suffering workers. His *Le Vrai Christianisme*[41] sold 2000 copies in 20 days and helped to retain some of his bourgeois adherents. Most important, Cabet abandoned his original idea that Icarie would develop gradually, through education, perhaps over 100 years, and began to urge the more Fourierist notion of setting up a model community immediately. Although some former Fourierists were won over to Cabet; many Icarians left the movement. Nearly 30 per cent of the subscribers of *Le Populaire* in November 1846 had withdrawn a year later. The paper began to print only one edition a week in April 1847.

Closely linked with the new messianic Christian tone in Icarianism,

Cabet's project for the establishment of a community in America was launched in association with the English utopian, Owen. Many resented the autocratic constitution proposed by Cabet for the community. Only 69 Icarians agreed to set off. Each had to supply 600 francs towards a homestead of 320 acres in the Red River area, but it emerged that Texas, not the land agent with whom they were negotiating, owned some of the land. Cabet was questioned by the police about the activities of one of his followers and was charged with swindling would-be settlers. The case was pending at the time of the February Revolution, when the settlers actually arrived in America. The leader of the largest and most influential artisan movement of the July Monarchy had put himself into a blind-alley, albeit socialist and republican, and one which few of his followers wished to pursue.

There were others who called themselves communist and thus earned the opprobrium of most other reformers. These included Laponneraye, the editor of Robespierre's speeches, who had been jailed after the 1834 'conspiracy'. Released in 1837, Laponneraye founded the journal *L'Intelligence*, in which he demanded an egalitarian society, '*l'égal répartition des charges et des avantages sociaux.*'[42]

Some socialists, including Cabet and Fourier, spoke up for women as equal members of society.[43] While never a champion of votes for women, Cabet wrote in defence of women workers, earning the thanks of Jeanne Deroin. Some writers and activists, mostly women, saw a parallel between the enfranchisement and liberation of male workers and female economic and political emancipation. Women fared ill in the First Republic, despite the elevation of feminine imagery with Marianne and the various underdressed goddesses. The Declaration of the Rights of man specifically only applied to men, as did the right to vote, join and address the various clubs. The First Republic made much of honouring women, as homemakers, as mothers and wives of citizens, but not as active republicans. The Civil Code, completed during the Consulate, reduced the status of women in marriage, especially their property rights. The Restoration permitted wealthy women to delegate their vote to a male in legislative elections, but the July Monarchy took that away.

It was the Saint-Simonians who reintroduced the question of the liberation of women. Enfantin gained the support of Eugénie Niboyet, Claire Bazard, Cécile Fournel, Jeanne Deroin, Suzanne Voilquin and others, some working class, some bourgeois. But the Saint-Simonian support for polygamy and polyandry shocked contemporaries and some of the members too. One working class associate who left

Enfantin's 'Family', Désirée Véret, founded *La Femme Libre*, selling at 15 centîmes an issue. It began: 'When there is talk of liberty everywhere, when the workers demand liberation, why should women be passive before this great wave of social emancipation?' After Enfantin's imprisonment on a charge of corrupting public morality, it changed its name to *Femme Nouvelle*. Cécile Fournel began *Foi Nouvelle, Livre des Actes*, which announced under its heading that it was published by women. There was a succession of such tiny, short-lived papers, initially inspired by Saint-Simonianism, later more by the writings of Fourier.[44]

Eugenie Niboyet (1796–1883) was an outstanding example of this generation of feminist journalists.[45] She was the daughter of a Protestant liberal doctor from Montpellier, whose family became enthusiastic supporters of Napoleon. Writing from a Christian and Saint-Simonian standpoint, she published critical studies of the prison system and education. Settling with her husband in Lyon, she founded the *Conseiller des Femmes*, to offer very practical advice to women on how to improve themselves in all directions, from health and general knowledge to fashion and household management. In January 1834 she started a society, *L'Athenée*, committed to the same end[46] which also ran a wide range of educational classes. Niboyet wanted to liberate women, through education, to be better mothers and household managers. She did not think that they should strive to enter professions.

A small group of Christian feminists founded the *Journal des Femmes* in 1832 to press for improvements in the education of girls to make them better wives and mothers. At 60 francs a year, it presumably attracted a wealthy readership and secured George Sand and Delphine Gay, wife of de Girardin, the populist editor of *La Presse*, among its journalists. Mme de Girardin also used a male pseudonym, vicomte de Launay. The monthly *Gazette des Femmes*, founded by Marie-Madeleine, daughter-in-law of Mme Herbinot de Mauchamps, a life-long feminist who had entertained Saint-Simon at her regular salon, survived from 1836 to 1838. It was run by women, also for a middle-class readership, but was primarily political in its orientation. It publicized women's rights according to the 1830 Charter. It demanded reform of the Civil Code to improve the status of women and to permit divorce. It demanded the enfranchisement of women on the same terms as men and the rights of women to enter the professions. In 1838 Marie-Madeleine and her husband were charged with offences to morality in their private life; he was condemned to 10 years, she to 18 months in jail.[47] (Inequality brought some benefits.)

The lowly status of many women in the world of work and of all women in politics and before the law was probably not helped by Saint-Simonian sponsorship. Although some socialists were sensitive to the gross exploitation of women in the workplace, others, like Proudhon, were downright abusive. The emancipation of women was far too much of a political firework for political reformers and republicans. Feminist women were ridiculed and caricatured. When they criticized the politics of Orleanism, they were hauled up before the courts, not as socialists or republicans, which many were, but as whores and procuresses.

Leroux was a utopian socialist who was more influential in his own time than subsequently.[48] He had been destined for the *école polytechnique* and engineering until his father's death forced him to earn his living. He worked first for a stockbroker, then a mason, finally training as a typesetter with a liberal publisher. He founded the *Globe* in 1824 and quickly became influenced by Saint-Simonian ideas. Like Saint-Simon in *Le Nouveau Christianisme*, Leroux hoped that class conflict could be superseded by spiritual brotherly love. From here he moved on to a romantic socialism in the 1830s and the secret societies, especially the *Droits de l'Homme*. He introduced a rather generalized socialist element into the society. Like Cabet Leroux rejected class conflict as the route to improve the lot of the unprivileged and hoped for eventual harmony. This harmony, or solidarity, between the classes would be attained, he argued, by a spiritual enlightenment. Leroux's socialism was essentially mystical. Like Cabet he tried experimental communities. He founded one at Boussac in the Creuse which had 80 members, each of whom received the same pay; all profits were to be reinvested.

The socialists so far discussed anticipated that wealthy individuals would finance model communities, or that working people would combine to help themselves. Louis Blanc volunteered the state as 'banker to the poor'. Blanc (1811–82) was unique among nineteenth-century socialists, being the only one to enter government, although he is mainly remembered for his writings. He is habitually categorized as a Jacobin socialist. He certainly developed an enthusiasm for Robespierre,[49] although never for violent revolution. Blanc was a journalist and one of the most lucid popularizers of socialist ideas in simple language.

Louis Blanc's father was a royalist[50] who found it expedient to serve the Empire. He was given a pension by the returned Bourbons, which was terminated in 1830. The family was subsequently poor. Louis however was educated at the *collège* at Rodez thanks to a scholarship. He became a tutor to the children of the liberal notable industrialist Frédéric Degeorge, owner of the *Propagateur du Pas-de-Calais*. Blanc wrote for the paper, and in 1834, with Degeorge's blessing, moved to Paris. His contributions to the *Propagateur* continued. Failing to gain a place with *Le National*, he joined the smaller *Bons Sens*, a democratic weekly paper.[51] Its tone suited Blanc, who was hostile to strikes and violent revolution as preached by Blanqui. He did not join the secret societies of the early 1830s. The *Bon Sens* attempted to educate its worker readers and printed a regular supplement of readers' letters, the *tribune des prolétaires*. When Rodde, one of the two owners of the paper, died shortly afterwards, Blanc had virtual editorial control. At 20 francs the subscription was higher than that of *Populaire*, but like the *Populaire* it was also sold by the street hawkers, for the giveaway price of 5 cents a copy.[52] In 1836, 1650 copies of *Bon Sens* were printed weekly, but this dropped to below 700 by 1838 as provincial subscriptions fell away and the paper was forced to close.

Like Cabet in the early 30s, Blanc tried to intervene directly in politics. In 1837 he helped to publicize an electoral committee headed by Dupont de l'Eure, Laffitte and Arago which tried, unsuccessfully, to unite the left in the election of that year. In January 1839 Blanc, in tandem with Bussac, the former editor of the defunct *Revue Républicaine*, started *La Revue du Progrès politique, social et littéraire*. This role marked him out as one of the leaders of the new republicanism.[53] The first edition set out the aims of the paper; universal suffrage, a unicameral legislature and subservient executive and fairer organization of work to give more reward to the workers. The philosophy of the paper was thus a combination of the political doctrines of 1790s Jacobinism and 1830s nascent socialism. Blanc concentrated on the analysis of contemporary social problems with a philosophy similar to that of Buchez, a combination of workers' cooperatives and representative government, which in the late 30s passed for Jacobinism. Leroux also had an impact on Blanc's thinking, with his belief in cooperatives and popular sovereignty and his conviction that socialist policies could only work with a republican form of government.

A selection of Blanc's articles were published a year later as *L'Organisation du Travail*, which gave a coherent, brief account of his solution to France's social ills. The book was an instant success, written in an emotional but clear, direct style, equipped with a simple message. The first printing of 3000 was sold out within two weeks and the next disappeared equally fast, assisted by the notoriety of the confiscation of part of the first edition. By 1847 it was in its fifth edition, doubled in size, to include his refutation of various criticisms.

L'Organisation du Travail was Blanc's solution to the misery of the poor in his society. He argued that poverty, the greatest evil in his day because it often led to crime, was the consequence of capitalist exploitation, yet capitalism was praised and justified by contemporaries in the name of free competition. Capitalism, in his view, was a recent scourge, encouraged by the bourgeois revolutions of 1789 and 1830, which in the name of individual freedom gave economic exploiters, 'the bourgeoisie' political ascendancy. For the vast majority, 'the prolet-ariat', the consequence was increasing vulnerability and dependence on wages. Men employed others to work for them at the cheapest possible rate in order to be able to sell the finished goods they produced competitively, constantly swelling the ranks of the proletariat and shrinking those of the bourgeoisie. Poverty could only be eliminated by radical social and political reform. The most urgent task, in his view, was the emancipation of the proletariat.

This would be achieved, not by a Babouvist revolution since Blanc had no stomach for bloodshed, but through state intervention. 'What the proletariat lacks to liberate itself, are the means of production; it is the government's job to provide them . . . the state is the banker to the poor.'[54] The state would lend capital to groups to set up social workshops, gradually to replace those owned by individuals. After the first year the workers would select their own leaders, share the profits and pay back the state, which would then adopt a more distant, supervisory role. Blanc assumed that this benevolent state would be a democratic republic, but wastes no ink over how this political change would be assured. Elsewhere he stipulated adult male suffrage; women would need extra education first, being strongly influenced by the Church.[55]

Having described his solution in a mere 15 pages, with great simplicity in comparison with the complexities proposed by many socialists, Blanc spends the rest of the book explaining why state intervention in the economy, a dramatic innovation for his day, was necessary. Capitalism was, he claimed, self-destructive, smaller firms being constantly forced into bankruptcy by the economies of larger; both the bourgeoisie and the proletariat were being reduced to misery, degradation and crime. He quotes figures for the very low wage rates paid to women workers in Paris and Nantes, using statistics collected by Drs Villermé and Guépin, the prefect in Lyon, Gasparin and Buret, to show that the capitalist system inexorably forced people to work for decreasingly adequate reward. He goes on to connect impossibly low rates of pay with a depressing 28 per cent increase in crime in Paris between 1832 and 1842,[56] the majority of villains coming from industrial occupations. Capitalism not only impoverished the individual, it destroyed the family because the mother was obliged to work for a wage, rather than rear her children.

In his concluding section Blanc elaborates on the mechanics of his proposal. Each state-initiated workshop could include a variety of trades. Workers would draw a wage. Profits would be used to provide for the old and sick, to help other industries and to buy equipment for new members. Outsiders could invest in the workshops at a fixed rate of interest. The state would act as a regulator to check price-cutting and stop the social workshops undercutting each other in the manner of traditional capitalists. Unreasonable competition would also be controlled by the creation of central workshops for each trade which would oversee the activities of supplementary groups. Fundamental to Blanc's thesis was an underlying belief in the potential of education to break down selfishness and replace it with a sense of common interest. Like other socialists Blanc writes optimistically of the growth of a sense of 'association', of 'solidarity' replacing destructive, self-interested capitalism, although Blanc has much less to say than most on these themes. He observes: 'The Industrial Revolution would be a profound moral revolution too.' He assumes that similar principles of cooperation would be applied to agriculture.

He describes his prescription for future happiness as a 'social revolution'. These changes were vital, first for moral reasons, because the present social order is too full of evils, misery and laziness; secondly because his proposal would benefit everyone; finally because it is a revolution which can be accomplished peacefully. His ultimate objective he calls 'fraternity'. The most valuable weapon in its achievement was education.[57] Like other socialists, Blanc was anticlerical, but not hostile to a Scripture-based Christianity. His God was Rousseauist. Blanc was also, like many of his fellows, intensely nationalistic.

In 1841 he published the first volume of his *Histoire de Dix Ans*. The *Revue* folded in 1842, to be succeeded briefly by the *Journal du Peuple*. Six months later Blanc founded the influential daily *La Réforme*, along with Arago, Cavaignac and Ledru-Rollin, forming a powerful quartet. Cavaignac, the leading spirit, persuaded the others to allow Blanc to draw up their statement of intent. Emphasis was placed on social reform; the right to work, the obligation of the state to provide work, the provision of free, compulsory, primary education. In November 1844 he drew up a *Petition des Travailleurs*, which secured 130,000 signatures and demanded an investigation into working conditions. Following Cavaignac's death a year later, Ledru-Rollin became more dominant at the paper. Blanc brought out the first two books of his 15-volume history of the French Revolution in 1847, but was still very involved in current politics. He supported the campaign for parliamentary reform and spoke at the Dijon banquet in November 1847.

On the eve of the 1848 Revolution Louis Blanc had taken over from Cabet as the leading socialist in France, with a broad following among Parisian workers and other artisans, for whom the role Blanc ascribed to the state was less an innovation than it must have seemed to his middle-class readers. Artisan groups such as the silkworkers in Lyon looked back to past times when the state, through its agents, had intervened to fix the *tarif*, the price for woven silk. To many artisans Blanc must have seemed to be recalling the state to a mediatory and supervisory role from which it had almost entirely escaped. His appeal to artisans was perhaps the restatement of tradition rather than a voyage into the unknown.

Proudhon espoused a totally different type of socialism, one which led naturally to anarchist, federalist and trade union developments, rather than the state-directed strategies of Louis Blanc. Pierre-Joseph Proudhon (1809–65) is best remembered for the aphorism, 'Property is theft!', which gave him the misleading reputation of being a single-minded extremist. Proudhon was almost unique among the early socialists, coming from a poor background. His mother's family were peasants, his father was a cooper in the Franche-Comté. However, education was important to the family. His father's cousin was Professor of Law at the University of Besançon, a Jacobin leader and a Freemason. Proudhon's mother encouraged him to attend the *collège* in Besançon, which he did until he was 17, although he never had the money to buy the necessary textbooks. He was then apprenticed to a printer. He printed Fourier's *Le nouveau monde industriel et sociétaire*, met the author and was influenced by his ideas. In 1839 Proudhon was awarded the Suard prize by the Besançon Academy, 1500 francs a year for three years, which gave him the economic opportunity and encouragement to move to Paris. He wrote first on grammar, then on the economy and politics. In 1840 he brought out *Qu'est-ce que la propriété?*, which displeased the Academy, the first and best-known of a large number of publications.[58] Proudhon was accused of undermining private property, but the jury in Besançon threw out the charge. In

Paris he met Marx, Bakunin and Herzen in the 1840s, the start of lasting friendships with the last two. Marx was keen on Proudhon's first book, but subsequently they could not agree. Proudhon thought Marx too doctrinaire. Proudhon did not become a full-time writer; when his scholarship ran out he went to work for a shipping company in Lyon where his employers were friends and left him time to write.

Proudhon was a very influential thinker; the founder of anarchism in France, he is often excluded from accounts of socialism, but he had a substantial impact on its development. He is remembered as a man of ideas more than a man of action, although he had a not-inconsiderable role in the Second Republic. He proclaimed himself both a republican and an anarchist, the former signifying no specific system, the latter simply meaning an opponent of a centralized regime dominated by one man or a small group.[59] He was, above all, a moralist.[60] He rejected violent revolution. He condemned socialists as unrealistic utopians,[61] yet his solutions to some of the social problems with which they were all preoccupied were in some respects not dissimilar. He rejected the state-dominated socialism of Louis Blanc; socialism had to come from the people.

Proudhon starts from the same preconceptions as many of his contemporaries: confidence in Enlightenment notions of the rationality of man; the belief that the 1789 Revolution in its early stages was progressive; an ever-present search for a solution to the social problems of industrialization. He was less convinced about the total rationality of man than other socialists, and in matters political was sometimes in accord with conservative contemporaries. But he rejected purely political solutions. In condemning capitalism socialists were consciously seeking the antithesis of traditional economics. His theory of mutualism offered a harmonizing equilibrium.[62] Mutualism was a sophisticated form of barter which involved the free association of producers engaged in the equal exchange of goods. Contracts between free individuals would replace capitalism, socialism and all forms of government. Why 'mutualism'? Proudhon worked in Lyon where the silkweavers organized themselves into a mutualist association, which may have suggested the term to him. He wrote a great deal, some of it as readable as the slickest advertising tract, some so dense as to be impenetrable. Only his first book was translated into English.

His most famous work, *Qu'est-ce que la propriété?* is easy to read, but even on first glance the reader is aware of gross and perhaps deliberate contradictions. The book is a good introduction to his basic ideas, which never changed substantially. Later editions were swelled by the author's refutation of socialists and others who took issue with him; in Proudhon's case these included Blanqui's brother, Adolphe, a liberal economist with a growing reputation who actually agreed with much of what Proudhon had to say.

The 'property' of Proudhon's title is 'private' property. It is never entirely clear what degree of private ownership he found tolerable. His criticisms were levelled at those who owned more property than they needed and used their wealth to exploit others. 'Surplus' property was, in his view, the enemy of equality and social harmony. But he was critical of communists who attacked the actual notion of private property. Proudhon liked to shock by his choice of words, always enjoying a verbal extremism which he was not prepared to translate into reality. He believed in liberty, he claimed, but he was not a democrat. He was an anarchist, but did not believe in chaos. For him, anarchy was simply the absence of a sovereign; society should be based on cooperation, not coercion. His ideal society was one of small landowners. Whenever he speaks of industry, it is always small-scale and artisanal.

Proudhon's prime objective in this, as in most of his works, is to define a just society and persuade his reader of its equity. 'I ask an end to privilege, the abolition of slavery, equality of rights, and the reign of law and justice, nothing else'.[63] All would agree, he asserts, that equality of conditions and equality of rights are identical and that therefore property rights are synonymous with robbery. Presumably the author was aware that almost none of his readers would agree! He claims that developments in modern times exacerbated this situation. The Revolutions of 1789 and 1830 grounded modern society on three principles: the sovereignty of human will, which he equates with despotism; inequalities of wealth and rank; rights of private ownership of property. Are these, he asks, in harmony with justice? The first self-evidently is not. Neither is the second; but it could easily be changed by eliminating the third. The Declaration of Rights stipulated that the right to property was inalienable but, Proudhon suggests, 'property and society are utterly irreconcilable institutions'. Property was incompatible with civil and political equality. He unequivocally states 'the right of property was the origin of evil on the earth'. If, he argues, the right of property is based on labour, then permanent ownership cannot follow. 'Without the abolition of property, the organization of labour is neither more nor less than a delusion.'

He takes issue with Fourier who argued 'to each according to his capital, labour and skill', on the grounds that such a division was essentially unequal. Inequality of talent should not, he claims, mean inequality of reward. Society could survive without its great artists, but not without its food producers. Private property and communism were habitually depicted as the only choices for society. Proudhon disliked both. While denying the right of an individual to have exclusive control over a piece of property, Proudhon was convinced that communism was as unfair and as riddled with inequalities. 'Communism is oppression and slavery'.[64] Society should be based on equality, law, independence and proportionality; this would be liberty. What did Proudhon mean by proportionality? It appears that what he is proposing is an equalizing process, but not egalitarianism. He now draws a distinction between property and possession. 'Suppress property, while maintaining possession, you will revolutionize law, government, the economy and institutions.' 'Profit is impossible and unjust'.[65] He was not opposed to moderate levels of private use of the land. Did this seal of approval stop short of outright ownership? Or is the difference between property and possession quantitative rather than qualitative? What Proudhon says is ambiguous, although his conclusion seems to lead towards the former definition.

Thus after 300 pages of invective and some of the most quotable phrases on the iniquity of private property, Proudhon's conclusion is a damp squib.

I ask, on the one hand, that property be left as it is, but that interest on all kinds of capital be gradually lowered and finally abolished; on the other hand, that the charter be maintained in its present shape, but that method be introduced into administration and politics.[66]

After one of the most uncompromisingly radical statements made by any of the early socialists, Proudhon seems to take fright from the logical conclusion of his criticisms. All he is asking for is lower interest rates and taxes on profit. He would retain the monarchy, asking only for less elitist attitudes from the king. Why? He realizes that there are few democrats in France and those who claim to be have ambitions to become kings. He wants change, but does not believe that the existing regime has to be overturned to achieve it. His delightful conclusion summarizes his actual approach. 'Property is like the dragon which Hercules killed: to destroy it, it must be taken, not by the head, but by the tail, – that is, by profit and interest.'[67]

Proudhon had set the tone of his philosophy, which he continued to develop while working for the Gauthier brothers in Lyon. In 1846 came

Système des contradictions économiques ou philosophie de la misère, to which Marx replied with *Misère de la philosophie.* On the eve of the 1848 Revolution, Proudhon was planning the launch of a newspaper, *Le Peuple.* He was convinced that he was one of the few who understood 'the people' and in return expressed faith in the collective wisdom of the same.[68] In reality during the July Monarchy his ideas were known only to specialists.

Whilst workers themselves were struggling for solutions, socialist writers had begun to develop a variety of theories in these years. There were two problems, the economic one of advancing capitalism, which socialists would solve by different forms of association, and in addition there was a social problem of conflicting socio-economic groups. For artisans these were specific; rivalry between merchants and masters, the proliferation of rural industry bringing conflict between rural and urban artisans, the employment of cheaper women workers downgrading jobs, and many others. Workers must have thought the socialists' definition of social conflict as 'bourgeois v. proletariat' hopelessly simplistic and inappropriate. The solutions postulated by artisans were pragmatic ways of coping with the lack of security of France's unpredictable and volatile economy. Most socialists also suggested peaceful solutions, even when the structures they proposed were radical. Very few wanted to expand and explode the social conflicts they described. Auguste Blanqui's revolutionary republican socialism was exceptional. The competition engendered by capitalism was seen as harmful, but also as unnatural. Most writers and artisan activists sought solutions which would neutralize or replace the conflict with equitable and fair economic relationships; the term most often used was the one initially suggested by Robert Owen, harmony. Association seemed to be the modern equivalent of traditional artisan groupings.

Socialist proposals for economic change were of four main kinds, association, private or state-financed, punitive egalitarian taxation, *phalanges* with private ownership or the communally-owned *Icarie.* Initially the most traditional, and the most appealing to contemporary workers, were developments of existing artisan organizations. Association as a way of combating the evils of competition seemed attractive to artisans trying to preserve their independence as technology made essential equipment increasingly expensive and left them, like the Lyonnais silkweavers and the Rouennais cotton producers, dependent on the merchants. But associations like that of the mutualist silkweavers in 1830–4 were disastrous failures, leading only to conflict with the merchants and troops alike, forcing *canuts* to abandon direct confrontation and socialists, disappointed with Orleanism, to turn to other alternatives.

Some continued to put their faith in cooperation and a variety of model communities, called variously mutualism, solidarity, community and harmony. Conversion by persuasion and careful education in altruism and social responsibility were recommended by all. The socialists of the 1830s and 1840s were moralists, not fighters. Some would have shared all property equally as Babeuf had suggested in the 1790s, or at least taxed everyone to produce a more egalitarian society (Proudhon); others, notably Cabet, would have tried to persuade property owners to give up private ownership; others hoped to end envy, arguments and poverty by creating associations of workers or peasants to run owner-cooperatives, either autonomously, or initially through state subsidy. Some republicans were also socialists and committed to radical change.

Socialists ranged in their political preferences from embryonic state socialists to anarchists. Blanc assumed that only a democracy would be sympathetic to working men. Fourier expected that his *phalanges* would be administered by a democratic council, but more on the lines of a Swiss canton than any French example. Cabet described an elaborate democratic framework, involving both highly centralized aspects along with de-centralized consultation, although Icarie was presided over by a single individual who seemed to wield considerable power. In the 1840s socialist ideas were already too diverse to be associated with a single political model. There was, perhaps, among socialists, a generalized and vague expectation that republican institutions would be more understanding of the problems of industrial and social change with which they themselves were absorbed, but Proudhon and Fourier in particular rejected the Jacobin-style central authority regarded as essential by Louis Blanc.

What impact did these socialist theorists, popularizers and journalists have on the political situation? The contrast with July 1830 is revealing. In 1830 initially the links between political and economic crises were almost nil. Since 1827 artisans had engaged in frequent protests about work shortages and food prices, but their expectations were limited to tax reforms and traditional charity handouts. Within the elite, fears of artisan demonstrations, plus their own disagreements about the solution to the economic recession, might well have persuaded the liberals to accept Charles X's Four Ordinances in July

1830. In 1848, by contrast, the proliferation of socialist theories predisposed artisans protesting about yet another economic crisis to expect active support from the political reformers, which one segment, those surrounding Ledru-Rollin and *La Réforme*, seemed willing to provide, although they too seemed prepared to back down when the government banned the Paris banquet. The two main innovations of the 1830s and 40s, the development of socialist ideas and the growth of artisan interest in the press and in cooperative worker associations, served to alarm the more timid middle-class reformers. In many respects the early socialists rendered the search for unity among republicans more remote, but in the long term the interest they aroused among the less well-off stimulated a new and lasting interest in a republican alternative. As in July 1830, artisans constituted the crowds who joined the demonstration to protest about the cancelled banquet and provoked firing by troops from which the revolution escalated. The workers' expectations had been refined and focused by the socialists. The 'right to work' had been popularized by Louis Blanc. State-financed worker cooperatives as well as short-term state charity, were seen as a solution to the 10,000 unemployed in the capital. The bulk of the population had other ideas. On this rock the Second Republic would founder.

8 Universal Suffrage and the 'Right to Work': The Second Republic, February–April 1848

Universal suffrage and 'the right to work' were proclaimed at the outset as the two basic principles of the Second Republic. This chapter will consider the problems encountered in trying to implement them up to the end of April 1848, the first in the election of a Constituent Assembly, the second in controlling escalating unemployment in the capital and other major towns.

There were barely half a dozen republicans in the last Orleanist Chamber of Deputies.[1] A slightly larger number proclaimed the Second Republic on February 24th. They visualized their long-cherished ideal as a regime of virtue, just as Robespierre had done in the 1790s. They believed that a republic could be established by liberating 'natural' rights in the context of republican institutions. The association of republicans with movements for both parliamentary and social reform in the 1840s accentuated their moral stance, but not their unity, and the high moral ground was uncomfortably empty of massed ranks of convinced republicans.

There were three main political problems for those who tried to build a republic in 1848. First, the *républicains de la veille*, the name given to those who were already republican 'on the eve' of the February revolution, had no agreed programme. Some, and especially those who subscribed to the ideas of *Le National*, wanted the substitution of a democratically elected assembly for the king, with no fundamental alteration in the structure of the economy and society. Others, especially the adherents of *La Réforme*, wanted social and economic as well as political change, but could not agree on how much. A small number were socialists, of a variety of warring persuasions. The literary fame of individual socialists often gave them a disproportionate influence, which alarmed more moderate republicans. Thus there was conflict from the first within the new government. Secondly, the republic was declared by a tiny number of Parisian radicals with the enthusiastic backing of a few towns, but otherwise only modest support from the provinces. The provisional government enfranchised all adult males who immediately responded by creating the third major political problem of 1848, electing a Constituent Assembly the majority of whose members had only become republican since February 24th. It was soon apparent that the bulk of the new Assembly had little sympathy with a republic and none at all with a 'social' republic. They were former monarchists who converted to republicanism after the February Revolution, *républicains du lendemain*, 'republicans of the next day'. They were as much opportunists as republicans as they had been when they were Orleanists or Legitimists. Their main intention was to retain their traditional control as *notables* and to act as a brake on all change.

The occasion of the February Revolution 1848 was a march, organized as a prelude to a Latin Quarter banquet, the climax of a season of suffrage-reform campaigning. When the government got wind of the march, which was to include unemployed artisans and malcontent students, the banquet was banned. On February 21st a meeting was held at the offices of *La Réforme*. The *gauche dynastique* reformers were prepared to cancel the banquet and Louis Blanc agreed. Ledru-Rollin also expressed the view that they were not ready to fight it out in the streets (which of course almost none of these middle-class reformers wanted anyway, given the threat to property and the host of uncomfortable and dangerous historic precedents). The meeting decided 80:17 to cancel the banquet. The demonstration went ahead. From 8 a.m. groups from the main artisan districts, new and old, of St Denis, St Martin, St Antoine, Temple, Belleville and from Ménilmort gathered at the place de la Madeleine.

They were joined by students from the Latin Quarter nearby. Why? Student agitation had been gathering momentum for several months. Exactly a year earlier students had commemorated the Polish revolution and tempers were frayed following bans placed on popular courses given by Mickiewicz, Michelet and Quinet. On January 3rd, 3000 students had marched to parliament to protest when Michelet's lectures were cancelled. Student newspapers also complained about the failure of the Orleanist regime to alleviate the problems of the economic crisis. The demonstrators of February 22nd were moved by economic and political considerations, and they and the radical politicians were closer in their expectations than had been their counterparts in July 1830. The impact of socialist-republican thinking ensured that the February Revolution would involve more than an extra 80,000 voters and minor revisions of the existing monarchist constitution.

However, although opposition politicians like Ledru-Rollin indulged in threatening rhetoric about the sovereignty of the people and social reform, the history of popular insurrection over more than half a century caused more apprehension than anticipation in the hearts of radical politicians. That the demonstration escalated out of control was mainly due to the government's loss of confidence. It was only when Guizot and Louis-Philippe failed to take a decisive lead after fighting had broken out, that expectations began to rise. Just as in 1830, meetings of radical critics then hastily rehearsed their agenda, this time exclusively in the offices of *Le National* and *La Réforme*. Earlier revolutionary experiences set a predictable pattern and the main actors were self-consciously imitative.

Troops were stationed around the Palais Bourbon to check the demonstration. That it spilled over into fighting and the overthrow of the regime was accidental, unplanned, but could not have been totally unexpected, given the history of the previous half-century. The Orleanist regime, itself born of revolution, was always fearful of popular upheaval. Apparently in a haphazard, unplanned fashion, nervous troops began to fire on the crowd and fighting developed. There were demands for the resignation of the government. Workers and students threw up barricades in various streets, mainly around the Palais Bourbon, but without any specific direction or immediate result. There was no escalation or major conflict on the first day.

National Guardsmen were called out to join the regular soldiers, but few showed up for duty. Next day, February 23rd, most legions were hostile to Guizot and declared for the banquet campaign.[2] By midday, Louis-Philippe was sufficiently worried that he replaced Guizot with Molé. The National Guard and the parliamentary opposition leaders under Barrot were satisfied and urged the crowds to disperse. But Molé, at 70, twice chief minister in 1836 and 1837, seemed an unlikely guarantor of parliamentary reform. Jubilation in the streets gave way to disappointment. Crowds of workers, National Guardsmen and students continued their protests and finally, towards evening, marched on the Ministry of Foreign Affairs. Their way was blocked by a company of the 14th regiment who refused to let them pass. Shots were fired, without any command apparently being given, and in the exchange of fire which ensued 52 were killed and 74 injured.

During the night, as protests increased, Molé was replaced by Thiers. The number of barricades grew rapidly to around 1500 and many armourers' shops were looted in the quest for ammunition and weapons. Marshal Bugeaud, in command of the troops, was notorious for his repressive tactics and did nothing to calm the situation. The increasing numbers of National Guardsmen on the barricades demoralized the soldiers who, as in 1830, also began to change sides. Around midday of the 24th the Tuileries palace was attacked and Louis-Philippe hastily abdicated in favour of his 9-year-old grandson, the comte de Paris. But crowds had invaded the parliament building where a scrappy debate considered first a regency under the liberal duchesse d'Orléans, then Dupont de l'Eure and Ledru-Rollin produced a list of names for a provisional government, which had been drawn up at *Le National* and included themselves, Lamartine, Arago, Crémieux, Marie and Garnier-Pagès.

A delegation moved on to the *hôtel de ville*, far more centrally located close to the main artisan districts of the capital than the parliament building, and a traditional crucible of revolution both in the 1790s and in 1830. Not to be outdone came the journalists from the rival, *La Réforme*, with their list, more radical and socialist than the one already accepted. Their candidates, Flocon, Louis Blanc and Albert Martin, always referred to as Albert, a mechanic and head of the society of the *Seasons*, were immediately welcomed along with Marrast, editor of *Le National*, and made secretaries of the new government by the canny Garnier-Pagès.

The provisional government quickly declared France a democratic republic and promised that a Constituent Assembly would be immediately elected by universal suffrage.[3] Republicans had always scorned the Orleanists for their hurried constitutional conclusion to the July Days in 1830 and were determined to allow the whole nation to be involved in deciding France's future. The death penalty was abolished for political offences, indicating that the republicans of France's Second Republic wanted to separate themselves from the Terror of the First. Slavery was also abolished in France's colonies. 'La République démocratique' was not enough for some of the staff of *Le Réforme*, and '*et sociale*' was added. Pressure from the journalists of *La Réforme* and from the large number of unemployed in the capital made the issue of unemployment paramount. Economic and financial problems came to overshadow other issues, such as the introduction of universal education, which had been so important to these same republicans during the July Monarchy, and to paralyse genuine debate. The presence of the socialist journalist, Louis Blanc, suggested that structural, rather than piecemeal, solutions might be attempted. On 25 February 1848 he persuaded a reluctant provisional government to decree:

> The Provisional Government engage themselves to guarantee the existence of the workmen by means of labour. They engage themselves to guarantee labour to every citizen.[4]

Under the pressure of crowds of workers surrounding the Chamber of Deputies, the provisional government agreed on February 26th to the setting up of National Workshops. Most of them looked to the traditional short-term emergency measures used in 1830 and in 1789.[5] Indeed some were so anxious not to appear innovative that, in their declaration creating workshops, they cited precedents for government intervention in the economy as far back as the reign of Henri IV.[6]

The determination to avoid even a whiff of socialism was reflected in their refusal to create a Ministry of Labour and the decision to appoint Blanc's critic, the staunch republican Marie, Minister of Public Works with the job of organizing workshops. Emile Thomas, equally hostile to Blanc's ideas, was made director of the workshops. However, Blanc was put in charge of an innovative venture, a Parliament of Industry, with delegates elected from the various trades, which was to meet at the Luxembourg Palace, to discuss the difficulties of the different sectors of the economy.

How was the transformation to democracy, now the cornerstone of early nineteenth-century republicanism, to be effected? Ledru-Rollin, the new Minister of the Interior, was a key figure. A lifelong republican and editor of *La Réforme*, well known for his insistence that a future republic should include major social reform (not socialism) as well as political change, he was the most radical member of the new provisional government until the names of Blanc and others were added as secretaries. His hero was Danton, 'the champion of the little man', whom he liked to think he resembled. His model republic was that of the Jacobins of 1793, although some said he only spoke of it with reverence to ensure it was never reborn.[7] He detested Bonaparte for trying to make himself the heir of the Republic. Ledru-Rollin wanted social reform, but kept a distance from the socialists and was distinctly apprehensive of popular unrest.

Ledru-Rollin sent an urgent despatch to the Orleanist prefects: 'A republican government has been set up. The Nation will be asked to sanction this decision.' In 1830 it had taken up to a week for the news of the revolution to reach the most remote departments, but in 1848 the completion of the new telegraph system meant that news could be transmitted throughout the country within a matter of hours. Following the example of the Orleanists in 1830, Ledru-Rollin embarked on a purge of prefects, subprefects and state prosecutors. In 1830 the administrative changeover was swift and mostly completed by local liberal electoral committees. In 1848 banquet campaigners formed a similar nucleus in 30 departments, but elsewhere there was no such alternative government waiting in the wings. Banquet campaigners were prominent in the new administration. In Nantes the indefatigable republican Dr Guépin took the lead and on February 28th Ledru-Rollin put him in charge of the department.[8] However, radicals were very divided among themselves and lacking the sophisticated organizational basis which local opposition newspapers had created a generation earlier. In some cases existing officials felt little personal loyalty to Louis-Philippe and experienced no twinge of conscience in taking a republican oath. Changes were therefore often slower, more piecemeal and more Paris-initiated than in 1830.

Ledru-Rollin gradually replaced prefects with officials who had similar duties, called commissioners (*commissaires*), in memory of the Convention. While deploring the ambitious self-seeking of 1830, Ledru-Rollin made 110 appointments for the 85 departments, including 24 general commissioners to oversee groups of departments in the style of the First Republic. Only a dozen of Louis-Philippe's subprefects survived.[9] Where possible Ledru-Rollin chose men with long republican pedigrees, but they were therefore usually short on administrative experience. Typically the new administrator might, if old enough, have been a *carbonaro*, a member of secret societies in the early 1830s, an opposition journalist, an officer in the National Guard and a supporter of the banquet campaign. A study of the 110 men appointed as commissioners judged 22 to be democrats in the style of *La Réforme*, 22 republicans of *Le National* variety, 22 moderate republicans like Lamartine (late converts?), 14 from the Orleanist *gauche dynastique* and 30 whose politics, apparently, remain unknown.[10] The commissioner was very likely to be a doctor or a lawyer; although bourgeois, he was usually less wealthy than his Orleanist predecessor. In the largest cities radicals, often officers in the National Guard, took over the main jobs, with the backing of the new commissioner, but elsewhere existing mayors often simply declared for the new republic and their conversion was taken at face value. Ledru-Rollin counselled restraint when it came to a total purge of minor posts on the lines of 1830. Outside the capital the old elites often went undisturbed, even in the immediate aftermath of the February Revolution.

By now there was a recognized post-revolutionary etiquette. Each commune was expected to send an address of welcome to the republic. The commune of Landes, Seine-Inférieure, responded enthusiastically on March 3rd; the republic had been proclaimed throughout the commune with drum accompaniment and had been well received (but the ceremony was presumably completely inaudible).[11] Sometimes the address of welcome was signed by the individual inhabitants of a commune and it is possible to guess at the limits of both patriotism and literacy. Later on subscriptions '*à la Patrie*' were launched, liberty trees were planted, for which the Minister of the Interior was carefully debited;[12] *fêtes patriotiques* were held with public buildings illuminated, dances, parades and banquets.[13]

In April Ledru-Rollin rallied the mayors: 'The new regime demands that all citizens unite in patriotism and fraternity to work to create a society in which all will be guaranteed happiness, security and the opportunity to achieve their full potential'.[14] Outspoken support for a republic was confined to Paris, a few big towns and some rural areas, where either poverty, or a dominant individual, or both, created radicalism. There was a core of republicans in most departments, whose loyalty to an altruistic and idealistic radicalism often went back throughout their careers, and often their families, with 1815 *fédéré* experience, the *charbonnerie*, Saint-Simonian affiliations and so on being a common inheritance. This was particularly marked among middle-class professional men, especially doctors. The latter were often the inspiration for local republicanism. The doctors at the hospital in Rouen sent one of the earliest pledges of loyalty: 'Committed to easing the sufferings of the poor, we have long held dear the principles which are now triumphant'.[15] One thinks immediately of Raspail, Buchez and Trélat, who were important nationally, but there were many others in the regions, including Turck in Epinal, the Béchets in Nancy,[16] Guépin in Nantes. They had a significant influence in the first few months of the Republic, but their radicalism and their socialist sympathies usually meant that they did not survive in office beyond the summer of 1848.

Popular radicalism was equally long-established and areas where popular support for the Republic was most marked in 1848 were those which had shown a continuing tradition of protest, such as Lyon.[17] Some of the poorest rural areas were the most left-wing, especially districts where artisan activities were seriously disrupted by the recession or where a substantial portion of the working population were seasonal migrants to Paris or some other large town, where they had encountered socialist ideas. Such an area was the Limousin where the socialist Leroux found a ready audience. He had set up a utopian socialist community at Boussac during the July Monarchy and was the first to proclaim the Republic there in 1848. He was elected mayor. Along with his brother he had a strong influence on the porcelain workers of Limoges. A *Société populaire* was formed in Limoges after the February Revolution, 59 per cent of whose members were workers, especially potters.[18] A long-lasting tradition of radicalism had begun.

Republicans often consciously imitated the 1790s, via the 1830s, in the choice of names and language for the huge growth of political societies and newspapers. Up to 300 new newspapers were launched in Paris and other towns in the early months of the republic. Their editors often had more enthusiasm than cash or readers and many had only a transient existence. In Paris over 200 clubs were set up with about 70,000 members to prepare for the elections to the Constituent Assembly and to 'watch over' the activities of the provisional government. Some were tiny, many ephemeral, but they were far more numerous than the clubs formed after the 1830 Revolution. Membership lists show that the republican leaders of the 1830s set them up; in Paris ten of the new chiefs were veterans of these times.[19] Two of the most substantial clubs were those of the seasoned revolutionary activists, Barbès, *Club de la Révolution*, and Blanqui's *Société républicaine centrale*. The two were now enemies, each blaming the other for their failure in 1839. The names of the republican clubs of the 1830s were reused. The *Société des Droits de L'Homme* was reborn. The idealist republican doctor Raspail resurrected the *Amis du Peuple*, more usually known as *Club Raspail* with perhaps 6000 adherents, although it was never formally constituted, to educate workers in republican ideas ready for the election. Raspail was an isolated figure, very critical of the lack of radicalism of the provisional government. Another man who had been a republican leader before 1848 was also to become sidelined. Cabet set up a club, the *Société fraternelle centrale*, which became one of the largest and most influential, with meetings of up to 5000 people.

The clubs recalled the Jacobins (three with this name) and other groups of the 1790s and sounded very radical, but they did not take a lead in popular unrest and spent most of their time on preparations for the April elections. In addition men from the different Parisian trades held frequent meetings, originally to elect delegates to the Luxembourg Commission, and persisted, stimulated both by the worsening economic crisis and the hope that the new regime would find a solution. Engineering, leather, building and metal trades were particularly active, as they were to be in the June insurrection.

Some clubs were formed, not to prepare for the elections, but to ask why universal suffrage included only half the adult population. Eugénie Niboyet founded a *Club des Femmes* in 1848 and set up a *Comité des droits de la femme* and a *Club d'emancipation des femmes*. The *union des travailleuses* carried on the efforts of Flora Tristan. New women's newspapers appeared, including *La Voix des Femmes*, founded by Niboyet, which was run as a collective by all the main women journalists interested in a socialist republic, including Suzanne Voilquin, Désirée Gay and Jeanne Deroin. In April 1848 a women's group took part in the *Commission de Travail* set up by the government. Crêches for working mums were discussed. Some specific workplace issues were approached; a maximum 12-hour day was decreed for washerwomen (who was to police the tubs and mangles?). The *Club des femmes*, which had bourgeois and worker members, discussed a wide range of issues including divorce; men were allowed to attend, but paid double the entrance fee. Hecklers interrupted their meetings and in June 1848 the club was banned. In June 1849 Daumier devoted a series of caricatures to ridiculing women's clubs.[20] Almost no one thought to include women in the vote. Some of the outstanding female republicans were hostile. The writer George Sand, who wrote some of Ledru-Rollin's most threatening and explosive election circulars to the departmental commissioners,[21] for all her socialism and personal disregard for conventional morality, did not urge votes for women. Indeed when proposed as a candidate by *La Voix des Femmes*, she spurned the proposal rudely. She wrote for *La Vrai République* and founded the short-lived *La Cause du Peuple* in April 1848. She was concerned about the consequences of poverty for working people, but believed that gradual progress, not class war, was the way forward and retired from politics after 15 May 1848. Jeanne Deroin pressed the cause of votes for women, in addition to support for unions of workers.

The idea of battalions of 'Amazons' was one of the rumours and mockeries of the Second Republic, just as it was of the First. *Les Vésuviennes* was founded on February 26th in Belleville by Borme, as a collective of working women committed to fighting for social reform. Borme claimed 5000 members throughout the country and led the women on marches to the *hôtel de ville*. De Beaumont found their bizarre militaristic activities excellent material for caricature.[22] *La Voix des Femmes* became hostile and Daniel Stern in her history of the revolution was scornful. The men of 1848 showed some sympathy with the problems of women workers, but had no more interest than those of 1792 in female suffrage and were just as scathing of female militancy.

The provisional government was determined to avoid the mistakes of 1830, when they thought that the new regime had been barely distinguishable from that which it replaced. Elections for a Constituent Assembly were initially called for April 9th, but radicals protested that time was needed to explain to the bulk of voters why they should vote for a republican regime. On March 16th a demonstration of around 150,000 workers, organized by the clubs and particularly by Cabet, marched to the *hôtel de ville* to demand deferment to the end of May and the removal of all troops from the capital. Cabet, a known communist, was seen as a real threat by conservatives. The election was delayed, but only by a few days. Cabet's name was removed from Ledru-Rollin's list of candidates, Icarians were hounded and Cabet retreated into an attempt to create a utopian community in the abandoned Mormon village of Nauvoo, Illinois.

The elections were put back, but only to Easter Sunday, April 23rd. The revised day was a curious choice for those seeking a republican assembly, for it was one of the small number of Sundays when large numbers could be guaranteed in church before voting. The argument over the date of the election turned on the issue of whether men were instinctively democratic and republican. The republicans had always maintained that the sovereignty of the people and universal male suffrage were natural rights. The Orleanists, of course, insisted that men had to learn to vote in their best interests, that only those with education (and wealth) understood enough to participate in politics. The more radical republicans, such as Blanqui, Barbès and Cabet, argued that reason and the experience of the 1790s showed that although sovereignty was natural and inalienable, a period of training would be needed. The republic should therefore defer voting and educate men in citizenship. But in February 1848 the historic memory of the Terror and hostility to anything which smacked of dictatorship, plus perhaps the realization that delay would alienate voters from the republic and hamper economic recovery, persuaded the provisional government to hold elections as soon as possible.

Ledru-Rollin assumed, along with all his colleagues, that all honest men, given the opportunity, would naturally be enthusiastic republicans. He believed that there would be no need to stage-manage elections in the style of the Orleanists. The commissioners' main job was impartially to prepare for the elections. Within a few days Ledru-Rollin was back-tracking on his initial evenhandedness. On March 8th he emphasized that since the destiny of France lay in the elections, commissioners had to ensure that only genuine republicans were elected, '*En un mot, tous hommes de la veille et pas lendemain*'. A few days later he continued: '*Quels sont vos pouvoirs? Ils sont illimités . . . Que votre mot d'ordre soit partout: des hommes nouveaux et, autant que possible, sortant du peuple*'.[23] This rapid change of mood was reflected in his choice of commissioners. The first were moderate republicans, later ones more radical and more obviously acting as electoral agents.[24] New 'super' commissioners appointed in April to oversee groups of departments were of this type. They were widely disliked and came into conflict both with existing staff and with local people. Their presence caused riots in Bordeaux, Périgueux, Marseille, Nantes and in the Aveyron and Ain. Commissioners and local people fell out in Besançon, Troyes and in the Yonne, Drôme and Somme. Commissioners and other officials came to blows in the Nord, Rhône and the Oise.[25] In the end the commissioners, many of whom were new, not only to their region but also to a senior administrative role, had little impact on voting in April, although 110 of them managed to secure their own election.[26]

Ledru-Rollin put aside 123,000 francs from his secret funds to spend on special delegates to the provinces who were to advertise the merits of a democratic republic. The project emanated from Barbès' *Club des Clubs* in Paris. Its committee, which included Ledru-Rollin's secretary Delvau, had grouped democratic clubs into a federation to publicize agreed lists of candidates. The committee appointed 450 delegates and Ledru-Rollin was persuaded to pay for their provincial mission, four or five to each department, although he was unaware of the connection with Barbès. Such crude propaganda was no more successful than a similar scheme in the army.[27]

The task of persuading the departments to vote for republicans was colossal given the survival in office of many Orleanist officials. In 1830 a general election had been delayed for ten months, during which time there had been two thorough administrative purges at all levels. In 1848 a full-scale administrative reshuffle was attempted in some areas. In the Isère 60 of the 133 municipal councils in the *arrondissement* of Vienne were purged, after appeals from the commissioner, but there simply was not time to copy this model nationally. There was often a lack of suitable republican, or even literate, alternatives. Thus the elections were run at grassroots level by the Orleanists. A typical comment was the despairing 'nearly everyone in an official position was working against us'.[28] Only the commissioners could be relied on to represent the Republic and they were no more in agreement than their superiors about what sort of republic they wanted.

The commissioners took their role as election agents very seriously, part educator, part propagandist. Emmanuel Arago, the radical lawyer who had been defence spokesman for Blanqui after the May 1839 insurrection, was appointed to Lyon.[29] Hamon, the sincere and well-meaning socialist appointed to Rennes, wrote to his 'citoyen ministre' in the first week of March explaining how he and other patriots were proceeding to ensure that republicans were chosen. First they had chosen an electoral committee in Rennes whose job it was to get other communes to set up groups. They had agreed on a list of candidates and were holding public meetings to overcome indifference. Some of the local bourgeoisie would have preferred a regency, while the legitimists were partly won over to the republic.[30] Two weeks later he was less confident. All the committees were in place but none were prepared to defer to the Rennes group: 'It's as if the monarchy were still in place. The department has dissolved away into its *arrondissements*.' Big public meetings, the press and roving commissioners to explain the republican case might help, but Hamon was convinced that April 9th was much too soon 'to overcome the little rebellions and petty parochialism'. There was a real danger that the candidates would be bourgeois and not all that republican. The result would be, '*une petite république anodine, une république bourgeoise* in which the only real change is in the title of the head of the executive'. The dominant local bourgeoisie were firmly '*républicains du lendemain* who don't want real democracy in social institutions, industrial organization and taxation and who are terrified at the prospect of social revolution'. Above all they lacked the 'ardent and devoted love' of the masses necessary for a republic.

Hamon tried to organize the local workers, setting up a committee of 2000 to discuss candidates and elections. But they were divided amongst themselves and not class conscious. Hamon's fears were justified. The agreed list of 14 candidates were all bourgeois. He begged for postponement of the election. The news of the Republic had been accepted with stupefaction and fear by the local middle class. In time they could get accustomed to it, but for the moment '*nous sommes dans le pêle-mêle*'.[31] Hamon persisted. He produced his own list of candidates in a proclamation to his fellow citizens in which he stressed his desire to 'advise, protect freedom and prevent intrigue. To create a democracy, we must believe in it, hope for everything from it, love nothing but it'. His list included members of the bourgeoisie, one worker and a primary school teacher.[32]

If the old elite in many departments found it difficult to come to terms with a republic, genuine republican candidates were not always easy to distinguish in the plethora of lists. The more moderate *National* contacted local committees and put forward a list of candidates for all departments on April 10th. Louis Blanc presented a more radical Luxembourg list. Local electoral committees added to the number. In Paris alone there were 2000 names. Less than two weeks before polling day Ledru-Rollin still did not know who was standing, let alone which were genuine republicans worthy of support. The new republicans were less prepared for an election than any government since 1814 with an electorate grown overnight from a quarter of a million to 9 million. The vast majority had never voted before and even the seasoned voters were puzzled by being asked to vote for a departmental list of candidates and not just a single member. Even the provision of sufficiently large and suitably located accommodation for the poll was a headache. The local church had to be ruled out. The problems were enormous; the adjoint to the mayor of Bourth (Eure) tried to set up groups in the little villages, using the local *garde champêtre* as convener, to interest people in voting.[33] Sometimes *instituteurs* took the task upon themselves. A few days before the election in Caenchy, Calvados, the local *instituteur* started classes in citizenship. Those who did not turn up found themselves receiving a 'fraternal' visit from him armed with his list of candidates.[34]

The clergy also took an active role in the elections.[35] This was nothing new; ultra-royalist candidates had the backing of the Church throughout the Restoration, although their contribution had been more discreet during the July Monarchy after numerous anti-clerical outbursts, in and after the 1830 Revolution. In contrast many clergy welcomed the 1848 Revolution and enthusiastically blessed this crop of 'trees of liberty'. Mgr Affre, archbishop of Paris, honoured the head of the provisional government, Dupont de l'Eure, with an official visit, a marked contrast to 1830 when the palace of the ultra-royalist Rohan-Chabot, then archbishop, was sacked, the archbishop himself having fled abroad. The Minister for Religion and Education, Hippolyte Carnot, encouraged the clergy to participate in politics. Montalembert had organized electoral committees for religious liberty in 1846 to fight state education, for what the Church called 'freedom of education' and they were ready to press their cause. But while some republicans accepted the intervention of the Church, socialists were hostile, and the zeal with which bishops addressed the task of supplying lists of candidates for the Constituent Assembly soon worried republicans of all kinds. After the elections, faced with many protests from local mayors, Hamon, commissioner in Rennes, reported that the influence of the clergy had been colossal and unstoppable in rural areas where people could neither read nor write, '*elle vote par parole*', exactly as instructed by the *curé*. The triumphant church-backed candidates were keen to stress their republicanism, but Hamon knew that they were not really republican.[36]

The elections were crucial, but economic problems could not wait for the Constituent Assembly. The mayor of one small commune in the Seine-Maritime added at the bottom of his poster which effusively welcomed the Republic a footnote urging citizens to give generously to a poor relief appeal vital in Rouen and its surrounding district where the cotton industry was severely depressed.[37] There were two aspects which demanded immediate attention. The allied problems of industrial recession and unemployment were made worse by the political effervescence set off by the Revolution itself. Secondly the republican propaganda of the *Amis du Peuple* and other societies and the links between socialist and republican ideas before February encouraged the expectation that a republic would bring social benefits for the poor, not just political democracy. These expectations were sometimes no more than vague and traditional aspirations of a world-turned-upside-down; the abolition of hated *droits réunis*, salt taxes, wine taxes; the end of the Forest Laws and the preservation of communal rights, notions that were present before the 1789 and 1830 Revolutions and in times of economic crisis, both the traditional subsistence crisis caused by harvest failure and the more recent combination of this with commercial and industrial recession. Those artisans influenced by Saint-Simonian and socialist notions were also looking for structured long-term solutions to repeated cyclical depressions and the perceived evils of capitalism. The provisional government was thus dressed in the garb of Fairy Godmother, except that for those within the economic establishment, social reform was more the threat of Satan than a welcome innovation. Was the government to settle for short-term palliatives or a Brave New World?

Worst of all, the Fairy Godmother was penniless.[38] Paris was becoming more unsettled as increasing numbers of unemployed moved there expecting the government's declaration of a 'right to work' to mean a job for them. There was a dramatic run on the Bank of France, whose gold reserves fell from 226 million francs in February to 59 million by mid-March. Garnier-Pagès, as Minister of Finances, proposed a temporary 45 per cent increase in direct taxation. Although the other members of the government were hesitant to impose a measure which would be likely to cause all taxpayers to detest the Republic, the 45 centîmes decree was passed. Exemption for the poorest taxpayers was promised but seldom materialized. True the hated salt tax was abolished, announced in April with huge posters in Brittany printed in French and Breton.[39] Wine taxes were also reduced, but this was small compensation for the immediate flat rate tax rise, which to many seemed to be destined to pay the idle unemployed of the capital and elsewhere. In addition Garnier-Pagès introduced a 1 per cent tax on mortgages and his successor Godechot proposed a progressive income tax, both of which were criticized as a socialist attack on property. Railway nationalization, seriously proposed during the July Monarchy and which seemed vital for the survival of the network as companies suspended dividend payments in the depression, was portrayed as the march of communism when Louis Blanc and the Luxembourg Commission approved it.

National Workshops were the traditional means of coping with large numbers of unemployed in times of economic difficulty. They were usually organized by the municipality, or since the Consulate by the prefect, and were normally financed by private or municipal funds, or a combination of both. Menial work, shovelling earth for road or canal projects, or even less constructive schemes, was offered in return for a small daily wage. These workshops were never meant to be more than a temporary stopgap, to find work for idle, and potentially disruptive hands. Such short-term solutions to economic deprivation were attempted in the 1790s and in 1830 in Paris and the provinces.[40] Similar schemes were tried before the February Revolution.[41]

The provisional government was obliged to do something which at least looked different and was more extensive and structured, partly because of the pressure from socialists, especially Blanc, and partly because of the numbers and vociferous demands of the unemployed. The male artisan population of Paris was about 200,000 in 1848. Estimates of those unemployed in the immediate aftermath of the February Revolution ranged from 10,000 to 49,000. There was no way of knowing how many were out of work at the time of the Revolution, nor how many had subsequently been left jobless. It was anticipated that perhaps up to 10,000 men were in urgent need of help. When the provisional government initially decreed the setting up of workshops the unemployed were instructed to report to their local town hall. Thousands of people besieged them and Marie claimed later that the mayors, frightened by the crowds, failed even to check their credentials, let alone take steps to find them work.[42]

The government, urged on by the moderate republican Cauchois-Lemaire, a friend of Emile Thomas's father, eagerly adopted Thomas's plan to create a semi-military hierarchy within traditional National Workshops. The government put a disused chateau at Monceau, in the north-west suburbs of Paris, at his disposal, at a stroke removing the threatening crowds from the centre and leaving the mayors free to organize the political aspects of the republic, particularly the elections. Marie furnished Thomas with up to 5 million francs credit, with more promised from secret funds if needed. Thomas, a young chemist with no republican antecedents and no embarrassing socialist baggage, approached the problem of organizing the unemployed in a vaguely Saint-Simonian spirit. He anticipated that disciplined workshops would have an improving moral impact on the unemployed, who would then no longer be a threat to the new government. He hoped to use students of his old college, the *Ecole Centrale*, to group the workers into disciplined brigades. Like Thomas, the *centraliens* rejected both the state socialism of Blanc and the Fourierist socialism of Considérant and students of the rival *Polytechnique*.[43] Thomas was convinced that effective administration and jobs for the men would remove the danger of social unrest. The basic workshop unit was a squad, consisting of ten men with an elected leader. A brigade was made up of five squads, with an elected brigadier. Four brigades were grouped into a *lieutenance*, while four *lieutenances* formed a company, under the direction of a captain. Three companies made up a *service*, run by a *chef de service*, himself subordinate to a *chef d'arrondissement*. All officers from captain upwards were *centraliens* appointed by Thomas.

This military structure was the sole extent of innovatory thinking. In other ways the workshops imitated traditional models. They tried to find jobs in public works schemes. Plans were laid to employ about 10,000 men in this way, each man being required to provide evidence from his landlord to the police that he was a Paris resident. The Police Commissioner would then issue him with a certificate which would allow him to enrol in a workshop which had a vacancy, from which he would then be entitled to between 1.5 and 2 francs per day,[44] 1 franc after March 17th, if no actual work was available. Officers were paid more; up to 3 francs a day for brigadiers. Bread, meat and soup, and free medical aid were made available. A nine-and-a-half hour day was to be worked. All this in theory, for ten times the projected number rushed to apply and at no stage could work be found for more than 10,000 men. The navvying work provided was not very appropriate for men accustomed to skilled work in Parisian luxury industries and supervision was lax. The government engineers, graduates of the *Ecole polytechnique*, who were required to organize the work, were unsympathetic both to the idea of the workshops and to working with their traditional rivals, the graduates and students of the *Ecole centrale*.

Marie himself was determined that the workshops should be no more than a transitory palliative. However, he did devise some laudable schemes, in particular a plan to use the men to prepare the ground for a rail route around the capital, which the new Assembly rejected. The huge cost of the massive dole appalled the Assembly and often caused violent resentment in the provinces. One tribute to Thomas's success, however, was that none of the men in the workshops took part in the 100,000-strong worker demonstration of March 17th, organized by the clubs to put pressure on the government to delay the elections. Thomas, warned of the event, managed to find work for everyone on that day.[45]

Thomas and Marie were less interested in the economic than in the political potential of the workshops. They hoped that disciplined and obedient members would police future popular demonstrations and would be a counterweight to the radical Luxembourg Commission. To this end Thomas encouraged the formation of a 400-strong *Réunion centrale des ateliers nationaux*, an unemployed workers' society (which carefully avoided the use of the term 'club'). Its members were to be elected from the brigades. Thomas also urged the men to join the National Guard and as many as 40,000 probably did. Meanwhile the *Garde Mobile*, launched shortly after the February Revolution, was pursuing the same end, of engaging loyalty to the Republic of the unemployed who had fought on the barricades in February.[46]

There were workshops in the provinces, but they were generally called simply *ateliers de charité* and there was even less pretence that they were in any way related to Blanc's theories; in traditional fashion they handed out a small dole. On hearing of the Parisian decrees, workers in the provinces also demanded the transformation of local *ateliers*, the recognition of the 'right to work' and the same rates of remuneration as in Paris, which often more than doubled the existing handout. The skilled unemployed enrolled. They were unhappy with the traditional labouring work provided in the workshops; some were acquainted with Blanc's writing or at least with his ideas and expected the social workshops he had described, not the old-style degrading charity. They believed that '*la république sociale*' owed them more, and some of the more idealistic middle-class local republicans encouraged them in their aspirations. Out-of-work craftsmen, including silkweavers in Lyon and tailors in Marseille, petitioned the government to set up state-subsidized or cooperative workshops. Few of the new public officials had the business expertise or the ideological disposition to oblige. Indeed many officials expected the Revolution itself to work miracles on the economy and were appalled both at the cost of workshops and the disruptive potential of those enrolled. The rates paid to the provincial unemployed were reduced, only local residents were allowed to enrol and there were repeated attempts to shut the workshops. Those in Reims were twice temporarily closed in March and April to expel disruptive members. In Rouen and Limoges, the heart of the depressed porcelain industry, they were the fulcrum of the rioting which followed the elections to the Constituent Assembly in April.

The scale of the problem for provincial towns was less than for Paris, which was by far the largest and fastest-growing industrial centre in France and where a total of 14.5 million francs was spent on the workshops.[47] The provincial workshops can be divided into three categories.[48] The need for emergency help was greatest in the largest industrial centres, both from the humanitarian and public order aspects. These included principally Rouen, Lille, Lyon, Limoges, St Etienne, Toulon, Marseille, Roubaix and Tourcoing. The government contributed about 2 million francs. The local elite, which on the whole had little contact with the working population, gave nothing. Workshops were large, wages rivalled those of Paris and the unemployed were often well-versed in socialist ideas. This last factor was the most crucial in attracting government attention and money; towns with a history of rebellion got most. Some commissioners showed real dedication and some a commitment to socialism which the central government did not welcome. In Rouen (Seine-Inférieure), the radical Deschamps, a former railway administrator on the line from Paris to Rouen, set up *L'Union des intérêts municipaux et industriels* with 1,500,000 francs capital. He was able to revitalize about 20 cotton firms employing 2500 workers. Deschamps also found temporary navvying jobs for nearly 16,000 on public works projects. But the poor relief budget soared to nearly 2 million francs.

In Lyon silkweavers persuaded the government to put up 6.8 million francs and order flags and other official items for the republic. But in total work was found for barely 100 of the 20,000 who declared themselves unemployed. In the surrounding countryside the government provided 300,000 francs to pay the wages of 3000 men building the Paris–Lyon railway. This was almost the only scheme to do anything for the rural poor. The naval arsenal workers of Toulon, who had a history of political radicalism[49] and where there was serious unemployment at the beginning of 1848, were guaranteed jobs for the whole of the year. In Nancy a workshop was set up with voluntary subscriptions. Out-of-work bargees on the local canal were set on to move the earth from the site of an old calvary, not a real job, but they received 1.50 francs a day. The women made underwear. After a short time the daily rate was lowered to 1.25 and the beneficiaries rioted.[50]

Marseille's experience of workshops was almost unique. This was due to two factors. First, public works projects, quite unconnected with socialist initiatives, were already a recognized large-scale employer of local and foreign labour. The July Monarchy had invested millions of francs in a scheme to canalize the Durance to bring fresh water to the city. Secondly local craftsmen were politically aware and had a long history of organization and activism.[51] Emile Ollivier, who was to be liberal chief minister under Louis-Napoleon, was the government-appointed commissioner in Marseille.[52] Ollivier was a young, eloquent and idealistic republican; he was sympathetic to the workers, less sensitive to the ambitions of the local *notables* and far less inclined than were the latter to use force against the workers. He failed to realize that he needed the confidence and cash of the elite to help the poor. His most important associate in 1848 was de Montricher, the chief government engineer, a far-seeing man who tried to turn the economic crisis into an opportunity to extend Marseille's public works programme and provide work for the jobless. Neither was inspired by socialist concepts, both were cripplingly impeded by the 17 million franc debt which the city had accrued in its earlier public works projects and the inability or unwillingness of the local elite to dig deep into its pockets to finance new schemes.

Following the February Revolution the city's tailors, bakers and shoemakers got together to organize a committee to put pressure on the government to organize work for the jobless.[53] As a start they persuaded the municipal council to expel foreigners from the project canalizing the Durance. On March 6 the municipal council, backed by the state and the local Chamber of Commerce, approved a 3 million franc plan to extend the canal and port schemes presented to them by

Montricher. The Chamber of Commerce offered a 200,000 franc loan, the municipal council voted another 200,000 francs to employ 1200 men on canal and road schemes. A week later over 2600 had been taken on but 3500 were still jobless. Ollivier launched a 1 million franc government subscription loan, but the local elite managed to raise only just under one-third.

The workers' response was violent. One man was killed during fights with foreign labourers on the canal scheme. There were riots in the workshops, demonstrations in front of the town hall and demands for higher wages. The government gave way; more foreigners were sacked, wages were raised from 1.75 to 2 francs a day, a record for the provinces, and two new workshops, providing 200 new jobs, were immediately opened. But tactics reminiscent of the Parisian workshops were also implemented in an effort both to cut costs and to reduce the opportunities for worker unrest. From April 8th men were marshalled into brigades of 30; a government official was made overseer of groups of three brigades with draconian powers to expel those who were recalcitrant and reduce the wages of the lazy. Only those resident in the town since February 1st were eligible for relief and wages were cut from 2.50 francs to 2. A march to the town hall led to a relaxation of this decree. Workers were to be paid for a six-day week, whether or not there was work, and an additional 400,000 francs were found for the canal and road schemes.

Both in Paris and the provinces there was a serious gap between the need for jobs and cash to do anything. There was constant conflict over whether this was a sticking-plaster or a surgical programme. The provisional government was intent upon temporary relief for the unemployed, suspicious of any structural change that might be thought socialist, but some of their officials, particularly *polytechnicien* engineers who had to find the jobs and a few prefects who were left to carry out policies, had somewhat Fourierist socialist sympathies. Workers were generally concerned with survival more than socialist discourse, though Lyon was a major exception. Their violence was directed first at foreign labour, although the government became a target later. This was partly because the socialist ideas of Blanc, Fourier and the rest had raised expectations even amongst men who had no specific socialist affiliation. It should also be remembered that traditionally workers did anticipate government assistance at times of crisis and tended to show their dissatisfaction by very direct means.

Socialist expectations were sidelined by the provisional government into the cul-de-sac of the Luxembourg Commission, or Parliament of

Industry. Louis Blanc, at the head of the Commission, was to analyse the workers' problems and make recommendations to the government. It was ironical that Blanc, whose *Organisation du Travail* had been hailed as the solution to the pressing problems of industry, was thus prevented from creating his social workshops and a much more conservative republican, Marie, was given free rein to run old-style temporary poor relief, dressed up as National Workshops. Few of the new republicans wanted radical social change, but they knew that the socio-economic situation of the capital was explosive. They could give the impression that Blanc-style socialist experimentation was in hand, in the workshops, while placating Blanc with a time-consuming irrelevance. Blanc was persuaded that he would have more influence at the Luxembourg than at the head of a conventional government ministry. What is surprising is that he accepted the deception of the National Workshops and never denounced the sell-out.

At first the Luxembourg Commission, an elected assembly of workers meeting at the old stamping ground of the Chamber of Peers in the Luxembourg Palace, must have seemed a real innovation. Nothing like it had been seen before. On March 1st 200 workers met at the palace, chosen in various ways from a range of Parisian trades. There was no formal standard procedure for election and no attempt to summon delegates from the provinces to Paris. Analogous gatherings were assembled in a number of provincial centres, including Lyon, Lille and Marseille.

Blanc was exceptionally popular with the crowds and was often referred to as 'the first worker in France'.[54] He proposed that the workers look at both the immediate and more long-term problems of industry. The Commission immediately addressed the vital question of conditions of employment. On its first day the assembly decreed the reduction of the working day by one hour to ten hours in the capital, eleven in the provinces, and the abolition of subcontracting, *marchandage*, which in the building trade left workers nominally self-employed, but effectively defenceless to protect their wages. The detested *livret*, which all workers had been obliged to carry since the First Republic, was abolished. The Commission had begun in an ad hoc fashion. Indeed Blanc had been startled by the demand for the abolition of *marchandage*. After the first day it was decided that members should be chosen from the various corporations in Paris, three from each, totalling 242. One from each group was to be present at the daily debates, the others only at the general assemblies. A comparable number of employers representing 77 trades were to join them. Ten were to be chosen to form a permanent committee to meet daily with the workers' group.

The Commission became a focus not just for those seeking the solution of the specific crisis of unemployment at that moment, but also for those who hoped for radical structural change as suggested by socialists over recent years. Blanc coopted leading economists, socialists and journalists onto the Commission to address and advise the delegates. Blanc's own brand of socialism not unnaturally prevailed.

After many interruptions to deal with specific issues, the Commission issued a list of its objectives. First, a Ministry of Labour should be created to organize a social revolution which would gradually and peacefully abolish the working class. Second, a Ministry of Progress should buy up all railway and mining companies; transform the Bank of France into a State Bank; centralize all insurance companies; create huge warehouses for the central exchange of goods by means of guaranteed paper money; open bazaars for retail trade. All of these concerns would be state-owned and run, their profits forming the budget of the Ministry of Labour to be used for the benefit of the workers. Workers' associations and agricultural colonies would be set up with the surplus to run profit-sharing workshops and to provide sickness and retirement pay. Workshops would, it was hoped, cooperate to eliminate all the evils of usury, capitalism, greed and wars and replace them with worker solidarity. The state would give the lead, but no one would be coerced and private ownership would continue outside these cooperative structures. In 1870 Louis Blanc still gave pride of place to this scheme in his own history of the 1848 Revolution.[55] It had no impact whatsoever on the policies pursued by any government in the Second Republic.

The Luxembourg Commission achieved its greatest successes as an arbiter of practical questions, in resolving disputes between masters and men, in the manner of the traditional *conseil des prudhommes*. Strikes threatened in a number of key trades which would have paralysed the economy of the capital, including baking and the roofers who were working on the new building to house the 900-man Constituent Assembly. In some cases the arbitration provided by the Commission was short-lived, especially in the numerous disputes over foreign workers, whose presence was particularly resented.

The Commission lacked an independent budget, but it set up a number of cooperative workshops, notably one to make uniforms for the National Guard. Parisian master tailors provided capital totalling

11,000 francs for a workshop in the old debtors' prison at Clichy, which gave work to more than 2000 unemployed tailors. They finished 110,800 uniforms in record time to Blanc's great satisfaction, working overtime on Sundays. An embroiderer's workshop was added to make the insignia for the uniforms. In both cases workers who proved less competent than others were retained on moral grounds.[56] A workshop of spinners and trimming experts was given the order for the epaulettes for the uniforms and managed to get a start-up advance of 12,000 francs from the Discount Bank. A saddlers' workshop was also founded in a former army barracks. They were given orders for saddles previously made in state-owned workshops in Saumur. These successful workshops are often forgotten. Blanc's more ambitious schemes for large-scale nationalization never saw the light of day.

The problem of the unemployed was intractable; both costly beyond any past experience and ideologically charged. It distorted and seriously impaired the future of the new republic. Meanwhile even the Luxembourg Commission became preoccupied with attempting to organize the workers' vote for its candidates for the Constituent Assembly. The headquarters of their electoral committee was established in the Sorbonne and a list of candidates prepared, separate from that of the provisional government. Their initial proposal was for a list entirely of workers, but Blanc persuaded them that this was impractical. Their final list included Blanc, Ledru-Rollin, Albert and the printer Flocon from the government's list, and their own candidates, Barbès, Sobrier, Deplanque, Vidal, Etienne Arago, Thoré, Caussidière, Leroux, Raspail and Lebon. Nearly all were socialists. The list was made public a few days before the election.

The election was well supported with an 84 per cent turnout. But universal suffrage was not enough to secure a republic. The elections were a catastrophic defeat for republicans of all kinds, particularly for the socialists. They underlined either the lack of appeal of a republican message, or the failure to indicate to new voters which were the genuinely republican candidates. They indicated widespread open hostility to expensive radical socialist projects. Among the genuine *républicains de la veille* were a mere 230 moderates and 55 radicals.[57] Ledru-Rollin came only 24th and Blanc 27th of the 34 members elected in the Seine. Only five socialists in all were elected for the Seine and these were men who were on other lists too. The majority of Parisian voters were not workers and the workers' vote was split between the Luxembourg and Thomas's National Workshop list. Thomas himself was hopelessly defeated with only 26,166 votes.[58]

The elections were a triumph for the *républicains du lendemain*, the moderates as they called themselves, although 'closet monarchists' might be a more accurate term. Of the 851 elected, 439 were Orleanists or Legitimists who had been active in politics before February. Electoral experience and local clout were the victors. The old elites found, perhaps a little to their surprise, that universal suffrage actually strengthened their hand. The old *notables* of the pre-revolutionary *pays légal* managed to survive the adoption of universal suffrage with no difficulty. The social composition of the Assembly was clue enough. Of the 880 deputies after by-elections, 325 were lawyers, 160 landowners, 99 army officers, 65 industrialists, 53 involved in commerce, 53 doctors; while only 18 were workmen and 6 foremen. Democracy helped the *notables*; 700 paid more than 500 francs tax a year, 80 per cent were over 40 and could have been deputies (165 were) before 1848.

Outside Paris there were pockets of isolated support for genuine republican candidates. These were concentrated in larger cities like Lyon where the artisans favoured radical candidates. The failure of the radicals sometimes led to serious unrest, notably in Rouen and Limoges where industrial depression aggravated the situation.[59] It is clear that it took more than economic grievances to make radical voters. In Troyes, where the artisan-organized hosiery industry was dominant and also in crisis and where the turn-out was 82 per cent, the men elected to the Constituent Assembly were socially undistinguishable from their Orleanist predecessors, indeed one had been an MP before the Revolution, four had been candidates and two were sons of MPs.[60]

By the end of April the situation in Paris, a handful of other large towns and in some country districts was far more volatile than in February. The economic crisis was worse and attempts to resolve it had created expectations of radical socialist initiatives among a tiny minority of the middle class and among workers, and horror of the threat of 'socialism' among the vast majority. In country districts there were riots against the 45 centîmes tax, as well as popular protests against hated old taxes and against the erosion of communal rights. The minority *républicains de la veille* were increasingly divided, most were satisfied with universal suffrage and a constituent assembly, but an element argued that the unemployment generated by the economic crisis offered an opportunity for significant social reform, at the least the acceptance of state responsibility to find work for those without jobs. The fragmentation and electoral failure of the republicans was amply displayed to 100,000 discontented unemployed in Paris and the

new conservative, mainly monarchist majority in the Constituent
Assembly.

9 The June Days; Bonapartism; The Decline and Fall of the Second Republic

Logically the decision of the new mass electorate to choose a Constituent Assembly containing a large majority of tepid post-February converts to republicanism meant that the new democratic Second Republic was likely to be stillborn. The *républicains de la veille* continued to hope that a republic would emerge, despite their minority position in the Assembly. They believed that a combination of 'natural' emergent republicanism and institutional change could confirm the republic. But divisions between long-term republicans, moderates and radicals were themselves becoming increasingly rigid. Given the composition of the Assembly, was it inevitable that France would have a conservative, near-monarchist, constitution?

The first problem for the Assembly when it met on May 4th was to ensure that its views would prevail. Republican tradition was ambiguous, indicating respect both for democracy and for the right of rebellion. Would the conservative decisions of the electorate, which radicals had feared, be respected? The Luxembourg Commission, the clubs and the members of the National Workshops were all very disappointed with the failure of radical candidates in the elections. The workshops contained over 100,000 unemployed. To the Assembly they were a real threat, epitomizing demands for a socialist republic and representing an insurrectionary tradition which could destroy them.

The Assembly quickly elected a five-man executive of moderate republicans, visibly less radical than the provisional government which it replaced: Marie, Arago, Garnier-Pagès, Lamartine, with Ledru-Rollin the most left-wing the last to be chosen. Most of the old ministers were retained. The moderate socialist Buchez, a *protégé* of Garnier-Pagès and enemy of Louis Blanc, was elected president of the

210

Assembly. Blanc demanded the creation of a Ministry of Progress, but was ignored. The Luxembourg Commission was closed down, although the *Comité central des ouvriers*, its electoral arm, retitled the *Comité des délégués du Luxembourg*, remained active. The task of investigating the problems of industrial and agricultural workers was taken over by a committee of the Constituent Assembly. Many of the clubs, both in Paris and the provinces, dissolved themselves once the business of the election was complete.[1]

Next was the turn of the workshops. The new Assembly was fearful of popular unrest and the assembled ranks of so many unemployed in workshops both in Paris and in the provinces were a cause of real concern. By May the numbers enrolled seemed overwhelming, particularly as no one knew the precise total. According to Thomas there were just under 88,000 in Paris, but a committee of enquiry set up after May 15th counted 115,000. By June 1848, 120,000 were enrolled in the workshops and another 50,000 had failed to gain acceptance. Non-Parisians made up 30,000. Even taking account that outsiders had flocked to the capital before restrictions were imposed to take advantage of the workshops, a high proportion of the normal Parisian artisan population was out of work in June 1848 and thoroughly discontented with what the workshops could offer.[2]

Trélat, who replaced Marie as Minister of Public Works, upon the latter's appointment to the new Executive Commission, impressed upon a hostile Thomas that the workshops had to go.[3] On May 13th the Executive Commission decreed that no more men should be admitted. All single males between 18 and 25 were to be enlisted into the army; those who refused were to be dismissed from the workshops.

On May 15th a radical demonstration of 20,000 led by Blanqui and Barbès occupied the Assembly. The ostensible motive was to secure French support for the Polish revolt.[4] Blanqui and Barbès were republicans in the insurgent tradition, who had led an abortive coup in 1839. At the *hôtel de ville* Barbès and Albert proclaimed a provisional government of themselves, Raspail, Ledru-Rollin and Louis Blanc, which left no doubt that the insurgents were trying to do far more than support Polish patriots. Blanc and Raspail did not help to initiate the unrest, but spoke at length to the crowd which occupied the Assembly. There was considerable delay in calling the National Guard and Buchez was blamed. Barbès and Albert led a march to join their associates at the Assembly, but by then the rising was over. Lamartine and Ledru-Rollin ordered their arrest. With difficulty Louis Blanc was able to convince his fellow deputies that he had been trying to calm matters, not incite rebellion. Raspail was charged and imprisoned. None of the republicans came out of May 15th well. Ledru-Rollin survived, but had clearly been tempted to join the rebels. The unity of February was gone; republicans were patently at war with each other in an Assembly where the majority was increasingly hostile to social reform.

While it is clear that Blanqui and Barbès had hoped to change the course and nature of the Republic on May 15th, it is unlikely that many of those who followed them were of the same mind. In contrast to earlier popular movements that year, nearly 75 per cent of the demonstrators, at least 14,000, were members of the workshops, marching with their workshop banners. They were disappointed at the failure of radical republicans in the April elections and apprehensive that the Assembly was unsympathetic to the workshops. They wanted jobs and expected the state to continue to provide a safety-net of a minimum income during the crisis and perhaps benevolent neutrality and some support subsequently. That is not to say that they were indifferent to politics. Parisian artisans had joined the *charbonnerie*, the secret societies of the 1830s, followed Cabet and other socialists; the better-off had experience of self-help in mutual-aid associations. They were aware that they could be a pressure group on the Assembly, but this was far from wanting to take over the state. There is no evidence that they shared Blanqui's expectations. In 1839 Blanqui had found artisans unreliable allies and on May 15th the workshop rioters posed no real threat; most deserted Blanqui within a few hours and rejoined their National Guard battalions, which stayed loyal to the government. Their director, Thomas, conscious that the new Assembly was against him and the workshops, may have done little to prevent their participation. If so, he played into the hands of the Assembly, for May 15th gave them good reason to act. The Executive Commission decreed the immediate implementation of the decision reached on the workshops two days earlier.

In the provinces there was disquiet among radical workers that the election had produced an assembly out of sympathy with the unemployed and scarcely republican in spirit. In Rouen the April election was won by moderates, including the government prosecutor Senard, who defeated the popular radical commissioner, Deschamps. Protest riots left 23 workers dead and 36 others injured. In Limoges workers overwhelmed the bourgeois National Guard, invaded the prefecture and held it for two weeks until May 18th. In Lyon, where four radical republicans had been elected and five of fourteen in the

Rhône contingent were artisans, the Assembly as a whole was a great disappointment. The moderate commissioner Emmanuel Arago resigned and was replaced by Bernard, who had been defended by Arago after the 1839 conspiracy. He struggled to control the Lyon workshops and the socialist-inclined club members, to prevent assaults on innovative weaving machines and on the government prosecutor and to secure the peaceful removal of a statue of Louis XIV from Bellecour, the main square in central Lyon.[5]

In the midst of popular unrest in many parts of France more violent than anything seen since the 1790s, on May 17th the Assembly elected its constitutional committee, composed of moderate *National*-style republicans and a few Orleanists, including Cormenin (president), Barrot, Marrast, Considérant, Dufaure and de Tocqueville. Their proposals, presented to the Assembly on June 19th, had to be put on one side until the issue of the workshops had been resolved.

Trélat, a long-standing republican and a worthy, altruistic doctor, who had both sympathy for and direct knowledge of the problems of the poor, was given responsibility for the workshops after the elections. He hesitated to apply the harsh decision of the Assembly taken after May 15th. A committee of engineering experts from the traditionally radical *Ecole Polytechnique* was called to offer advice. In their report on May 20th they applauded 'the right to work' and recommended a Fourierist solution of government loans to private industry to regenerate the economy, including railroad construction, in the doldrums since the onset of the economic crisis. The government was appalled and suppressed the report, so successfully that it was subsequently forgotten for 100 years.[6] Some of the more modest suggestions were implemented on May 24th; Thomas was obliged to resign and hustled away to Bordeaux. All workshop members who had not lived in Paris for at least six months or who had refused jobs were summarily dismissed. They were to be drafted into provincial public works projects and those who remained were to be paid piecerates, which would deny them any income if there were no jobs.

Such plans were dependent on economic recovery and there was no sign of that. A sense of crisis among workshop members was intensified by the build up of troops around the capital and in other major cities. With some justice the members felt besieged. Together with delegates from the old Luxembourg Commission, they secured the election of Leroux and Proudhon in by-elections to the Assembly on June 4th. On June 13th their joint committee issued a proclamation to the workers of Paris urging support for the 'democratic and social republic'. Rumours that the workshops were to be completely shut down flew around the capital and there were constant demonstrations and meetings, despite draconian decrees banning public gatherings. Meanwhile the Assembly's Labour Committee, which represented a broad spectrum of opinion, including for a time Blanc and the legitimist comte de Falloux who was determined on closure,[7] was in earnest but inconclusive debate.

On June 20th the Assembly finally decided to dissolve the workshops. Two days later the *Moniteur* announced that workers were to be drafted into the army or moved to the provinces; by June 24th 400 had gone. A protest demonstration to the Assembly, planned by men from the workshops, and possibly also from the Luxembourg Commission, began on June 22nd at 8 a.m., too early to catch anyone but Marie, who was determined on closure. Repeated marches that day culminated in a 100,000-strong meeting at the Place du Panthéon. Demonstrations continued the next day, during which the government decided against trying to arrest the leaders. A state of siege was declared and a military campaign was begun under General Cavaignac, made temporary head of the government. The workshops were to be closed within three days. That evening the marchers began to build barricades in eastern Paris and what had begun as a workshop protest became much more complex.

The June Days had begun. They were a spontaneous, virtually leaderless insurrection, a protest against the imminent disappearance of the only means of livelihood for the unemployed. How many fought? Marx, in his study *Class Struggles in France 1848–50*, suggested that up to 50,000 took part. Probably the figure was nearer 20,000. Who participated? Workshops members, but many were persuaded to stay off the streets by the good faith which the government demonstrated in continuing to pay the dôle throughout the insurrection. Some idea of the participants can be gauged by the composition of the workshops themselves. Thomas estimated that nearly 9000 were unskilled labourers. The rest belonged to the traditional Parisian crafts: 6300 were joiners, over 4000 masons and nearly 4000 were painters – indicative of the depressed state of house-building and repair. Nearly 3000 were locksmiths, 2500 turners and the same number were barrelmakers. Shoemakers, tailors, jewellers, hatters made up a high proportion of the rest. Over 7600 did not state their jobs.[8] Tocqueville claimed that the rebels had links with a criminal underworld and Taine was to take up the same story. In reality the insurgents' only crime was poverty. Of those arrested nearly 67 per cent were skilled workmen, particularly from the building, metalworking, clothing and furniture trades, while just over 10 per cent were shopkeepers.[9]

What were their aims? How far were the June Days an attempt to press on with the Revolution begun in February, to secure the 'social' republic? How far were they a protest born of misery and economic deprivation? The closing of the workshops was central and encapsulated both issues, immediate survival and the long-term direction of the Republic. The immediate objective of the rising was an attempt by the unemployed in Paris to oblige the Assembly to retain the workshops. The workers' grievances were not simply those of temporary unemployment, but concerned a range of long-standing and often-rehearsed complaints about structural and technical changes in industry.[10] The participants were influenced by socialists, especially by Blanc, whom they considered betrayed them by refusing his support. Some undoubtedly had been convinced by Blanqui's faith in insurrection, but most marched as a pressure group, not as a class war against the existing republic.

In June 1848 very few, in or out of the workshops, wanted state-run workshops as a permanent measure. But the government's failure to pursue long-term social reform and its hostility to the workshops meant that the participants also believed that they were defending the idea of a 'social' republic which had been pushed aside after the elections. The republican government had espoused a repressive strategy similar to that pursued during the July Monarchy in Lyon and the rue Transnonain in 1834. The worker protesters were isolated in June 1848. The 1830 and the February Revolutions had been artisan and student risings quickly taken over by an educated middle-class group, whereas June was a revolt of working men, organized in the workshops, which attracted almost no support within the middle classes, even from established socialists.[11]

The traditional insurrectionary leaders, Barbès and Blanqui, were noticeably absent, in jail or in exile after May 15th. Proudhon and Blanc were hostile and continued to attend the debates of the Assembly. The violence of the June Days was as distasteful to most socialists as to more moderate republicans. To contemporary socialists the June Days were the result of the failure to implement socialist measure. The insurgents were the victims of the absence of a social programme. Specifically the rebellion happened because the government finally decided to close the workshops in an economic situation when alternative means to provide sustenance were lacking.

June came about, not because of demands for socialist measures, nor because the new regime was totally unsympathetic to the unemployed, but because of the incompetence, first of the provisional government and then of the Executive Commission. The government failed to limit access to the Paris workshops to the unemployed of the capital and failed to provide adequate provincial schemes. It is significant that two-thirds of those arrested in June were from the areas around Paris, not from the capital itself. To the government the workshops became a major obstacle to the creation of a republic; an expensive and an ever-present threat of violent intervention. The government hesitated for over a month to implement its decision to disband the workshops, meanwhile amassing troops in and around Paris. The government contributed far more than the unemployed to determining that the problem would end in a military confrontation.

The June barricades confirmed the fears of conservatives that the workers were intent on civil war, not just against the Republic, about whose future they were fairly indifferent, but against the established social order. De Tocqueville neatly summed up their worries in his memoirs. 'In truth it was not a political struggle, but a class struggle, a sort of "Servile War".'[12] The government, chivvied by the conservative majority in the Assembly, insisted that the republic itself was under attack. They believed they were justified in reconquering artisan Paris with a military campaign. The commander Cavaignac was a man of impeccable republican pedigree, whose military expertise, so much the worse for the insurgents, had been gained in Algeria. The government had been nervously massing troops in and around the capital since May 15th, using the completed rail links. There were 20,000 garrisoned in Paris, thanks to the new forts, 10,000 in the new republican *garde mobile*, 2600 republican guards and 2000 regular Parisian police. In the surrounding areas there were an additional 15,000 men at the ready. The Parisian National Guard was available.[13] National Guardsmen also arrived from 53 departments, which was of considerable psychological significance, given the hostility in rural areas to the 45 centîmes tax. Six days of bitter street fighting ensued. How many were killed? The conservative estimate of the prefecture of police was 1460, but the actual figure must have been several times that, making the June Days the bloodiest fighting ever recorded in the capital to that date.[14] Around 15,000 were arrested, of whom 5000 were sent to Algeria. On July 3rd the workshops were closed.

A number of France's larger provincial towns continued to experience similar hopes, frustration and violence as Paris.[15] Disappointment over the election of moderates led to fears that workshops would be in jeopardy. In Marseille by early May up to 5000 were being found work, but Marseille's financial crisis obliged Ollivier to replace daily wages with piecework. When the angry workers invaded the Council Chamber on May 4th, the council responded by throwing them out of the workshops. At the end of May the municipal council unsuccessfully petitioned the central government for a 4.5 million franc loan for road and canal schemes, announcing that there were still 9000 unemployed without help. Rumours that the workshops were to close were rife at the end of May when 100 men were laid off one of the road schemes. Balance-sheets were ordered for each workshop with a view to closure. Apprehension grew in mid-June when about a hundred Parisian workers arrived with tales of the imminent dissolution of their workshops. From June 12th there were almost nightly protests and on June 18th 400 workers invaded the prefecture, led by Chauvin, leading light of the local Montagnard club.

Chauvin and other leaders were arrested, the Parisians were expelled. The workers hesitated, but on June 22nd 2000 marched on the prefecture. In a major clash in the old part of the town 12 were killed, 13 injured and 414 were arrested, of whom only 70 had participated in this last riot. In 1849, 153 were finally tried, of whom only 4 were members of the workshops. The bulk of those arrested were radical politicians. On July 10th Cavaignac demoted the Marseille commissioner, Ollivier, who had been both too radical and too indecisive, to the minor and non-radical Haute-Marne. By the end of September all the workshops set up since February were gone. Ambitious projects, more humanitarian than dogmatically socialist, had failed, leaving the Marseille workforce disenchanted and social cleavages much greater.[16]

Elsewhere there were protests, but more muted. In Lyon fighting continued in the main silk district of the Croix Rousse for several weeks, but Bernard proved an adept commissioner and the government was careful to honour its orders for flags and committed itself to a 5 million franc payment which helped the silk industry. By the end of May weavers were sufficiently optimistic to leave the workshops and reopen their own premises. There was no echo of the Parisian insurrection in Lyon.[17] In Limoges a strengthened garrison allowed the prefect to close workshops which had included 3700 workers in April and to harass the radical republican club. In the Eure, the 200 weaving operatives at the Waddington textile mill downed tools on June 22nd, but the issue was not socialism or workshops, though there was an underlying nervousness about jobs. Eight female Scots weavers had been brought over to teach the local women how to operate new weaving machines. The Scots were roundly accused of both incompetence and immorality and threw one of their trainees into the water. The local weavers appealed to the prefect to intercede; the foreigners left.[18] Popular unrest had its Luddite and chauvinistic, as well as its socialist side.

Cavaignac believed that the Republic was the victor in June. The son of a regicide and brother of the republican leader in the 1830s, Cavaignac was firmly committed to a democratic republic. In the first week of July memorial services were held to honour those who died in June 'defending the republic'. In Brest, Finistère, the church was not big enough to contain all those who turned up for the service, in which a tricolour flag bordered with black was flown.[19] At the end of June Cavaignac recommended a new government to the Assembly. It marked the exclusion of republicans committed to a 'social' republic. Jules Bastide, old *carbonaro* and republican journalist, continued at Foreign Affairs, Bethmont, defender of republicans in the July Monarchy, stayed at Justice, Goudchaux returned to Finance. Senard, the moderate republican leader in Rouen who had helped put down the worker protests to the moderate April elections, took the Interior Ministry. The Assembly would not allow Carnot to stay at Education.[20]

Cavaignac appointed a commission of enquiry into the June Days, which reported on August 3rd. Its president was Odilon Barrot, backed by a collection of provincial Orleanists. Quentin-Bauchart, who had proposed dictatorial powers for Cavaignac, made the report to the Assembly. On August 25th Blanc faced a parliamentary enquiry, chaired by Marrast. The Assembly condemned him to deportation by 504 votes to 252, but he had already left for Britain, where he was to remain until the end of the Second Empire.

The Assembly may have been relieved to inter the 'social' republic, but socialist ideas, often of a Fourierist imprint, were far from dead. In July 1848 the Assembly felt obliged to vote 3 million francs credit to cooperatives and preferential treatment on public works contracts. Buchez was a leading figure in their creation, although his influence subsequently declined and *L'Atelier* ceased publication in July 1850. In deliberate contrast to Blanc's theories, these cooperatives were capitalist in inspiration and a 5–6 per cent rate of interest on investment was projected. Proudhon, whose ideas on how to finance industry were also very different from those of Blanc, exerted a brief influence on public opinion after the June Days. A critic of the provisional government, Proudhon founded *Le Représentant du Peuple* and his practical solutions to the worsening economic crisis quickly became well known and popular. Up to 40,000 copies were sold daily. Many articles, on subjects such as unemployment and poverty, were turned into short, cheap pamphlets. Proudhon argued, to popular acclaim, that the answer to repeated economic crises lay in eliminating exorbitant interest rates. He founded a bank to offer interest-free credit in the spring of 1848 which attracted 27,000 subscribers. Proudhon was elected to the Constituent Assembly for Paris in June 1848 with the help of the workshops' committee, but he condemned the June rebellion[21] and wrongly blamed Blanc.[22] On July 8th he proposed to the Assembly's Finance Committee, of which he was a member, a 33 per cent reduction of all rents for a three-year period to help economic recovery. Property-owners were scandalized by his scheme: 'an affront to the moral order, an attack on private property'. Only the Lyon silkworker Greppo voted for him, with 691 against.

Meanwhile the democratic republic was obliged to defend itself by becoming increasingly indistinguishable from the old monarchy. Riots against the temporary 45 centîmes tax grew worse in the provinces. The government's answer everywhere was the traditional one of force. The telegraph and the complete rail links made control easier. In the following months railway lines and bridges had to be patrolled to prevent sabotage.[23] The freedom of the press, proclaimed in February, was eliminated at the beginning of August by the reintroduction of caution money. An editor had to deposit 24,000 francs with the authorities before he could publish. Proudhon roundly condemned this' as a muzzle for all but the very rich editor and printer. Publication of his *Représentant du Peuple* was halted three times in three days in August 1848, following the addition to the title of the paper, 'What is the producer? Nothing. What should he be? Everything! What is the capitalist? Everything! What should he be? Nothing!' The paper was forced to close. It was succeeded by *Le Peuple*, printed at first as a weekly, then as a daily. In October 1848 he addressed a banquet of 2000 in Paris on the need for permanent revolution and direct action.

> Révolution de 1848, comment te nommes-tu? – Je me nomme *Droit au Travail?* – Quel est ton drapeau? – *L'Association!*
> – *Ta devise?* – *L'Egalité* devant la fortune! – Où nous mènes-tu? – A la *Fraternité*! – Salut à toi, Révolution![24]

Instead, a conservative republican regime was being moulded. Many commissioners had been elected to the Assembly, leaving gaps, and others had proved too socialist, like Ollivier and Guépin. The title of prefect was restored and the new officials tended to be old Orleanists. Municipal elections at the end of July gave mixed results. In many areas they reinforced the return or even simply the continued retention of power by the *notables*; 35,000 of the 65,000 new mayors or their deputies had held a similar post during Louis-Philippe's reign. In Troyes, a hosiery town hit by the depression, the old pre-revolutionary municipal council, Orleanist in its politics, was strongly representative of wealthy business interests. None resigned after February. When it came to the municipal elections only the better-off third of the electorate bothered to vote. Fourteen of the old members were elected. A glance at the average tax roll of the 'new' municipal councillors compared with the old reveals the lack of change. The 1846 average was 580 francs, that of 1848 was 500 francs.[25] But elsewhere, in areas where radicals had done best in April, especially in the Midi and the Centre, the municipal elections were a triumph for 'red' republicans. Elections to the departmental general councils followed a similar pattern.

In September 17 by-elections were held to fill gaps in the Assembly left by a number of earlier multiple elections. The Cavaignac government made no bones about appointing official government candidates.[26] Fifteen of the new deputies were royalists, another was Louis-Napoleon, chosen by five departments, elected first in June, but denied a seat. As in June he had no support from the press, either republican or conservative, but was carried forward by the legend of his uncle and a poster campaign, which presented him as a candidate to reconcile social conflicts. He was not allowed to enter France to campaign. After his election the newspapers condemned the spontaneous popular vote he had attracted as an unthinking response; some thought he took votes which would otherwise have gone to socialists, some thought his appeal was to anti-republicans. His modest acceptance of the oath to the Republic when he took his seat reassured everyone that he was no threat.

The constitution was the most pressing issue for the Assembly. Discussion of the constitutional committee's proposals was curtailed by the June Days and only resumed at the end of August, when the elimination of any reference to 'the right to work' seemed the most urgent issue. It was not until the first week in October that the Assembly returned to the question of political arrangements including the presidency. The committee, with some dissent, had recommended that there should also be a president elected by universal suffrage.

Radicals, like Pyat, did not want a president at all, moderates were divided between election by the legislative assembly and by the people. Tocqueville reproached those republicans who were opposed to the democratic election of a president with a lack of faith in universal suffrage itself, a view which Lamartine echoed in a famous speech on October 6th. Having been elected in ten departments a few months earlier, Lamartine was not without some hope of being chosen. Conservatives, not yet backers of Louis-Napoleon, opted for universal suffrage because they were convinced that Cavaignac was bound to win if the Assembly elected the president and because the local elections had been so reassuring to them. The possible candidacy of Louis-Napoleon and its accompanying threat to the Republic was in everyone's minds and a ban on members of former ruling families was discussed. Louis-Napoleon modestly reassured the Assembly. The decision for universal suffrage was made on October 10th, with the proviso that if no candidate secured a majority of votes cast and at least 2 million votes, the Assembly would elect the president from among the five candidates who obtained most votes.[27]

The rest of the constitution was designed more as an antidote to fears than an expression of hopes. The constitution-makers were clearly conscious of trying to learn lessons from the distant, but terrifying disasters of the First Republic, as well as the more recent problems of May and June 1848. They tried to steer a mid-course between the dictatorship of an assembly and of one man. Democracy was an inevitable and tolerable component. On the whole the national and local elections showed that democracy held no terrors for the established elite. Article 1 of their new constitution declared 'Sovereignty lies in the citizens of France and is inalienable and imprescriptible. No one person or group can exercise it.' There was little disagreement that a republic should have a unicameral legislative assembly. Its 750 members, representatives, not delegates, were to be elected by direct, male and secret suffrage for three years. Voters had to be at least 21, candidates 25. Deputies could not hold public office. The president was to appoint the government, but to prevent him becoming too powerful, he was not allowed to stand for immediate re-election. The new constitution was approved on November 4th by a majority of 739 to 30, Proudhon being the only one of the 16 most radical deputies to vote against it. He argued that the president had been given too much power and he had little faith in elected assemblies.

Who was to be president? When the decision on universal suffrage was made, it was assumed, by all except the most radical deputies, that

Cavaignac would be chosen. But the constitution-making months were marked by the growing electoral success of Louis-Napoleon, Napoleon's great-nephew, and awareness of this overshadowed the debate, despite his denials. His increasing popularity in 1848 was in some ways surprising; he had twice failed to seize power during the reign of Louis-Philippe. He had totally failed to associate himself with the powerful Bonapartist legend. Bonapartism had a broad patriotic, nationalist appeal in early nineteenth-century France, compelling at elite, but especially at popular levels. Napoleon was portrayed as the saviour of the Revolution in popular songs, plays, novels and paintings. Republicans could honour him without embarrassment. He was also respected as the man who had brought 'order' to the Revolution. The memoirs he had dictated to Las Cases on St Helena went through six editions between 1823 and 1842. Bonapartism had become such a vague, amorphous, classless sentiment that Louis-Philippe turned part of the palace of Versailles into a museum to the emperor. In 1833 a statue of Bonaparte was placed on the top of the Vendôme column, symbolically linking Napoleon to 1789 and 1830. The return of Napoleon's ashes to France, one of the emperor's last requests, was organized and funded by popular subscription. Louis-Philippe encouraged one of his sons to preside over the installation of the ashes in Les Invalides in 1840, which became a shrine to the Empire. On Sunday 20 December 1840, 200,000 visited the tomb.

On 27 February 1848, with no hypocrisy, *Le National* reminded its readers that Napoleon had declared on St Helena, '*Avant cinquante ans, l'Europe sera cosaque ou républicaine*'.[28] Maybe, but for the moment Bonapartism was unquestionably the most powerful mass political sentiment, overshadowing the appeal of the Republic because it was merely an historic memory and sentiment, requiring no decision or action. It engaged the emotions of literate and illiterate alike, but had a particular impact on those newly enfranchised in April. There was nothing to touch the universality of popular Bonapartism.

Napoleon's great-nephew seemed no threat whatsoever to the Republic in 1848. Neither as conspirator nor· as a politician did he strike much of a figure. In 1839 he had brought.out a short account of the Empire in which, echoing Napoleon's own memoirs, he claimed that Napoleon had only been a dictator because of the demands of war, and had been a liberal at heart.[29] The volume was translated into several languages, cheap editions were printed and Lamartine speculated that half-a-million copies were sold. It was a tribute to the legend, not the author. Few were convinced by the thesis of a 'liberal' emperor.

The republican Laponneraye ridiculed his claims. He did not deny Napoleon's contribution, 'Your uncle was a soldier who offered his sword to the Revolution'. But it was important not to make unreasonable philosophical, and above all dynastic claims. 'You have heard that your uncle is venerated; you think that your name entitles you to the same homage; it's like the tale of the donkey who bears sacred relics on its back. People honour the relics, but ridicule the donkey.'[30]

Why did people begin to take the 'donkey' seriously after the February Revolution? Louis-Napoleon's first attempt to enter France at the end of February was repulsed, but Bonapartist propaganda began to appear, several candidates for the Constituent Assembly reminded voters that they had served the emperor, and two of his nephews were elected for Corsica. Louis-Napoleon was a different matter; his attempted coups condemned him as 'a Pretender' and no friend of republicanism. However, the patriotic memory of the Empire was enough to secure his election in June, while he was still in London, in four constituencies, including artisan Paris. Perhaps the artisans had heard of Louis-Napoleon's appeal for an attack on poverty, written in 1844.[31] The press, a few ephemeral Bonapartist publications aside, was uniformly hostile. The Assembly refused to allow him into France, some deputies concerned that he was intent on reviving an empire, some more worried that he had attracted widespread support among the workers. Only his obvious mediocrity and apparent lack of imperial ambition made them more tolerant in September.

In preparation for the September by-elections 400 or so conservatives formed the *Réunion* of the *rue de Poitiers*, which included Barrot, the vicomte de Falloux, Faucher, Fould, some former centre-left Orleanists and some legitimists. The dominant figures were Berryer, Molé and Thiers. Their successes in September behind them, they turned to the presidency. They were aware that they could neither agree on a common candidate of their own nor could they hope to win. On October 26th Louis-Napoleon had been forced to admit that he intended to stand. A few days later Thiers addressed the *Réunion*, urging them to agree to back the obvious winner, otherwise an indecisive poll would mean that the choice would be left to the Assembly which would choose Cavaignac. Because a successful candidate would have to be known to everyone, Thiers convinced most of them that the *Réunion* had to back Louis-Napoleon, even though at that point they had no contact with him and he was hostile to them. An increasing number of conservative *notables* and their newspapers accepted Thiers' judgement. Why? Many of the *notables* believed that Louis-Napoleon was indeed simply a donkey, with a famous name (cartoonists delighted in copying Laponneraye's image). The name was indispensable because it was known to the newly enfranchised peasant masses who still believed that Napoleon had epitomized aspects of the 1789 Revolution which they applauded. This, and Louis-Napoleon's own apparent lack of either charisma or message, convinced some of the leading conservative *notables* that he was the least dangerous and most malleable candidate.

There were four republican candidates, of which Cavaignac was the most conservative. He was little known outside Paris and there his military victory in June was hardly likely to endear him to many of the voters. Those who recognized his name more than his recent reputation would associate it with his republican family. Lamartine, the next most conservative candidate, had not distinguished himself as Minister of Foreign Affairs and was probably the only person to be confident of his success in December. Ledru-Rollin was backed by a group of popular societies, *La Solidarité Républicaine*, organized by Martin Bernard, Delescluze and Pyat, which was supposed to guarantee him nationwide support. But its first publicity did not appear until December 3rd.[32] Ledru-Rollin fought on a ticket of 'peaceful' social reform, which by then must have seemed a contradiction in terms, especially given the backing of Pyat, who was a partisan of violent social revolution. The most radical candidate was Raspail, stil in jail awaiting trial after the May 15th demonstration.[33]

This was the first election when officials were simply there to see fair play, with no official candidate, although some showed a personal preference for Cavaignac. But few thought he had any chance outside the large towns.[34] Until shortly before the poll, when there was a perceptible landslide towards Louis-Napoleon, local factors and rivalries seemed to dominate preferences. In Morbihan, as in the other Breton departments, the clergy dominated elections, rejecting Louis-Napoleon as a demagogue. All that the subprefect of Lorient could say was that if the *parti reactionnaire* went for Cavaignac, which seemed the most likely, the 3000 democrats of the *Club de la rue de Vauban* would vote for Ledru-Rollin; if the clergy pushed for Louis-Napoleon, the democrats would move on to Cavaignac.[35] In other parts of Brittany some bishops supported Louis-Napoleon. All sides put their faith in democracy. On December 15th, after the voting was finished, but the result was as yet unknown, *L'Auxiliaire Breton* quoted *Le National* with approval that whoever had been chosen would be *'la volonté du pays'*.[36]

The election of Louis-Napoleon to the presidency on December 10th marked the total defeat of the February republicans. It was a public display of their disunity and lack of popular appeal. He secured 5,434,226 votes out of the 7,327,345 votes cast (74 per cent), giving him a majority of 3.5 million votes over all the other candidates. Cavaignac came second with 1,448,107. No one else was a serious contender. Ledru-Rollin got 370,119 votes, Raspail 36,920, Lamartine 17,910 and Changarnier, senior military commander in Paris, 4790.[37] There were notable differences between departments, but Louis-Napoleon was defeated only in a few remote areas such as Finistère.[38] (See Map 2, Appendix Three.)

In the Limousin, where radical republicans had done well in April, and where he was presented as a social reformer, Louis-Napoleon secured a higher than average poll in December. In France as a whole the new president was supported by 54.4 per cent of the whole electorate, in Creuse his vote was 69.2 per cent and in 735 rural districts the Bonapartist vote was almost unanimous. In some areas where the number of migrant workers was very high (thus the area was very poor) he gained 100 per cent of the votes. Louis-Napoleon was also successful in artisan Limoges itself, more so than in any other departmental capital, with 71.5 per cent, compared with 59.4 per cent in Lyon and 40.7 per cent in Nantes.[39]

Louis-Napoleon's gratitude to the *Réunion* was marked by the appointment of a government which suited them and included no republicans. Odilon Barrot became head of the government, Faucher, another former left-wing Orleanist, became Minister of the Interior and the legitimist Falloux took over Education. This was an important turning point; a determined effort was made to eliminate republicans from public office. By January 1850 Faucher had dismissed or shuffled to obscurity 95 prefects and 249 subprefects, the biggest purge of republicans being accomplished before the legislative elections of May 1849, by which time 49 of the most radical prefects had gone. In March–April alone 20 prefects and 103 subprefects were disposed of.[40] Faucher brought back experienced Orleanist officials, briefly unemployed during the more radical phase of the republic. Only moderate republicans were left among the prefects. But mayors, often the most radical officials, were untouchable, because they were now elected, not appointed.

The official republic may have been shunted towards the right, but the comparative freedom of the early part of the Second Republic allowed a variety of socialist experiments and developments. The 'right to work' may have been excluded from the republican constitution, but the old republican concept of 'fraternity' in its new socialist clothing continued to have a profound appeal. The idea that 'fraternity' could best be developed by establishing associations of like-minded people was fundamental to socialism. Associations of a vaguely 'socialist' imprint prospered, attracting large numbers of artisans, with some middle-class support. In total about 50,000 members joined 300 socialist associations from 120 trades during the life of the republic.[41] They were met by unremitting hostility from conservatives, but were also made very vulnerable through lack of capital. Blanc's ideas on social workshops were followed by a group of Parisian tailors. Mutual-aid societies and producer and consumer cooperatives continued to grow. A Society of United Corporations had been launched by members of the Luxembourg Commission including Vincard and Dupas to try to create a central organization to encourage the formation of cooperatives. In August 1849 the Union of Worker Associations was formed. The Union sought to provide mutual credit and an impressive total of 104 associations joined. Its organizers, including Jeanne Deroin, corresponded with Blanc and also with Proudhonists. A Saint-Simonian, Deroin linked the emancipation of workers and women's political rights.[42] She was imprisoned when the democ-soc committee in the Seine included her and George Sand in their candidate list for the May 1849 legislative elections. Sand rejected the candidacy totally and Deroin got 15 votes.[43] After the election she turned her full attention to the Association, which was under siege from the government. In May 1850 it was forced to close.[44]

Mutual-aid schemes continued to expand: from 262 in Paris in 1846, during the Second Republic there were 348 in the capital and 114 in Lyon. It was not unusual to find the local mayor at the head. Consumer cooperatives were also attempted in Lyon, Nantes and Reims. In Lyon one of the three cooperatives in existence in 1849 opened nine shops selling household goods at modest prices. The society consisted of shareholders and used notes redeemable for goods. In Reims the *Association Rémoise* tried to create a nationwide network of consumer cooperatives linked with mutual-aid insurance and planned to add a producer cooperative. It attracted widespread support in northern and north-eastern France. In Reims there were 5000 members who paid 50 centîmes to join and 15 centîmes each week. An equal number joined from the surrounding area. It was organized in 21 corporations each of which elected its own officials. As well as providing mutual-aid insurance, including finding work for unemployed members, the cooperative bought coal, oil and food for its consumer cooperative and set up a cooperative bakery. A weavers' and a tailors' cooperative were founded. The society also ran a newspaper, *L'Association rémoise*, with 1000 subscribers, which backed democ-soc candidates in the election of May 1849. A sister society in Sedan also started a cooperative restaurant.[45]

In Nantes *La Fraternelle Universelle*, a Proudhonian mutual aid society, was started in May 1848 by the irrepressible Guépin. A membership fee of 1.50 francs a month provided sickness benefit, pensions and 2 francs a day unemployment pay for its 700 members until the prefect forced it to close in November 1850. Like many such plans it was rooted in *compagnonnage* structures and only those holding a *livret* could join. Similar schemes operated in Lorient, Rennes, Brest, Angers, Tours, Lyon and Paris. Guépin also organized a cooperative bakery which forced private bakeries to reduce their prices so much that they banded together to get the prefect to close it down. A later project survived until a fire in 1862.[46] In April 1849 the municipal council of Caen started an association, presided over by the mayor, to help the unemployed and sick. Worker members, grouped by trade, paid 10 centîmes weekly, non-workers 50 centîmes minimum. Medical services were provided for members, who had to be local residents. The unemployed might be found jobs, or given money or necessary goods.[47] Practical democratic mutual-aid schemes like these were numerous. They were based on earlier ideas, sometimes dating back to *compagnonnage* roots, sometimes to the mutual-aid schemes of the early nineteenth century. There was also an input from the socialist thinkers and the existence of a republican regime was an encouragement in the early days of the Second Republic.

At the beginning of 1849 Proudhon began to set up a second bank, the *Banque du Peuple*. The day after Louis-Napoleon had taken his presidential oath, Proudhon remarked in *Le Peuple* that 'today democracy and socialism have no greater enemy than Bonaparte'.[48] In March 1849 he was sentenced to three years imprisonment and fined 10,000 francs. His bank project never matured. From his prison Proudhon wrote for *La Voix du Peuple*, until it was forced to close in May 1850. His *Idée générale de la Révolution* was published in 1851. It was an immediate success; the first edition of 3000 sold instantly and a second edition was produced.

L'Idée générale described Proudhon's ideal republic, which was very different from that of 1848. The book was dedicated to the 'bourgeoisie' and stressed the need for reconciliation between the classes, the abandonment of violent political revolution in favour of gradual social revolution. Capitalism should be dismantled, not by violent revolution, but gradual change; once this had been completed, government would become an irrelevance. The socialist society which would eventually emerge would consist of democratic, self-governing groups. The state would disappear. To Proudhon the absence of the strong state was the republic, which must have seemed quite contradictory to Jacobins.

> To be governed is to be kept in sight, inspected, spied upon, directed, law-driven, numbered, enrolled, indoctrinated, preached at, controlled, estimated, valued, censured, commanded by creatures who have neither the right, nor the wisdom, nor the virtue to do so.[49]

Proudhon's mutualist ideas had an impact on the various worker associations of the time, and his attack on the centralized state also had an appeal to those who resented the interference of Paris, but it is doubtful whether Proudhon's logical conclusion, that the republic meant the elimination of the state as such, had many sympathizers.

The very small number of workers and peasants who actively participated in national politics were mostly Proudhonists. These included Perdiguier, the son of a peasant who was also a cabinet-maker, who himself became first a cabinet-maker and then a teacher of technical drawing and was elected to the 1848 Assembly for Paris. Anthime Corbon, a woodcarver, who was elected as a deputy for Paris to the Constituent Assembly, was the son of an artisan in the Haute-Marne, who worked for a local weaver from the age of seven, moved to printing and in 1840 he was with *L'Atelier*. One might add Greppo and Joseph Benoît, both from rural origins, elected in 1848 to represent Lyon. All were from essentially rural or artisan backgrounds. None had any experience of factory industry, though some had knowledge of centres like Belleville.[50] Martin Nadaud, the mason from the Creuse most often cited because he actually published his memoirs,[51] was a republican socialist, a member of the *Droits de l'Homme* and the *Saisons* in the 1830s, an Icarian, then a democ-soc. He was elected to the Legislative Assembly and set up a successful masons' cooperative in Paris.[52]

The small number of workers and peasants actively involved in national politics, and the list is pretty well complete if Albert, Louis Blanc's artisan supporter on the Luxembourg Commission, is remembered, was the inevitable consequence of the newness of democratic institutions added to the enormous expense of political activity. The democratization of politics was in its infancy; the masses were enfranchised, but they and the politicians assumed that members of parliament would still be chosen from the wealthy elite. Nor was there at any time during the Second Republic, despite the June Days, the idea that a worker ought to be elected to represent worker interests. Indeed, after the June Days it was assumed that the state would not concern itself with problems such as employment, and artisans concentrated on the creation of their own mutual-aid societies. But their aims were specific and limited. Proudhon's broader, anarchist ideas that the centralized state should be eliminated by institutional change had little impact.

Most republicans were far too keen to gain control of the state to want to destroy it. The scale of Louis-Napoleon's unexpected success in 1848 and the realization that he had made an enormous appeal to peasants and the less well-off generally, awoke republicans to the need to work together for the legislative elections in May 1849. The radicals, often called the 'Mountain', the group around Ledru-Rollin which liked to remember Jacobin republican antecedents, began to work with supporters of Louis Blanc, Leroux, the Fourierists under Considérant, Lamennais and even Blanqui's men. The alliance was tentative, there were still big differences, but the link was the essential first step for republicans which had been absent a year earlier. They were agreed on broad issues; the urgent need to educate men for universal suffrage, social strategies, including the right to work and the creation of cooperatives, and the need to rediscover a primitive Christianity as a moral foundation for society. Their twin beliefs in a democratic and social republic earned them the rather inelegant name 'democ-soc'. Their enemies referred to them as reds, democrats, socialists or, simply, extremists.

The basis for their union was Ledru-Rollin's December election committee. With membership lists looking very like those of the secret societies of the July Monarchy, a mix of professional middle classes, shopkeepers and artisans, by January 1849 *La Solidarité Républicaine* had created 353 branches in 62 departments. Police reports fretted that they had 30,000 members.[53] In Metz there were four '*cercles*', all authorized, one of which was a 'democratic' offshoot of the post-February republican club, itself the heir of July Monarchy formations.[54] It should come as no surprise to find that one of the organizers was Emile Bouchotte, *négociant*, former mayor, who had been foremost in all the radical groups of the July Monarchy. There were 96 members, middle-class professionals and landowners along with 36 workers.[55] On January 10th Faucher formally banned *La Solidarité Républicaine*, claiming it was a 'state within a state',[56] but the ban had only limited success. No public political meetings were allowed but the democ-socs simply transformed themselves into electoral committees in preparation for the May elections.

The democ-socs published small pamphlets and pocket-sized almanacs sold, as always, by public hawkers. The *Almanach Démocratique et Social* of 1849 (50 centîmes a copy, 100,000 printed) contained brief articles by all the main socialists who a year earlier would have refused to share a platform.[57] Dedicated to Fourier, it included tiny pieces by Lamennais, Leroux, Raspail and Proudhon. Many of the pamphlets were written by Pyat, a journalist, Ledru-Rollin's commissioner in the Cher and a member of the Constituent Assembly. They demanded progressive income tax, the abolition of indirect taxes on necessities, widespread nationalization of primary industries and utilities, free and compulsory primary education and army reform to make it truly representative of the 'nation-in-arms'.

The democ-socs were becoming more aware, since the presidential election, of the importance of the peasant vote. Their demands for the end of indirect taxes and for state loans at modest rates were attractive to small-scale producers who were often in hock to money-lenders at crippling 15 per cent rates of interest. The democ-socs publicized their cause and candidates at banquets, a familiar device, except that theirs cost only 80 centîmes, for paté and wine – and speeches! At a banquet to celebrate the February Revolution in 1849 Pyat addressed 'Peasants of France' urging them to realize their strength, '24 million out of 35 million' and to cooperate with the workers '*Que le blouse grise des champs entend avec la blouse bleue des villes*' and vote for those candidates who would be real friends of the Republic.[58]

Conservative support for the new president was opportunistic and the conservative alliance very fragile. The presidential election encouraged conservatives to shrug off their *républicain du lendemain* disguises, but it did not make them Bonapartists. They were very divided, not just between legitimists, Orleanists and Bonapartists, but on regional and personal grounds too. The term 'Party of Order' began to be used to describe them, recalling the Orleanist slogan 'Liberty and Order', itself an indication that they dare not, for the moment, openly proclaim themselves enemies of the Republic. The Party of Order was an alliance of convenience. Their rationale was defensive, to oppose social reform, protect private property and to uphold an elitist concept of the state, which would deny the right to strike, to form worker associations and so on.

The obstacles to selecting agreed conservative candidates for the Assembly were substantial. Elections were seldom a simple contest between the Party of Order and the Mountain. The correspondence between the Minister of the Interior, Léon Faucher and his prefects, who had the job of trying to persuade local *notables* to settle on a single candidate, is very revealing. Faucher recognized the danger of appearing to create a list of 'official' candidates and urged his officials to try to find a middle way. His most used comment was 'we do not want a White mountain any more than a Red mountain'.[59] Between the most conservative 'whites' and the 'reds' were 'blues'; it all made for a colourful election.

The alliance of the *notables* won, although the unity and regional strength of the democ-socs alarmed them. Roughly 450 of the 715 deputies were conservatives, 75 were moderate republicans and about 200 were democ-socs. There were more republicans than a year earlier but the proportions of moderates and radicals were reversed. The democ-socs secured 2.36 million votes compared with 3.5 million for the conservative coalition.[60] (See Map 3, Appendix Three.) They won absolute majorities in 16 departments and over 40 per cent of the vote and 154 out of 196 seats in the Centre, the Lyon area and Alsace. They also did well in the Mediterranean departments. The departments most favourable to them included the Basses-Alpes, Var, Hérault, Aude, Pyrénées-Orientales, Ariège, Gers, Lot-et-Garonne, Dordogne, Corrèze, Haut-Vienne, Cher, Vienne, Nièvre, Allier, Ain, Jura, Saône-et-Loire plus the largest industrial towns and their surrounding area. All republicans, moderate and democ-soc did poorly in western and northwestern, eastern, north and northeastern France, with the exception of the departments of the Nord, Bas-Rhin and Seine-Inférieure. Ledru-Rollin was victorious in five departments, including Paris where he came second to Lucien Murat, Louis-Napoleon's cousin. His personal vote this time totalled 2 million. The turnout was much lower than a year earlier and over 3.25 million out of almost 10 million voters failed to vote.

The results of the election pleased no single group. The government was disappointed with its failure to dominate. Not infrequently prefects would explain that the large proportion of mayors '*au parti extrême*' gave them little hope of success.[61] In April 1848 many voters must have accepted at face value assurances given by candidates that they were

'republican'. By May 1849 it was much more obvious what conservatives wanted to preserve. The democ-socs themselves had learned fast
that disunity was disastrous. Their successes in May 1849 were due to
the absence of open conflict between them.

Democ-socs were deeply disillusioned by this further encounter with
democracy. In a speech to the Legislative Assembly on 12 June 1849,
Ledru-Rollin declared: '*Je crois au suffrage universel, c'est ma foi; mais je
crois aussi qu'il y a quelque chose de supérieur au suffrage universel qui pourrait se
tromper . . . C'est le droit eternel et la justice, c'est je ne sais quoi, qui est la
conscience humaine.*' If this were violated, a man would, he claimed, have
the right to rebel, even against a government based on universal
suffrage.[62] During acrimonious exchanges that day the democ-socs
tried to impeach the government for breach of the constitution, whose
preamble promised support for other nations. A French expedition to
the Papal States in the spring, supposedly to head off an Austrian
defence of the Pope, seemed likely to achieve the opposite result.

The next day 120 deputies signed a petition against government
foreign policy and Ledru-Rollin, with some reluctance, led a critical,
but unarmed demonstration of about 8000. Seven were killed in violent
repression by the troops. A state of siege was declared once more in the
capital and in the surrounding 11 departments. There were many
arrests, including 30 of the radical-socialist deputies. Ledru-Rollin
escaped along with Considérant and Pyat, and fled to England. He was
criticized then and later for his failure to stand his ground. Did he want
to? One of his unforgettable comments dates from that occasion: 'I am
their leader; I must follow them.' There was conflict in a number of
provincial centres including Strasbourg, Valence, Grenoble, Toulouse
and Perpignan. Fighting between the Lyon workers and the soldiery
turned into a full-scale battle on June 15th. More than 50 were killed
and 800 arrested.[63] A state of siege was declared in the Rhône and
neighbouring departments. Large numbers of people were arrested
throughout the country, in Bordeaux, the Haut-Rhin, the Aube, the
Haute-Saône and elsewhere.

On 24 June 1849 all political clubs, even unofficial *cercles* and
chambrées, were forced to close or go underground. By mid-June only one
of the two republican clubs in Lorient, Morbihan, was still extant and
that was a mere shadow of its former self. Its 150 members were mostly
workers at the port. Their meetings consisted of reading aloud from the
newspapers and some talks, which the subprefect thought pretty
tame.[64] In Metz the *club démocratique* simply moved its meeting place
from time to time, but its membership and leadership were relatively

unchanged in April 1851.[65] The republican club in Caen was the *Société philanthropique*, its newspaper the *Haro*. The prefect forced the society, which had 183 members, to close in December 1850. It instantly reopened as a mutual-aid society, with a weekly subscription of 25 *centimes*, but no regular meeting-place. It made no attempt at concealment; membership lists were published and it was well supported throughout the area.[66] The leading figure was Pont, editor of the *Haro*. Its members were mostly workers from the suburbs, supported by a number of middle-class republicans, including cloth merchants and some local landowners, referred to by the workers as 'aristocrats of democracy'.[67]

Cooperative associations of all kinds were forced to disband. Censorship of the press was stiffened in both 1849 and 1850. Public hawkers were prevented from selling radical literature; trees of liberty were chopped down, all reminiscent of the early 1830s. Some republican mayors and schoolteachers were dismissed. Prefects were encouraged to investigate all reports of democ-soc attitudes with a zeal which became a veritable witch-hunt in areas where the republicans retained support and organization. In some cases National Guard battalions were disbanded.

There was the usual purge of officials. After the 1849 election 48 mayors or assistant mayors were dismissed. In 1850 another 265 were sacked. Between April 1849 and February 1851, 276 municipal councils were forcibly dissolved. In addition in 1850 1200 'dangerous' primary school teachers were fired.[68] To underline the return to conservatism, and protect against the influence of radical schoolteachers, the Falloux Law of March 1850 permitted the expansion of church run schools. But the increasing conservatism of the regime was not entirely to the taste of the Party of Order, who found that the president was far less complaisant than they had hoped. In October 1849 the Barrot ministry was replaced by the first government chosen by Louis-Napoleon, of which he was effectively the head and including his own men such as Rouher and Fould.

Repressive action by the government after June 1849 sharpened the sense of confrontation and hostility. Radical societies and publications were forced underground wherever possible, but continued to thrive in favourable areas such as Paris, Lyon, Marseille, the Massif Central and the south where working men knew of radical ideas either because they worked as migrant labour in Paris or Lyon, as was the case of the Massif Central, or because they were part of a culture of small-scale farmers and artisans producing for a market in a social situation where they met together regularly to discuss a variety of issues, including politics. Above all radical ideas had an impact where the Church did not.

Within 18 months of the declaration of the Second Republic many of the outstanding republican leaders had been forced into exile. Abroad they were even more at odds with each other. In 1850 the former socialists, Blanc, Leroux and Cabet, tried to cooperate to relaunch Cabet's *Populaire*. Blanc, still in exile in London, eventually withdrew, Leroux tried to keep his own *Revue Sociale* afloat and Cabet was left alone to battle with police persecution of the *Populaire*. Those in exile were not only cut off from the mainstream of thinking in Paris, but were very poor. Blanc had great difficulty publishing his prolific writing, even in Belgium. Together with a group of other exiles he set up a Fraternal Society of Democrats and Socialists, but the 900 impecunious exiles soon quarrelled. In exile and adversity radicals like Ledru-Rollin and socialists like Blanc redoubled their internecine rivalries, each convinced that the other had ruined the Republic.

Schemes for a perfect democracy proliferated in isolation. In 1851 Ledru-Rollin and Charles Delescluze set up a *Voix du Proscrit* which recommended that all legislation should be discussed by democratically elected delegates and voted by the whole nation meeting in small local councils, a proposal reminiscent of Icarie. Blanc was very hostile and in *Plus des Girondins* (1851) demanded that they should work simply for government based on popular suffrage. He was at odds with many of the radicals, who were intent on minimum government, whereas Blanc continued to suggest public ownership.[69] Blanc went some way towards meeting Ledru-Rollin, proposing in *La République une et indivisible* (1851), annual elections and accepting the idea of a referendum for the constitution itself and any amendments. None of the exiles had any impact on the Republic or subsequent empire.

However, republicans at home could not be ignored. The success of the conservative backlash was patchy. There were limits on the information against individuals which could be gathered by a prefect who was habitually a stranger in his department. With only sketchy police coverage, he was dependent on the gendarmerie, whose strength was no more than 18,000 before 1852.[70] To the horror of conservatives, 21 democ-socs were chosen in by-elections in March 1850, including the novelist Eugène Sue. The conservatives now resorted to the electoral tactics of the Bourbon Restoration. A commission of 17 conservatives, of whom Thiers was a dominant figure, sought to exclude the 'dangerous' classes; as Thiers put it 'real Republicans fear the mob, the vile mob (*la vile multitude*) that has . . . delivered over to every tyrant the liberty of every Republic'.[71] In May 1850 universal suffrage, the central pillar of republican ideology under the Orleanists and the basic unifying force of the new republic, was undermined by a three-year instead of a six-month residence requirement for all voters. One-third (3 million) of the electorate, it was assumed the most radical because mobile through poverty, was thus disenfranchised, leaving an electoral register of 6,800,000 and the Republic in tatters. This had a particularly marked impact on larger towns, which attracted migrant labourers. The electorate of Rennes was cut from 9500 to 3500, that of Besançon cut from 8000 to 3000 and two-thirds of the voters in the Nord were disenfranchised.[72] The Republic had been identified with democracy, both as an ideal and in frequent elections since April 1848. The masses had learned to associate their right to vote with a republic. There were petitions against the new law, signed by 23,000 in the Gard alone.[73] Ironically, the revision committee also toyed with making voting compulsory; the abstention rate had risen from 16 per cent in April 1848 to as high as 50 per cent. Prefects were consulted and none felt that the government would gain from such a change.

Conservatives tried to organize their own propaganda machine against an opposition which they identified as socialist (it would have been indelicate to say republican since France was still a republic). In July 1849 an *Association pour la propagande anti-socialiste et pour l'amélioration du sort des populations laborieuses* was announced in Paris. Its committee consisted of a range of deputies including Berryer and de Broglie (vice-presidents), Molé (president), Montalembert and Thiers. The prefects acted as recruiting agents. It tried to create an antidote to socialism. The Moselle group gave 1000 francs to help the children of 'honest and hardworking' workers. A year later there were groups in Pas-de-Calais, Metz, Charente-Inférieure, Rennes, Seine-et-Oise (2 groups), Seine-et-Marne, Seine, Saône-et-Loire, Grenoble, Basses-Alpes, Basses-Pyrennes and the Jura. In Finistère a weekly paper, *Le Dimanche*, subscription 6.50 francs a year, was aimed at workers and small farmers to inform them about the progress of the society and its charitable works, 'and specially dedicated to the defence of religion, the family and property'. Anti-socialist songs were circulated and there were plans for a popular almanac.[74]

Conservatives were so determined to eliminate radical resistance that the re-election of Louis-Napoleon, specifically forbidden in the constitution, was viewed as the most desirable option. In the spring of 1850, 52 of the departmental general councils, urged on by their prefects, voted in favour of constitutional revision. In 1851 the number rose to 79. In June 1851 the prefects were ordered to organize revision petitions. They were to establish a 'representative' committee of five in the *chef-lieu* of each canton, including on each a worker, a small and big landowner, someone involved in commerce and other business to launch the petition.[75] One secured over 1 million signatures. The campaign for revision concluded with a parliamentary vote in July 1851 in which the proposal to allow Louis-Napoleon to stand for a second term gained a vote of 446:278, a very clear majority, but insufficient for constitutional revision.

Between December 1848, when Louis-Napoleon was elected president and December 1851 when he seized permanent power through a coup d'état, conservative elements conspired, legislated and administered to smother the democratic republic. Louis-Napoleon was given the opportunity to present himself as the defender of democracy. During the autumn of 1851 he proposed the restoration of universal suffrage, but this was rejected by the Assembly. Conservatives were hoodwinked by tales of a 'red' rebellion planned for November 30th. The rebels were expecting British help. Prefects were urged to arrest anyone who seemed dangerous and to alert the local gendarmerie and forest guards. What effect such rallying cries evoked is hard to judge; a similar one had been sent out in April and although the bugle was sounded down the line, nothing untoward was noted,[76] unsurprisingly when it was in fact Louis-Napoleon who was planning action.

Louis-Napoleon's coup d'état was executed as a military exercise, two of the chief organizers, together with Morny, Interior Minister from the morning of the coup, being Maupas, Police Minister, and Saint-Arnaud, War Minister. The Second Republic really ended on 2 December 1851, the anniversary of the battle of Austerlitz, although its formal demise was delayed for a year. The operation involved 30,000 troops, and 220 deputies were arrested (where were the other 38 who had voted against revision?), including Barrot, de Tocqueville and Falloux. The president proclaimed that he was acting in defence of the Republic and that anyway there had been a large majority in favour of him standing for re-election. Any argument that such a constitutional 'revision' was universally popular should have been dispelled by the unprecedented scale of resistance in many parts of France and by the number of arrests and condemnations.

The ensuing four months witnessed equally unprecedented political repression. On December 3rd barricades went up in traditional centres of artisan radicalism in Paris, such as the area around the *hôtel de ville*,

St Martin, rue Rambuteau, rue Transnonain, but no more than 1200 turned out. The ferocity of the repression can be gauged by the fact that one-third of the protesters were killed on the spot. The government had laid the ground for the coup with great care, learning lessons from both 1830 and 1848. In areas where resistance might be expected mobile columns of troops were drafted in, making full use of the telegraph system and the new rail network. The response to the coup in the provinces was very varied. In northern France, although there were republican groups, there was little popular protest. In Calvados the news of the coup had provoked 'minor acts of vengeance' and for a few days in December 1851 subprefects were ordered to send daily reports, but they had so little to say that the order was cancelled. Caen had an active republican club and a vigorous mutual-aid society. On the eve of the coup delegates from the club were about to leave for a conference in Paris. Crowds gathered to complain about the coup, the republicans protested to the mayor, but the National Guard patrolled the streets, with extra troops in reserve. There was no trouble.[77]

Southern France reacted spontaneously with far more force. Some departments were already in a state of siege, including the Drôme, Ardèche, Cher and Nièvre. Tens of thousands in two dozen departments in the centre and south rose against the coup, including seven in the south-east, two in the south-west and three in the centre. Rebellion began in the small towns, but included many rural communes. Revolutionary communes were declared in 100 centres, which went beyond past experience, even that of 1830 when one commentator had talked of France dissolving into thousands of little republics.[78] The *chef-lieux* of one department and twelve *arrondissments* were seized by rebel armies of over 1000 in thirteen cases. The government squashed these uncoordinated, civic rebellions with mobile columns, graphically recalled by Zola in *La Fortune des Rougon*. A state of siege was declared immediately in the 32 rebel departments including (grouped by region) Seine, Seine-et-Oise, Oise, Seine-Inférieure, Eure, Eure-et-Loir, Loire-et-Cher and Loiret; in the Centre Aube, Yonne, Nièvre, Cher, Allier, Loire, Saône-et-Loire and Aveyron; in the east Bas-Rhin and further south Jura, Ain, Rhône, Basses-Alpes, Isère, Drôme and Ardèche; in the Midi Vaucluse, Var, Gard, Hérault, Gers, Lot-et-Garonne, Lot and Gironde.[79] (See Map 4, Appendix Three.)

What were the main concerns of the rebels? Government supporters stressed immediate economic issues. Of those arrested 44 per cent worked in agriculture, 48 per cent in various crafts and commerce;[80] 80 per cent of the rebel communes were in rural areas where peasants were producing goods for a market economy which were extremely sensitive to price fluctuations in times of crisis. Although the industrial sector had recovered from the mid-40s depression by 1851, agricultural prices had remained low and peasant producers, unable to pay their debts to urban moneylenders, were sometimes threatened by expropriation. However, an exclusively economic explanation of their rebellion is inadequate. Peasants in wheat-producing areas who were suffering from low prices rose in revolt; wine-producers in similar circumstances did not, although they had been volatile in the 1830s. Conversely some prosperous areas rebelled.

Political factors were far more important. Five members of parliament were sentenced to deportation, 65 were expelled as 'leaders of socialism' and eighteen others were made temporary exiles because of their opposition. The rebels declared themselves defenders of the Republic; article 68 of the constitution declared the president guilty of high treason if he dissolved the National Assembly. The rebels claimed that they were acting in the name of the 'general will' which, given the coup, was the only remaining legal centre of authority. Violence was rare in their takeover of town halls. The rebel departments were those where the democ-socs had been most active in the 1849 elections, had gone underground in the time-honoured tradition of secret societies and had suffered more than average harassment by the authorities. That is not to say that secret democratic societies only existed in rebel Provence or Languedoc. Democratic clubs were common in about 700 communes in December 1850, 500 in the south-east and 50–100 in the south-west, with 90 in the Var alone. Peasants were numerous, 'We wouldn't have any forest guard, any fishing guard, any priest. We would lower taxes, we would divide the commons', was the motivation of one peasant in southern Ardèche.[81]

There were other reasons. The Protestants of the Gard and elsewhere, traditional supporters of the Revolution in earlier bloody conflicts in the 1790s and in 1815–16, were active in the societies. They were appalled by the prospect of the vengeance the legitimist–Bonapartist alliance would exact after the coup.[82] Above all, the repeated declarations of communal autonomy were protests against the constant interference of Paris in local affairs. It was no coincidence that the departments which rose were some of the ones with a pronounced tradition of communal autonomy. The centralizing march of the bureaucratic state, which had become increasingly interfering since December 1848, was not to their taste.

An extended round-up of known republicans persisted long after the original coup. On January 18th Morny, shortly before his replacement by Persigny, sent a 'very confidential' instruction to all his prefects demanding information on socialists and those 'totally opposed to the government or likely to cause trouble'. Special arrangements were made for the most hostile departments where a state of siege had already been declared. Mobile columns arrested suspects and terrified local communities. Government prosecutors had to send regular reports to the Minister of Justice. At the beginning of February 1852 the Minister of War was empowered to create special commissions (*commissions mixtes*) in each department to deal with opponents. The commissions consisted of the prefect, government prosecutor and military commander. They were able to impose summary punishment including transportation to Cayenne or Algeria. Those worthy of mere exile were to be sent with all speed to Belgium or England. In all 27,000 were arrested, 9000 of whom were deported to Algeria. Republicans later suggested that government statistics deliberately underestimated those punished and Jules Simon estimated that a realistic figure might be as high as 100,000.[83]

The response to demands for such unprecedented legal terrorism was very varied. In some places a mere handful of known socialists were rounded up. Often republicans had already been incarcerated. In Audelys, Eure, the subprefect ordered five arrests on 4 January 1852 including a tailor, a carpenter, a gardener and a public hawker, who were accused of being members of a secret society, distributing socialist literature and indulging in seditious conversations.[84] Some local officials, for a variety of reasons, were reluctant to arrest anyone. The prefect in Evreux received a barrage of 'very confidential' demands, all of which he seems to have ignored. The Calvados prefect refused to arrest anyone, on the grounds that it would be counter-productive.[85] On March 29th the *commissions mixtes*, which had not been welcomed by the jealous officials who had to serve on them, were disbanded.

Worker self-help associations such as the *Travailleurs-Unis* at Lyon were closed. Only 15 of 299 such organizations in existence on December 2nd survived.[86] The usual arboreal persecution was ordered. A number of young sapling trees of liberty, planted with ceremony after February 1848, were felled. Their timber was to be given to the needy; republican memorials and inscriptions were to go. Lists were made of all communes to prove that these humourless instructions had been followed. One zealous subprefect noticed that a number of trees dating back to 1793 still survived, but was told that these should only be touched if local mayors agreed that they could be removed without fuss, which presumably after nearly 60 years of vigorous growth would have been tricky.[87] Street names were checked. In Caen the Place Royale had been transformed into Place de la Révolution de 1848 and had to be renamed, but Caen scored some points; it already had a rue Napoleon.[88]

At the time of the coup Louis-Napoleon had a mixed, mainly conservative, but not a Bonapartist administration. Only 9 of the 86 prefects were Bonapartists and perhaps an additional 16 had been won over to him; 52 had begun as Orleanist officials, 14 in the early stages of the Second Republic. On the news of the coup 8 resigned, including the prefect of Finistère who put up posters condemning the coup and orchestrated an official protest by the general council of the department. Six prefects were dismissed. A number of influential magistrates made their protest by giving nominal sentences to republicans arrested after the coup. Throughout all branches of the centralized administration sympathizers were promoted and republicans, from doctors to café-owners, were deprived of their livelihood.[89]

Louis-Napoleon insisted that he had acted in the name of democracy, which he restored at a stroke. He reintroduced the plebiscitary system of his great-uncle, claiming that it was the pinnacle of democratic consultation. The military coup was immediately followed by a plebiscite on 20 December 1851, in which Louis-Napoleon secured 7.5 million votes in support of his decision to make himself president for life. Mayors were ordered to distribute printed affirmative ballot papers to all voters; dissidents, of whom there were 650,000, had to write their own in full view of the civic authorities and their fellow citizens. This device continued throughout the Empire, refined so that voting cards printed 'yes' were delivered to the homes of each voter, with an additional pile in the hall where voting took place.[90]

The republican constitution was revised by a commission in which Rouher had a leading voice. Article 1 asserted: 'The Constitution recognizes, confirms and guarantees the great principles proclaimed in 1789, which are the basis of the public law of the French people'.[91] The Revolution was ostensibly honoured, the Republic ignored and Louis-Napoleon's great-uncle imitated. In a proclamation on 14 January 1852 introducing the 'revised' constitution, Louis-Napoleon remarked that since France had been governed throughout the century by imperial institutions which covered everything except the political framework, there was a good case for devising matching political institutions. Legislative power was to be shared by an elected assembly, a new nominated Senate and Louis-Napoleon, who was to be president for ten years. The president and assembly were once more to be elected by universal suffrage, the president was also permitted to appeal directly to the nation in plebiscites, but press censorship was reinforced. The council of state was to propose all legislation, as in the days of the Empire. The legislative assembly was merely to discuss and vote laws and taxes; it could not even question ministers. The president could summon, adjourn and dissolve the Assembly at will. An upper chamber or Senate was created whose members were to be appointed for life by the president and would habitually include marshals, cardinals, admirals and so on. Centralization, which had been progressively relaxed between the fall of Napoleon I and December 1848, was reinforced. Mayors and local councils were again to be appointed by the government. Following the decree on constitutional revision an election was held in February 1852 for a new legislative assembly. Unsurprisingly, given that they were specifically banned from the polls, only three republicans were elected.

The biggest single issue in the failure of the republican 'apprentice-ship' of 1848–52 was not the absence of republicans, but discord among them, particularly over the issue of social reform. Radicals and moderates were irreconcilable, moderates and *républicains du lendemain* failed to find any common ground. Instead existing forces more attune to creating, shaping and echoing mass opinion took over; the Church, then Bonapartism manipulated by Louis-Napoleon. Louis-Napoleon, unlike the republicans, lost no time in capturing and organizing the new instruments of the modern centralized state which were the gifts of the Industrial Revolution, the telegraph and the railway system. These, combined with loyal troops and police, were the tools Charles X and Louis-Philippe had lacked. Republicans, who had committed them-selves to universal suffrage as the central prop of a republic, became fatalistic, as in the debate on the constitution, or sceptical of mass voting, like Dr Guépin of Nantes, who began to wish that the new republic had imposed a voting qualification, not of wealth, or residence, but education.

Louis-Napoleon succeeded, both in his initial election as president and in his subsequent coup, because the conservative elites never wanted a democratic republic, but could not agree on an alternative to him. They controlled France during the remaining years of the Republic and the subsequent Empire in harness with a Bonapartist regime which they tolerated rather than welcomed. The coup of December 1851, which Louis-Napoleon hoped would liberate him from the *notables*, put him further into their hands. The resistance to the coup enabled the president to claim that he had saved France from the 'reds' and civil war, but the consequent repression ensured that republicans would be Louis-Napoleon's intransigent enemies, leaving him more exposed to the demands of the *notables* than before.

10 From the Silent Years to Bloody Week: Republicans 1852–1871

On 7 November 1852 an empire was formally and officially re-established. At one level the Second Empire marked the virtual disappearance of republicanism, particularly in the 'silent years'[1] of strict government censorship and rigid republican abstention in the 1850s and early 1860s. Many of the senior figures, including Ledru-Rollin and Blanc, were in exile and even in 1870 there were only 30 republicans in the Legislative Assembly. In May 1870 a leading young republican, Gambetta, admitted the plebiscite on liberal reform confirmed the continuing popularity of Louis-Napoleon. Yet the declaration of a republic in September 1870 aroused no opposition, except from radical republicans. In what ways did the aspirations of republicans change during the Empire? There were marked similarities between the parliamentary system of the Empire in 1870 and the republic created after its fall. This chapter will also ask to what extent the Empire itself was in process of being transformed into a republic by 1870, and if so, in response to what pressures.

The Empire was an uneasy compromise between the *notables* and Louis-Napoleon. Louis-Napoleon's willingness to combat radical republicanism and the absence of an agreed alternative sustained their tolerance of his regime. On the other hand Louis-Napoleon created an empire which from the outset he claimed would be authoritarian only for a limited period. Uniquely among French rulers in the nineteenth century, he not only promised to liberalize, but actually succeeded in effecting a major political transformation in the 1860s. Other regimes became increasingly conservative, the Second Empire more parliamentary and open. Former Orleanists welcomed the growing emphasis on the Assembly. Gradually more moderate republicans also began to tolerate the liberal empire. The reformed Empire was destroyed by military defeat, not by political opposition or revolution.

The Bonapartist legacy had been vital for Louis-Napoleon's initial presidential electoral victory, but the Empire was never to become Bonapartist. Although he modelled himself on how he though his great-uncle would have behaved if the pressure of war had not intervened, Louis-Napoleon did not welcome the creation of a Bonapartist party, but circumspectly, since many Bonapartists did not warm to him, always presented himself as the representative of the 'nation' and not a narrow group. The Legislative Body, consisting of a mere 261 in 1852, rising to a modest 292 by 1869, contained a large number of 'official' candidates, until the concept was abandoned in 1869. But 'official' did not imply 'imposed', simply prefectoral affirmation of the choice of local *notables*. Louis-Napoleon had to coexist with a critical Legislative Body of wealthy (52 per cent had an annual income of 30,000 francs or more) old Orleanists who had been Guizot's *gauche dynastique* opponents, over a third of whom were former officials or army officers. Only about a third of them had long-standing Bonapartist sympathies, and these were for Napoleon, not his great-nephew. Most of these Bonapartists had held official posts, or had been deputies under Louis-Philippe.[2] They were delighted to have escaped a 'red' republic, consistently put themselves forward for re-election to the Assembly, but they were not docile. The emperor's liberal reforms were in part a response to demands made by the Legislative Body itself. Louis-Napoleon survived because he was more desirable to the wealthy *notables* than the republic they feared would have to be his replacement. His skill rested on his ability to engage the tolerance of the wealthy without antagonizing the less rich beyond endurance, a task made easier by a period of the most rapid economic growth in the century.

Nor was the administrative personnel of the Empire Bonapartist. There was no dramatic and thorough administrative 'revolution' in 1852. In part this was because there had been a gradual replacement of republicans since the summer of 1848. But the reality was that the centralized administrative machine was a mirror-image of the Legislative Body. In 1852 the prefect of the Haute-Garonne who was responsible for 983 subordinates, 629 of whom were legitimists, 241 Orleanists with 50 or so republicans and about the same number of Bonapartists, requested the replacement of five opponents among his officials. He secured only three of the changes he requested.[3] The same pattern of almost apolitical compromise can be seen in the departmental general councils. In 1870 prefects calculated that whereas only

16 per cent of the members were opponents of the Empire, a mere 24 per cent were *ralliés*, who had become active supporters of the regime, while the vast majority were quite indifferent to politics.[4]

Democracy, embraced with some hesitation by the republicans since the 1830s, was hijacked and made an integral part of the regime of their enemy, the Empire, by two strategies, one spurious, one more genuine. Napoleon I's idea of plebiscites was revived. Only the emperor could call a plebiscite and he always secured large majorities. Within a fortnight the declaration of an empire was confirmed by a plebiscite in which 7.75 million voted yes and only 253,000 no, with 2 million abstentions, mostly in the Rhône valley and the west. Even in 1870, when familiarity if nothing else might have tarnished the image, there was an overwhelming affirmative vote. To reinforce the plebiscites, Louis-Napoleon made regular visits to the different regions, delivering anodyne, patriotic and encouraging homilies. These speeches were immediately turned into huge posters and reproduced ad infinitum; 1200 copies of the speech he made at Bordeaux in October 1852 were ordered by the prefect in Rouen (14 of them are still in the departmental archives).[5] But plebiscites were detested with good reason by the republicans among others, as a denial of democracy. They offered no choice, no alternative, but merely an opportunity to affirm the decisions of the emperor. A more convincing litmus test of democratic intent was the restoration of full universal suffrage, although major centres of opposition such as Paris and Lyon lost their elected local councils. Official candidatures, press censorship and restrictions on associations muzzled opposition.

The repression of 1851–2 alarmed republicans, most of whose leaders were forced into exile, if they were not already in prison. Gradually they began to regroup, in traditional formations. Secret societies were important to them, but they were obliged to be very cautious. The most successful were the apparently casual gatherings in cafés and informal *chambrées* and welfare-orientated mutual-aid societies. In Bas-Languedoc alone the numbers of these three types of groupings grew to 1457 in 1858, an increase of 47 in one year.[6] Opposition societies tended to be turned into male voice choirs to escape the law. Gatherings to mark the funerals of leading republicans were tolerated, with military escorts. In 1853 there were three such occasions, for Marrast, François Arago and, with only 24 hours' notice, 25,000 workers followed the cortège of Madame Raspail. A year later police and troops prevented workers attending Lamennais' funeral. Press censorship was also intensified, leaving only the circumspect Havin's

Siècle, the *Charivari* and, from 1854, the cautious *Revue de Paris*, run by Ulbach.[7]

Republicans never made an impressive showing in legislative elections during the Empire. In the 1852 elections, held immediately after the repression and before the actual declaration of an empire, republicans were not allowed to stand as candidates. They responded by continuing their strategy of abstention embarked on during the Second Republic itself to signal their disapproval of government policy. Just over 5 million of the 6,200,000 who turned out voted for government candidates, an impressive total until abstentions are considered. There were nearly 10 million registered voters, thus only 53 per cent of the whole electorate actually voted for the official candidates.[8] In 26 departments government candidates were elected by a minority of the electorate. The abstention rate was highest in towns and concealed many resentful republicans, as well as some Orleanist critics. In Strasbourg, Sedan, Lisieux, Amiens, Bourg (Ain), La Rochelle and Aix two-thirds refused to vote. There were high abstention rates in Vierzon, Cher (81 per cent), St Etienne (75 per cent), Bordeaux (70 per cent) and Marseille (54 per cent). A poll of 50 per cent was not uncommon.[9]

Abstention was chiefly a republican strategy; the 250 opposition candidates were mostly legitimist. Opposition was geographically concentrated. In 40 per cent of the constituencies there was no real contest; in 40 per cent there was some opposition, but the real fight centred on the remaining constituencies, located in the west, north and south-east. Here votes for opponents totalled 471,000, for the government 835,000.[10] The Church was an unreliable ally of the regime. The clergy in the Loire-Inférieure (Brittany) took voting slips for their own candidate printed 'in the name of religion and Our Lord' to the homes of their parishioners and used the confessional as an opportunity to reinforce their opposition to the Bonapartist candidate.[11] On the other hand only six opponents were actually elected, of whom three were republicans, the rest legitimists. Carnot and Cavaignac, elected for Paris, and Hénon for Lyon, wrote from exile refusing the oath to the regime, and were excluded.[12]

Meanwhile the leading figures in the Second Republic were in exile. Ledru-Rollin remained in Britain after his escape from Paris in June 1849, writing critical assessments of the emperor and meeting other exiles from time to time. He never became reconciled to the Empire and condemned those republicans who did, even Ollivier, who formally amnestied him in 1870. The socialists were the most persistent exiles.

Proudhon emerged from a three-year jail sentence in 1852 to continue his prolific criticism. In 1858, after a new sentence had been imposed, he fled to Belgium, where he remained until 1862. The day after Louis-Napoleon's election as president Cabet set sail for America. Icarianism had collapsed in France and he hoped to rescue the American venture. However, in 1850 he was forced to return to answer charges of mismanagement of the Icarian movement. During 1851 he joined Leroux and Blanc to found *La République populaire et sociale*, but the coup d'état forced it to close. Opposed to the coup, he found little consolation in the Icarian producer-cooperatives in Lyon and elsewhere in France.[13] He returned to America, quarrelled with the well-established colony at Nauvoo, where his authoritarian attitudes were resented, and in 1855 moved to another experiment in St Louis, where he died shortly afterwards. Nauvoo survived until the end of the century. Leroux and Blanc founded a socialist community on Jersey in the 1860s; Considérant embarked on a similar project in America. Life in exile was hard for Leroux who survived in part on donations from other socialists. Blanc remained in Britain for the entire Second Empire and had no political links with France. He urged republicans to refuse all contact with the Empire. He became British correspondent for the *Temps*. In 1869 he refused the request of democrats in St Etienne to stand as their candidate in the legislative elections, although he supported the candidature of Henri Rochefort against his old enemy Jules Favre. Radicals in the Seine tried to persuade Blanc, Barbès and Ledru-Rollin to enter the lists on their behalf in the same election, but to no avail.

Totally intransigent exiles like Ledru-Rollin, Blanc and the writers Quinet and Victor Hugo were the exceptions. Between 1854 and 1856 republicans condemned and exiled after the coup were released and formed the basis for a new movement. In the election of 1857 superficially little had changed. Nearly 86 per cent of those who voted favoured official candidates (a slight increase), while the abstention rate remained high at 35.5 per cent, but the abstainers were not the same groups as five years earlier. Many republicans had come to regard abstention, which they had pursued in local as well as legislative elections, as valueless. From London Ledru-Rollin and Blanc urged them to take part in the campaign, although Blanc continued to claim that taking an oath to the regime would be 'suicide' for republicans. On the other hand Havin, editor of *Le Siècle*, suggested that republicans could take the oath.

An electoral committee was formed, headed in turn by Buchez, Carnot and Garnier-Pagès and including Cavaignac, Jules Simon,

Bethmont, Arnaud, Charton, Degousée, Corbon, Sain, Reynaud, Vacherot and Hérold.[14] Despite a lack of finance and the divisions between Havin and the committee, republicans fielded about 100 candidates who attracted between them half a million votes. Five were elected, along with eight Independents. All of the republicans were elected in Paris where they took half of the seats in the central districts. In the provinces their candidates had been the local and national leaders in 1848. Cavaignac was backed by twelve constituencies, Carnot by five and some voted for Garnier-Pagès, Lamartine and Raspail. Where there was no obvious local candidate, republicans abstained, sometimes with dramatic results. In the industrial town of Decazeville only 640 out of 3009 voters went to the polls.[15] Carnot and Goudchaux refused to take the oath and Cavaignac died before the session opened. Some months later by-elections for these three added Picard and Jules Favre, the defender of Orsini, the would-be assassin of the emperor. Ollivier, Darimon, Jules Favre, Picard and Hénon (for Lyon) entered parliament. In contrast, very few legitimist and Orleanist opponents saw any point in contesting the elections and opposition votes consequently slumped in the west.

A year later French republicans were blamed for the attempt by the Italian, Orsini, to assassinate the emperor and a law of general security was passed, allowing the incarceration of those arrested merely on suspicion of subversive intent. They could be held and disposed of without trial, heavier penalties were inflicted and greater use was made of deportation. Prefects were encouraged to arrest up to 20 suspicious characters and in total nearly 400 were jailed in the provinces, 100 in the capital. A cross-section of republicans, or simply those regarded as trouble-makers, were rounded-up. In Paris the victims were young journalists and highly skilled artisans; elsewhere lawyers and doctors were imprisoned along with workers. An analysis of those jailed in the Eure revealed a journeyman joiner, a cabinet-maker, a draughtsman, a tinsmith, a blacksmith, two day labourers, four shoemakers, a piano-maker, a spinner, a carpenter, a commercial broker and a lawyer (*avocat*); all from occupations with a tradition of independence. The age range of the 16 is interesting; five were in their fifties, six in their forties, four in their thirties and only one was in his twenties – certainly not young hotheads. Their offences were membership of a secret society or insults to the emperor.[16] Recently repatriated exiles found themselves once more in Guyana or Algeria as prefects often struggled to find enough 'dangerous' republicans within their area. Press censorship was intensified, the main victim being the *Revue de Paris*.

However, some of Louis-Napoleon's policies, notably his support for Italy, were attractive to republicans, who began to see their role as one of constitutional opposition. In 1859 came an amnesty from the emperor to coincide with his alliance with Piedmont and his military intervention, apparently in support of Italian liberation. Many of the exiles accepted the opportunity to return home. Ten years later there was a second amnesty and others went back to France. The result was to produce more divisions at first, but gradually some old republicans began to find common cause with a younger generation.

The republicanism of the 1860s was not a rehash of 1848, although continuity was stressed and the First Republic continued to be the ideal. A new generation of republicans was emerging, centring around Gambetta (whose hero was Danton) and Ferry, which was determined to shake off the conspiratorial image never sought by more than a minority, and focus on parliament, the courts and the press. Middle-class republicans, inspired by writers like Quinet, were above all concerned with the issue of liberty. Conspirators were still present; Blanqui had been released in 1859 to be rearrested in 1861 for conspiracy. He had some influence upon Clemenceau. In 1865 he escaped to Belgium. Proudhon, writing prolifically, captured the interest of a new generation, including Gambetta. His followers, under the direction of Longuet, founded a periodical *Rive Gauche*, to which Flourens contributed, but which was forced to publish abroad.

In the provinces the few papers with republican sympathies included the *Phare de la Loire* in Nantes, the *Progrès* in Lyon and the *Gironde* in Bordeaux. The *Phare* in particular was given considerable leeway by the regime and published articles by Quinet, Michelet and others. Outside Paris the lead was taken far more by artisans and minor officials, rather than the old bourgeois republican elite, who were more hesitant than in 1848. The parliamentary republicans had new rivals in their attempts to secure support from the growing working class. By the early 1860s the Workers' International had a quarter of a million members in France. It placed class unity and international solidarity above the quest for a particular form of government. Although they secured some support among French workers, the most successful organizations, especially after 1864, continued to be those pressing first for material benefits for their members.[17]

In the 1863 election campaign the old leader Garnier-Pagès made a railway-borne pilgrimage to more than 60 towns to persuade republicans to abandon abstention, a prime objective if they were to become a force in the Legislative Assembly. This Catch 22 decision implied an unwelcome acceptance, or at least tolerance, of the regime and a dilution of republican fervour. Carnot and Simon were persuaded, but some leading figures like Proudhon still insisted that republicans could not take an oath to the regime, despite his own friendship with Prince Napoleon. The main leaders quarrelled openly and formed rival campaign committees. Garnier-Pagès organized a 'consultative' committee under his leadership which included, from the 1848 generation Carnot, Marie, J. Simon, Corbon, Crémieux, Charton, Martin, and from the new generation Dréo, Ferry, Floquet, Durier, Clamageran and Hérold. There was criticism that republicanism had become exclusively middle-class. Electoral alliances contracted with liberal opponents of the Empire like Thiers and Berryer, whose candidatures eventually won the support of republicans and the electorate, would have been inconceivable in the Second Republic and were disdained by the more intractable republicans.

Despite these conflicts republican representation rose to eight. Favre, Ollivier, Darimon and Picard were joined by Pelletan and J. Simon plus two editors, Havin and Guéroult. They gained 12 per cent of the vote nationally and in areas with an active republican club the figure reached 50 per cent. The opposition, liberal and republican, was in a majority in all towns of more than 40,000 inhabitants. The republicans did best in Paris, but Hénon and Jules Favre were chosen by Lyon, Marie by Marseille, Dorian by St Etienne, Magnin in the Côte-d'Or and Glais-Bizoin in Côtes-du-Nord. Two Parisian by-elections in 1864 saw the return of two leaders of the Second Republic, Garnier-Pagès and Carnot.[18] Despite these successes the Parisian republican electoral committee was successfully prosecuted as an illegal organization, because it was 25-strong instead of 20. Jules Favre proffered the standard republican defence that the right to hold such meetings was an essential part of universal suffrage.

Thiers, now a democrat, but not yet a republican, was the most notable member of the left-wing opposition in the new Assembly. Jules Favre was the most eloquent of the republicans. Jules Simon, a leading academic who also had the ear of the Parisian workers through the social surveys he had conducted and published, soon emerged as the dominant republican. The old leaders of 1848, Carnot, Marie, Garnier-Pagès, were far less impressive. They were moderates in the Assembly; they presented themselves as liberal democrats and cohabited amicably with Thiers and Berryer, jointly signing a project to decentralize provincial administration.

Republicans also began to contest local elections with a variety of allies. In Bas-Languedoc in 1864 and 1865 in alliance with old allies, the legitimists, they secured 100 seats out of 900 in municipal elections, including 7 out of 27 seats in Nîmes. By the end of the Empire in this region they were making progress in villages rather than big towns; education and anti-war strategies were vote winners.[19] Elsewhere, for instance in the Charente, republicans considered Bonapartists their natural allies as joint partisans of 1789 and the two worked together in municipal elections to contrive the defeat of all monarchists.

From 1860 to 1861 Louis-Napoleon embarked on a series of reforms, not in response to pressure from the tiny number of republicans in the Legislative Assembly, but because 'official' deputies had been demanding greater power for the Assembly since its inception. He also hoped that social reform would stifle the link between complaining workers and republicans. The Assembly was allowed to make an annual address summarizing its preferred legislative programme; its debates were to be published in full; government representatives could be asked to address the Assembly. In 1861 the government was no longer to be allowed to raise loans additional to those provided in the Budget, which extended parliamentary control over finance.[20]

The emperor exceeded the expectations of the Legislative Assembly, which wanted no more than the enhancement of parliamentary power, by a broader scheme of liberalization. Having successfully robbed the republicans of their monopoly of democracy, he produced a package of social reform more radical than many republicans would have sought. As the economy grew rapidly in these years, so did the working population. Proudhon's ideas on worker organization and self-help remained popular, particularly in Paris. In 1862 a worker delegation attended the International Exhibition in London and, in concert with English workers, laid the foundations for a Proudhonist international association of workers. A year later a manifesto demanded the right to present worker candidates for the legislative elections.

Louis-Napoleon, alarmed by the links between French workers and the International Working Men's Association, embarked on an innovative programme of social legislation, which did little to persuade urban workers of the value of the Empire but which did achieve one of the emperor's objectives, that of dividing middle-class republicans. Louis Napoleon was always careful to maintain and to develop a populist image, which, while anti-socialist, nonetheless involved active concern for the social welfare of the population. He never stopped claiming that his 'noble and great mission' was 'to bring about improvements in the interests of the poor'.[21] In 1864 his reform of industrial relations legislation was drafted by a converted republican, Emile Ollivier. Prolonged strikes in mining, textiles and the iron industry were the background to the legalization of unions and strikes. The emperor's approach was a novel reversal of the repressive strategy of the July Monarchy and unique in Europe at that time. Responding to Saint-Simonian advisers, Louis-Napoleon also tried to initiate state provision for workers which would dilute the appeal of socialist schemes. State encouragement to private charitable ventures was accompanied by a plan for compulsory state insurance against sickness, and the draft of a scheme to provide old age pensions.

If the emperor's economic and social concepts were too limited to please workers, they terrified traditional businessmen who had no time for the *Credit Mobilier* and free trade treaties. A series of startling financial scandals, in reality linked more to the arrival of Californian and Australian gold in Paris than to Louis-Napoleon's attempts to encourage small firms, caused traditional businessmen to deplore financial innovation and workers to renew their condemnation of capitalism. The grumblings of the latter intensified as wages demonstrably failed to keep pace with profits and prices. In 1867 economic problems led to an increase in popular criticism. In Elbeuf the high price of food contributed to a couple of local quarryworkers pinning a note on the mayor's door 'We want bread at 3 sous a pound, or the . . . of a mayor of Elbeuf will see blood and shot'. One was jailed for a year. There were other incidents, minor in themselves, typified by a small, handwritten poster ornamented with the drawing of a red flag which urged the declaration of a 'red' republic.[22]

The International continued to develop. In 1866 a branch was started in Lyon[23] and the first International congress was held in Geneva, attended by Proudhonist Parisian workers and Blanquist Parisian students, who quarrelled. The next congress, held in Lausanne in 1867, produced even more furious conflict, this time between German and French delegates. In 1867 there was an attempt to disband the French section following a republican demonstration at Manin's tomb. It was obvious that the project for international proletarian accord had made little progress and was no threat. But working class militancy on more specific, material complaints was a different matter; in 1869–70 a pronounced wave of strikes undermined confidence, but reassuringly for Louis-Napoleon, was greeted with only very muted enthusiasm from republicans.

Despite their disputes and very modest following, did republicans launch a 'war against the Empire' from 1868 onwards, as Weill suggested, or were his claims merely wishful thinking? As a background to this 'war' the emperor's failing health and foreign policy in Mexico and the German States were cited. In this context, the continuance of liberal reforms was seen as contributing to the downfall of the regime. While it is true that de Tocqueville and other contemporaries were convinced that a governing system was never in more danger than when it sought to improve itself, the sustained legislative programme of the 1860s surely cannot be dismissed as the whim of a declining autocrat, but must be seen as, in part, a response to the demands of the dominant *notables*. In 1867 ministers were allowed to address the Assembly and deputies could question them. Of prime significance was the relaxation of the censorship of the press and public meetings. Two new papers were started, the moderate liberal *Electeur*, edited by Ferry and backed by Favre, Picard and Hénon, and the more outspokenly democratic *Réveil* of Delescluze, the old Jacobin, and Ranc, a young radical. Delescluze opposed the compromise with Orleanist and legitimist opponents of the Empire into which the moderates had been drawn. Other papers followed, including Rochefort's *Lanterne*, whose criticism was so intense that after a time he was forced to print it in Brussels.

There were limits to the impetus for liberalization. Religious and political associations were still required to seek the sanction of the prefect. However, electoral meetings were now permitted during the run-up to an election. In the Bas-Languedoc some friendly societies founded in the 1860s became overtly political as did a number of new lecture societies. There was even a *Société des Droits de l'Homme* in the Gard in May 1869. Local councils, even more apolitical than normal in the early years of the Empire, became increasingly critical. They condemned official candidatures which were subsequently abandoned for the election campaign in 1869. Gambetta, Delescluze and others openly questioned the legality of the Empire. The coup d'état came under new scrutiny and was declared illegal in a trial of those who subscribed to a monument to Baudin, the deputy killed in the Parisian protest to the 1851 coup.

Republicans fought the 1869 election with unprecedented freedom, but as a consequence, with increased internal wranglings. The more radical, often the younger generation republicans, would not tolerate alliances, either with liberal monarchists, or even with republicans who were willing to work within the Empire. They put up Bancel, an 1849 deputy, banished after the coup, to fight against Ollivier in Paris. Garnier-Pagès, Marie and Favre were criticized as bourgeois and too conservative. Gambetta stood in Belleville, armed with a lengthy manifesto of republican demands. He roundly informed his audience that political reform had to be first on the republican agenda. He gave enough support for social reform to hold his working-class vote and maintain, he hoped, a bourgeois alliance. The number of votes cast in France as a whole against government candidates in legislative elections rose to 3,355,000, compared with 4,438,000 for government sympathizers, with 2,291,000 abstentions.[24] Former government candidates began to demand reform. Only 80 of those elected in 1870 claimed to be Bonapartists and 30 republicans were elected by the major towns. However, republicans continued to find little support in rural areas, except in parts of the Midi and the east.

The victories of Gambetta and Ferry signalled the arrival of a new generation of republicans, although Favre, Garnier-Pagès, Simon, Pelletan and Thiers were all re-elected. Despite the presence of the old socialist Raspail and the outspoken Rochefort in the new Chamber, the general tone of the republican group was still overwhelmingly moderate, but even less in concert than ever. Increased tolerance by the regime allowed a greater range of dissent to be expressed. The example of Bas-Languedoc indicates that the republicans were very divided in the late 1860s. The old bourgeois leaders were regarded with some suspicion by workers and reciprocated with similar sentiments.[25] The Limousin elections showed that worker support for a republic had not evaporated. The republicans began to pick up votes in districts with a large migrant population of stonemasons where their vote rose to 38 per cent, but on the whole rural districts remained firmly committed to the Empire. The republican share of the total poll in the area in 1869 was a mere 11 per cent. What is most striking about the Limousin, where in general Louis-Napoleon did well, was the continuity of opinion.

In the summer of 1869, the Rouher government, under attack from an alliance of 116 critical deputies, reluctantly introduced a reform programme, before resigning to avoid a full-scale debate in the Assembly on these proposals. The Assembly was granted the right to initiate legislation. Ministers were allowed to be members of either the Assembly or Senate and both bodies were permitted to question ministers. The Assembly was to elect its own officers and the Senate's debates were to be published. The Budget was to be discussed and voted in sections, not simply en bloc. The Assembly was to decide on trade treaties, a sensitive issue with industrialists who had been hurt by free trade. With such legislation the authoritarian Empire was melting into a parliamentary state. There were considerable tensions in the

Assembly and the new chief minister, Ollivier, had minimal control, but France was no longer dominated by one man. Ollivier introduced additional liberal measures. The government's right of arbitrary arrest was ended, jury trials for press offences were introduced, stamp duty was repealed and the obligation of workers to carry a *livret* abolished. Mayors had to be members of their municipal councils and local councils were to elect their leaders and publish their debates.

Republicans were not satisfied with this programme but, in isolation, were too divided and small a group to count. The emperor's right to call a plebiscite in circumstances of his choosing, including constitutional reform, was retained. Ollivier opposed a plebiscite on the reform programme, but had to give way. In the early months of 1870, during discussions on reform, Paris, Marseille, Montauban and other towns were shaken by unrest over industrial problems and the repercussions of the murder of the republican journalist Victor Noir by Prince Pierre Bonaparte. Both the prince and Louis-Napoleon's severest critic, Rochefort, were arrested, together with 400 demonstrators. Blanqui and Flourens urged revolution, to the acute embarrassment of the majority of republicans. Troops were sent to put down strikes, notably at the Schneider works in Le Creusot. However the plebiscite went ahead with ease. Voters were asked to confirm their support for the whole 'liberal' Empire and 7.3 million voters did so, with 1.5 million rejections. But in line with past experience urban centres were the least enthusiastic. In the Limousin as a whole 73.5 per cent voted yes, 2.5 per cent no. In Limoges 25.3 per cent voted yes, 49 per cent no.[26] (See Map 5, Appendix Three.)

The role of the Legislative Assembly had been enhanced in the reforms of the 1860s, although the retention of the imperial plebiscite emasculated some of the benefits. Reformers turned their attention to local liberties, promised by the new government. Ollivier established a sub-committee led by Odilon Barrot.[27] This was not specifically a republican issue. Throughout the 1860s writers from de Tocqueville, Michelet and Quinet to Proudhon and in 1868 Prévost-Paradol,[28] had criticized the increased centralization of the Empire. Not only major cities, but even tiny communes had lost their right to elect their mayor, who was nominated from Paris and did not even have to be an elected member of the municipal council. By such a means universal suffrage was often a sham. In 1865 a Nancy-led committee of landowners and former civil servants which included monarchists and republicans with such diverse figures as Louis Blanc, Ferry and Simon, urged decentralization and condemned the growing power of the state.

However, Louis-Napoleon was left in no doubt of the importance of centralization to his survival by the republicanism of the major cities in all elections. In early April 1870 Barrot's committee recommended by one vote that mayors should be elected by their municipal councils. The proposal was ignored by the government.

To what extent were republicans distinctive in their approach and united in their strategies? By 1869 many had tacitly accepted the increasingly parliamentary regime and were content to try to reform it further in concert with former monarchist *notables* who now called themselves simply liberals. Republicans were united on a number of issues. They continued to regard plebiscites as a travesty of democracy. They still wanted the abolition of indirect taxes and the protection of communal rights. They avoided debate on more controversial social questions. Little was said about the liberation of the proletariat; strikes were an embarrassment, not a clarion call to action. There was nothing whatsoever in the demeanour of republicans in 1870 to indicate that a republic was imminent. If the emperor had not made the mistake of going to war in the summer of 1870, losing disastrously and being captured by the Prussians, there is no reason to doubt that the parliamentary Empire would have survived.

The republicans in the Assembly made no attempt to conduct a war against the emperor. Instead, in the summer of 1870 they supported that against Prussia, head of the new North German Confederation, being convinced, like most contemporaries, that it was a war to defend France against the aggressive ambitions of Bismarck. Republicans took an increasingly dominant role in the debates of the Assembly during the campaign, urging the arming of the *garde nationale mobile* in Paris. The old republican call for the creation of a 'nation in arms' through the enlargement and arming of the National Guard was made by Picard, but repulsed. Ferry demanded full publicity to engage the sympathies of the whole nation[29] as a cascade of defeats during August shattered the confidence of an army inferior in numbers and equipment.

On September 4th, following Louis-Napoleon's defeat and capture at Sedan, the republicans pressed the Assembly to declare that the Empire was at an end. They proceeded to the *hôtel de ville*, as was traditional, to proclaim a republic. A governing commission was set up, consisting of republicans, with the exception of Trochu, the popular monarchist military governor of Paris. It included Gambetta, Favre, Ferry, Picard, Garnier-Pagès, Crémieux, Jules Simon, Etienne Arago (who was made mayor of Paris), Rochefort, Glais-Bizoin, Dorian,

Magnin, General Le Flô and Admiral Fournichon. Few of the republicans from the imperial Assembly were left out, but militants like Blanqui and Blanc, the latter of whom only returned after the emperor's deposition, were not included. Blanc complained bitterly that only those who had taken the oath of allegiance to Louis-Napoleon thought themselves fit to govern a republic.[30]

The new Government of National Defence committed itself to continuing the war. By September 19th the Prussians were surrounding Paris, which was isolated from the rest of France in siege conditions. The government, with Gambetta as its effective leader, was moved first to Tours, then to Bordeaux. The Parisians, a high proportion of whom were enrolled in the 350,000-strong National Guard, deplored what they regarded as the pusillanimous lack of patriotism of the government. On October 31st Blanqui led an unsuccessful radical demonstration. Cooped up behind their fortifications, Parisians waited for the Prussians to attack, but the latter preferred to enlarge their huge swathe of conquest in provincial France. While Parisians ate rats, the army continued to fail. An attempted sortie by Parisian troops and Guardsmen on 22 January 1871 revealed their powerlessness to everyone but themselves.

The authority of the new central government was tenuous, even in territory free from the invading armies. Those towns which had been wayward during the Empire ignored the new government and began to run their own affairs. Marseille and Lyon rebelled, on a scale unprecedented since the 1790s.[31] From September 5th Marseille's municipal council virtually declared home rule, creating a Committee of Public Safety and appointing an acting prefect. Over the next few months a constant battle continued between radicals and moderates for control of the city.[32] Gambetta sent Esquiros to be his man, but he sided with local radicals in persecuting Jesuits and monarchists. Esquiros, a democratic socialist journalist in Marseille and left-wing deputy during the Second Republic, in self-imposed exile from the 1851 coup until 1869 when he was elected to the Assembly for Saône-et-Loire, quickly abandoned his initial opposition to the war. In September he helped to organize an ephemeral defensive League of the Midi among the 13 neighbouring departments. Municipal elections gave the victory to the moderates, but more radical republicans continued to make demands. Esquiros was forced to resign at the beginning of November.

In Lyon a Committee of Revolutionary Action was formed during the summer of 1870, which on the news of Sedan took over the city, flew the red flag and declared a republic a day earlier than in Paris, with no bloodshed. Their new Committee of Public Safety was moderate, including the veteran republican Hénon, ousted in the 1869 legislative elections by a radical rival. The leaders of the local branch of the International were left out, although some members of the group were included.[33] The committee showed no serious interest in socialist measures, however. They worked on the assumption that decentralization would be the main priority of the new republic. Thus, rather tongue-in-cheek, they refused to recognize Gambetta's prefect, the teacher and writer Challend-Lacour, simply acknowledging him as a representative of the Provisional Government. The Committee concentrated on preparing Lyon to fight the Prussians. They abolished the long-detested *octroi*, despite the fact that half their revenue came from it. They were manifestly anti-clerical; clergy were required to do military service, some religious orders were suppressed and no church bells were to be rung. On the insistence of Challend-Lacour, municipal elections were held and Hénon was elected mayor. On September 28th an abortive socialist rising followed the arrival of the anarchist Bakunin and an unpopular wage-cut for workers repairing Lyon's fortification. Rebuffed, Bakunin left for Marseille and Challend-Lacour's authority was accepted by the municipal council, eager for his support in their quarrel with the local military commander.

What was at stake? In part, the disputes were ideological; republicans were at loggerheads over the sort of republic to be created, whether radical, centralized or the reverse. But personal enmities, local issues and arguments between representatives of the various branches of administration began to predominate. Meanwhile national defence strategies proved ineffectual and ineffective; the Prussians confirmed their control of 40 departments, including the major industrial areas. On January 28th an armistice was signed, which the Parisians and Gambetta detested. He resigned and in the February elections for an assembly to make peace, all of the 43 deputies chosen in Paris and headed by Louis Blanc were radicals, who wanted to continue the fighting. Elsewhere the elections were a triumph for the traditional *notables*, a predictable response from a nation anxious to end an unwinnable war. Of the 650 new deputies who met in Bordeaux 400 were monarchists, 20 were Bonapartists, 78 were moderates and only 150 were republicans. It seemed that yet another attempt to create a permanent republic would fail ignominiously. But the main brief of this assembly was to end the war. On February 26th Thiers, the candidate elected in the largest number of constituencies and thus chosen as head of the executive, signed the preliminaries of a peace settlement in which France gave up the whole of Alsace, except Belfort, and a large part of Lorraine and agreed to submit to an army of occupation until an indemnity of 5 milliard francs was paid. On March 1st, as the Prussians paraded in triumph through Paris, the Treaty of Frankfurt was ratified by the Assembly by 546 votes to 107, the only dissentients being the radical republicans elected by the main cities.

The war was over, but before a new form of government could be finalized, the Assembly determined to return France to normal. They declared the formal deposition of Louis-Napoleon and decided to move to Versailles, considering Paris too unsettled. Their attempt to return the capital to equilibrium was hasty and conceived in ignorance, betraying the majority's fear of Parisian radicalism. A large proportion of the adult male population of the capital had enrolled in the National Guard during the siege. Such a large body was no longer needed and from February 15th the 1.50 franc daily allowance for Guardsmen was cut to 30 centimes, and was only to be given to those otherwise destitute. The measure was logical but uncaring. During the siege the economy of Paris had come to a halt and the National Guard allowance had been the only means of support for many families. After the siege it would take time for the economy to recover, especially as workshop owners who had not fled before the siege left as soon as it was over. The decrees of the Assembly of March 7th, lifting the moratorium on the huge number of goods deposited in state pawnshops during the siege, and on rents and overdue debts, showed a peculiar insensitivity to the economic stagnation of the capital. Within a week, over 150,000 bankruptcies had been declared among the small shopkeepers and workshop owners. Economic misjudgements aside, Parisians, especially the National Guardsmen, sustained during the siege by their patriotism, could not accept defeat, detested the peace treaty and were incensed by Prussian military parades through streets they had not conquered.[34] Meanwhile, in conformity with the Treaty, the troops stationed in Paris during the siege were given ten days' pay at the beginning of March and moved out.

On March 15th, aware that the government meant to repossess the capital on its return from Bordeaux, 215 of the 254 battalions of the National Guard in Paris elected a central committee to try to protect their interests. On March 18th Thiers sent troops into Paris to seize cannon from the heights of Montmartre. This was either a disastrous error of judgement or deliberate provocation, for the cannon belonged to the National Guard and had been paid for by public subscription during the siege and built in the capital. The Parisian mayors backed Thiers, but many of the troops did not and the attempt was a total and bloody failure, in which the generals Lecomte and Clement Thomas were shot. Thiers ordered the evacuation of Paris.

The next day the central committee of the National Guard established itself at the traditional radical heart of the capital, the *hôtel de ville*, and with the support of some of the many political clubs which had sprung up during the siege, decided to hold elections on March 26th for a Commune for Paris. Their decision consciously recalled the republican traditions of the 1790s, when France had also been invaded by the Prussians and there had been discord among the revolutionaries. What propelled them in defiance was not so much a sense of history or a common ideology, for their loyalties were varied, but the sense that they had been abandoned all along the line, during the siege, the defeat and with the peace settlement.[35] They claimed that Thiers' evacuation left the capital without a government. In their proclamation of March 18th the National Guard committee declared:

> The proletarians of Paris, amidst the failures and treasons of the ruling classes, have understood that the hour has struck for them to save the situation, by taking into their own hands the direction of public affairs.[36]

Marx eagerly quoted the proclamation in a different sense, to show that the Commune was a class war.[37] In reality a large proportion of the middle-class population had fled during the siege and after and barely half the electorate voted. Workers, primarily artisans, predominated among the quarter-million or so voters, and the 90 men elected represented them more than any previous assembly, local or national, had done, 35 being themselves artisans. Politically the Commune represented all strands of anti-Thiers opinion, including Blanquists, Proudhonists and Jacobins. As the situation worsened, more extreme views came to hold sway. At its most moderate, the Commune expressed the demand of Parisians for civic autonomy denied them throughout the Empire, at its most extreme it was an attempt to spark the decentralization of France. Some members were convinced from the outset that they were in a state of civil war with Thiers, others hoped to negotiate. Thiers never wavered from his view that the Commune was a treasonable socialist rebellion. Proudhonist socialists were enthusiastic supporters, although other socialists, such as Louis Blanc, were hostile.[38] The small number of Marxists were at first uncertain whether the Commune was indeed a proletarian revolution. There were some socialists within the Commune, but its social provisions were as much geared to revitalizing the economy as socializing it. Opponents condemned decrees encouraging workers to take over abandoned workshops as an attack on private property, but the Bank of France, it is true given little choice, agreed to underwrite the transient regime.[39]

However, while the Communards issued practical decrees for recovery and idealistic ones to reform social inequalities, the government in Versailles refused all negotiations and planned a military campaign to take Paris. Only in late April did the Communards accept that they could not influence the shape of the new republic, merely fight for their lives. By then Thiers had been able to gather sufficient troops to launch a full attack, and to control the defiance of other towns, which were not always in sympathy either with him or the capital.

The Commune was brought to an end by the army, in what has been known ever since as 'bloody week', 22–28 May 1871, a massacre surpassing that of the June Days 1848. Versaillais and Communard forces battled for the control of Paris street by street. The death toll among Communards was 25,000, for the army 900. Many Communards were summarily shot after capture. Estimates are very varied, often related to the sympathies of the writer. Some say that 2000 soldiers died. Certainly 40,000 Communards were arrested, of whom 270 were condemned to death and 26 actually executed, while 400 were deported. During the last days of the fighting many public buildings were destroyed by fires, some accidental, some started by the Communards to halt advancing troops.[40] Thus Thiers at the head of the elected assembly reasserted control of France's most rebellious city in the usual manner, using the army, but in a battle more costly than any of the Franco-Prussian war. The manner of the defeat of the Commune created not only an international socialist legend[41] – Marx after some hesitation, entitled his account of it a 'civil war'[42] – but also a legacy of bitterness on both sides which has not yet been obliterated. Paris remained in a state of siege until 1878.

The Paris Commune had only modest repercussions in other major towns such as Marseille and Lyon where conflict amongst republicans and between the municipality and the central government had been in progress since the summer of 1870. The Paris Commune sent delegates to ask for support. Sympathizers in Marseille, fairly quiescent since the municipal elections in November, invaded the prefecture, captured the prefect, Cosnier, and set up a Revolutionary Departmental Commission with the blessing of the National Guard. They assured the moderate republican local administration that their quarrel was not with them but with Thiers, but, unconvinced, the municipal council asked Versailles for a 'real' republican prefect and withdrew their backing from the Departmental Commission. The delegate from Paris, Landeck, urged support for the Paris Commune and with 2000 men tried to resist the army reinforcements sent against him. An artillery bombardment brought Marseille's support for Paris to an end at the beginning of April.[43]

Lyon, which had contributed 10,000 additional volunteers and an extra 12 million francs for armaments to the war effort in addition to the quota demanded by the government, far more than any other city, had been as appalled as Paris by the decision to give in to the Prussians. On the news of the election of the Paris Commune, the new prefect, Valentin, urged obedience to Versailles. On March 22nd the National Guard and radical republicans pressed the mayor, Hénon, to agree to create a commune in Lyon, to which he replied that Lyon already had a perfectly good one. By the end of the day the centre of the city, the *hôtel de ville* and the prefecture were in the hands of the radicals, although the National Guard remained loyal to the mayor. In effect the radicals had no quarrel with Hénon, but with the Prussians encamped in nearby Dijon. Like him their main concern was national defence and their main emotion was frustrated patriotism. Within two days the mayor was back in full control.[44] The Paris Commune had a transitory influence elsewhere. Communes were set up briefly in Limoges and a handful of other towns but on the whole Paris was not regarded as an example to be emulated, rather as a threat to stability and a danger to be feared, particularly in view of the Prussian occupation.

The crushing of the Paris Commune probably contributed much to the creation of a stable republic, even though it was four years before the constitutional laws of the Third Republic were completed. Republicans were still very divided on their ideal republic, but left-wing aspirations, whether Blanquist or Proudhonist, were no longer a factor in realistic future plans. Paris and the militants who had backed its Commune could be discounted in any definition of the republic. None of the Parisian deputies to the National Assembly supported the Commune. The degree of uncertainty about France's political future was less than might appear from the unwillingness to rush into print with a new constitution. Thiers claimed that this was a 'republic without republicans', but he exaggerated. The assembly of monarchists had been elected to make peace, not a monarchy, and in addition they could never have settled on a claimant. The by-elections of July 1871 were more indicative of public opinion when republicans secured 99 of the 114 vacancies.[45] The old exiles of the Second Republic were among them. Ledru-Rollin returned in September 1870 a sick man. He was elected to the Assembly in February 1871, but resigned. Louis Blanc, a revered socialist veteran, became a founder of the moderate radical socialist movement. The republican leadership had passed to the generation trained in the Empire. Although still arguing, moderates were in control. Using the model of the liberal Empire in which they had served their apprenticeship, they calculated and compromised with the monarchist *notables* to create a conservative republic, tolerable to the elite and just about democratic enough when laced with anti-clerical policies and a secular state education system to be a convincing heir of the First Republic. (See Map 6, Appendix Three.) Born tentatively, of defeat and civil war, this Third Republic was to prove the most enduring regime since 1789.

Conclusion

In 1814 a republic was not considered; in 1871 nothing else was seriously contemplated. What did this signify? This volume has addressed the question by attempting to define the norms and assumptions of republicans, how the historic experience has been presented since 1814, the conflicting traditions created by the revolutionary years, the emergence and development of radical attitudes during the Constitutional Monarchy, the input of socialist thinking, the 'apprenticeship' of 1848–52, the growth of confidence in parliamentary institutions in the 1860s which brought together the formerly warring heirs of the 1789 tradition, the significance of the Commune and the establishment of a stable republican regime in the 1870s.

The relationship between the 1789 Revolution and republicanism, the interconnections and differences between the insurrectionary tradition and nineteenth-century revolutionary upheaval, the links and chasms between elite and popular republicanism and the significance of different regional experiences have been evaluated within a chronological framework.

The large and growing number of monographs on local and other specific aspects of this topic and the demise of the previously ubiquitous (at least in France) Marxist interpretation of nineteenth-century French revolutions, makes a new synthesis of the development of republicanism in the nineteenth century essential. The revisionist attempt to demolish Marxist revolutionary theory has made some inroads into historians' attitudes to the nineteenth century. The Marxist bourgeois revolution has sunk almost without trace, although the same cannot be said for the middle classes themselves. Investigation into the political aspects of both the 1789 and the 1830 Revolutions has confirmed the control of a traditional elite mainly, but not entirely,

264

bourgeois. Marxist notions of proletarian revolution, never of course intended, by nineteenth-century commentators, to mean the insurrection of an exclusively factory workforce, have been shown to be inappropriate, in the way in which they were applied by Marx to the June Days and Paris Commune. Neither of these events was an aspect of a class war but, like the 1830 Revolution, both were violent movements of sections of the artisan community in the capital protesting about particular issues. The complexities of popular unrest, rural as well as urban, have been thoroughly rehearsed in recent years. The significance of traditional socio-economic norms and newer socialist doctrines is usually stressed alongside both the desire of some protestors to restore perhaps a rather idealized concept of the traditional economy and the demand of others for a slice of more modern proto-capitalist action. In each instance a small group rose to criticize and try to influence government policy.

What has replaced Marxist dogma for historians of nineteenth-century France? In some ways the answer lies in suggesting, as this volume has done, a different initial question. Marx never applied his theoretical framework of economic change and its relationship to revolution as rigidly to post-1789 France as did some later Marxists, and they never applied it as rigorously as revisionists began to suggest in the 1960s. The socialist historians of the Third Republic were patriots first and their account of republicanism was the story of the liberation of the French people. In the 1980s historians of France, both in Britain and North America and in France itself, re-emphasized the significance of these ideas of liberation in 1789 and the importance of specific political issues along with the intervention of a variety of economic factors in the nineteenth century. Socio-economic factors have not been excluded from history, but the diversity of class definition and the importance of particular issues to different branches of the economy and the regions are now observed, enrichening and deepening our understanding of the past.

The attack on Marxism since the 1960s has led French historians to put more stress on patriotism. This present volume insists on the importance of socio-economic factors in nineteenth-century revolutions and examines, and questions, the notion that the creation of the Third Republic in 1871 signified the survival and triumph of an eternal republican ideal. The idea of the republic was unspecific in 1814. The Napoleonic Empire quintessentially claimed to be the climax of patriotic endeavour and its propagandists emphasized only the negative aspects of the earlier Republic, focusing as the Directory had done, on the negative coercion and bloodshed of the Terror in the Jacobin republic. The broad altruistic and idealistic principles of 1789 and the Declaration of Rights which encapsulated them were claimed by constitutional monarchists as their inheritance and were not seen as uniquely republican.

At the outset of this investigation Weill's premiss that almost no one wanted a republic in 1814 because the memory of the First Republic was so bloody and divisive seemed convincing. However his claim that the Third Republic was an inevitable consequence of the development of a republican movement seemed a mere wish-fulfilment. A glance at the handful of republicans in Louis-Philippe's last Chamber of Deputies, the failure to secure an assembly favourable to a republic in 1848, the mere 30 republicans in Louis-Napoleon's Legislative Assembly in 1870, not to mention the minority of republicans in the 1871 assembly elected after the declaration of a republic, hardly seemed the stuff from which a durable republic could ever be constructed. Rather it appeared that very few Frenchmen wanted a republic in 1848 and that in 1871 a republic was adopted because all the other alternatives had failed.

The clue to the actual significance of France's nineteenth-century political instability lies in regional investigations which display the underlying continuity of commitment to the 1789 Revolution. While it might be tempting to scorn the lack of principle of a politician such as Adolphe Thiers, several times government minister in the July Monarchy, opposition deputy during the Second Empire and head of government in the Third Republic, the constant repetition on a local scale of Thiers' career pattern suggests an explanation rooted in a little more than self-seeking political ambition. Throughout this present investigation frequent reference has been made to individuals whose careers spanned the 1790s, the Empire, the First Restoration, the Hundred Days and the July Monarchy, frequently including membership of one of the patriotic federations of 1815, the *carbonari*, often Saint-Simonism and *Aide-toi*. After 1830 a number of factors led to divisions, including both the response of individuals to the experiment with an Orleanist Monarchy and differing attitudes to what was termed 'the social question' and socialism itself. Some former *carbonaros* became staunch Orleanists, some stayed loyal to Louis-Philippe until 1848 but wanted reforms, some became overt republicans and a minority opted for socialism.

In 1830 the white flag of the Bourbons was furled in favour of the revolutionary *tricolore*. Its three stripes might be said to correspond, very roughly and rather fancifully, to three main tendencies which emerged. Within this spectrum the most radical joined societies such as *Amis du Peuple* or the *Société des Droits de l'Homme*, served in the National Guard, backed the banquet campaign of 1847 and became commissioners and deputies in 1848–51 (they were to be dubbed the 'reds' or democ-socs by the Party of Order in 1849); they, or their sons or other relatives were active republicans in the late 1850s and 1860s and founders of the Third Republic and the Radical-Socialist party after 1870. The least radical resigned their membership of *Aide-toi* in March 1831, voted for Guizot throughout the 1840s, a number were elected to the assemblies of the Second Republic as conservatives, being joined by some of the moderate legitimists who had also sat in July Monarchy assemblies and had ignored the backward-looking *'émigration à l'intérieur'* of some of their fellows (the 'whites' of the 1849 election campaign); they adorned the assemblies of the Second Empire as official candidates until 1869 and were the backbone of the most conservative side of the Third Republic, preferring the Senate to the elected chamber. In the 1960s their heirs must have become Gaullists. In between were Thiers' followers, the *gauche dynastique* of the 1840s, elected in large numbers to the Constituent Assembly of 1848 and its successor in 1849 (the 'blues'). They formed the liberal opposition in Louis-Napoleon's Legislative Assembly and were crucial to the success of the Third Republic.

While the *tricolore* conveniently includes all three colours, the differences between the groups are often emphasized when the instability of nineteenth-century politics is under observation. The fragility of governments was as much a feature of the Third and subsequent republics as it was of the First Republic and the Orleanist Monarchy. Beneath the vulnerability of governments, there was an inherent stability based, perhaps partly on the slowness of economic change in these years, and consequent social stability, but perhaps also on mutual respect for the basic principles of the 1789 Revolution, however vaguely defined.

1789 meant a revolution in ideas, in institutions and individual opportunities, which a quarter of a century of upheaval and war made irreversible. Those who supported 1789 shared a common belief in the potential for change and the confidence that change was progress (even if that confidence had its limits). Factional labels, Girondin and Jacobin, *résistance* and *mouvement*, moderate republican and democ-soc, indicated differences which were bitterly divisive in particular situations but which were relatively superficial in comparison with the initial commitment of an individual and his family to 1789 in broad terms. Ancien regime historians might well comment that, judged on such a Richter scale, 1789 itself was also incidental, and that such a broad commitment pre-dated the Revolution, but that is, mercifully, beyond the scope of this investigation.

Historians of the late twentieth century are once again inclined to stress the philosophical content of this commitment or consensus as the product of the Enlightenment. Regional studies reveal particular factors; the independent patrician traditions of Alsace which underlay the liberalism of its elite; traditions of communal autonomy in areas such as the Var which led to democ-soc sympathies in 1848; Protestant areas were invariably republican.

A bourgeois republican tradition can also be sustained by the investigation of families in their locality. Although the red herring of the Marxist entrepreneurial bourgeois revolutionary has been thoroughly grilled by revisionists, sections of certain professional groups showed pronounced radical tendencies in the nineteenth century, especially lawyers and doctors. Was this the product of 1789, or do these attitudes pre-date the Revolution? After all, the *parlements*, the senior appeal courts in the ancien regime, took the lead in political argument with the Bourbons in the eighteenth century. Investigations of the *parlement* of Toulouse and that of Paris[1] indicate that many senior lawyers abandoned such radical tendencies in the 1790s. However, their anxiety to maintain their professional and corporate status, which the revolutionaries and their nineteenth century successors attacked with even more fervour than had the ancien regime Bourbons, meant that they resisted the encroachments and demands of an increasingly centralized state, whether Jacobin, Directorial, Bonapartist or either species of post-revolutionary monarchist. In trying to assert their independence and the independence of their courts, magistrates could find themselves defending the freedom of the press and the right of association, leading the *Aide-toi* in the defence of the principle of free elections and sometimes becoming overtly republican in the 1830s. Doctors, not dissimilarly driven to defend the independence of their profession, were also moved by Saint-Simonian humanitarian impulses and the deficiencies of the liberal state towards radicalism and republicanism.

The numerous examples which have been noted in the present volume along with the evidence of countless personal dossiers of state servants in the *Archives Nationales* confirm, not the conspiracy theory of the right-wing historians of a 'grand bourgeois' takeover in the 1790s,[2] nor the revisonist belief in a consolidated post-revolutionary elite, but that the Revolution created dynasties of pro-1789 civil servants, most of whom were middle-class, who provided a firm and stable structure despite the volatile appearance of nineteenth-century France. As de Tocqueville sadly observed, the Revolution's onslaught on centralization led to an even more centralized state, and the fault was not all that of one ambitious general. The dramatic expansion of bureaucratic employment during the 1790s[3] continued throughout the nineteenth century and revolutions were always accompanied by even more job-seekers than insurgents.

Although the republican tradition which was treasured by enthusiasts from the 1830s onwards was self-consciously Jacobin and the Jacobin republic of the early 1790s had striven for centralized control, regional radicalism, often coordinated by lawyers, was based on rivalry with the capital and resentment of Parisian interference. The examples of Lyon, Marseille and other cities are well known, from the work of the outstanding generation of English doctoral students in the 1960s who rewrote the provincial history of the 1790s, to the impressive work of French and North American historians on the regional history of the nineteenth century. With the temporary collapse of central authority in 1830, 1848 and 1870–1 departmental capital cities and sometimes smaller towns seized the opportunity to appoint their own officials and often their decisions were rubber-stamped by the new revolutionary regimes. Sustained periods of resistance to Paris persisted, spectacularly, but not uniquely in larger towns like Lyon. But a centralized system also offered rich pickings and those who sought power in their localities were not unhappy to have it sanctioned in Paris. A centralized system coupled with a weak centre was a significant feature of nineteenth-century France. Radicals saw no contradiction between support for a republic and criticism of Parisian interference, a tendency still not uncommon in the Fifth Republic. Decentralization remains an ideal more honoured in the breach than the achievement.[4]

If the Revolution had meant jobs, it also meant the chance to buy cheap land and this fundamental underpinning of republicanism may be far more significant than the ideas of the *philosophes*. In England the sale of church land had been conducted by the Crown and reinforced the royalism of landed families whose influence endures to this day and supports the survival of a monarchy in Britain. In France the Church became the central pillar of a monarchist counter-revolution and the purchase of church and *émigré* lands committed families permanently to the Revolution. Both of these statements are of course wild generalizations and revisionist historians of France have noted that *émigré* families did buy back family land, and presumably sometimes bought church land through agents. The relationship between permanent commitment to the Revolution and the purchase of *biens nationaux* is a very complex question and only the surface of it has been touched, despite extensive research.[5] The proportion of land owned by the Church in pre-revolutionary France varied from between less than 1 per cent in parts of the Corrèze to over 20 per cent in the Aisne, but the national average was around 10 per cent. All of this was sold. Far less noble land was sold and on average the nobility lost perhaps 5 per cent of its lands during the Revolution, in 1814 still owning about 20 per cent of the land of France. Much of the land sold in the 1790s was bought by wealthy former office-holders with the compensation they obtained when they were obliged to give up venal offices. The purchase of these *biens nationaux* would obviously be a factor in the survival of revolutionary preferences but, as a single issue, its significance had huge regional variations, about which little is known despite a substantial number of regional histories. The systematic study of land purchase is laborious and apt to be overtaken in notarial records by the appetites of generations of rats.

The inheritance of the Revolution was far more than a distant memory or a nightmare in 1814. The institutional changes of the revolutionary decades survived and are in place to this day. It has been said that the Bourbon Restoration was the Empire without Napoleon. Put another way, it was the Republic plus a king. France did not become a republic in 1814, less because of the contradictory political inheritance of the revolutionary years and certainly not, as Weill suggested, because of an absence of republicans, but because she was defeated and occupied and her enemies thought a Bourbon monarchy would keep the peace. But the victorious Allies were content to preserve the institutional framework which had been constructed over 25 years. In addition, many old republicans who had served Napoleon helped to define the 1814 constitutional settlement. This compromise ensured that most of the institutional changes of the revolutionary and imperial years would survive and placed a parliamentary constitutional bridle on the brothers of the guillotined Louis XVI. The new king adopted Napoleon's civil servants as part of the deal. The muted degree of support for the Bourbons was clearly shown by the ease with which Napoleon was able to recover control during the Hundred Days.

Louis XVIII's initial attempts at compromise were scuppered by the Hundred Days. To a certain degree the *fédéré* movement cemented the alliance between Bonapartist and republican, making them both less palatable to the king and less tractable, but the merging of revolutionary and Bonapartist loyalties long preceded the Hundred Days. More significantly, the ease with which Napoleonic officials, who had been employed by the king in 1814, swore loyalty to Napoleon again in 1815, put the king in the hands of ultra-royalists, eager for revenge not compromise. The ultras never secured substantial support in the country, but from 1822 their leader, the future Charles X, gained ascendancy over his brother and the influence of the ultras began to exceed their numbers in the Chamber of Deputies. The ultras were not interested in compromise but sought confrontation with the Anti-Christ of revolutionary France by challenging the settlement of 1814. The liberal defenders of the constitution sought refuge in both conspiratorial and parliamentary tactics and by 1830 dominated the Chamber of Deputies.

But tales of an old aristocratic monarchist France at war with a new bourgeois country were ultra-royalist anachronisms. While the vast majority preferred to maintain a constitutional monarchy because they knew they could not agree amongst themselves on an alternative and were fearful of popular upheaval, their monarchism was entirely pragmatic. The small number of Orleanists were, after all, led by the banker Jacques Laffitte, and the duke of Orleans was his richest client. While these liberals would have denied they were republicans, their monarchism was pure opportunism, their only real commitment being to the very vaguely defined principles of 1789.

An overtly republican movement quickly revealed itself after the 1830 Revolution. The decision to cobble together the Orleanist monarchy was the opportunistic response of liberal notables who were determined to protect the tangible material and institutional benefits they had gained from the 1789 Revolution. Those who became dissatisfied with Louis-Philippe were hopelessly divided on alternatives. Some wanted to bring about a republican seizure of power with the support of the poor through conspiracy and violence. Most were so afraid of the masses that they preferred evolutionary change and the development of parliamentary powers. Some were eager for varying degrees of social reform and a few were utopians seeking a perfect model new society. Most were terrified of socialism.

Alongside the arguments of the educated, these years witnessed frequent expressions of popular unrest related to gradual economic change and repeated cyclical depression. Some artisan and peasant groups took to the streets to protest about such matters as specific political issues, taxation, the defence of communal institutions, and complaints about machines. Most of these demonstrators, like the liberal *notables*, looked back to the 1789 Revolution as a time of hope, if not fulfilment. On occasions, particularly up to 1834, when government repression intensified, they worked with sections of the educated middle classes in republican clubs. In both 1830 and 1848 political revolutions were the product of the coincidence of elite political criticism of the regime, *Aide-toi* and the liberals in 1830, the banquet campaign in 1847–8, with heightened popular unrest due to sustained economic crisis. On both occasions, however, the key to the collapse of the regime lay in neither of these factors; the economic crises seemed to be abating somewhat in both periods and middle-class political critics were terrified of violence. What was conclusive was the inability of both Charles X and Louis-Philippe to hold their capital city. As much as anything else the revolutions were made by geography and panic. The central right bank of Paris was the heart of government and luxury industry, including newspapers, in which opposition papers predominated. Neither Charles X nor his successors seemed able to deploy enough troops effectively to control a volatile mixture in narrow streets which were easy to defend and hard to conquer. France was highly centralized but at this point governments lacked adequate means, and the confidence, to impose their will in a crisis.

Thus in 1848 Louis-Philippe lost Paris and those who had been active in the banquet campaigns tried to establish themselves in power. Only a minority were overtly republican before the Revolution, but this may have signified little. Even the word republic was banned from the press after 1835. In February 1848 there was little alternative to a republic. There was positive support for a republic in Paris and the larger cities and growing evidence of popular support in certain rural areas. Once more, however, there were too many conflicting ideas on how to define a republic. Republicans agreed to introduce a democratic electoral system and were in accord that social problems, including unemployment, should be addressed. But how to tackle short-term social problems and how to define long-term objectives sank republicans in a morass of conflict. A democratic vote did not produce a republican assembly. The democratically elected president was the self-proclaimed heir of Bonaparte. Although many liberals and republicans had retained Bonapartist sympathies after 1814, very few supported Louis-Napoleon. His retention of power was based on the Bonapartist folk-memory of peasants and the opportunism of the old elites, who backed him because they thought that otherwise a democratic system would dilute their own power base. Louis-Napoleon manipulated the idea of democracy to sideline republicans and other opponents. Only in the 1860s did a broad coalition of moderate republicans and left-wing Orleanists emerge, while more extreme leaders, especially the socialists, were in exile. It was based on the quest for parliamentary power and left social questions on one side.

What was the relationship between the republicanism of the wealthy and those who were disenfranchised until 1848? Occasional glimpses of protest in police records indicate that the revolutionary and imperial years were looked back on as the golden age of the Continental System by some who worked in textiles, especially silk, the metallurgical trades, wine production and similar businesses, although the overall impact of the period had often been retrograde and negative. Countless violent protests against indirect taxes and government commercial policy after 1814 were frequently Bonapartist rather than republican, but there can be no doubt that small-scale producers thought of the whole period in a favourable light compared with the impact of commercial protectionism after 1814. The most influential single element was the artisan communities of the large cities, especially Lyon, but in particular central Paris, the fastest-growing industrial centre for most of the nineteenth century, dominated by luxury trades which were vulnerable in the frequent cyclical depressions.

The radicalism of artisans and peasants can be explained by their opposition to government taxation policies, the pressure of economic change or the repeated cyclical depressions of the nineteenth century. The detailed research into particular communities completed in the 1970s and 1980s revealed a variety of economic grievances and experiences and suggested that economic explanations for popular radicalism are crucial, even if they do not add up to the concerted proletarian revolution anticipated by Marxists. In addition the guillibility or naïveté of the less well-educated perhaps created a willingness to accept the double-talk of ambitious middle-class politicians. French historians stress that the most important single factor in popular republicanism in the nineteenth century was the egalitarian and liberal tradition of the 1789 Revolution. The revolutionary enthusiasm of the less well-off, fed by the night of 4 August 1789, and subsequent mythology, apparently survived the disappointments of less favourable revolutionary strategies. The election of Louis-Napoleon in 1848 might be cited to support the idea of the survival of popular patriotism, except that the most consistently republican areas rose against him in 1851 and voted against him throughout the Second

Empire. The political commitment of the less well-off is difficult to analyse and quantify because of the relative lack of evidence. There were artisan newspapers from the 1830s onwards, popular almanacs, songs and poetry, there are even a tiny number of memoirs. But the political views of the less well-off are often seen through the distorting mirror of their better-educated and wealthier fellow-citizens, especially novelists such as Zola who, out of altruism or profit, concerned themselves with social questions. The case for the patriotism of the masses cannot be substantiated by surviving evidence.

What is most apparent in this study of nineteenth-century republicanism is the continuity of a revolutionary tradition in the careers of individuals, their families, in communities and regions. No agreed political model emerged from the revolutionary and Napoleonic years. Defeat in 1814 meant that the emergence of a republican alternative was disputed and long-delayed in monarchist Europe, but those who had worked with the Revolution at any stage found it difficult to accept the Restored Bourbons after the failure of the First Restoration. Things might have been different if Napoleon had not escaped from Elba, if Louis XVIII's policy of conciliation had been sustained and the ultras contained, and if liberal catholic ideas had triumphed in the Catholic Church.

Counting heads is not very revealing. The tiny number of actual republicans in elected assemblies before 1871 were depressed by two factors. The centralized state held enormous and growing opportunities for patronage which local *notables* were keen to tap. Charles X's successors learned from his disastrous failure to exploit this advantage. In addition, paranoid about opposition (the negative side of the revolutionary tradition), the state regulated and rigorously policed the public expression of criticism, even in the Liberal Empire. Above all republicans were their own worst enemies; critical of both monarchies and the Second Empire, they were united only in what they did not like, but very divided about alternatives. The spectre of the Terror, the *enragés* and of Babeuf long confused a republic with violence and the dispossession of property-owners. A democratic republic would only succeed in a country where the majority of voters were small property-owners if innovative social reform was not on the agenda.

Ironically, Blanqui's theories notwithstanding, the political volatility of the nineteenth century itself delayed the acceptance of a republic. The frequent (although comparatively bloodless) collapse of centralized authority, in 1830, 1848 and 1870, worked against the radical minority who were catapulted into power. On each occasion a change of regime was the result of the nervousness of the Establishment. Radicals took over: liberals in 1830, republicans in 1848 and 1870. They were cast in the guise of agents of revolution and consequently were pressed by those who wanted even more extreme measures and criticized by those who feared all change. The Third Republic avoided revolution; like the Second Empire, it was eventually destroyed by war. Its creation was due partly to the determined repression of radical opinion in Paris, Lyon and elsewhere and to the absence of any credible alternative. But above all its survival depended on republicans forgetting a good deal they had held dear in revolutionary tradition, working with former monarchists they had hated during the Second Republic and settling for a parliamentary regime, the basis of which had been laid down in the 1860s. The Third Republic was the Empire without Louis-Napoleon but it was not a republic without republicans.

Notes

Chapter 1. The Republic: Idea and Image

1. M. Agulhon, 'La République de Gauche à Droite', a talk given at the Modern French History Seminar, *Institut Français*, London, 5 December 1992.
2. *Le Monde*, 16 October 1992.
3. F. Furet, J. Juilliard and R. Rosavallon, *La République du Centre: la Fin de l'exception française* (Paris, 1988).
4. *Esprit des Lois*, II, 1.
5. J. J. Rousseau, *Contrat Social*, III, 1.
6. J. Godechot, *Les Révolutions (1770–1799)* (Paris, 1963), pp. 203–47; R. R. Palmer, *The Age of the Democratic Revolution*, 2 vols (Princeton, NJ, 1959, 1964).
7. T. C. W. Blanning, *The French Revolution in Germany: Occupation and Resistance in the Rhineland, 1792–1802* (Oxford, 1983).
8. P. Higonnet, *Sister Republics* (Cambridge, Mass., 1988), p. 278.
9. Judith Shklar and B. Vincent, in F. Furet and M. Ozouf (*sous direction de*) *Le Siècle de l'avènement républicain* (Paris, 1993).
10. P. Nora (*sous direction de*) *Les Lieux de mémoire*. 3 vols, 1984–1993: vol. III *La France. 1. Conflits et partages 2. Traditions 3. De l'Archive à l'emblême* (Paris, 1993).
11. M. Agulhon, *Marianne. Les Visages de la République* (Paris, new edn. 1992); first edn. trans. *Marianne into Battle. Republican Imagery and Symbolism in France 1789–1880* (Cambridge, 1981), pp. 30–7.
12. M. Ozouf, *La Fête révolutionnaire, 1789–1799* (Paris, 1976).
13. L. Duguit and H. Monnier, *Les Constitutions et les Principales Lois Politiques de la France depuis 1789* (3rd edn. Paris, 1915), pp. 1–3.

14. L. Jaume, *Les Déclarations des droits de l'homme; du début 1789–1793 au préambule de 1946* (Paris, 1989); M. Gauchet, *La Révolution des Droits de l'Homme* (Paris, 1989).

15. Olympe de Gouges, *Déclaration des droits de la femme* (Paris, 1791), reprinted in Olympe de Gouges, *Oeuvres* (Paris, 1986).

16. Duguit and Monnier, *Les Constitutions*, pp. 36–8.

17. L. Jaume, *Le Discours jacobin et la démocratie* (Paris, 1989); L. Jaume 'Les Jacobins et l'opinion publique', in S. Berstein and O. Rudelle (eds), *Le modèle républicain* (Paris, 1992), pp. 57–69.

18. Duguit and Monnier, *Les Constitutions* pp. 66–9. The *Acte Constitutionnelle du 24 juin 1793* had 35 clauses.

19. Duguit and Monnier, *Les Constitutions*, pp. 78–80. Constitution of 5 Fructidor Year III, 22 August 1795; the constitution of the Directory was preceded by a 'Declaration des Droits et des Devoirs de l'homme et du citoyen'.

20. Duguit and Monnier, *Les Constitutions*, pp. 184–5.

21. Duguit and Monnier, *Les Constitutions*, pp. 196–7.

22. Duguit and Monnier, *Les Constitutions*, pp. 213–14.

23. Duguit and Monnier, *Les Constitutions*, pp. 233–6.

24. Duguit and Monnier, *Les Constitutions*, pp. 274–80.

25. Duguit and Monnier, *Les Constitutions*, pp. 314–42.

26. P. Campbell and B. Chapman, *The Constitution of the Fifth Republic* (Oxford, 1958) (trans. and commentary).

27. R. Alexander, *Bonapartism and the Revolutionary Tradition in France. The Fédérés of 1815* (Cambridge, 1991).

28. M. David, *Le Printemps de la Fraternité. Gènese et vicissitudes (1830–51)* (Paris, 1992).

29. P. M. Pilbeam, *The 1830 Revolution in France* (London, 1991), pp. 99–120.

30. J. de Maistre, *Considérations sur la France* (Geneva, 1796), p. 69.

31. A. de Tocqueville, *The Old Regime and the French Revolution*, trans. S. Gilbert (New York, 1955), p. 6.

32. F. Furet, 'Edgar Quinet', in F. Furet and M. Ozouf, *The Transformation of Political Culture 1789–1848*, vol. 3 of *The French Revolution and the Creation of Modern Political Culture* (Oxford, 1989), p. 617.

33. J. Michelet, *Histoire de la Révolution*, I, p. 25 cited by L. Gossman, 'Michelet and the French Revolution', in Furet and Ozouf, *Transformation of Political Culture*, p. 645.

34. P. Birnbaum, *'La France aux Français'. Histoire des haines nationalistes* (Paris, 1993).

35. L. C. Jennings, *France and Europe in 1848: A study of French Foreign Affairs in time of Crisis* (Oxford, 1983).

36. *Discours prononcé par M. Gambetta au banquet de la Jeunesse*, St Germain, nd [1869], 16 pp. Anodyne address – anti-Bonapartist, pro-universal suffrage.

37. Typical was Cavaignac's defence speech, *Cour d'Assises de la Seine, Procès du Droit d'Association, audience du 15 décembre 1832* (Paris, 1832), pp. 19–20.

38. Colin *procureur-général* Dijon to *garde des sceaux*, 20 Sept. 1833. *A[rchives] N[ationales]* BB18.1338.

Chapter 2. Historians and the Republic

1. L. Orr, *Headless History. Nineteenth-century French Historiography of the Revolution* (Ithaca and London, 1990), p. 20.

2. E. L. Newman, 'Lost illusions: the Regicides in France during the Bourbon Restoration', *Nineteenth-Century French Studies*, X (1981–2), 45–72. The complete list, 'Barrière', *Catalogue Générale des Imprimés*, Bibliothèque Nationale (*BN*).

3. P.-T. Durand de Mailland, *Histoire de la Convention Nationale* (Paris, 1825); Barrière et Berville (eds), *Papiers inédits trouvés chez Robespierre, Saint-Just, Payan etc.*, 4 vols (Paris, 1828); L. Thiessé, *Débats de la Convention Nationale*, 5 vols (Paris, 1828). Newman, 'Lost illusions', p. 57.

4. A. Thiers, *Histoire de la Révolution française*, 10 vols (Paris, 1823–7); F. Mignet, *Histoire de la Révolution française* (Paris, 1827).

5. P. Buonarroti, *Conspiration pour l'Egalité dite de Babeuf, suivie du procès auquel elle donna lieu*, 2 vols (Brussels, 1828).

6. E. Cabet, *La Révolution de 1830 et la situation présente* (Paris, 1831); J. J. L. Blanc, *Révolution française. Histoire de Dix Ans*, 5 vols (Paris, 1841–4).

7. E. Cabet, *Histoire populaire de la Révolution française 1789–1830* (Paris, 1840).

8. L. de Bonald, *Réflexions sur la Révolution de 1830* (presenté par F. Bastier, new edn Paris, 1988); J. de Maistre, *Considérations sur la France* (1796).

9. Cabet, *La Révolution de 1830*, p. 119.

10. E. Quinet, *Le Christianisme et la Révolution française* (Paris, 1846).

11. P. Buchez and P. C. Roux, *Histoire parlementaire de la Révolution française* (Paris, 1837).

12. J. Michelet, *Histoire de la Révolution*, 7 vols (Paris, 1847–53).

13. A. de Lamartine, *Histoire des Girondins*, 3 vols (Paris, 1847); trs. *History of the Girondists* (London, 1913), vol. 1, 1.

14. J. J. L. Blanc, *Histoire de la Révolution* (Paris, 1847).

15. A. Esquiros, *Histoire des montagnards* (Paris 1847).

16. L. de la Hodde, *Histoire des sociétés secrètes et du parti républicain de 1830 à 1848* (Paris, 1850).

17. A. de Lamartine, *Histoire de la Révolution de 1848*, 2 vols (Paris, 1849).

18. K. Marx, *The Class Struggles in France 1848 to 1850* (Moscow, n.d.; trans. from German edn 1895).

19. A. de Tocqueville, *Recollections* (trans. G. Lawrence, New York, 1971), pp. 169–206.

20. A. de Tocqueville, *The Old Regime and the French Revolution*, trans. S. Gilbert (New York, 1955).

21. F. Furet, *Interpreting the French Revolution*, trans. (Cambridge, 1984).

22. Tocqueville, *Recollections*, pp. 205–6.

23. Tocqueville, *Recollections*, pp. 5, 52.

24. P. Thureau-Dangin, *Royalistes et Républicains. Essais historiques sur des questions de politique contemporaine* (Paris, 1874).

25. Thureau-Dangin, *Royalistes et Républicains*, p. 337.

26. G. Weill, *Histoire du parti républicain en France de 1814 à 1870* (Paris, 1900).

27. Weill, *Le Parti républicain*, pp. 524–30.

28. I.-A. Chernov (Tchernoff), *Le Parti républicain sous la monarchie de juillet. Formation et evolution de la doctrine républicaine* (Paris, 1901); I.-A. Chernov (Tchernoff), *Associations et sociétés secrètes sous la Seconde République, 1848–51* (Paris, 1905); I.-A. Chernov (Tchernoff), *Le Parti républicaine au coup d'état et sous la second empire* (Paris, 1906).

29. G. Perreux, *Aux Temps des sociétés secrètes. La Propagande républicain au début de la Monarchie de Juillet, 1830–35* (Paris, 1931).

30. For example, A. Tuetey, *Publications sur la Révolution à Paris. Répertoire des sources manuscrites* and M. Tourneux, *Publications sur la Révolution à Paris. Bibliographie de l'histoire de Paris*. To their many volumes, which leave little to chance in revolutionary Paris, should be added Tuetey, *Archives Parlementaires*.

31. A. Cobban, *Historians and the Causes of the French Revolution* (Historical Association pamphlet, G.2. revised, London, 1965); C. Nicolet, *L'Idée républicaine en France 1789–1924. Essai d'histoire critique* (Paris, 1981), pp. 96–101.

32. C. Seignobos, *La Révolution de 1848 – le Second Empire (1848–59)*, vol. 4 of *Histoire de la France Contemporaine*, ed. E. Lavisse (Paris, 1921), pp. 82–3. His conclusions are criticized by F. de Luna, *The French Republic under Cavaignac* (Princeton, NJ, 1975).

33. J. Lhomme, *La Grande Bourgeoisie au pouvoir 1830–1880* (Paris, 1960).

34. G. Lefebvre, *La Révolution française* (Paris, 1951); A. Soboul, *Précis historique de la Révolution française* (Paris, 1962: Eng. trans. 1975).

35. G. Lefebvre, *The Great Fear of 1789; Rural Panic in Revolutionary France* (trans. London, 1973) is a brilliant evocation; A. Soboul, *Les Sans-culottes parisiens de l'An II* (Paris, 1958) where detailed evidence does not always suit the dogma.

36. The challenge was launched in A. Cobban, *The Myth of the French Revolution* (inaugural lecture, University College, London, 1955; reprinted in *Aspects of the French Revolution* (London, 1968). The final version of his redefinition is A. Cobban, *The Social Interpretation of the French Revolution* (London, 1968).

37. G. Ellis, 'The Marxist interpretation of the French Revolution', *English Historical Review*, XCIII (1978), 353–76; P. M. Pilbeam, *The Middle Classes in Europe 1789–1914; France, Germany, Italy and Russia* (London, 1990), pp. 210–23.

38. G. Chaussinand-Nogaret, *Une Histoire des élites* (Paris, 1975).

39. D. C. Higgs, *Nobles in Nineteenth Century France. The Practice of Inegalitarianism* (Baltimore, MD, 1987).

40. D. H. Pinkney, *The French Revolution of 1830* (Princeton, NJ, 1972); P. M. Pilbeam, *The 1830 Revolution in France* (London, 1991).

41. A. J. Tudesq, *Les Grands Notables en France 1840–1849. Etude Historique d'une psychologie sociale*, 2 vols (Paris, 1964); B. Leclère and V. Wright, *Les Préfets du IIe. Empire* (Paris, 1973).

42. R. D. Price (ed.), *Revolution and Reaction. 1848 and the Second French Republic* (London, 1975); R. D. Price, *The French Second Republic; A Social History* (London, 1972); C. Tilly and L. Lees, 'Le peuple de Juin 1848', *Annales: Economies, Sociétés, Civilisations* (1974), 1061–91; M. Traugott, *Armies of the Poor. Determinants of Working-Class Participation in the Parisian Insurrection of June 1848* (Princeton, NJ, 1985).

43. R. Tombs, 'Paris and the rural hordes; an exploration of myth and reality in the French Civil War of 1871', *Historical Journal* (1986); J. Rougerie, *Le Procès des Communards* (Paris, 1964).

44. M. Agulhon, *La République au village*. Trans. *The Republic in the Village* (Cambridge, 1982); A. Corbin, *Archaisme et modernité en Limousin au XIXe. siècle* (Paris, 1975); P. Vigier, *La Seconde République*

dans la région alpine, 2 vols (Paris, 1963); R. Aminzade, *Class, Politics and early Industrial Capitalism. A study in Mid-nineteenth-century Toulouse* (Albany, New York, 1981); P. M. Jones, *Politics and Rural Society. The southern Massif Central c. 1750–1880* (Cambridge, 1985).

45. Corbin, *Archaisme et modernité en Limousin.*

46. A. Soboul, *Problèmes paysans de la Révolution française 1789–1848* (Paris, 1976).

47. Vigier, *La Seconde République dans la région alpine.*

48. Agulhon, *La République au village.*

49. Corbin, *Archaisme et modernité en Limousin.*

50. Aminzade, *Class, Politics and early Industrial Capitalism.*

51. J. Merriman, *The Agony of the Republic. The Repression of the Left in Revolutionary France 1848–51* (New Haven, CT, 1978).

52. M. L. Stewart-McDougall, *Artisan Republic: Revolution, Reaction and Resistance in Lyon 1848–1851* (Kingston and Montreal, 1984), pp. 156–9.

53. See below, ch. 7.

54. T. W. Margadant, *French Peasants in Revolt. The Insurrection of 1851* (Princeton, NJ, 1979); Merriman, *Agony of the Republic.*

55. E. Weber, *Peasants into Frenchmen. The Modernization of Rural France 1870–1914* (London, 1977); E. Weber, 'The Second Republic, politics and the peasant', *French Historical Studies*, 11, 4 (1980), 522–50.

56. E. Zola, *La Fortune des Rougon* (Paris, 1981; first pub. 1871).

57. Weber, 'The Second Republic, politics and the peasant'.

58. Margadant, *French Peasants in Revolt.*

59. Jones, *Politics and Rural Society.*

60. W. Edmonds, *Jacobinism and the Revolt of Lyon, 1789–93* (Oxford, 1990), p. 304.

61. A. Soboul, *Comprendre la Révolution: Problèmes politiques de la Révolution française 1789–97* (Paris, 1981).

62. R. Robin, *La Société française en 1789: l'exemple de Semur-en-Auxois* (Paris, 1970).

63. F. Furet, *Penser la Révolution française* (Paris, 1978). Trans. as *Interpreting the French Revolution* (Cambridge, 1981).

64. F. Furet, *La Gauche et la Révolution au milieu du XIXe. siècle. Edgar Quinet et la question du Jacobinisme 1865–70* (Paris, 1986).

65. F. Furet and M. Ozouf, *The Transformation of Political Culture 1789–1848*, vol. 3 of *The French Revolution and the Creation of Modern Political Culture* (Oxford, 1989).

66. F. Furet (ed.), *The Influence of the French Revolution on Nineteenth*

Century Europe (Oxford, 1989); F. Furet, *L'Héritage de la Révolution française* (Paris, 1989).

67. K. Baker, *Inventing the French Revolution* (Cambridge, 1990).
68. Nicolet, *L'Idée républicaine en France*.
69. F. Furet, J. Juilliard and P. Rosanvallon, *La République du Centre: la fin de l'exception française* (Paris, 1988).
70. See in particular D. H. Pinkney, *Decisive Years in France 1840–47* (Princeton, NJ, 1986) although the absence of political issues from this discussion may indicate some reservation in his resuscitation of the Orleanists. H. A. C. Collingham, *The July Monarchy. A Political History of France, 1830–1848* (London, 1988) has some kind words to say, but is too dismissive of the left.
71. F. Furet, *Revolutionary France 1770–1880* (trans. Oxford, 1992) pp. 281–3.
72. M. Traugott, *Armies of the Poor. Determinants of Working-Class Participation in the Parisian Insurrection of June 1848* (Princeton, NJ, 1985).
73. M. Agulhon, *1848 ou l'apprentissage de la république 1848–1852* (Paris, 1973).
74. Furet, *Revolutionary France 1770–1880*, p. 537.
75. S. Berstein and O. Rudelle, *Le Modèle républicain* (Paris, 1992).

Chapter 3. The Legacy of the First Republic and the Napoleonic Empire

1. M. Vovelle, *The Fall of the French Monarchy 1787–1792* (Cambridge, 1984), p. 117, first published as *La Chute de la monarchie, 1787–1792* (Paris, 1972); R. Griffiths, *Le Centre perdu. Malouet et les 'monarchiens' dans la Révolution française* (Grenoble, 1988).
2. E. Lever, 'Le mythe du complot sous le règne de Louis XVI (1789–92)', Modern French History Seminar, *Institut Français*, 22 May 1993. Mme Lever is preparing a biography of the duke of Orleans.
3. L. Duguit and H. Monnier, *Les Constitutions et les Principales Lois Politiques de la France depuis 1789* (Paris, 1915), pp. 7–13.
4. F. Furet, *Revolutionary France 1770–1880* (trans. Oxford, 1992), p. 78.
5. T. Tackett, *Religion, Revolution and Regional Culture in Eighteenth-Century France: The Ecclesiastical Wrath of 1791* (Princeton, NJ, 1985); J. McManners, *The French Revolution and the Church*

(London, 1969); C. Langlois and T. Tackett, 'A l'épreuve de la Révolution (1770–1830)' in F. Lebrun (ed.), *Histoire des catholiques en France du XVe. siècle à nos jours* (Paris, 1980).

6. A. Forrest, *The French Revolution and the Poor* (Oxford, 1981).

7. O. Hufton, *Women and the Limits of Citizenship during the French Revolution* (Toronto, 1992).

8. A useful summary of the counter-revolution can be found in J. Roberts, *The Counter-Revolution in France 1787–1830* (London, 1990). See also M. Winock (*sous direction de*), *Histoire de l'extrême droite en France* (Paris, 1992).

9. T. C. W. Blanning, *The Origins of the French Revolutionary Wars* (London, 1986), pp. 69–76.

10. Duguit and Monnier, *Les Constitutions*, p. xxvi.

11. D. M. G. Sutherland, *France 1789–1815. Revolution and Counter-Revolution* (London, 1985), p. 155.

12. M. Bouloiseau, *The Jacobin Republic 1792–1794* (trans. 1983), pp. 47–8.

13. *French Revolutionary Speeches*, 424.

14. Duguit and Monnier, *Les Constitutions*, pp. 78–118.

15. L. Delbez, *Les Grands Courants de la pensée politique française depuis la XIX siècle*, p. 24.

16. P. Buonarroti, *Conspiration pour l'Egalité dite de Babeuf, suivie du procès auquel elle donna lieu*, 2 vols (Brussels, 1828), p. 270.

17. 'Manifesto of the Equals' in Buonarroti (above), p. 314.

18. C. H. Church, *Revolution and Red Tape: the French Ministerial Bureaucracy 1770–1850* (London, 1981); D. Woronoff, *The Thermidorian Regime and the Directory 1794–1799* (trans. 1984), pp. 192–5.

19. A very clear account in I. Collins, *Napoleon and his Parliaments, 1800–1815* (London, 1979).

20. A splendid chart of the various institutions and their relationships can be found in G. Ellis, *The Napoleonic Empire* (London, 1991), pp. 20–1.

21. Duguit and Monnier, *Les Constitutions*, 'Constitution de la République Française du 22 Frimaire an VIII (13 décembre 1799)', pp. 118–23.

22. Duguit and Monnier, *Les Constitutions*, pp. 144–5.

23. G. Lefebvre, *Napoléon* (Paris, 1935, trans. New York, 1990).

24. B. D. Gooch (ed.) *Napoleonic Ideas. Napoleon III. Des Idées Napoléoniennes par le Prince Napoléon-Louis Bonaparte* (1967), pp. 34–5.

25. Collins, *Napoleon and his Parliaments*, pp. 19–22.

26. E. L. Newman, 'Lost illusions: the Regicides in France during the Bourbon Restoration', *Nineteenth-Century French Studies*, X (1981–2), 46.

27. J. Godechot, *Les Institutions de la France sous la Révolution et l'Empire* (Paris, 1951); Ellis, *The Napoleonic Empire*, pp. 27–8.

28. L. Bergeron and G. Chaussinand-Nogaret, *Les Masses de Granit* (Paris, 1979).

29. G. K. Anderson, 'Old nobles and *Noblesse d'Empire* (1814–1830); in search of a conservative interest in post-revolutionary France' (unpublished paper, University of Glasgow, March 1993).

30. W. Edmonds, *Jacobinism and the Revolt of Lyon, 1789–93* (Oxford, 1990).

31. G. Bossenga, *The Politics of Privilege. Old Regime and Revolution in Lille* (Cambridge, 1991).

32. J. Tulard, *Napoleon. The Myth of the Saviour* (trans. 1985), p. 81.

33. Church, *Revolution and Red Tape*.

34. A succinct survey can be found in Ellis, *The Napoleonic Empire*, pp. 33–49. See also L. Bergeron, *France under Napoleon* (trans. Cambridge, 1981; French edn 1972); R. B. Holtman, *The Napoleonic Revolution* (Philadelphia, 1967).

35. Sutherland, *France 1789–1815. Revolution and Counter-Revolution*, p. 396.

36. Sutherland, *France 1789–1815*, p. 400.

37. B. Constant, *Principes de Politique* (Paris, 1815), p. 1110.

38. B. Constant, *Principes de Politique*, repr. in *Oeuvres de Benjamin Constant* (Paris, 1957), pp. 1110–79.

39. 'Acte Additional aux Constitutions de l'Empire', 22 April 1815, Duguit and Monnier, *Les Constitutions*, pp. 190–1.

40. R. Alexander, *Bonapartism and the Revolutionary Tradition in France. The Fédérés of 1815* (Cambridge, 1991).

41. P. Thureau-Dangin, *Le Parti libéral sous la Restauration* (Paris, 1888), pp. 15–31.

Chapter 4. Conspirators and Parliamentarians: Republicans 1814–1830

1. F. Guizot, *Des moyens de gouvernement et des moyens d'opposition dans l'état actuel de la France* (Paris, 1821). A preliminary assay into the nature of nineteenth-century republicanism, P. M. Pilbeam, 'Republicanism in early C19[th] France, 1814–35', *French History* (1991), 30–47. I am grateful to Oxford University Press for

permission to incorporate this material into the next two chapters.

2. G. Weill, *Histoire du parti républicain en France de 1814 à 1870* (Paris, 1900), p. 1; G. Weill, 'L'Idée républicaine en France pendant la Restauration', *Revue d'histoire moderne*, II (1927), 321–48.

3. A regrettably unpublished account came to a similar conclusion. E. L. Newman, *Republicanism during the Bourbon Restoration in France, 1814–1830* (PhD, University of Chicago, 1969). I am very grateful to the author for generously providing me with a microfilm of this informative work.

4. J. Roberts, *The Counter-Revolution in France 1787–1830* (London, 1990) presents a lucid and indispensable analysis.

5. J. de Maistre, *Considérations sur la France* (Neuchâtel, 1796), p. 69.

6. J. M. Sherwig, *Guineas and Gunpowder. British Foreign Aid in the Wars with France 1793–1815* (London, 1969).

7. A brief account of the process in A. Jardin and A. J. Tudesq, *Restoration and Reaction 1815–48* (Cambridge, 1983), pp. 3–13. Originally published as *La France des Notables 1815–48*, 2 vols (Paris, 1973).

8. L. Duguit and H. Monnier, *Les Constitutions et les Principales Lois Politiques de la France depuis 1789* (3rd edn, Paris, 1915), pp. 179–82.

9. Duguit and Monnier, *Les Constitutions*, pp. 182–90.

10. N. Richardson, *The Personnel of the French Prefectoral Corps under the Restoration* (PhD 4712, Cambridge, Feb. 1964), p. 106.

11. G. K. Anderson, 'Old nobles and *Noblesse d'Empire* (1814–1830); in search of a conservative interest in post-revolutionary France' (unpublished paper, University of Glasgow, March 1993).

12. R. S. Alexander, 'The Federations of 1814 and the continuity of anti-Bourbon personnel, 1789–1830', *Proceedings of the Annual Meeting of the Western Society for French History*, vol. 17 (1990), p. 288.

13. S. Neely, 'Rural politics in the Early Restoration; Charles Goyet and the liberals of the Sarthe', *European History Quarterly*, XVI (1986), 313–42.

14. R. S. Alexander, *Bonapartism and the Revolutionary Tradition in France. The Fédérés of 1815* (Cambridge, 1991), pp. 1–62.

15. Alexander, *Bonapartism*, pp. 94–5.

16. Alexander, *Bonapartism*. Also 'Republicanism in Restoration France', an unpublished paper given to the annual conference of *French Historical Studies*, University of Texas at El Paso, March 1992.

17. Roberts, *The Counter-Revolution in France*, pp. 3 and 115–16.

18. L. de Bonald, *Théorie de l'éducation sociale et de l'administration publique* (1796).
19. de Maistre, *Considérations sur la France*.
20. B. Fitzpatrick, *Catholic Royalism in the Department of the Gard, 1814–52* (Cambridge, 1983); D. Resnick, *The White Terror and the Political Reaction after Waterloo* (Cambridge, Mass., 1966); D. C. Higgs, *Ultra-royalism in Toulouse from its Origins to the Revolution of 1830* (Baltimore, MD, 1973), pp. 55–7; Jardin and Tudesq, *Restoration and Reaction*, p. 24.
21. An indication of some aspects of Restoration Bonapartism can be gained from B. Ménager, *Les Napoléons du Peuple* (1988).
22. F. Bluche, *Le Bonapartisme* (Paris, 1980).
23. E. Guillon, *Les Complots militaires sous la Restauration* (Paris, 1912), pp. 6–38.
24. P. Chalmin, *L'Officier français de 1815 à 1870* (Paris, 1957), pp. 69–73.
25. R. Holyrood, 'The Bourbon army 1815–30', *Historical Journal*, XIV, 3 (1971), 540.
26. *Compte annuel* 1818. AN F1cIII Moselle 9. P. Leuilliot, *L'Alsace au début du XIXe. siècle. Essai d'histoire politique, économique et religieuse, 1815–30*, I (Paris, 1959–60), p. 81.
27. 10 October 1815. AD Ille-et-Vilaine, 1M98.
28. Anderson, 'Old nobles and *Noblesse d'Empire* (1814–1830).
29. P. Buonarroti, *Conspiration pour l'égalité dite de Babeuf* (Brussels, 1928).
30. A. B. Spitzer, *The French Generation of 1820* (Princeton, NJ, 1987), an elegantly written modern comparison. The Third Republican historians Thureau-Dangin and Charléty were inclined to make similar observations.
31. See Spitzer, *French Generation*.
32. 'Discours prononcé à l'ouverture de cours de l'histoire de la philosophie, 13 décembre 1815' (Paris, 1816) trans. by and quoted in Spitzer, *French Generation*, pp. 91–2.
33. Stendhal, *Le Rouge et le Noir*. Written in 1828, the novel is readily available in English, cf. the Penguin edition translated and with introduction by Margaret R. B. Shaw.
34. Spitzer, *French Generation*, pp. 9–45.
35. D. W. Johnson, *Guizot. Aspects of French History 1787–1874* (London, 1963), pp. 119–21.
36. Spitzer, *French Generation*.
37. See Spitzer, *French Generation*, ch. 1.

38. P. Gerbod, *Paul-François Dubois, universitaire, journaliste et homme politique, 1793–1874* (Paris, 1967).
39. P. Thureau-Dangin, *Le Parti libéral sous la Restauration* (Paris, 1888), p. 70.
40. D. L. Rader, *The Journalists and the July Revolution in France* (The Hague, 1973), p. 19.
41. F. Parent, 'Les cabinets de lecture dans Paris; pratiques culturelles et espace social sous la Restauration', *Annales*, 34 (1979), 1016–38.
42. I. Collins, *The Government and Newspaper Press in France 1814–81* (London, 1959).
43. *Association pour le refus de l'impôt.* A substantial correspondence exists, *AN* F7.6742 and F7.6754.
44. *Journal de Carion*, 28 October 1829.
45. *L'Annonciateur Boulonnais*, 3 December 1829. *AN* F7.6742.
46. P. M. Pilbeam, *The Middle Class in Europe 1789–1914; France, Germany, Italy and Russia* (London, 1990), pp. 173–209.
47. E. Trélat, *De la Constitution du corps des médecins et de l'enseignement médical* (Paris, 1828).
48. G. de Bertier de Sauvigny, *Le comte Ferdinande de Bertier et l'énigme de la congrégation* (Paris, 1948).
49. G. Weill, 'Les mémoires de Joseph Rey', *Revue historique*, 156 (1928).
50. S. Neely, *Lafayette and the Liberal Ideal, 1814–24. Politics and Conspiracy in an Age of Reaction* (Carbondale, Ill., 1991).
51. E. Guillon, *Les Complots militaires sous la Restauration* (Paris, 1912), p. 140.
52. 5 February 1822 to *garde des sceaux. AN* BB30.241.
53. Reports on *Conspiration de l'Est* can be found in prefectoral accounts of local happenings, e.g. in *AN*. F7.9682, *Situation des départements de 1814 à 1830*. This series is organized on a departmental basis. Likewise judicial reports occur in *AN*. BB30 where they are grouped according to *cours royaux*. BB30.237 and 240 provide useful accounts.
54. *AN*. BB30.237.
55. L. de la Hodde, *Histoire des sociétés secrètes et du parti républicain de 1830 à 1848* (Paris, 1850).
56. R. J. Rath, 'The *carbonari*: their origins, initiation rites and aims', *American Historical Review*, 69 (1963), 353–70.
57. A. Calmette, 'Les carbonaris en France sous la Restauration', *La Révolution de 1848*, x (1913–14), 135; J. A. Faucher and A. Ricker,

Histoire de la franc-maçonnerie en France (Paris, 1967), p. 274; E. Trélat, 'La Charbonnerie', *Paris Révolutionnaire*, II (1838), pp. 275–341.

58. Prefectoral report to Minister of Interior, 10 March 1822, *AN* F7.6686.

59. Trélat, 'La Charbonnerie', pp. 227–52.

60. Alexander, *Bonapartism*, p. 180.

61. A. Spitzer, *Old Hatreds and Young Hopes. The French Carbonari against the Bourbon Restoration* (Cambridge, 1971); J. M. Roberts, *The Mythology of the Secret Societies* (London, 1972); Calmette, 'Les carbonaris en France sous la Restauration', *La Révolution de 1848*, IX (1912–13), X (1913–14).

62. *AN.* F7.6686; BB30.241.

63. Trélat, 'La Charbonnerie', p. 217; Grillon, *Complots militaires*, pp. 144–51.

64. 5 February 1822, *AN* BB30.241.

65. 6 December 1822, *AN* BB30.241.

66. Ibid., 11 April 1823.

67. *AN* BB30.239.

68. Prefect to Minister of Interior, a selection of regular reports 1822, principally 1 January, 3 January, 25 January, 5 March. Also *procureur-général* to *garde des sceaux*, 1 January 1822, *AN.*BB30.240.

    A. Brandt, 'Quelques aspects de la vie politique à Mulhouse sous la Restauration', *Bulletin de la société industrielle de Mulhouse*, 101 (1935), 351; L. Delabrousse, 'Les députés de l'Alsace sous la Restauration', *Revue Alsacienne* (1883–4), 62.

69. Report to Minister of Interior, 3 January 1822, *AN* BB30.240.

70. *Procureur-général* to *garde des sceaux*, 14 August 1822, *AN* BB30.240.

71. Augustin-Joseph Caron (1774–1822).

72. H. Wahl, 'Les manifestations de l'opposition libérale et les complots militaires dans le Haut-Rhin sous la Restauration', *Revue d'Alsace*, 92 (1953).

73. Grillon, *Les Complots militaires*, pp. 159–172.

74. Spitzer, *Old Hatreds and Young Hopes*; C. Robert, *Les Quatre sergents de la Rochelle* (Paris, 1849); P. Dethomas, *Le Procès des quatre sergents de la Rochelle* (Paris, 1912).

75. D. Porch, *Army and Revolution. France 1815–48* (London, 1974).

76. Stendhal, *Lucien Leuwen* (first pub. 1836).

77. de Corcelle, *Documents pour servir à l'histoire des conspirations, des partis et des écrits* (Paris, 1831), *BN* La38.3.

78. Faucher and Ricker, *Histoire de la franc-maçonnerie*, p. 271.

79. St Die, *Les Amis Incorruptibles des Vosges*, 25 December 1829. *BN, Fonds Franc-maçonnerie*.

80. P. Barral, 'La Franc-maçonnerie en Lorraine au XIXe. et XX siècle', *Annales de l'Est* (1970), 13.

81. Barral, 'La Franc-maçonnerie en Lorraine', p. 15.

82. Police and *Procureur-général*'s reports 8 June 1823, *AN* BB30.241, BB6.258; Strasbourg failed to stir, BB30.250.

83. H. de Saint-Simon, *Le nouveau Christianisme*, ed. H. Desroche (Paris, 1969).

84. P. M. Pilbeam, *The 1830 Revolution in France* (London, 1991), pp. 13–36.

85. P. Rosanvallon, 'Les Doctrinaires et la question du gouvernement représentative', in F. Furet and M. Ozouf (eds), *The Transformation of Political Culture 1789–1848* (Oxford, 1989), p. 420.

86. E. de Waresquiel, 'Les Voyageurs français en Angleterre pendant la Restauration', Modern French History Seminar, *Institut Français*, London, 13 February 1993. Waresquiel's study of the political life of the Restoration was published at the end of 1993.

87. G. A. Kelly, 'Liberalism and aristocracy in the French Restoration', *Journal of the History of Ideas* (1965), 509.

88. P. Rosanvallon, 'Les Doctrinaires et la question du gouvernment représentatif', pp. 412–13.

89. L. Delbez, *Les Grands Courants de la pensée politique française depuis la XIX siècle,* pp. 23–49.

90. E. Harpaz, *L'Ecole Libérale sous la Restauration* (Geneva, 1968), p. 14.

91. F. R. vicomte de Chateaubriand, *De la Monarchie selon la Charte* (London, 1816).

92. *Archives Parlementaires*, 7 March 1829, pp. 269–72.

93. M. Hartmann, 'The sacrilege law of 1825 in France, a study in anti-clericalism and myth-making', *Journal of Modern History* (1972), 35.

94. S. Kent, *The Election of 1827 in France* (Cambridge, Mass., 1975), pp. 25–30.

95. Chamber of Deputies, 19 March 1829. *Archives Parlementaires*, LVII, p. 637.

96. Pilbeam, *1830 Revolution in France*, pp. 13–36.

97. 'Liste des électeurs de l'arrondissement de Remiremont d'après la liste générale du Jury dressée en 1829'; 'Liste nominatif des électeurs de l'arrondissement de Mirecourt'; Etat Nominatif des Electeurs de l'arrondissement de St Dié, dressé en exécution de la

lettre confidentielle de M. le Préfet, 1 juin 1830'. *AD* Vosges, *série* M. Elections.

98. Kent, *The Election of 1827 in France*, p. 65.
99. Kent, *The Election of 1827 in France*, pp. 88–92.
100. P. M. Pilbeam, 'The growth of liberalism and the crisis of the Bourbon Restoration, 1827–32', *Historical Journal*, 252 (1982), 351–66.
101. Weill, *Le Parti républicain*, p. 26.
102. Cauchois-Lemaire, *Notice personnelle à consulter par les électeurs qui voudraient connaître les titres de Cauchois-Lemaire à la candidature pour la prochaine assemblée constituante*, *BN Nouvelles Acquisitions Françaises*, 22889.
103. Neely, 'Rural politics in the Early Restoration'.
104. Alexander, *Bonapartism*, p. 152.
105. Kent, *The Election of 1827 in France*.
106. *Aide-toi, Manuel de l'électeur en fonctions*. *BN* Lb49 1330. There is a fairly representative collection of the *Aide-toi* pamphlets 1827–30 in the *Bibliothèque Nationale*.
107. P. M. Pilbeam, 'The economic crisis of 1827–32 and the 1830 Revolution in Provincial France', *Historical Journal* (June 1989), 319–38.
108. *Archives Parlementaries*, 6 February 1829, debate on king's speech opening the session, 44–60.
109. Leuilliot, *L'Alsace au début du XIXe siècle*, vol. 1, p. 509.
110. *Archives Parlementaires*, LVIII, pp. 190–1.
111. Ibid., 8 April 1829, p. 251.
112. *Aide-toi, le ciel t'aidera*, 25 August 1829. *BN* Lb49.1096.
113. Prefectoral reports January 1829, *AD* Calvados M16212.
114. His speech was circulated to all prefects, e.g. *AD* Puy de Dôme M62.
115. E.g. *Aide-toi*, 15 April 1830. *BN* F7.6718.
116. 18 April 1830. *AN* F7.6718.
117. P. L. Duvergier de Hauranne, *Histoire du gouvernement parlementaire*. 10 vols (Paris, 1857–72), vol. 10, p. 463.
118. Leuilliot, *L'Alsace*, vol. 1, pp. 494, 512.
119. Reports of *procureur-général* September 1829. *AN* BB18.1175, 1176.

Chapter 5. Revolution and Popular Unrest: Republicans 1830–1835

1. The details of the revolution in Paris are dealt with admirably in D. H. Pinkney, *The French Revolution of 1830* (Princeton, NJ, 1972). P. M. Pilbeam, *The 1830 Revolution in France* (London, 1991) puts the revolution in a broader time-scale and adds a regional dimension.

2. P. Duvergier de Hauranne, *Histoire du gouvernement parlementaire en France*, 10 vols (1857–72), vol. 10, p. 705.

3. *Code Pénal, 12 février 1810. Les Cinq Codes de l'Empire* (Paris, 1812), section 7, p. 636.

4. Minister of Interior to prefect, 28 January 1832, *AD* Vosges 8M6bis.

5. *Manifeste de la société des Amis du Peuple*, 30 July 1830.

6. L. de la Hodde, *Histoire des sociétés secrètes, 1830–48* (Paris, 1850), p. 37.

7. *Procès du Droit d'Association. Cour d'Assises de la Seine. Audience du 15 décembre 1832* (Paris, 1832).

8. G. Perreux, *Aux Temps des sociétés secrètes. La Propagande républicain au début de la Monarchie de Juillet, 1830–35* (Paris, 1931), p. 63.

9. P. M. Pilbeam, 'The emergence of opposition to the Orleanist Monarchy, August 1830–April 1831', *English Historical Review* (1970), 12–28.

10. Perreux, *Aux Temps des sociétés secrètes*, pp. 53–8.

11. *Association pour l'instruction libre et gratuite du peuple* (1833).

12. G. Frambourg, *Le docteur Guépin, 1805–73* (Nantes, 1964), pp. 70–4.

13. I. Collins, *The Government and Newspaper Press in France, 1814–1881* (Oxford, 1959).

14. G. Weill, *Histoire du parti républicain en France de 1814 à 1870* (Paris, 1900), pp. 75–6.

15. Chaper to Minister of Interior, 25 November 1832. *AD* Fonds Chaper 2J3.

16. *Procureur-général* Dijon to *garde des sceaux* 20 September 1833. *AN* BB18.1338.

17. P. Gonnet, *La Correspondance d'Achille Chaper 1831–40* (Dijon, 1970).

18. Chaper to Minister of Interior 25 November 1832. *AD* Fonds Chaper 2J3.

19. Weill, *Le Parti républicain*, pp. 111–18.

20. La Hodde, *Histoire des sociétés secrètes*, p. 69.

21. C. Langeron, *J. Demontry, sa vie et sa mort* (Brussels, 1850), pp. 9–11.
22. *AN* BB18.1328.
23. *AD*.8M6bis.
24. *AN* F7.3983.
25. *AD* Fonds Chaper. 2J10.
26. *AD* Bas-Rhin 3M52.
27. B. H. Moss, 'Parisian workers and the origins of republican socialism 1830–3' in Merriman, *1830 in France.*
28. Mayor Metz to prefect, 25 January 1834. *AM* Metz 1D37.
29. *AD* Bas-Rhin 3M39.
30. *AD* Jura M18.
31. *AD* Côte-d'Or FC.2J3.
32. Archives Municipales, Metz.1D37.
33. *AD FC* 2J3. 24 November 1833.
34. Prefect Saône-et-Loire to Minister of Interior 17 March 1834. *AD* Saône-et-Loire 51M27.
35. Weill, *Le Parti républicain*, p. 86.
36. E. Bourloton, G. Cogny and A. Robert, *Dictionnaire des parlementaires français* (Paris, 1889–91), I, pp. 541–2.
37. E. Cabet, *La Révolution de 1830 et la situation présente* (Paris, 1831), pp. 107–10.
38. Ibid., p. 121.
39. C. H. Johnson, *Utopian Communism in France* (Ithaca, 1974), p. 34.
40. E. Cabet, *93 n'est pas la République* (Paris, *sd*); reprinted in *Revolutions du XIXe. siècle*, 1st series, vol. 8 (no page numbering).
41. *Société des Droits de l'Homme. Petit Catéchisme Républicain* (Paris, 1832).
42. Quoted in Weill, *Le Parti républicain*, p. 43.
43. Chardonneret, 'Les représentations des événements de la Révolution française 1830–48' in M. Vovelle, *Les Images de la Révolution française. Actes du colloque du 25–27 octobre 1985 à la Sorbonne* (Paris, 1988), p. 329.
44. Chardonneret, in Vovelle, *Les Images*, p. 331.
45. P. Buonarroti, *Conspiration pour l'Egalité dite de Babeuf, suivie du procès auquel elle donna lieu*, 2 vols (Brussels, 1828).
46. U. Trélat, *Buonarroti*, reprinted in *Les Révolutions du XIX siècle*. Série 2, 6 (n.d.), 3.
47. *Buonarroti's History of Babeuf's Conspiracy for Equality with the author's reflections on the causes and character of the French Revolution* . . . trans. Bronterre (ed.), *The Poor Man's Guardian* (London, 1836).

48. Trélat, *Buonarroti*, p. 15.
49. P. Buonarroti, *Mémoires de N. F. Gracchus Babeuf; Tribun du Peuple; précédés de l'ouvrage ayant pour titre: Conspiration pour l'egalité dite de Babeuf* etc., 4 vols. *Prospectus*. 7pp.
50. Trélat, *Buonarroti*.
51. Cf. E. Eisenstein, *The First Professional Revolutionist. F. M. Buonarroti* (Cambridge, Mass., 1959); A. Galante Garrone, *Ph. Buonarroti et les révolutionnaires du XIXe. siècle* (Paris, 1975).
52. Buonarroti, *Mémoires de N.-F. Gracchus Babeuf, Prospectus*, p. 2.
53. A. Laponneraye (ed.), *Oeuvres de Maximillien Robespierre* (Paris, 2 vols, 1832; 3 vols, 1840–2).
54. *Société des droits de l'homme et du citoyen*, Paris, *BN* Lb51,1784.
55. *Archives parlementaires* (2nd series, 1800–1860, LXXXV), p. 459.
56. C. Teste, *Project de constitution républicaine et déclaration des principes fondementaux de la société*, p. 108.
57. *Procès du Droit d'Association. Cour d'Assises de la Seine. Audience du 15 décembre 1832* (Paris, 1832), pp. 19–20.
58. *Société des Droits de l'Homme, Déclaration des Droits de l'Homme et du Citoyen, avec des commentaires par le citoyen Laponneraye* (23rd reprint since August 1830, n.d.).
59. D. Weiner, *Raspail, Scientist and Reformer* (New York, 1968), p. 47.
60. *Manifeste des Amis du Peuple*, 31 July 1830.
61. I.-A. Chernov (Tchernoff), *Le Parti Républicain sous la Monarchie de Juillet. Fondation et évolution de la doctrine républicaine* (Paris, 1901), p. 89.
62. U. Trélat, *Anniversaire des 27, 28, 29 juillet 1830* (Paris, 1831).
63. E. Cabet, *La Révolution de 1830 et la situation présente* (Paris, 1831), pp. 137–44.
64. P. M. Pilbeam, *The 1830 Revolution in France* (London, 1991), pp. 170–6.
65. *Dialogue entre une presse méchanique et une presse à bras, recueilli et raconté par une vieille presse en bois* (Paris, 1830); G. Bourgin, 'La crise ouvrière à Paris dans la seconde moitié de 1830', *Revue Historique* (1947), 203–14.
66. C. H. Johnson, 'Economic change and artisan discontent: the tailors' history, 1800–48', in R. D. Price, *Revolution and Reaction. 1848 and the Second French Republic* (London, 1975), pp. 87–113.
67. E. Coornaert, *Les Compagnonnages en France du moyen âge à nos jours* (Paris, 1966); D. Garrioch and M. Sonenscher, '*Compagnonnages*, confraternities and associations of journeymen in eighteenth century Paris', *European History Quarterly*, 16 (1986), 25–45.

68. It has been suggested that societies themselves formed the basis for artisan militancy. W. Sewell, 'La confraternité des prolétaires: conscience et classe sous la Monarchie de Juillet', *Annales: Economies, Sociétés, Civilisations* (1981), 650–71; W. Sewell, *Work and Revolution in France: the Language of Labour from the Old Régime to 1848* (Cambridge, 1980).

69. M. D. Sibalis, 'The mutual-aid societies of Paris 1789–1848', *French History*, 3 (1989), 1–30.

70. Prefect Gasparin to Minister of Commerce 18 March 1833. *Gasparin Papers AM*. Lyon.

71. R. J. Bezucha, *The Lyon Uprising of 1834* (Cambridge, Mass., 1974), p. 102.

72. *AN* F1C I 33, Reports of Paris police and departments 1831, 1832.

73. 18 September 1833, *AN* BB18.1388.

74. Cavaignac's final defence speech in the *Procès du Droit d'Association. Cour d'Assises de la Seine. Audience du 15 décembre 1832* (Paris, 1832), p. 22.

75. Gendarmerie report, Vosges. *AN* F7.4215.17.

76. 22 February 1834 *AD*.

77. Marc-Dufraisse, *Société des Droits de l'Homme; Association des Travailleurs* (Paris, n.d.).

78. A. Guépin, *Histoire de Nantes* (Nantes, 1837); A. Guépin and C. E. Bonamy, *Nantes au XIXe. siècle* (Nantes, 1835).

79. E. Cabet, *Nécessité de populariser les journaux républicains* (Paris *sd* [1833]).

80. Weill, *Le Parti républicain*, p. 80.

81. *AD* 8M6bis. 30 November 1833.

82. M. Lyons, *Le Triomphe du livre. Une Histoire sociologique de la lecture dans la France du XIXe. siècle* (1987), p. 145.

83. Gendarmerie commander Truchi to Chaper, 2 December 1833. *AD* 8M29.

84. Minister of Interior to prefects, 22 March 1832. *AD* Vosges 8M6bis.

85. *Correspondance du préfet Gasparin*, vol. 2. *Documents Gasparin AM* Lyon.

86. F. Guizot, *Mémoires pour servir à l'histoire de mon temps* (Paris, 1858–67), II, pp. 505–12.

87. An accessible and balanced modern account can be found in Bezucha, *Lyon Uprising of 1834*.

88. *Société Amis du Peuple, La Voix du Peuple* (Paris, December 1831).

89. 6 November 1831. *Bulletin des Lois*, 9th series, Part 3, 1831, no. 116, 31.

90. Weill, *Le Parti républicain*, p. 92.

91. Prefectoral reports October 1833–March 1834. *AD* Seine-Maritime 4M 2703.

92. *Association lyonnaise des Droits de l'Homme et du Citoyen, Au Peuple. Le Peuple souffre parce qu'il ne gouverne pas* (Lyon, n.d.), p. 2.

93. *AD* Rhône M257.

94. W. Edmonds, *Jacobinism and the Revolt of Lyon, 1789–93* (Oxford, 1990).

95. Bezucha, *Lyon Uprising of 1834.*

96. [Gasparin, prefect], 'Recit de l'insurrection de Lyon en avril 1834, écrit en mai 1834', Guizot, *Mémoires pour servir à l'histoire de mon temps*, III, p. 425; L. Blanc, *History of Ten Years, 1830–40* (1845), II, p. 243.

97. *Archives de la Guerre*, Vincennes. E5.46.

98. *Cour des Pairs. Affaire du mois d'avril 1834. Rapport fait à la cour par Girod de l'Ain*, vol. 3, p. 327. *AN* CC 575.

99. *Archives de la Guerre*, Vincennes, E5.46.

100. *AN* CC575.

101. *AN* CC583; *AD* Jura M18.

102. G. Weill, *Le Parti républicain*, p. 130.

103. Miran to president *cour des pairs* 28 December 1835. *AN* CC582.

104. *AN* CC576.

105. Chaper to Minister of Interior, 30 July 1834. *AD FC*.2J3.

106. Chaper 27 November, 26 December 1834. *AD* Côte-d'Or FC 2J3.

107. AD Saône-et-Loire 51M28.

108. R. J. Goldstein, 'Censorship of caricature in France, 1815–1914', *French History*, 3 (1989), 71–107.

109. *Loi sur les crimes, délits et contraventions de la presse*, 9 September 1835, *Bulletin des Lois* IX *sèrie* I, vol. 6, p. 247.

110. *AD* Bas-Rhin 3M52 July 1834.

Chapter 6. The Republic Outlawed: Insurrection and Reform 1835–1848

1. An earlier version of the following pages devoted to Blanqui and the insurrectionary tradition was given as a paper to the Annual Conference of the French Historical Studies society, March 1992, and subsequently published in the *Modern and Contemporary France Review* (no. 3, 1993). I am grateful to the session chairman,

Professor John Rothney and to the commentator Professor Edward Newman for their valuable remarks.

2. A. Blanqui, *Manuscripts Blanqui. BN*.1850 quoted in S. Molinier, *Blanqui* (Paris, 1984), p. 31. All translations from the French are my own.

3. P. Buonarroti, *History of Babeuf's Conspiracy* (trans. London, 1836), p. 106.

4. W. Sewell, 'Beyond 1783: Babeuf, Louis Blanc and the Genealogy of "Social Revolution" ' in F. Furet and M. Ozouf, *The French Revolution and the Creation of Modern Political Culture* (Oxford, 1989), pp. 509–526.

5. Cf. M. Agulhon (ed.), *Blanqui et les Blanquistes* (Paris, 1986); M. Dommanget, *Les Idées politiques et sociales d'Auguste Blanqui* (Paris, 1957); S. Bernstein, *Auguste Blanqui and the Art of Insurrection* (London, 1971); A. Spitzer, *The Revolutionary Theories of Louis-Auguste Blanqui* (New York, 1957).

6. D. B. Weiner, *Raspail, Scientist and Reformer* (New York, 1968).

7. Accused on 10 January 1832 at the assize court of the Seine were the main leaders of the *Amis de Peuple*: Raspail, Gervais, Blanqui, Thouret, Hubert, Trélat, Bonnias, Pagniol, Juchault and Delaunay. *Défense du Citoyen Louis Auguste Blanqui devant la Cour d'Assises* (1832), p. 4.

8. *Défense du Citoyen Louis Auguste Blanqui devant la Cour d'Assises* (1832), pp. 5–15.

9. I.-A. Chernov (Tchernoff), *Le Parti républicain sous la Monarchie de Juillet. Fondation et évolution de la doctrine républicaine* (Paris, 1901), p. 343.

10. Weill, *Le Parti républicain*, pp. 169–70. See also F. A. de Luna, 'Barbès' in Newman, *Historical Dictionary*, vol. 1, pp. 61–2.

11. S.-A. A. Barbès, *Quelques Mots à ceux qui possèdent, en faveur des prolétaires sans travail* (Paris, 1837).

12. Weill, *Le Parti républicain*, pp. 168–9.

13. *AD* Bas-Rhin 3M53.

14. *AD* Bas-Rhin 3M39.

15. *Cour des Pairs. Attentat du 12–13 mai 1839. Acte d'Accusation* (Paris, 1839), pp. 49–51.

16. *Cour des Pairs*, p. 41.

17. *Cour des Pairs*, pp. 62–3.

18. *Cour des Pairs*, pp. 68–76; *Le Moniteur* 13 May 1839.

19. C. Latta, 'L'Insurrection de 1839' in Agulhon, *Blanqui et les Blanquistes*, p. 78.

20. *Cour des Pairs*, pp. 5–6.
21. *Cour des Pairs*, pp. 44–5.
22. M. Dommanget, *Auguste Blanqui. Des Origines à la Révolution de 1848, premiers combats et premières prisons* (Paris, 1969), pp. 178–238.
23. *Annales du parlement français*, 8 May 1839 (Paris, 1839).
24. T. Thoré, *La Verité sur le parti démocratique* (Paris, 1840), pp. 32–3.
25. D. C. McKay, *The National Workshops. A Study in the French Revolution of 1848* (Cambridge, Mass., 1933), p. xx.
26. J. Howorth, 'The myth of Blanquism under the Third Republic 1871–1900', *Journal of Modern History*, 48 (1976).
27. A. Blanqui, 'Instruction pour une prise d'armes' in S. Molinier, *Blanqui* (Paris, 1948), p. 32.
28. Molinier, *Blanqui*, p. 18.
29. J. J. Baughman, 'The French Banquet Campaign of 1847–8', *Journal of Modern History*, xxxi, 1 (1959), 1–15.
30. An excellent account of Guizot's final government in R. L. Koepke, 'The failure of parliamentary government in France, 1840–48', *European Studies Review*, 9 (1979), 433–55.
31. A. Gourvitch, 'Le Mouvement pour la réforme électorale', *La Révolution de 1848*, vols XI–XIV (1914–18). See also A. J. Tudesq, *Les Grands Notables en France 1840–1849. Etude historique d'une psychologie sociale* (Paris, 1964), vol. 1, pp. 516–27.
32. C. F. M. de Remusat (ed. C. H. Pouthas), *Mémoires de ma vie* (Paris, 1959), vol. III, p. 416.
33. Koepke, 'The failure'. Figures are taken from the Guizot-inspired Paul Thureau-Dangin, *Histoire de la Monarchie de Juillet*, 7 vols (Paris, 1884–92). See also D. W. Johnson, *Guizot, Aspects of French History 1787–1874* (London, 1963).
34. H. A. C. Collingham, *The July Monarchy. A Political History of France, 1830–1848* (London, 1988), pp. 289–302.
35. *Journal des Débats*, 16 February 1842. All of his speeches reprinted in F. P. G. Guizot, *Historie parlementaire de la France*, 5 vols (Paris, 1863–4).
36. David Longfellow, 'Garnier-Pagès' in Newman, *Historical Biography*, vol. 1, pp. 443–4.
37. R. Schnerb, *Ledru-Rollin* (Paris, 1948).
38. A. Jardin and A. J. Tudesq, *Restoration and Reaction 1815–1848* (Cambridge, 1983), p. 104.
39. C. Dupin, *Forces productives et forces commerciales de la France* (Paris, 1827).

40. R. D. Price, *Revolution and Reaction. 1848 and the Second French Republic* (London, 1975), pp. 7–8.

41. J. Dautry, *1848 et la deuxième république* (Paris, 3rd. edn 1977), p. 22.

42. R. L. Koepke, 'The short, unhappy history of progressive conservatism in France, 1840–1848', *Canadian Journal of History*, xviii (1983), 189–90.

43. P. Duvergier de Hauranne, *De la Réforme parlementaire et de la réforme électorale* (Paris, 1847).

44. Koepke, 'Short, unhappy history', pp. 204–6.

45. Prefect to Minister of Interior, 7 June 1847. *AD*.Loire-Inf. 55J2.

46. L. Chevalier, *La Formation de la population Parisienne au XIXe. siècle* (Paris, 1950), p. 40.

47. J. Vidalenc, 'A propos de la campagne des banquets', *Congrès des sociétés savantes* (Rouen, 1956), *Section d'histoire moderne et contemporaine*, pp. 679–89.

48. C. H. O. Barrot, *Mémoires posthumes de Odilon Barrot* (Paris, 1875), vol. 1, p. 214.

49. Baughman, 'The French Banquet Campaign', p. 3.

50. Baughman, 'The French Banquet Campaign', p. 9.

51. Schnerb, *Ledru-Rollin*, p. 12.

52. A. J. Tudesq, *Les Grands Notables en France 1840–1849. Etude Historique d'une Psychologie Sociale* (Paris, 1964), vol. 2, p. 969.

53. Schnerb, *Ledru-Rollin*, p. 11.

54. A. Jardin and A. J. Tudesq, *La France des notables 1815–48* (Paris, 1973), vol. 1, p. 246.

55. J. Bruhat, *Les Journées de Février 1848* (Paris, 1948), p. 6.

56. Duvergier de Hauranne, February 7 1848, Chamber of Deputies, *Annales du parlement français*, vol. 10 (1849), p. 187.

57. Jardin and Tudesq, *La France des notables 1815–48*, vol. 1, p. 246. They mention only 50 banquets in 28 departments.

58. Alexis de Tocqueville (1805–59) was to be elected to both the Constituent and Legislative Assemblies and was briefly imprisoned after Louis-Napoleon's coup in December 1851.

59. *Chambre des Députés; Annales du parlement français* 27 January 1848 (1849), pp. 108–9 (also quoted in his *Souvenirs*).

60. *Annales du parlement français*, vol. 10, pp. 186–270.

61. Daumier, 'Voyage à travers les populations empressées', *La Caricature*, 14 August 1834, reproduced in C. F. Ramus, *Daumier. 120 Great Lithographs* (New York, 1979).

Chapter 7. Socialist Utopians and Reformers before 1848

1. T. Thoré, *La Verité sur le parti démocratique* (Paris, 1840).
2. D. W. Lovell, 'The French Revolution and the origins of socialism: the case of early French socialism', *French History*, 6 (1992), 185–205.
3. E. Berenson, *Populist Religion and Left-wing Politics 1830–1852*, (Princeton, 1984), p. 69.
4. A readable, brief survey of the early socialists in D. W. Lovell, 'Early French socialism and class struggle', *History of Political Thought* (1988), 327–48.
5. A useful and accessible survey in T. Judt, 'The French labour movement in the nineteenth century', *Marxism and the French Left* (Oxford, 1989), pp. 24–224. The case for traditional influences on workers in W. Sewell, *Work and Revolution in France: the Language of Labour from the Old Régime to 1848* (Cambridge, 1980; the socialist influence in B. H. Moss, *The Origins of the French Labour Movement: The Socialism of Skilled Workers, 1830–1914* (Berkeley, 1976).
6. E.g. M. Nadaud, *Mémoires de Léonard, ancien garçon maçon* (Paris, 1895).
7. A clear and well-organized account of his ideas in English in F. E. Manuel, *The New World of Henri Saint-Simon* (Cambridge, Mass., 1956).
8. A. Bayet and F. Albert, *Les Ecrivains politiques du XIXe. siècle* (Paris, 1924), p. 155. This book provides an old but excellent brief summary of his ideas with extracts from his works.
9. H.de Saint-Simon, *Le Nouveau Christianisme* (first pub.1825), ed. H. Desroche (Paris, 1969).
10. H. de Saint-Simon, *Catéchisme des industriels* (Paris, 1823–4).
11. *Doctrines de Saint-Simon. Exposition* (1828–30).
12. E. Faguet, *Politiques et Moralistes du dix-neuvième siècle* (Paris, 1898), vol. 2, 81.
13. Fourier, *Théorie de Unité Universelle* (Paris, 1822), vol. 1, p. 199; quoted in Bayet and Albert, *Les Ecrivans*, pp. 229–30.
14. F. C. M. Fourier, *Le Nouveau Monde industriel et sociétaire* (Paris, 1829). Extracts from various works in translation in F. C. M. Fourier, *Harmonian Man. Selected Writings of Charles Fourier*, ed. M. Poster (London, 1971); sensitively chosen extracts and a succinct introduction to Fourier's thought in French in Bayet and Albert, *Les Ecrivains*, pp. 205–43.

15. Fourier, *Harmonian Man.*
16. Fourier, *Harmonian Man*, pp. 165–6.
17. F. C. M. Fourier, *Political economy made easy. A sketch . . . exhibiting the various errors of our present political arrangements.* Presented to the London Cooperative Society by the translator (London, 1828).
18. *La Fausse Industrie morcelée, répugnante, mensongère et l'antidote, l'industrie naturelle, combinée, attrayante, véridique, donnant quadruple produit* (Paris, 1835–6).
19. V. P. Considérant, *Principes du socialisme. Manifeste de la démocratie au XIXe. siècle* (Paris, 1847).
20. V. P. Considérant, *Destinée sociale*, 2 vols (Paris, 1834–8).
21. R. Owen, *Report to the Country of Lanark* and *A New View of Society*, ed. V. A. C. Gatrell with a lucid introductory essay (London, 1969).
22. R. A. Mandel, *J. B. André Godin and the Familistère of Guise, 1817–1888* (PhD, University of Toronto, 1978).
23. Philippe-Joseph-Benjamin Buchez (1796–1865). For a brief account of his contribution see A. Cuvillier, *P.-J.-B. Buchez et les origines du socialisme chrétienne* (Paris, 1948). His papers are conserved in *Bibliothèque historique de la ville de Paris*, including his correspondence with his father.
24. For a useful summary of the whole century see ch. 2, Judt, *Marxism and the French Left* and of the first half-century W. Sewell, 'Property, labor and the emergence of Socialism in France, 1789–1848' in J. Merriman, *Consciousness and Class Experience in Nineteenth-Century Europe* (New York, 1979).
25. F. Tristan, *L'Union ouvrière* (first pub. 1844; Paris 1967).
26. Berenson, *Populist Religion*, p. 46.
27. J. Maitron, *Dictionnaire biographique du mouvement ouvrier français* (Paris, 1964), I, pp. 333–6.
28. E. Cabet, *Histoire populaire de la Révolution française 1789–1830*, (Paris, 1840).
29. E. Cabet, 'Comment je suis communiste' 16 pp.; pamphlet reprinted in *Les Révolutions du XIX siècle*, série 2, vol. 5.
30. E. Cabet, *Voyage en Icarie* (Paris, 1840), vol. 1, pp. 8–45.
31. Cabet, *Voyage en Icarie*, vol. 1, pp. 59–65.
32. Cabet, *Voyage en Icarie*, vol. 1, p. 404.
33. Cabet, *Voyage en Icarie*, vol. 1, pp. 122–75.
34. Cabet, *Voyage en Icarie*, vol. 1, pp. 297–329.
35. Cabet, 'Comment je suis communiste' 16 pp.
36. M. Ozouf, 'La Révolution française au tribunal de l'utopie', in F.

Furet and M. Ozouf, *The Transformation of Political Culture 1789–1848*, p. 568.

37. Cabet, *Voyage en Icarie*, vol. 2, p. 502.
38. Cabet, *Voyage en Icarie*, vol. 2, p. 502.
39. C. H. Johnson, *Utopian Communism in France. Cabet and the Icarians 1839–51* (New York, 1974), pp. 78–145.
40. Cabet *Voyage en Icarie*, vol. 2. pp. 503–4.
41. E. Cabet, *Le Vrai Christianisme suivant Jésus-Christ* (Paris, 1846).
42. A. Laponneraye, 'Catéchisme Démocratique', *Extrait de L'Intelligence, Journal de la Réforme Sociale.*
43. E. Cabet, *La Femme.*
44. L. Adler, *Les Premières Journalistes (1830–1850)* (Paris, 1979), pp. 19–73.
45. L. S. Strumingher, *Women and the Making of the Working Class* (Montreal, 1979).
46. C. Moses, 'Saint-Simonian men/Saint-Simonian women: the transformation of feminist thought in 1830s France', *Journal of Modern History*, 54 (1982).
47. Adler, *Les Premières Journalistes*, pp. 102–8.
48. A welcome recent assessment is J. Viard, *Pierre Leroux et les socialistes européens* (Avignon, 1983).
49. L. A. Loubère, *Louis Blanc; his life and his contribution to the rise of French Jacobin Socialism* (Evanston, Ill., 1961), p. 9.
50. J. Vidalenc, *Louis Blanc* (Paris, 1948), pp. 7–8.
51. The *Bon Sens* (1832–9) was started in 1832 by Cauchois-Lemaire.
52. 'Bon Sens', P. McPhee in Newman, *Historical Dictionary*, vol. 1, p. 120.
53. Vidalenc, *Louis Blanc*, p. 14.
54. J. J. L. Blanc, *Organisation du Travail*, in J. A. R. Marriot, *The French Revolution of 1848 in its Economic Aspect*, I (Oxford, 1913), p. 14.
55. *Revue du Progrès social*, II, 15 October 1839; quoted in Loubère, *Louis Blanc*, p. 36.
56. Loubère, *Louis Blanc*, p. 53.
57. Loubère, *Louis Blanc*, p. 117.
58. R. Hoffman, *Revolutionary Justice: the Social and Political Theory of P. J. Proudhon* (Chicago, 1972), pp. 20–7. Hoffman offers an accessible introduction and provides a useful bibliography.
59. P. J. Proudhon, *Qu-est-ce que la propriété?* (Paris, 1840), p. 335.
60. E. Dolléans and J. L. Puech, *Proudhon et la Révolution de 1848* (Paris, 1948), p. 5.

61. P. J. Proudhon, *Système des contradictions économiques ou philosophie de la misère* (Paris, 1846), p. 391.
62. S. Edwards, *Proudhon. Selected Writings* (London, 1969), pp. 54–5. These selections provide a fair account of his thought.
63. Proudhon, *Qu'est-ce que la propriété?* p. 14.
64. Proudhon, *Qu'est-ce que la propriété?* p. 261.
65. Proudhon, *Qu'est-ce que la propriété?* pp. 285–6.
66. Proudhon, *Qu'est-ce que la propriété?* p. 448.
67. Proudhon, *Qu'est-ce que la propriété?* p. 453.
68. Dolléans and Puech, *Proudhon*, p. 12.

Chapter 8. Universal Suffrage and the 'Right to Work': The Second Republic, February–April 1848

1. M. Agulhon, *1848 ou l'apprentissage de la république 1848–1852* (Paris, 1973), p. 18. This is an excellent introduction to the republic. It has been translated into English, but is better read in French.
2. J. Bruhat, *Les Journées de février 1848* (Paris, 1948), pp. 29–32.
3. R. Price, *The French Second Republic. A Social History* (London, 1972) provides an invaluable introduction to social issues and the same author edited an indispensable collection of essays, *Revolution and Reaction. 1848 and the Second French Republic* (London, 1975).

   R. Huard, *Le Suffrage universel en France, 1848–1946* (Paris, 1991) investigates the way in which universal suffrage was interpreted.
4. Quoted in J. A. R. Marriott, *The French Revolution of 1848 in its Economic Aspect* (Oxford, 1913), p. lx.
5. D. H. Pinkney, 'Les ateliers de secours à Paris (1830–31). Précurseurs des Ateliers Nationaux de 1848', *Revue d'histoire moderne et contemporaine*, 12 (1965).
6. D. C. McKay, *The National Workshops. A Study in the French Revolution of 1848* (Cambridge, Mass., 1933), p. 12.
7. Schnerb, *Ledru-Rollin*, p. 68.
8. *AD* Loire-Inférieure 1 M 516.
9. A. Cobban, 'Administrative pressure in the election of the French Constituent Assembly, April 1848', *Bulletin of the Institute of Historical Research*, xxv (1952), 136.
10. P. Haury, 'Les commissaires de Ledru-Rollin en 1848', *La Révolution française*, lvii (1909), 450.

11. *AD* Seine-Maritime 1M180.
12. Prefect Morbihan to Minister of Interior 31 July 18484.*AD* Morbihan M680.
13. *AD* Côtes-d'Armor April–May 1848 1M330bis.
14. *AD* Côtes-d'Armor 1M330bis.
15. 3 March 1848 1M165, *AD* Seine-Maritime.
16. G. Richard, 'Une famille de médecins révolutionnaires à Nancy sous la Monarchie de Juillet. Les docteurs Béchet', *Revue Médicale de Nancy* (Nancy, 1961), 867–98.
17. An impeccable account of the Lyon situation in M. L. Stewart-McDougall, *Artisan Republic: Revolution, Reaction and Resistance in Lyon 1848–1851* (Kingston and Montreal, 1984).
18. A. Corbin, *Archaisme et modernité en Limousin 1845–80*, 2 vols (Paris, 1975).
19. P. Amann, 'The Paris Club Movement in 1848', in Price, *Revolution and Reaction*, p. 118.
20. C. F. Ramus, *Daumier. 120 Great Lithographs* (New York, 1979), p. 73. Daumier produced a series of 11 lithographs, *Les Banqueteers*, in June 1849 deriding clubs for women, and the men who sat at home and minded the children.
21. J. Pommier, *Les Ecrivains devant la Révolution de 1848* (Paris, 1948), p. 53).
22. L. S. Strumingher, 'Les jolies femmes d'Edouard de Beaumont', paper given at the annual conference of the Western Society for French History, October 1992.
23. 12 March 1848, Circular to commissioners, *Moniteur Universel*.
24. H. Machin, 'The prefects and political repression: February 1848 to December 1851', in Price, *Revolution and Reaction*, pp. 282–3.
25. Haury, 'Les commissaires de Ledru-Rollin', pp. 461–70.
26. Cobban, 'Administrative pressure', p. 145, fn.7. A lower figure of 67 is mentioned by Price, *Revolution and Reaction*, p. 28.
27. Comments on the 'secret' mission to the Nantes regiment, Commissioner Loire-Inférieure 12 April 1848, *AN* BB30.323.
28. Cobban, 'Administrative pressure', p. 143.
29. Stewart-McDougall, *Artisan Republic*, pp. 49–50.
30. 5 or 6 March 1848. *AD* Ille-et-Vilaine 3M157 Hamon papers.
31. 21 March 1848. Ibid.
32. 25 April 1848 *AD* Ille-et-Vilaine 3M157.
33. 26 March 1848 *AD* Eure 1M246.
34. *AD* Calvados M2855.
35. A. Cobban, 'The influence of the Clergy and the "Instituteurs

Primaires" in the election of the French Constituent Assembly, April 1848', *English Historical Review*, LVII (1942), 334–44.

36. 25 April 1848 *AD* Ille-et-Vilaine 3M157.

37. 5 March 1848 1M165 *AD* Seine-Maritime.

38. O. Heywood, 'The financial policy of the provisional government', *The Idea of Revolution in 1848* (unpublished PhD, University of London, 1975; a revised version of one section will shortly appear in *History*).

39. *AD* Côtes d'Armor 1M330bis.

40. Pinkney, 'Les ateliers de secours à Paris (1830–1), pp. 65–70.

41. T. R. Christofferson, 'The French National Workshops of 1848: the view from the Provinces', *French Historical Studies* 11,4 (1980), 550–20.

42. R. Gossez, *Les Ouvriers de Paris*, I, *L'Organisation, 1848–51* (Paris, 1967).

43. Vidalenc, *Louis Blanc* pp. 44–5.

44. E. Thomas, *Histoire des Ateliers Nationaux* (Paris, 1848), pp. 29–30.

45. McKay, *National Workshops*, pp. 20–33.

46. M. Traugott, *Armies of the Poor. Determinants of Working-Class Participation in the Parisian Insurrection of June 1848* (Princeton, 1985).

47. McKay, *National Workshops*, p. 167.

48. Christofferson, 'The French National Workshops', pp. 505–20.

49. M. Crook, *Toulon in War and Revolution. From the Ancien Régime to the Restoration, 1750–1820* (Manchester, 1991).

50. C. Schmidt, *Des Ateliers nationaux aux barricades de juin* (Paris, 1948), pp. 66 7.

51. W. Sewell, 'La confraternité des prolétaires:conscience et classe sous la Monarchie de Juillet', *Annales:Economies, Sociétés, Civilisations* (1981), 650–71.

52. T. Zeldin, *Emile Ollivier and the Liberal Empire of Napoleon III* (Oxford, 1963). For his earlier career see T. Beck, 'Ollivier' in Newman, *Historical Dictionary*, vol. 2, pp. 761–2.

53. Christofferson, 'French National Workshops', pp. 513–20.

54. Loubère, *Louis Blanc*, p. 97.

55. L. Blanc, *Histoire de la Révolution de 1848*, vol. 1, p. 161, quoted in Vidalenc, *Louis Blanc*, pp. 37–9.

56. Blanc, *Histoire de la Révolution de 1848*, vol. 1, p. 191.

57. F. de Luna, *The French Republic under Cavaignac* (Princeton, 1975), pp. 110–17.

58. Loubère, *Louis Blanc*, p. 115.

59. Corbin, *Archaisme et modernité*, vol. 2, p. 778. See below ch. 9, pp. 361–2.

60. C. Cock, *Troyes and the Aube under the July Monarchy* (unpublished PhD., University of Reading, 1973).

Chapter 9. The June Days; Bonapartism; The Decline and Fall of the Second Republic

1. P. Amann, *Revolution and Mass Democracy: the Paris Club Movement in 1848* (Princton, 1975).

2. D. C. McKay, *The National Workshops. A Study in the French Revolution of 1848* (Cambridge, Mass., 1933), p. xii.

3. McKay, *National Workshops*, p. 74.

4. L. C. Jennings, *France and Europe in 1848; A Study of French Foreign Affairs in Time of Crisis* (Oxford, 1973).

5. M. L. Stewart-McDougall, *Artisan Republic: Revolution, Reaction and Resistance in Lyon 1848–1851*, pp. 76–8.

6. C. Schmidt, *Des Ateliers nationaux aux barricades de juin* (Paris, 1948), p. 28. The unsigned report was rediscovered in the *Bibliothèque Nationale* by McKay. See his *National Workshops*, p. 85.

7. McKay, *National Workshops*, p. 115.

8. Cf. Schmidt, *Des Ateliers nationaux*, p. 65, reprints Thomas's complete analysis.

9. A useful brief survey in R. D. Price, *The French Second Republic: a Social History* (London, 1972), pp. 155–92. See also R. Gossez, *Les Ouvriers de Paris*, I, *L'Organisation, 1848–51* (Paris, 1967).

10. C. Tilly and L. Lees, 'Le peuple de Juin 1848', *Annales. Economies, Sociétés, Civilisations* (1974), 1061–91.

11. Tilly and Lees, 'Le peuple de Juin 1848', p. 1062.

12. A. de Tocqueville, *Recollections*, trans. G. Lawrence (New York, 1971), p. 169.

13. Schmidt, *Des Ateliers nationaux*, pp. 45–6.

14. F. de Luna, *The French Republic under Cavaignac* (Princeton, 1975), p. 149.

15. J. Vidalenc, 'La province et les journées de juin', *Etudes d'histoire moderne et contemporaine*, 2 (1948), 83–144.

16. T. R. Christofferson, 'The French national workshops', *French Historical Studies* 11, 4 (1980), 505–20.

17. Stewart-McDougall, *Artisan Republic*, pp. 87–8.
18. June–July 1848; exchange of angry letters between Waddington, prefect and mayor, *AD* Eure 1M246.
19. Subprefect Brest to prefect Finistère, 6 July 1848. *AD* Finistère 3M154.
20. de Luna, *French Republic under Cavaignac*, pp. 176–87.
21. P. J. Proudhon, *Confessions*, pp. 168–9, quoted in Mary B. Allen, 'P. J. Proudhon in the Revolution of 1848', *Journal of Modern History*, xxiv (1952), 12–13.
22. *Correspondance*, II, pp. 285–9, quoted in E. Dolléans and J.L. Puech, *Proudhon et la Révolution de 1848* (Paris 1948), pp. 32–5.
23. Prefect Eure to Minister of Interior, 29 November 1848 *AD* Eure 1M246.
24. 'Toast à la Révolution', *Le Peuple*, 17 October 1848.
25. C. Heywood, 'The revolutionary tradition in Troyes, 1789–1848', *Journal of Historical Geography*, 16 (1990), 108–20.
26. *AD* Côte-d'Or MIII53,54 (old classification).
27. L. Duguit and H. Monnier, *Les Constitutions et les Principales Lois Politiques*, p. 239.
28. A. J. Tudesq, *L'Election présidentielle du 10 décembre 1848* (Paris, 1965), pp. 13–21.
29. Louis-Napoleon, *Des Idées Napoléoniennes*, 1939, trans. B. D. Gooch, *Napoleonic Ideas* (New York, 1967).
30. A. Laponneraye, *Réfutation des Idées Napoléoniennes* (Paris, 1839), pp. 30–1.
31. Louis-Napoleon, *L'Extinction du paupérisme* (Paris, 1844).
32. Schnerb, *Ledru-Rollin*, p. 29.
33. His trial was delayed for ten months; he was eventually sentenced to six years' imprisonment.
34. Hamon, commissioner Ille-et-Vilaine to Minister of Interior 29 October 1848, *AD* Ille-et-Vilaine 3M154.
35. 7 November 1848, *AD* Morbihan M680.
36. *AD* Ille-et-Vilaine eM154.
37. General Changarnier (1793–1877) had a very successful career in North Africa and was elected to the Assembly in 1848. He had a reputation for legitimism and was the candidate for conservatives who could not stomach Louis-Napoleon.
38. *AD* Finistère 1M154.
39. A. Corbin, *Archaisme et modernité en Limousin 1845–80* (Paris, 1975), vol. 1, pp. 734–41.
40. *Bulletin Officiel du ministère de l'intérieur, 1848, 1849.*

41. B. H. Moss, *The Origins of the French Labour Movement* (Berkeley, 1976), pp. 80–1.

42. J. Moon, 'The *Association fraternelle et solidaires de toutes les associations*', *Western Society For French History*, Annual Conference, October 1992.

43. L. Abensour, *Histoire générale du féminisme* (Paris, 1921), p. 215.

44. Loubère, *Louis Blanc*, pp. 162–3.

45. J. Merriman, *The Agony of the Republic* (1978), pp. 68–72.

46. G. Frambourg, *Le docteur Guépin 1805–73* (Nantes, 1964), p. 236.

47. *AD* Calvados M2861.

48. *Le Peuple*, 22 December 1848.

49. Proudhon, *Idée générale*, pp. 245–6.

50. E. Dolléans, 'Vie et pensée ouvrières entre 1848 et 1871', *Revue historique* (1947), 69.

51. Martin Nadaud, *Mémoires de Léonard, ancien garçon maçon* (Paris, 1895).

52. J. Maitron (ed.), '*Nadaud*', *Dictionnaire biographique du mouvement ouvrier français, 1789–1864*, vol. 3; also excellent brief account by C. H. Johnson in Newman, *Historical Dictionary*, vol. 2, pp. 735–7.

53. Berenson, *Populist Religion*, p. 93.

54. Police commissioner Metz 25 January 1849, *Archives municipales* Metz 2I137.

55. 1 September 1848 *AM* Metz 2I137.

56. *AN* F1a*2098.

57. *Almanach Démocratique et Social* (Paris, 1849).

58. *AD* Calvados M2855.

59. Faucher papers, *AP, Archives Nationales*. T. Zeldin, 'Government policy in the French general election of 1849', *English Historical Review* (1959).

60. E. Berenson, *Populist Religion and Left-wing Politics in France 1830–1852* (Princeton, 1984), p. xiii.

61. Prefect Dordogne to Minister of Interior, 25 April 1849, *AN* F1cIII Dordogne 5.

62. Quoted in Schnerb, *Ledru-Rollin*, p. 51.

63. Stewart-McDougall, *Artisan Republic*, p. 131.

64. 16 June 1849 *AD* Morbihan M518.

65. 11 April 1851, *AM* Metz 2I137.

66. *AD* Calvados M2861.

67. *AD* Calvados M2855.

68. Merriman, *Agony of the Republic*, pp. 106–21.

69. Loubère, *Blanc*, p. 150.

70. H. Machin, 'The prefects and political repression: February 1848 to December 1851', in Price, *Revolution and Reaction*, p. 291.
71. J. P. T. Bury and R. P. Tombs, *Thiers 1797–1877. A Political Life* (London, 1986), pp. 126.
72. Reports from government prosecutors June and July 1850, *AN* BB18.1468.
73. R. Huard, *Le Mouvement républicain en Bas-Languedoc 1848–81* (Paris, 1982), p. 66.
74. 1849–1850 *AD* Finistère 1M178.
75. 19 June 1851 Minister of Interior to prefects. *AD* Loire-Inf. 1 M 516.
76. 1M180 *AD* Seine-Maritime.
77. *AD* Calvados M2855.
78. Journal of Nicholas Louet, 8 August 1830, *AD* Haute-Marne 2J401, 4814.
79. Weill, *Le Parti républicain*, p. 361.
80. An extremely useful table of all arrests by department and occupation in R. D. Price, *The French Second Republic; A Social History* (London, 1972), pp. 291–295.
81. T. W. Margadant, *French Peasants in Revolt. The Insurrection of 1851* (Princton, 1979), p. 141.
82. Margadant, *French Peasants in Revolt*, pp. 236–317.
83. J. Simon, *Souvenirs de 2 décembre* (Paris, 1874), p. 90, quoted in Weill, *Le Parti républicain*, p. 363.
84. *AD* Eure 1M182.
85. Prefect Calvados to Minister of Interior, 25 March 1852. *AD* Calvados M2855.
86. Weill, *Le Parti républicain*, pp. 398–9.
87. *AD* Calvados M2855.
88. Police commissioner Caen to prefect 9 January 1852. *AD* Calvados M2855.
89. V. Wright, 'The coup d'état of December 1851: Repression and the limits to repression', in Price, *Revolution and Reaction*, pp. 310–11.
90. Prefect Indre to Minister of Interior, 12 November 1852, *AN* F1cIII Indre 3. Prefect Manche to Minister of Interior, 13 October 1852, F1cIII Manche 4.
91. Quoted in A. Plessis, *The Rise and Fall of the Second Empire 1852–1871* (Cambridge, 1987; trans. of *De la Fête Impériale au mur de fédérés, 1852–71* Paris, 1979), p. 12, which gives a succinct and analytical account of the period.

Chapter 10. From the Silent Years to Bloody Week: Republicans 1852–1871

1. Weill, *Le Parti républicain*, p. 397.
2. A. Plessis, *De la Fête Impériale au mur des fédérés, 1852–71* (Paris, 1979), p. 51.
3. Plessis, *De la Fête*, p. 61.
4. Plessis, *De la Fête*, p. 72.
5. *AD* Seine-Maritime 1M180.
6. R. Huard, *Le Mouvement républicain en Bas-Languedoc 1848–81* (Paris, 1982), p. 118.
7. Weill, *Le Parti républicain*, pp. 410–13.
8. T. Zeldin, *The Political System of Napoleon III* (London, 1958), p. 39.
9. Prefect Haute-Loire to Minister of Interior, 3 August 1852, *confidentielle, AN* F1cIII Haute-Loire 3.
10. Zeldin, *Political System of Napoleon III*, p. 40.
11. Report subprefect Chateaubriant 4 March 1852, *AD* LI 1M100.
12. Weill, *Le Parti républicain*, p. 401.
13. C. H. Johnson, *Utopian Communism in France. Cabet and The Icarians, 1839–51* (Ithaca, NY, 1974), pp. 260–99.
14. Weill, *Le Parti républicain*, p. 416.
15. Zeldin, *Political System of Napoleon III*, pp. 70–4.
16. 10 June 1858, *AD* Eure 1M183.
17. Corbin, *Archaisme et modernité*, vol. 2, pp. 842–906.
18. Weill, *Le Parti républicain*, pp. 478–83.
19. Huard, *Le Mouvement républicain en Bas-Languedoc*, pp. 139–141.
20. W. H. C. Smith, *Second Empire and Commune: France 1848–1871* (London, 1985), p. 24.
21. Prefect Ariège to Minister of Interior, acknowledging and widely publicizing such claims, 27 February 1852, *AN* F1cIII Ariège 4.
22. 30 October 1867, *AD* Seine-Maritime 1M181.
23. M. Moissonnier, 'La Section lyonnaise de l'Intérnational et l'opposition ouvrière à la fin du Second Empire, 1865–70', *Cahiers d'Histoire*, 10 (1965), 275–314.
24. A. Plessis, *De la fête*, p. 209.
25. Huard, *Le Mouvement républicain*, p. 236.
26. Corbin, *Archaisme et modernité*, vol. 1, p. 885.
27. O. Barrot, *De la Centralisation et de ses effets* (Paris, 1863).
28. L. A. Prévost-Paradol, *Le France Nouvelle* (Paris, 1868).

29. *Compte Rendu.* Session of 1870, pp. 403–12.
30. Vidalenc, *Louis Blanc*, p. 64.
31. L. M. Greenberg, *Sisters of Liberty. Paris and the reaction to a centralized state 1868–71* (Cambridge, Mass., 1971).
32. A. Olivesi, *La Commune de 1871 à Marseille et ses origines* (Paris, 1950).
33. M. Moissonnier, *La première Internationale et la commune à Lyon* (Paris, 1972).
34. R. Tombs, *The War against Paris* (Cambridge, 1981).
35. A lucid exploration of the range of sympathies in R. Tombs, 'Prudent rebels: the 2nd *Arrondissement* during the Paris Commune of 1871', *French History*, 5 (1991), 393–413.

   For a summary of recent writing on the Commune see the useful review article by R. Tombs, 'L'année terrible 1870–1871', *Historical Journal*, 35 (1992), 713–24.
36. *Journal Officiel*, 21 March 1871; quoted in S. Edwards, *The Paris Commune, 1871* (London, 1971), pp. 155–6.
37. K. Marx, *Civil War in France* (London, 1872), p. 37.
38. Loubère, *Louis Blanc*, p. 224.
39. Edwards, *Paris Commune 1871.*
40. Tombs, *War against Paris.*
41. E. Schulkind, *The Paris Commune: the View from the Left* (London, 1972); J. Rougerie, *Le Procès des Communards* (Paris, 1964).
42. Marx, *Civil War in France.*
43. Greenberg, *Sisters of Liberty*, pp. 190–201.
44. Greenberg, *Sisters of Liberty*, pp. 245–81.
45. J. Goualt, *Comment la France est devenue républicaine. Les élections générales et partielles à l'Assemblée nationale 1870–1875* (Paris, 1954), p. 116.

Conclusion

1. M. P. Fitzsimmons, *The Parisian Order of Barristers and the French Revolution* (Cambridge, Mass., 1987), p. 194.
2. E. Beau de Lomenie, *Les Responsabilités des dynasties bourgeoises*, 4 vols (Paris, 1964).
3. C. H. Church, *Revolution and Red Tape. The French Ministerial Bureacuracy 1770–1850* (London, 1981).

4. P. Deyon, *Paris et ses Provinces. Le Défi de la décentralisation 1770–1992* (Paris, 1993).

5. Brilliantly tabulated in C. Jones, *The Longman Companion to the French Revolution* (London, 1988), pp. 282–3.

Appendix One: Chronological Table

1787	Feb.	Assembly of Notables
1789	May	Estates General
	July	Fall of Bastille
	Aug.	Abolition of Feudal Dues
		Declaration of Rights of Man
	Oct.	March to Versailles
	Nov.	Decrees on Church
1790	July	Civil Constitution of Clergy
1791	June	Flight to Varennes
	Sept.	CONSTITUTIONAL MONARCHY BEGINS
	Oct.	Legislative Assembly
1792	Apr.	Declaration of War
	June	Invasion of Tuileries (royal palace)
	Aug.	Revolution 10 Aug.; king suspended
	Sept.	September Massacres
		CONVENTION meets
		REPUBLIC declared. Year I of Republic
1793	Jan.	Execution of king
	Apr.	COMMITTEE OF PUBLIC SAFETY
	June	Girondins defeated; Jacobin Constitution
	Sept.	YEAR II of Republic
1794	July	Robespierre arrested and executed
1795	Aug.	Constitution of Year III
	Oct.	DIRECTORY begins

1796–9		French military victories
		Babeuf's Conspiracy of the Equals
1799	Nov.	Coup d'état 18 Brumaire
	Dec.	Constitution of Year VIII
		CONSULATE. Napoleon First Consul
1802	Apr.	Concordat with Papacy
	May	Napoleon Consul for life
1804	Mar	Civil Code
	May	EMPIRE proclaimed
	Dec.	Napoleon crowned
1808	Dec.	Invasion of Spain
1812		Invasion of Russia
1814	Apr.	Napoleon abdicates
		FIRST RESTORATION OF BOURBONS LOUIS XVIII KING
	May	Treaty of Paris
	June	Constitutional Charter
	Sept.	Congress of Vienna
1815	Mar.	EMPIRE. NAPOLEON'S 100 DAY RULE
	June	Battle of Waterloo. Napoleon's second abdication
		SECOND RESTORATION OF BOURBONS
		White Terror
	Aug.	*Chambre Introuvable* elected
	Nov.	Second Treaty of Paris
1816	Sept.	Dissolution of *Chambre Introuvable*
		Legislative Elections
		Economic crisis
		Conspiracies
1820	Feb.	Murder of duc de Berri
	June	Law of Double Vote
1821		Death of Napoleon
		Charbonnerie
	Dec.	Villèle government
1822	Mar.	Four Sergeants of la Rochelle conspiracy
1824	Mar.	Ultra election victory
	Sept.	LOUIS XVIII dies; Charles X king

1825	Apr.	Sacrilege law
	Apr.	Indemnification of *émigrés*
	May	Coronation of Charles X

1827	Apr.	National Guard dissolved
		Economic crisis
		Aide-toi, le ciel t'aidera
	Nov.	Elections

1828	Jan.	Resignation of Villèle
		Martignac government

1829	Aug.	Ultra government
	Nov.	Polignac chief minister

1830	June	Elections
	July	25th: Four Ordinances
	July	27–29th: Three Glorious Days Revolution in Paris
	July	31st: Duke of Orleans lieutenant-general
		Amis du Peuple & *Droits de l'Homme* formed
	Aug.	2nd: Charles X abdicates
	Aug.	ORLEANIST MONARCHY
		9th: LOUIS-PHILIPPE KING OF THE FRENCH PEOPLE
	Sept.	Riots in provinces

1831	Feb.	Anti-clerical riots
	Mar.	Casimir Périer chief minister
	July	Legislative Elections
	Nov.	Revolt in Lyon

1832		Cholera
	June	Popular unrest at funeral of Lamarque

1833		Education Law

1834	Feb.	Law against public hawkers
	Apr.	Law against Associations
		Revolt in Lyon
	Apr.	Rue Transnonain massacre
	June	Legislative Elections – defeat of left
		Society of the Families

1835	May	'Grand Conspiracy' trial
	July	Fieschi bomb plot
	Sept.	Press Laws

1836	Oct.	Louis-Napoleon in Strasbourg
1837		Society of the Seasons
1839	May	Society of Seasons' rising
		Louis-Napoleon, *Les Idées Napoleoniennes*
1840		Napoleon to Les Invalides
		Louis-Napoleon at Boulogne
		First Banquet Campaign
		Guizot government
		Proudhon, *Qu'est-ce-que la propriété?*
1842	July	Legislative Elections
1845		Economic crisis
1846	Aug.	Legislative Elections
1847	July	Banquet Campaign
1848	Feb.	23rd: Revolution in Paris. Guizot resigns
		24th: Louis-Philippe abdicates
		SECOND REPUBLIC PROCLAIMED
		Universal suffrage decreed
	Mar.	Radical demonstration Paris
	April	23rd: Election of Constituent Assembly
	May	15 Demonstration in Paris & Provinces
	June	22–26 June Days. Cavaignac government
	Nov.	4th: Constitution of Second Republic
	Dec.	10th: Election of Louis-Napoleon as President
1849	May	Elections to Legislative Assembly
	June	Unrest in Paris, Lyon,etc.
1850	Mar.	Falloux Law on Education
		Democ-soc election victories
	May	Suffrage restrictions
1851	Dec.	2nd: Coup d'état
		Republican insurrection in south
	Dec.	14th: Plebisicite
1852	Jan.	Constitution
	Feb.	Legislative Elections: 3 republicans chosen
	Nov.	Plebisicite
	Dec.	SECOND EMPIRE PROCLAIMED

1858		Election: 5 republicans
1860		Constitutional reform
1863		Election: 8 republicans
1864		Industrial Relations law
1867		Constitutional reform
1869		Election: 30 republicans. Ollivier government
1870	May	Plebiscite on constitutional reform
	July	War with North German Confederation
	Aug.	Invasion of France and defeats
	Sept.	1st: Louis-Napoleon surrenders at Sedan
		4th: REPUBLIC – GOVERNMENT OF NATIONAL DEFENCE
	Sept.	19th: Paris besieged
	Oct.	Government to Tours
		Rising in Paris; revolts in Marseille, Lyon, etc.
1871	Jan.	19th: Parisians fail to lift siege
	Jan.	28th: Armistice
	Feb.	8th: Election of National Assembly
		Thiers government
	Mar.	Peace of Frankfurt
	Mar.	18th: Montmartre guns
	Mar.	28th COMMUNE PROCLAIMED
	May	21–28 Bloody Week
	May	28th End of Commune
	Aug.	Rivet Law: Thiers president of the Republic

Appendix Two: Biographical Sketches

Albert, pseudonym of Alexandre Martin (1815–95), was the son of a peasant, who became a tool-and-dye maker in a button factory after serving an apprenticeship with his uncle, a machinist, in Paris. He was a leader of the revived society of the Seasons in the 1840s, well known enough in 1848 to be made the token worker in the provisional government. Vice-president of the Luxembourg Commission, he was noted for his silent support of Louis Blanc. Elected to the Constituent Assembly, he was arrested after joining the demonstration of May 15th. Albert spent four years on Belle-Ille and was finally amnestied in 1859. He refused the oath to Louis-Napoleon and worked as an inspector for the gas company. He failed to be elected either to the National Assembly or the Senate after 1871, but was honoured with a state funeral.

Arago, François (1786–1853) was the son of a peasant from the Pyrénées-Orientales who became a financial official during the Revolution. François was a brilliant scientist at the *Ecole Polytéchnique* and, at the age of 23, the *Académie des Sciences*. He was a republican member of the Chamber of Deputies from the 1830 Revolution for the rest of his life.

Arago, Etienne (1802–92),brother of François, *carbonaro*, insurgent in 1830, 1832 (June) and 1834; journalist at *La Réforme*; director of Post Office 1848, resigned at Louis-Napoleon's election; took part in June rising 1849 and was out of France until amnesty of 1859; mayor of Paris September 1870.

Arago, Emmanuel (1812–96), main defence lawyer in July Monarchy radical trials; fought in February 48; commissioner Lyon; ambassador

Berlin, resigned on Louis-Napoleon's election; deputy and senator 1869–death.

Audry de Puyraveau, Pierre-François (1773–1852), deputy 1822–37, 1848–death; very active in provisional government July Days and choice of Louis-Philippe; disillusioned, a founder of *Droits de l'Homme*; defender of 1834 accused; moderate in 48.

Barbès, Sigmund-Auguste-Armand (1809–70), born in Guadeloupe of mixed parentage, Barbès moved with his family to France at the age of five. He worked closely with Blanqui, sharing lodgings. He was a club activist in 1848, by now at odds with Blanqui, a member of the Constituent Assembly in 1848, a participant with Blanqui in the demonstrations of May 15th; subsequently jailed and self-exiled.

Bastide, Jules (1809–79), lawyer, *carbonaro*, insurgent in July Days 1830, June 1832, self-exile in London; defender of accused of 1834; journalist, then editor (1836) *Le National*; social catholic 1846; active in February 48, elected April 48, moderate republican foreign minister May 48 and supporter of Cavaignac, out on Louis-Napoleon's election and not re-elected to parliament.

Bazard, Saint-Armand (1791–1832) was awarded the legion of honour as a National Guardsman defending Paris from Allied invasion in 1815. Along with other clerks and fellow students, Buchez, Flottard and Joubert, he organized the *Amis de la Verité* in 1818 and the *charbonnerie* in 1821. An editor of both the *Producteur* and later *L'Organisateur*, he became a founder of the Saint-Simonist movement. In 1831 he left when Enfantin led the movement into doctrines of free love and also seduced Bazard's wife.

Blanc, Jean-Charles, father of Louis, was like his father involved in trade, fought, with his father, against the *montagnards* in Lyon at the time of the Convention. Both were subsequently imprisoned and the grandfather guillotined. It was thanks to his wife's family that he entered imperial service.

Blanc, J.J. Louis (1811–82), opposed the Paris Commune and in November 1872 he became president of the moderate Republican Union and worked with Clemenceau. He contributed to the Radical daily *Rappel*. He was still hailed as one of the main leaders of socialism in 1879, although by then French socialist groups were becoming more extreme, partly through the influence of the International. His hope of cooperation between classes seemed futile to a new generation of workers' leaders. Blanc himself is often thought of as the founder of radical socialism.

Carnot, Lazare Hippolyte (1801–88). His father was a famous revolutionary general, member of the Convention and minister of war during the Revolution. Hippolyte was a fan of Saint-Simon, a fighter in the 1830 Revolution and a republican deputy from 1839 to 1848. He was Minister of Education after the February Revolution.

Carrel, Nicolas Armand (1800–36), *carbonaro* in Belfort and Spanish adventures, journalist, then editor of *Le National* who quickly became disillusioned with Louis-Philippe and was killed by Emile de Girardin in a duel over their newspapers.

Cauchois-Lemaire, Louis-Auguste-François (1789–1861) was a journalist who, unlike many of his fellows, tried a variety of political affiliations: Bonapartist in 1814, when he was editor of *Le Nain Jaune*, one of the founders of *Le Constitutionnel* in 1819, the first to propose the duke of Orleans as France's William of Orange, a member of *Aide-toi*; and the republican editor of *Bon Sens* when Louis-Philippe actually became king. On retirement in 1840, he became royal archivist and completed one volume of a history of the July Revolution. In 1848 he was a conservative republican.

Caussidière, Louis-Marc (1808–61), son of an artisan who was active in the First Republic, he followed his father and fought in the St Etienne rising in 1834, amnestied 1837; in *Saisons*, involved in *La Réforme*, February Revolution 48; socialist, prefect of police 48, elected 48, against June Days, but forced into exile in London.

Cavaignac, Godefroy-Eleonore-Louis (1800–45), republican leader in the 1830 Revolution and prominent among republican clubs subsequently, was the son of Jean-Baptiste Cavaignac, the Jacobin member of the Convention, and like him spent some time in the Second Restoration in enforced exile in Brussels. Back in Paris to study law, he was an early member of the *charbonnerie*. Together with Bastide and Carnot, he founded the republican *Société des Francs-Parleurs*, which then merged with *Aide-toi*. He was one of the leaders of the attack on the Tuileries on 29 July 1830, became a captain in the National Guard but, disappointed with Louis-Philippe, became a leader of the *Amis du Peuple*. Frequently prosecuted and also acquitted because of his eloquent republicanism, he became president of the *Droits de l'Homme* when the *Amis* was forced to close in 1833. Arrested after the so-called conspiracy of 1834 he was one of the main spokesmen in the trial the following year. He escaped from prison shortly afterwards and fled to England, where he became the correspondent for *Le National*. Amnestied in 1840, he was editor of the shortlived, radical *Journal du Peuple*. He also wrote for Louis Blanc's *Revue du Progrès*.

Cavaignac, Louis-Eugène (1802–57), brother of Godfrey, *carbonaro*, *Ecole Polytechnique* and army (protected by uncle who rallied to Restoration); moved to Algeria in 1832 because of radical views.

Corcelle, Claude Tircuy de (1768–1843). From minor noble stock; army in 1789, he joined the prince de Condé's *émigré* army. Back in France 1799, he became National Guard commander in the Rhône in 1813, was in addition a *fédéré* leader in 1815 and banished by the Bourbons. In 1819 he became liberal deputy for the Rhône. In 1830 he proposed a national vote on the new monarchy, with which he was never well pleased. His son, also a Restoration radical, married Lafayette's grand-daughter, who was also Charles de Rémusat's sister, and was a lifelong member of the Chamber of Deputies.

Delescluze, Charles (1809–71) Jacobin socialist; *Amis du Peuple*, 1834 rising and journalist; commissioner of Nord until May 48 – too radical, in June 49 rising and London exile; to France December 51, Devil's Island to 1859; insurrectionary and deputy 1871, died on Commune barricades.

Deroin, Jeanne (1805–94), seamstress, educated in evening classes in Paris, socialist and feminist in Second Republic; condemned May 1851 and fled to London.

Destutt de Tracy, Comte A.-L.-C. (1754–1836). Born into an old court noble family, he was jailed during the Terror because of his support for moderate revolutionary policies, became a leading *idéologue* in the Directory, a Napoleonic Senator (1799–1814), a member of the *charbonnerie* in the Restoration and an active member of the Chamber of Peers.

Dubois, Paul-François (1793–1874), was successively a member of the *charbonnerie*, a teacher, a brilliant journalist on the *Globe* and a much admired Director of the *École Normale Supérieure* (1840–52), dismissed by Louis-Napoleon.

Dupont de l'Eure, Jacques-Charles (1767–1855), son of a merchant; lawyer in Revolution; very independent; deputy 1814 and Hundred

Days vice-president of Chamber; deputy 1817–May 1849. Minister of Justice 1830 but became disillusioned.

Duvergier de Hauranne, Prosper (1798–1881), an enthusiastic *doctrinaire* liberal during the Restoration, facilitated Louis-Philippe's accession to the throne, was elected to the Chamber of Deputies in 1831 and became a supporter of the *mouvement*. He supported Thiers against Guizot in the 1840s and was a major voice in the reform campaign. He was an opponent of Louis-Napoleon as president and emperor and retired from politics in December 1851 to write his 10-volume *Histoire du gouvernement parlementaire en France*.

Esquiros, Henri F.A. (1812–76), was a member of a prosperous bourgeois family, educated in a seminary, who as a follower of Victor Hugo became a poet and, influenced by Louis Blanc, a democratic socialist politician. A prolific writer, he wrote a history of the Convention (1842), supported the insurgents in June 1848 and fled to England. At the end of 1848 he was active among the socialists of Marseille and in the spring of 1850 was twice elected (the government invalidated his first election) as a radical socialist to the Legislative Assembly for the Saône-et-Loire. He fled France at the coup of 1851 and remained in England until 1869, when he was elected to the Assembly. He opposed the war of 1870. Briefly Gambetta's wayward prefect in Marseille, he joined Raspail in calling for a revolutionary onslaught on the Assembly of 1871, but later encouraged republicans to support the Thiers' government, as the only alternative to a monarchy. In 1876 he was elected on the extreme left of the Assembly by the Bouches-du-Rhône, signing Hugo's proposal of an amnesty for the Communards.

Flocon, Ferdinand (1800–66), was the son of an employee in the telegraph system. He was a member of the *charbonnerie* and his radicalism along with his skills as a printer gave him work with *Le Constitutionnel* and *Le Courrier Français* and the editorship of the latter. After 1830 he was a member of the *Amis du Peuple*, contributed to *La Tribune* and was well known for his enthusiasm for Robespierre before becoming main editor of *La Réforme* in 1843. A member of the provisional government in 1848 and Minister of Agriculture, he supported General Cavaignac in the June Days. Cavaignac did not keep him in the government and he was not re-elected in 1849. He returned to journalism with the *Démocrate du Bas-Rhin*. He fled to Switzerland after the 1851 coup and spent the rest of his life as a bookseller and translator.

Garnier-Pagès, Etienne-Joseph-Louis (1801–41), an established Parisian lawyer by the late Restoration, he was one of the organizers of *Aide-toi, le ciel t'aidera*, active in resistance to the July Ordinances of 1830, after which he had hoped for a democratic republic. He was elected for the Isère in a by-election in December 1831 and soon became a leading spokesman for radical suffrage reform.

Garnier-Pagès, Louis-Antoine, brother of the acknowledged leader of the republican group, Etienne, who had died in 1841.

Grégoire, Henri-Baptiste (1750–1831), an *abbé*, was elected by the First Estate in 1789; he became a constitutional bishop, was elected to the Convention and remained constant to his republicanism.

Guépin, Ange (1805–73), came from a long-established family of Breton lawyers, a branch of which was of Huguenot origin. His father had supported the Girondins in the early 1790s, but survived Jacobin imprisonment to resume his career as an official and was elected a member of parliament during the Hundred Days. Guépin studied medicine in Paris, where he joined the *charbonnerie* and got to know Trélat, Buchez and Leroux. He was strongly influenced, as were many who were in the *charbonnerie*, by Saint-Simonian ideas and the newspaper *Le Globe*, then being edited by Chevalier. He became an eye specialist in Nantes, where he joined the liberal opposition to Polignac and took a leading role in fighting against the prefect during the July Days in 1830.

Hernoux, Etienne (1777–1858), is a typical example of the continuity of revolutionary tradition. His father Charles, like him a local *négociant*, was elected by the Dijonnais Third Estate in 1789 and served later on the *conseil des anciens*. Etienne was first proposed as mayor of Dijon in 1812, was appointed in the Hundred Days, imprisoned at the Second Restoration and subsequently deputy 1817–24 and 1829–37. After the 1830 Revolution he was restored as mayor, appointed to the general council of the department, a body over which he presided until 1842. He was one of the richest men in the department, paying 4504 francs in direct tax in 1834. A liberal in the Restoration, he became a vigorous *mouvement* critic of the Orleanist régime after the appointment of Casimir Périer.

Ledru-Rollin, Alexandre-Auguste (1807–74), son and grandson of the Ledrus, he added his grandmother's name Rollin to avoid confusion with another lawyer. Editor of *La Réforme* and a republican deputy, he was a leading figure in the February Revolution, the Minister of the Interior in the provisional government and member of the Executive Commission from May to June 1848. Presidential candidate in December 1848, he was subsequently leader of the democ-socs until June 1849, when his participation in a march protesting at the government's foreign policy forced him to leave France. Ledru-Rollin remained in exile for 20 years, excluded from amnesties in 1859 and 1869. The Ollivier government of 1870 permitted him to return to France, but he was too ill to join in the government of 4 September 1870. He was chosen for the National Assembly in February 1871 but resigned and was elected for the last time in 1874.

Leroux, Pierre (1797–1871). Destined for the *Ecole Polytechnique*, family poverty forced him into a variety of jobs, finally settling as a typesetter for a liberal printer. A Saint-Simonian until 1831, he joined the *Droits de l'Homme*, turning its attention to socialist concerns. Mystic and shrewd critic of contemporary society, Leroux continued to mix practical politics and somewhat obscure philosophy throughout his life.

Marie, Alexandre-Thomas (1795–1870). A liberal in the Restoration, Marie quickly became a republican after 1830. A lawyer, he defended the republicans accused in 1832. In 1837 he joined Garnier-Pagès and Ledru-Rollin in an electoral committee. From 1842 he was a member of the Chamber of Deputies and took part in the Banquet Campaign of 1847. After a ministerial career in the Second Republic he opposed Louis Napoleon and returned to his legal career.

Nadaud, Martin (1815–99). The man-of-the-people always trotted out to illustrate the democratic character of nineteenth century republicanism is Nadaud, not because of his political activities, but because he had the wisdom to publish his memoirs. He is invariably cited as the quintessential artisan. Born in the Creuse, Limousin, like many from this impoverished area he travelled to Paris where he joined the *Société des Droits de l'Homme* and the *Saisons* and then became a convert to Cabet's Icarian communism. He was elected for the Creuse to the Legislative Assembly in 1849 where he spoke for and voted with the democ-socs. A founder of a successful masons' cooperative in Paris, he was forced into exile by the Empire. Nadaud was and remained an independent artisan, indeed he was so disgusted to find that his cooperative had been taken over by a number of wealthy masons when he was amnestied in 1859, that he went back to Britain and stayed there until the end of the Empire. After the fall of Louis-Napoleon he was momentarily prefect in his native Creuse. He was elected for the Creuse from 1876 until 1889 where he supported the Opportunists. Nadaud was important as an exception, a curiosity. His career in no way illustrates the involvement and integration of working people into the Republic.

Ollivier, Emile (1825–1913), was an accomplished republican politician and lawyer. His father, Demosthenes, had been in the *charbonnerie*, was arrested, and was a close friend of Ledru-Rollin, Leroux and Armand Carrel. Ollivier's grandmother was a keen legitimist. Emile won a scholarship to the *lycée* Saint-Barbe and went on to train as a lawyer. His father urged Ledru-Rollin to appoint his son, also an enthusiastic and fluent republican, rather than him, to be commissioner, then prefect, in Marseille. Demoted to the Haute-Marne after the June Days, he was dismissed after the election of Louis-Napoleon, when he had supported the candidacy of Lamartine, despite protests from his department. He continued to express his eloquent faith in fraternity. In 1849 he was arrested by Haussmann, prefect of the Var, for speaking on behalf of republican parliamentary candidates. Although acquitted, he retired temporarily from politics. His father, a left-wing member of the Constituent Assembly in 1848, was banished from France and his brother, a republican newspaper editor, was killed in a duel with a legitimist. He was to be elected to Louis-Napoleon's *corps législatif* and agreed to form a government in 1869, a triumph for the emperor.

Pyat, Aimé-Félix (1810–89), trained as a lawyer like his father, but unlike his legitimist father he was a liberal from the outset and fought in the July Days. He became a radical playwright and also wrote widely for the republican press.

Raspail, François-Vincent (1794–1878), a doctor, concerned with public health and the welfare of the poor; republican leader also in 1848 Republic and deputy for Marseille in Third Republic.

Rey, Joseph (1799–1855), lawyer, social and educational reformer, Owenite socialist and ultimately a communist who hoped his better society could be founded on consent, was disbarred by the Restoration and modestly appointed by the July Monarchy.

Sand, George (1804–76) pseudonym of Aurore Dudevant (née Dupin), daughter of the aristocratic Dupin de Francuel, aide-de-camp to Napoleon and a camp follower whose own father was a Parisian birdseller, broke away from a wealthy background and marriage to live a bohemian republican life in Paris, dressed as a man, supported herself by her writing, had various flamboyant affairs with famous litterati (de Musset, Chopin, etc.) and made many friends among socialists, such as Louis Blanc and Leroux. She was a prolific novelist (60 books), playwright (25 plays) and essayist.

Thierry, Augustin (1795–1856), a graduate of the *École Normale*, he was Saint-Simon's secretary and collaborator on a number of publications for two years from 1814. He moved to the liberal journal *Censeur européen*, writing a number of articles in which he compared his own time with that of seventeenth-century revolutionary Britain. From 1820 he wrote for the *Courrier Français*, urging a new approach to the writing of the history of France, stressing the heroic role of the French nation in its search for liberty. He then devoted himself to a history of the Norman Conquest of Britain, in the writing of which Armand Carrel worked as his secretary. An enthusiastic Orleanist, he became librarian to the duke of Orleans in 1834 and published a collection of documents on the history of the Third Estate.

Trélat, Ulysse (1798–1879), a doctor like Raspail and others of his generation who worked with a social conscience among the poor, a *carbonaro*, member of *Aide-toi* and secret societies of the early 1830s; he was active in 1848, the Paris Commune and on the municipal council of Paris until 1874.

These sketches include only radicals who figure prominently in the main book. It is not intended to be an exhaustive biographical dictionary. Where appropriate details are in the text, and only a partial, or no, biography given here. Use in conjunction with the index.

Details are taken from a wide range of sources, archival, memoirs, individual biographies and biographical dictionaries. Among the latter the most valuable is E. L. Newman (ed. with R. L. Simpson), *Historical Dictionary of France from the 1815 Restoration to the Second Empire*, 2 vols (New York, 1987). In French see also J. Maitron, *Dictionnaire Biographique du Mouvement Ouvrier Français*, 3 vols (Paris, 1964–6) and the indispensable E. Bourloton, G. Cogny and A. Robert, *Dictionnaire des Parlementaires Français*, 5 vols (Paris, 1889–91).

Appendix Three: Maps

The Maps

It should be noted that in 1830 only *c*.90,000 men were qualified to vote whereas Maps 2, 3, 5 and 6 represent the attitudes of a mass (male) electorate. The maps indicate that changes in regional orientation from 'right' to 'left' and vice versa are related to economic performances as well as to the memories and experiences of politics and religious preferences. Above all they show the lack of precision of *all* the terms used. Maps look precise but are only impressionistic. With that proviso, their indications are of value.

75% Left – Liberals

75% + Right Wing – Royalists and Ultras

Map 1 The victory of the liberals; the elections of June and July, 1830. The map shows the degree to which the Polignac government alienated voters even in traditionally royalist western areas

Source: T. D. Beck, *French Legislators 1800–1834* (University of California Press, Berkeley, Los Angeles, London, 1974), p. 105

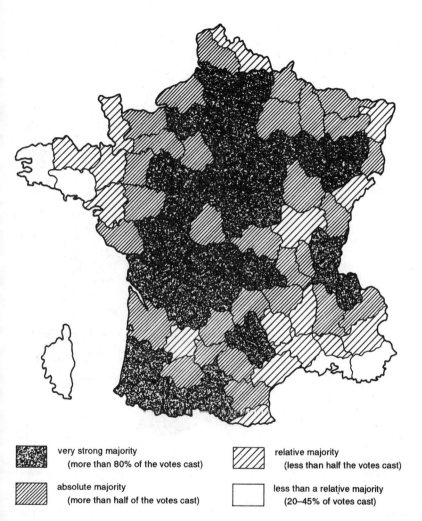

very strong majority
(more than 80% of the votes cast)

relative majority
(less than half the votes cast)

absolute majority
(more than half of the votes cast)

less than a relative majority
(20–45% of votes cast)

Map 2 The Second Republic: the presidential election, 10 December 1848:
Bonapartist memories – the vote for Louis-Napoleon

Source: A. J. Tudesq, *L'Election présidentielle de Louis-Napoléon Bonaparte, 10 décembre 1848*
('Kiosque' series – Colin, Paris, 1965), p. 253

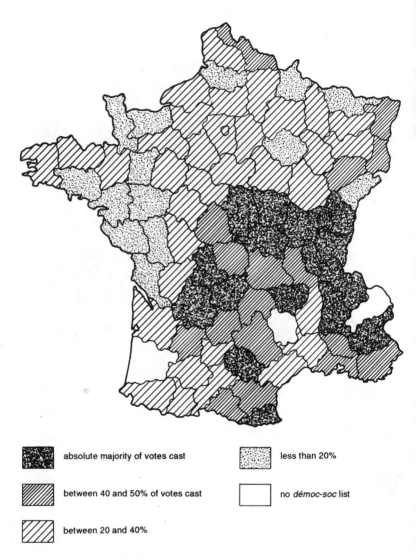

absolute majority of votes cast		less than 20%	
between 40 and 50% of votes cast		no *démoc-soc* list	
between 20 and 40%			

Map 3 The Second Republic: votes for radical-republicans (democ-socs) in legislative election, 13 May 1849

Source: M. Agulhon, *The Republican Experiment 1848–1852* (Cambridge University Press, 1983), p. 145

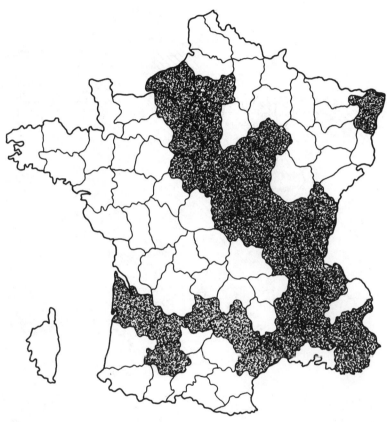

 State of siege declared by Louis Napoleon after coup in 32 departments

Map 4 Republican resistance to the coup d'état of December 1851 (compare with Map 3)

Source: G. Weill, *Histoire du parti républican en France de 1814 à 1870* (Paris, 1900), p. 361, fn 2

fewer than 25% of registered voters

35 – 59%

25 – 34%

over 50%

No votes cast in the plebiscite of 8 May 1870

Map 5 Criticism of the Second Empire: 'No' votes cast in plebiscite of 8 May 1870 on constitutional revision – an indication that voters thought the changes too modest and sought a more 'republican' empire

Source: A. Plessis, *The Rise and Fall of the Second Empire, 1852–1871* (Cambridge University Press, 1987), p. 167

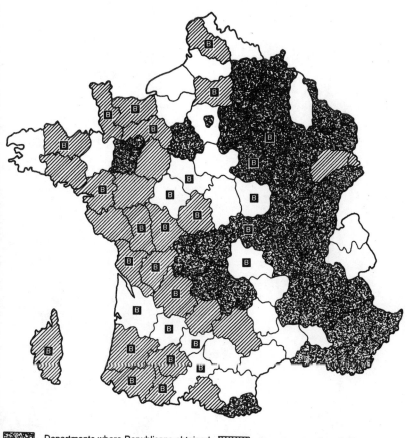

Departments where Republicans obtained 60 per cent or more of vote in 1876

Departments where half or more of deputies elected in 1876 belonged to Right

B   Departments where Bonapartists obtained 20 per cent or more of vote in 1876

Map 6 The republican vote in the early Third Republic, 1876

Source: R.D. Anderson, *France 1870–1914* (London, Routledge, 1977), p. 54

Bibliography

Manuscript Sources

ARCHIVES NATIONALES (*AN*)
BB. Justice.

Reports of government prosecutors:
BB3.1476
BB6.258.

Correspondence of magistrates on public opinion:
BB18.1175, 1176; BB18.1354B; BB18.1467; BB18.1468; BB18.1476.

Assize court reports:
BB20.54; BB20.72.

Reports on public opinion from government prosecutors:
BB30.237; BB30.239; BB30.240; BB30.241; BB30.250; BB30.319;
BB30.321; BB30.322; BB30.323; BB30.327; BB30.377.

F. Correspondence between central government and departments:
F1a*678; F1a*679; F1a*680; F1a*2098; F1a*2099; F1a*2100;
F1a*2101.

F1cI 33; F1cII56; F1cII57; F1cII58; F1cII97; F1cII98; F1cII99;
F1cII100; F1cII101; F1cII102; F1cII103.

F1cIII Allier 3; F1cIII Aisne 7; F1cIII Ariège 4; F1cIII Aveyron 5;
F1cIII Bas-Rhin 4; F1cIII Bas-Rhin 15; F1cIII Bouches-du-Rhône 4;
F1cIII Calvados 6; F1cIII Dordogne 5; F1cIII Finistère 9; F1cIII

Gironde 4; F1cIII Haute-Loire 3; F1cIII Hérault 4; F1cIII Indre 3; F1cIII Jura 14; F1cIII Loir-et-Cher 8; F1cIII Loire 4; F1cIII Loire-Inférieure 4; F1cIII Loiret 4; F1cIII Lot 5; F1cIII Manche 4; F1cIII Marne 3; F1cIII Mayenne 4; F1cIII Meurthe 6; F1cIII Meuse 6; F1cIII Nièvre 3; F1cIII Pas-de-Calais 6; F1cIII Vienne 4; F1cIII Vosges 6; F1cIII Var; F1cIII Vaucluse 4; F1cIII Yonne 4; F1cIII Yonne 10; F1cIV8.

Gendarmerie reports:
F7.6686, F7.6742. F7.9682

DEPARTMENTAL ARCHIVES (*AD*)

Calvados, Caen
Repertoire for M and Z series in typed and bound volumes. Does not use customary system of classification. Cf. R. Gandilhon, 'La série M', *Revue Historique* 1969, 147–62; G. Bernard, *Guide des Archives du département du Calvados* (Caen, 1978).
1848 M2855; Second Republic M2856; Second Empire M2860, M2861, M2868, M2921, M2926

Côtes d'Armor, St Brieuc
B. Salou, *Répértoire numerique de la sous-série 6 M* (St Brieuc, 1987).
Second Republic 1M259; Second Empire 1M260; 1848 1M330bis; 1851 1M331, 1M332, 1M333; Second Empire 1M334, 1M335, 1M336, 1M337, 6M826, 6M936.

Eure, Evreux
Second Empire politics: 1M132, 1M134–1M139; 1M147, 1M148
Second Empire 1M182, 1M183. Commune 1M184
July Monarchy 1M235–245; 1848 1M246; Second Republic 1M248–262.
1M345, 346, 347, 352, 353.

Finistère, Quimper
J. Charpy, *Guide des Archives du Finistère* (Quimper, 1973).
J. Charpy, *Archives de Kernuz* (Quimper, 1879).
1M: 1M170 Enquêtes sur les fonctionnnaires 1857–1940; Surveillance de l'opinion 1M178 1848–52 (a very useful file), 1M179 1852–70, 1M180 1870–6 includes meeting of International at Brest and the response to the Paris Commune; 1M200 Surveillance des cultes;

1M209 Proclamation de la République, etc. 1848–52; 1M210 coup of 1851; 1M211 Second Empire adresses to Emperor 1859; 1M212 Third Republic 1870–1939; 1M263 War of 1870–1 circulaires, affiches, etc.

3M Elections: 3M144 1850–1, 3M154 Presidential Election 1848, 3M157 Elections Mar–Nov.1848, 3M158 Elections 1849, 3M159–3M191 Elections 1850–69

100 J *Archives de Kernuz*. Documents on the ancien regime, 1789 Revolution and Empire amassed by A.Chatellier (1797–1855) and his son and son-in-law, historian and prefect.

Haute-Marne, Chaumont
2J Collection Louet. Journal des événements qui se sont déroulés à Paris, à Chaumont . . . 15 septembre 1791 jusqu'à 1847, 11 volumes.

Ille-et-Vilaine, Rennes
A typed catalogue.
1M: Esprit public, huge files on *chouannerie* and July Monarchy but Second Republic and Empire a total blank.
1M98; 1M157 Voyage de l'Empéreur 1858.

3M Elections: 3M154 Elections Dec.1848 very informative prefectoral reform on opinion; 3M157 Extremely useful papers of Hamon, commissioner 1848 Elections April 1848; 3M159 Elections of May 1849.

Loire-Inférieure
1M92 Plebisicites 1851–70; 1M100 Elections législatives 1811–87, some interesting reports on Second Empire; Police générale. Correspondance. Situation politique 1M516 1848–52, 1M517 1853–9; 1M518 1860–63; 1M519 1864–70; 1M520 1870.
Private papers of prefect, Achille Chaper 1840–7: 55J1, 55J2. Very informative.

Morbihan
Typed catalogue – very limited.
Cabinet de préfet, Affaires générales, Police Politique 1814–67 M500; 1843–65 M518; 1847–53 M680 most informative of these files; 1861–73 M681, M686 (a little on resistance to Third Republic).

Seine Maritime (Seine-Inférieure) Rouen
A printed *Répértoire numérique et détaillé de la série M. Administration générale et économique du département 1800–1940*, volume II, 6M à 10M.

Situation politique: 1M165 1848; 1M166–7 Second Empire; 1M168 1848 Revolution and Second Republic; 1848 Revolution 1M180; Second Empire 1M181; Third Republic 1M182; War of 1870, preparations to fight 1M212, 1M213, 1M214, 1M215.
Elections: 3M212 15 April 1848; 3M223 Plebiscite May 1870.
Rapports de police: 4M117 1838–54; 4M133 Jan–Nov.1870; 4M134 1871.
Associations politiques: July Monarchy 4M2685; 1848 Revolution 4M2686; Second Empire 4M2687; 4M2703; Commune 4M2704.

All archival references given above are in addition to those recorded in P.M. Pilbeam, *The 1830 Revolution in France* (London 1991), pp. 216–225 which cover 31 departments *c.*1814–*c.*1848.

Printed Sources, Newspapers, Pamphlets

Pamphlets

Les Révolutions du XIXe siècle is a 43-volume collection of contemporary radical pamphlets photocopied and reprinted in Switzerland by *Editions d'Histoire Sociale (EDHIS)*, Paris, covering the period 1830–72. It is an unparalleled source and includes radical, republican and socialist material, election propaganda, the proceedings of political trials, individual copies and occasionally whole runs of newspapers. The volumes are organized thematically and each is preceded by a short list of contents and followed by an index of names. In the third series which covers the Second Republic (the series are not actually numbered), there is a very brief introduction by Maurice Agulhon and volume 1 of the fourth and final series has both an introduction and a short bibliographical essay.

There is no indication where any of the pamphlets are now located, beyond a note of thanks to a number of libraries including the *Bibliothèque Nationale* and the *Archives Nationales*. Nor is there any explanation for the rationale of the choice of themes and individual pamphlets, beyond a comment by Maurice Agulhon that Jacques Rougerie had contributed much in their selection and that there had been a positive effort to include inaccessible material, a decision which at times makes the selection somewhat unbalanced. The title of the whole series *Les Révolutions du XIXe. siècle* has a curiously old-fashioned tone; these pamphlets might have been selected by Georges Weill himself. They present a somewhat deterministic and 'intellectual' approach to the subject of revolution.

Nonetheless *Les Révolutions* are an Aladdin's cave for students of republican and socialist politics. Most of the pamphlets and trial records quoted here, with a few exceptions such as the 1835 monster conspiracy trial and some regional material, have been taken from these series. Unfortunately the absence of page numbers in the individual volumes makes it impossible to give sensible references. I make no pretence that I have done more than sample the volumes.

Les Révolutions du XIXe. siècle:
First series. 1830–4. 12 volumes (Paris, 1974).
    I, Les Associations Républicaines 1830–34.
    II, La Société des Amis du Peuple 1830–32.
    III, La Société des Droits de l'Homme et du Citoyen 1832–4.
    IV, Naissance du mouvement ouvrier 1830–4.
    V & VI, Le mouvement social à Lyon 1830–4.
    VII, Écrits de Ph. Buonarroti, etc.
    VIII, Cabet et les publications du Populaire 1831–4.
    IX, Le propagande républicaine en province 1830–4.
    X, La presse républicaine devant les tribunaux 1831–4.
    XI, Les républicaines devant les tribunaux 1831–4.
    XII, Feuilles populaires et documents diverses 1830–4.

Les Révolutions du XIXe. siècle:
Second series. 1834–48. 12 volumes (Paris 1979).
    I–II, Le Mouvement Ouvrier 1834–1848.
    III–IV, La Propagande Socialiste 1834–1848.
    V, Cabet, le Communisme icarien de 1840 à 1847.
    VI–VIII, Révolutionnaires et Néo-Babouvistes 1835–1847.
    IX–XI, Les procès des sociétés secrètes devabt la Cour des Pairs. L'insurrection de Mai 1839. L'attentat Darmès 11 Mai 1840. L'attentat Quénisset 13 Septembre 1841.
    XII, Feuilles populaires et documents diverses 1835–1848.

Les Révolution du XIXe siècle:
Third series. 1848. *La Révolution Démocratique et Sociale*, 9 volumes (Paris, 1984).

Les Révolutions du XIXe siècle:
Fourth and last series. 1852–72. 10 volumes (Paris, 1988).
    I, Les Républicains sous le Second Empire, introduced by M. Cordillot.

II–IV, Les sociétés ouvrières.
V, L'Association Internationale des Travailleurs en France.
VI, De la Révolution du 4 septembre 1870 à l'insurrection du 18 mars 1871.
VII, La Commune de Paris.
VIII, Les mouvements républicaines et communalistes de Province.
IX, 'La Mutualité, Journal du Travail' 1865–1866.
X, Affiches, feuilles populaires et documents divers 1852–1872.

Other Printed Material

Various years of the *Almanach Royal, Almanach National.*
Annales du parlement français.
Bulletin Officiel du ministère de l'intérieur, 1848, 1849.
Code Pénal, 12 fév 1810. Les Cinq Codes de l'Empire (Paris, 1812).
Cour des Pairs. Affaire du mois d'avril 1834. Rapport 1835. 4 vols (Paris, 1835).
Duguit, L. and Monnier, H., *Les Constitutions et les Principales Lois Politiques de la France depuis 1789* (3rd edn Paris, 1915).
Tourneux, M., *Publications sur la Révolution à Paris. Bibliographie de l'histoire de Paris.*
Tuetey, A., *Publications sur la Révolution à Paris. Répértoire des sources manuscrites.*
Tuetey, A., *Archives Parlementaires.*
Annuaires in a number of departments – see specific Notes.

A number of national and local newspapers, departmental *annuaires* and *almanachs* were consulted on particular issues and some specific references can be found in individual Notes.
Memoirs and philosophical and political tracts of contemporaries are included in the following list of secondary works because otherwise the extended choronological compass of this study led to arbitrary bibliographical divisions.

Secondary Works
Abensour, L., *Histoire générale du féminisme* (Paris, 1921).
Actes du colloque Gracchus Babeuf (Amiens, 1989).
Adler, L., *Les Premières Journalistes (1830–1850)* (Paris, 1979).
Advielle, V., *Histoire du Gracchus Babeuf,* 2 vols (Paris, 1884).
Aftalion, F., *The French Revolution. An Economic History* (Cambridge, 1990).
Aguet, J.P., *Contribution à l'histoire du mouvement ouvrier français: les grèves sous la Monarchie de Juillet, 1830–47* (Geneva, 1954).

Agulhon, M., *1848 ou l'apprentissage de la république 1848–1852* (Paris, 1973); rather misleadingly translated as *The Republican Experiment* (Cambridge, 1983). All references are to French edition.

Agulhon, M. (ed.), *Blanqui et les Blanquistes* (Paris, 1986).

Agulhon, M., *La République au village*; trans. *The Republic in the Village* (Cambridge, 1970).

Agulhon, M., *Histoire Vagabonde*, 2 vols (Paris, 1988), includes '1830 dans l'histoire du XIXe. siècle français'.

Agulhon. M., *Marianne. Les Visages de la République* (Paris, new edn 1992).

Agulhon, M., *Une Ville ouvrière au temps du socialisme utopique: Toulon de 1815 à 1851* (Paris 1970).

Alazard, J., 'La population ouvrière sous la Monarchie de Juillet', *Revue du Mois*, 10 November 1911.

Alazard, J., 'Le mouvement politique et social à Lyon entre les deux insurrections de novembre 1831 et d'avril 1834', *Revue d'histoire moderne* (1911).

Alazard, J., 'Les causes de l'insurrection lyonnaise de novembre 1831', *Revue historique*, cxi (1912).

Alexander, R.S., *Bonapartism and the Revolutionary Tradition in France. The Fédérés of 1815* (Cambridge, 1991).

Alexander, R.S., 'The federations of 1814 and the continuity of anti-Bourbon personnel, 1789–1830', *Proceedings of the Annual Meeting of the Western Society for French History*, vol. 17 (1990).

Allen, M.B., 'Proudhon in the Revolution of 1848', *Journal of Modern History* (1952), 1–14.

Almanach Démocratique et Social (Paris, 1849).

Amann, P., *Revolution and Mass Democracy: the Paris Club Movement in 1848* (Princeton, NJ, 1975).

Amann, P., 'The Paris Club Movement in 1848', in Price, *Revolution and Reaction* (London, 1975), pp. 115–131.

Amann, P., 'The changing outlines of 1848', *American Historical Review*, 6 (1963), 938–53.

Aminzade, R., *Class, Politics and early Industrial Capitalism. A Study in Mid-nineteenth-century Toulouse* (Albany, NY, 1981).

Anderson, G.K., 'Old Nobles and *Noblesse d'Empire* (1814–30); in search of a Conservative Interest in Post-Revolutionary France' (unpublished paper, University of Glasgow, March 1993).

Anderson, R.D., *France 1870–1914. Politics and Society* (London, 1977).

Armengaud, A., *Les Populations de l'Est-Aquitaine au début de l'époqe contemporaine* (Paris, 1961).

Bagge, D., *Les Idées politiques sous la Restauration* (Paris, 1952).

Baker, K., *Inventing the French Revolution. Essays on French Political Culture in the Eighteenth Century* (Cambridge, 1990).

Barral, P., 'La Franc-maçonnerie en Lorraine au XIXe. et XX siècle', *Annales de l'Est* (1970).

Barrière and Berville (eds), *Papier inédits trouvés chez Robespierre, Saint-Just, Payan, etc.* 4 vols (Paris, 1828).

Barrot, C.H.O., *Mémoires posthumes de Odilon Barrot*, 4 vols (Paris, 1875, 1876; pub. by C.Duvergier de Hauranne and others).

Barrot, C.H.O., *De la Centralisation et de ses effets* (Paris, 1863).

Bastid, P., *Les Institutions politiques de la Monarchie parlementaire française 1814–1848* (Paris, 1954).

Baughman, J.J., 'The French Banquet Campaign of 1847–8', *Journal of Modern History*, xxxi, 1 (1959), 1–15.

Bayet, A. and Albert, F., *Les Ecrivains politiques du XIXe. siècle* (Paris, 1924).

Berenson, E., *Populist religion and left-wing politics in France 1830–1852* (Princeton, 1984).

Berenson, E., 'A new religion of the Left: Christianity and Social Radicalism in France 1815–48', in Furet and Ozouf, *The French Revolution and the Creation of Modern Political Culture* (Oxford, 1989), pp. 543–60.

Bergeron, L., *France under Napoleon* (trs. Cambridge, 1981; French edn 1972).

Bernstein, S., *Auguste Blanqui and the Art of Insurrection* (London, 1971).

Berstein S. and Rudelle O. (eds), *Le Modèle républicain* (Paris, 1992).

Bezucha, R.J., *The Lyon Uprising of 1834* (Cambridge, Mass., 1974).

Birnbaum, P., *'La France aux Français'. Histoire des haines nationalistes* (Paris, 1993).

Blanc, J.J.L., *Histoire de la Révolution* (Paris, 1847).

Blanc, J.J.L., *Histoire de la Révolution de 1848* (Paris, 1870).

Blanc, J.J.L., *Organisation du travail* in J.A.R. Marriot, *The French Revolution of 1848 in its Economic Aspect*, I (Oxford, 1913; first pub. as book Paris, 1840).

Blanc, J.J.L., *Révolution française. Histoire de dix ans*, 5 vols (Paris, 1841–4).

Blanc, J.J.L.. *La République une et indivisible* (1851).

Blanning, T.C.W., *The Origins of the French Revolutionary Wars* (London, 1986).

Blanqui et les Blanquistes, Actes du Colloque Blanqui, Société d'histoire de la révolution de 1848 et les révolutions du dix-neuvième siècle (Paris, 1986).

¡luche, F., *Le Bonapartisme* (Paris, 1980).

¡lum, C., *Rousseau and the Republic of Virtue: the Language of Politics during the French Revolution* (Ithaca, NY, 1986).

¡onald, L. de, *Théorie de l'éducation sociale et de l'administration publique* (Paris, 1796).

¡onald, L. de, *Réflexions sur la Révolution de 1830*, presenté par F. Bastier (Paris, 1988).

¡ossenga, G., *The Politics of Privilege. Old Regime and Revolution in Lille* (Cambridge, 1991).

¡ourgin, G., 'La crise ouvrière à Paris dans la seconde moitié de 1830', *Revue Historique* (1947), 203–14.

¡ourloton, E., Cogny, G. and Robert, A., *Dictionnaire des parlementaires français*, 5 vols (Paris, 1889–91).

¡outon, A., *Les Luttes ardentes des francs-maçons Manceaux pour l'établissement de la République, 1815–1914* (Le Mans, 1966).

Bruhat, J., *Les Journées de février 1848* (Paris, 1948).

Brustein, W., *The Social Origins of Political Regionalism in France 1849–1981* (Berkeley, 1988).

Buchez, P. and Roux, P.C., *Histoire parlementaire de la Révolution française* (Paris, 1837).

Buonarroti, P., *Conspiration pour l'Egalité dite de Babeuf, suivie du procès auquel elle donna lieu*, 2 vols (Brussels, 1828).

Buonarroti's History of Babeuf's Conspiracy for Equality with the author's reflections on the causes and character of the French Revolution . . . trs. Bronterre, editor of *The Poor Man's Guardian* (London, 1836).

Bury, J.P.T. and Tombs, R.P., *Thiers 1797–1877. A Political Life* (London, 1986).

Cabet, E., *Histoire populaire de la Revolution française 1789–1830* (Paris, 1840).

Cabet, E., *La Femme, son malheureux sort dans le société actuelle, son bonheur dans la communauté* (8th edn, Paris, 1848).

Cabet, E., *La Révolution de 1830 et la situation présente* (Paris, 1831).

Cabet, E., *La Révolution de 1830 et la situation présente expliquée et éclairée par les révolutions de 1789, 92, 99 et 04 et par la Restauration*, 2 vols (Paris, 1833).

Cabet, E., *Le Vrai Christianisme suivant Jésus-Christ* (Paris, 1846).

Cabet, E., *Voyage en Icarie [Voyage et aventures de Lord Villiam Carisdall En Icarie. Traduit de l'anglais de Francis Adams par Th. Dufruit]* 2 vols (Paris, 1840).

Calmette, A., 'Les carbonaris en France sous la Restauration', *La Révolution de 1848*, ix (1912–13), x (1913–14).

Campbell, P. and Chapman, B., *The Constitution of the Fifth Republic*, trans. and commentary (Oxford, 1958).

Carlisle, R.B., 'Saint-Simonian radicalism: a definition and a direction', *French Historical Studies*, 5 (1968), 430–45.

Carrel, A., *Histoire de la contre-révolution en Angleterre sous Charles II et James II* (Paris, 1827).

Cavaignac, G., 'La Force révolutionnaire', *Paris Révolutionnaire*, 1 (1838).

Charlton, D.G., *Secular Religions in France 1815–70* (Oxford, 1963).

Charton, C., 'Souvenirs de 1814 à 1848', *Société d'Emulation des Vosges*, XIV (1872).

Chateaubriand, F.R. vicomte de, *De la Monarchie selon la Charte* (London, 1816).

Chaudonneret, M.C., 'Les representations des evenements de la Révolution Française 1830–48' in Vovelle, *Les Images* (Paris, 1988).

Chaussinand-Nogaret, G., *Une Histoire des élites* (Paris, 1975).

Cherest, A., *La Vie et les oeuvres de A.-T. Marie, avocat, membre du Gouvernement provisoire* (Paris, 1873).

Chernov (Tchernoff), I.-A., *Le Parti Républicain sous la Monarchie de Juillet. Fondation et évolution de la doctrine républicaine* (Paris, 1901).

Chernov (Tchernoff), I.-A. *Associations et sociétés secrètes sous la Seconde République, 1848–51* (Paris, 1905).

Chernov (Tchernoff), I.-A. *Le Parti républicaine au coup d'état et sous le second empire* (Paris, 1906).

Chevalier, L., *La Formation de la population Parisienne au XIXe. siècle* (Paris, 1950).

Christofferson, T.R., 'The French national workshops of 1848; the view from the provinces', *French Historical Studies*, 11, 4 (1980), 505–20.

Church, C.H., *Europe in 1830* (London, 1983).

Church, C.H., *Revolution and Red Tape. The French Ministerial Bureaucracy 1770–1850* (London, 1981).

Cobb, R., *Police and People. French Popular Protest 1789–1820* (Oxford, 1970).

Cobban, A., 'Administrative pressure in the election of the French Constituent Assembly, April 1848', *Bulletin of the Institute of Historical Research*, xxv (1952), 133–59.

Cobban, A., 'The influence of the Clergy and the "Instituteurs Primaires" in the election of the French Constituent Assembly, April 1848', *English Historical Review*, LVII (1942), 334–44.

Cobban, A., *Historians and the Causes of the French Revolution*, Historical Association pamphlet, G.2. revised (London, 1965).

Cobban, A., *The Social Interpretation of the French Revolution* (London, 1968).

Cock, C., *Troyes and the Aube under the July Monarchy* (unpublished PhD, University of Reading, 1973).

Cole, A., *French Electoral Systems and Elections since 1789* (Dartmouth, 1989).

Collingham, H.A.C., *The July Monarchy. A Political History of France, 1830–1848* (London, 1988).

Collins, I., *The Government and Newspaper Press in France, 1814–1881* (Oxford, 1959).

Collins, I., *Napoleon and his Parliaments, 1800–1815* (London, 1979).

Considérant, V.P., *Destinée sociale*, 2 vols (Paris, 1834–8).

Considérant, V.P., *Principes du socialisme. Manifeste de la démocratie au XIXe. siècle* (Paris, 1847).

Constant, B., *Principes de Politique*, repr. in *Oeuvres de Benjamin Constant* (Paris, 1957).

Contamine, H., *Metz et Moselle de 1815–1870*, 2 vols (Nancy, 1932).

Contamine, H., 'La Révolution de 1830 à Metz', *Revue d'histoire moderne*, IV (1931), 115–23.

Corbin, A., *Archaisme et modernité en Limousin 1845–80*, 2 vols (Paris, 1975).

Corcelle, C.T. de, *Documents pour servir à l'histoire des conspirations, des partis et des écrits* (Paris, 1831).

Coornaert, E., *Les Compagnonnages en France du moyen âge à nos jours* (Paris, 1966).

Crook, M., *Toulon in War and Revolution. From the Ancien Régime to the Restoration, 1750–1820* (Manchester, 1991).

Cuvillier, A.,*P.-J.-B.Buchez et les origines du socialisme chrétienne* (Paris, 1948).

Daline, V., *Gracchus Babeuf à la veille et pendant la Grande Révolution Française, 1785–1794* (Paris, 1976).

David, M., *Le Printemps de la fraternité. Génese et vicissitudes (1830–51)* (Paris, 1992).

Delbez, L., *Les Grands Courants de la pensée politique française depuis le XIX siècle* (Paris, 1970).

Dethomas, P., *Le Procès des quatre sergents de la Rochelle* (Paris, 1912).

Deyon, P., *Paris et ses provinces. Le défi de la décentralisation 1770–1992* (Paris 1993).

Dolléans, E., *Histoire du mouvement ouvrier*, 3 vols (Paris, 1936–53).

Dolléans, E., 'Vie et pensée ouvrières entre 1848 et 1871', *Revue historique* (1947).

Dolléans, E. and Puech, J.L., *Proudhon et la Révolution de 1848* (Paris, 1948).

Dommanget, M., *Auguste Blanqui. Des Origines à la Révolution de 1848, premiers combats et premières prisons* (Paris, 1969).

Dommanget, M., *Les Idées politiques et sociales d'Auguste Blanqui* (Paris, 1957).

Dommanget, M., *Auguste Blanqui et la Révolution de 1848* (Paris, 1972).

Doyle, W., *Oxford History of the French Revolution* (Oxford, 1989).

Dubois, J., *Le Vocabulaire politique et social de la France de 1869 à 1872* (Paris, 1962).

Dupeux, G., *Aspects de l'histoire sociale et politique du département de Loir-et-Cher, 1848–1914* (Paris, 1962).

Dupuy, A., *1870–1. La Guerre, la Commune et la Presse* (Paris, 1959).

Durand de Mailland, P.-T., *Histoire de la Convention Nationale* (Paris, 1825).

Duroselle, J.B., *Les Débuts du catholicisme social en France (1822–1870)* (Paris, 1951).

Dutacq, F., *Histoire politique de Lyon pendant la Révolution de 1848* (Paris, 1910).

Dutacq, F. and Latreille, A., *Histoire de Lyon de 1814 à 1940*, vol. III of A. Kleinclausz, *Histoire de Lyon* (1952).

Duveau, G., *1848: The Making of a Revolution* (New York, 1967).

Duvergier de Hauranne, P., *De la Réforme parlementaire et de la réforme électorale* (Paris, 1847).

Duvergier de Hauranne, P., *Histoire du gouvernement parlementaire en France*, 10 vols (Paris, 1857–72).

Edmonds, W., *Jacobinism and the Revolt of Lyon, 1789–93* (Oxford, 1990).

Edwards, S., *The Paris Commune 1871* (London, 1971).

Ellis, G., 'The Marxist interpretation of the French Revolution', *English Historical Review*, xciii (1978), 353–76.

Ellis, G., *The Napoleonic Empire* (London, 1991).

Elwitt, S., *The Making of the Third Republic. Class and Politics in France 1868–1884* (Baton Rouge, 1975).

Esquiros, A., *Histoire des montagnards* (Paris, 1847).

Fabre, J.R.A., *La Révolution de 1830 et le véritable parti républicaine*, 2 vols (Paris, 1833).

Faguet, E., *Politiques et moralistes du dix-neuvième siècle*, 3 vols (Paris, 1890–9).

Fasel, G., 'The wrong Revolution: French republicanism in 1848', *French Historical Studies*, 8 (1974), 654–77.

Fitzpatrick, B., *Catholic Royalism in the Department of the Gard, 1814–52* (Cambridge, 1983).

Fitzsimmons, M.P., *The Parisian Order of Barristers and the French Revolution* (Cambridge, Mass., 1987).

Forrest, A., *The French Revolution and the Poor* (Oxford, 1981).

Forrest, A. and Jones P., *Reshaping France. Town, Country and Region during the French Revolution* (Manchester, 1990).

Forstenzer, T.R., *French Provincial Police and the Fall of the Second Republic* (Princeton, NJ, 1981).

Fortescue, W., *Alphonse de Lamartine. A Political Biography* (London, 1982).

Fourier, F.C.M., *Le Nouveau Monde industriel et sociétaire* (Paris, 1829).

Fourier, F.C.M., *Political economy made easy. A sketch . . . exhibiting the various errors of our present political arrangements.* Presented to the London Cooperative Society by the translator (London, 1828).

Fourier, F.C.M., *Théorie de unité universelle* (Paris, 1822).

Fourier, F.C.M., *Harmonian Man. Selected Writings of Charles Fourier*, ed. M. Poster (London, 1971).

Frambourg, G., *Le Docteur Guépin 1805–73* (Nantes, 1964).

Furet, F., *Interpreting the French Revolution*, trans. (Cambridge, 1984).

Furet, F., *La Révolution de Turgot à Jules Ferry 1770–1880* (Paris 1988; trs. Oxford, 1992 as *Revolutionary France 1770–1880*).

Furet, F. (ed.), The Influence of the French Revolution on Nineteenth Century Europe (Oxford, 1989).

Furet, F., *L'Héritage de la Révolution française* (Paris, 1989).

Furet, F., *La Gauche et la Révolution au milieu du XIXe. siècle. Edgar Quinet et la question du Jacobinisme 1865–70* (Paris, 1986).

Furet, F., 'Le catechisme révolutionnaire', *Annales; Economies, Sociétés, Civilisations* (1971), 255–89.

Furet, F. and Ozouf, M., *The Transformation of Political Culture 1789–1848* vol. 3 of *The French Revolution and the Creation of Modern Political culture* (Oxford, 1989).

Furet, F. and Ozouf, M. (*sous direction de*) *Le Siècle de l'avènement républicain* (Paris, 1993).

Furet, F., Juilliard, J. and Rosavallon, R., *La République du Centre: la Fin de l'exception française* (Paris, 1988).

Galante, Garrone A., *Ph. Buonarroti et les révolutionnaires du XIXe. siècle* (Paris, 1975).

Garrioch, D. and Sonenscher, M., '*Compagnonnages*, confraternities and associations of journeymen in eighteenth century Paris', *European History Quarterly*, 16 (1986).

Gauchet, M., *La Révolution des Droits de l'Homme* (Paris, 1989).

Gauthier, F., *Triomphe et mort du Droit Naturel en Révolution 1789–1795–1802* (Paris, 1993).

Gerbod, P., *Paul-François Dubois, universitaire, journaliste et homme politique, 1793–1874* (Paris, 1967).

Godechot, J., *Les Institutions de la France sous la Révolution et l'Empire* (Paris, 1951).

Godechot, J., *La Presse ouvrière 1819–1850* (Paris, 1966).

Godechot, J., (ed.), *La Révolution de 1848 à Toulouse et dans la Haute-Garonne* (Toulouse, 1949).

Godechot, J., *Les Révolutions (1770–1799)* (Paris, 1963).

Goldstein, R.J., 'Censorship of caricature in France, 1815–1914', *French History*, 3 (1989), 71–107.

Gonnet, J.P., 'Esquisse de la crise économique en France de 1827–32,' *Revue d'histoire économique et sociale*, xxxiii (1955), 249–92.

Gonnet, P., *La Correspondance d'Achille Chaper 1831–40* (Dijon, 1970).

Gordon, D.M., *Merchants and Capitalists. Industrialization and Provincial politics in mid-nineteenth-century France* (Alabama, 1985).

Gossez, R., *Les Ouvriers de Paris*, I, *L'organisation, 1848–51* (Paris, 1967).

Gossez, R., 'Presse parisienne à destination des ouvriers, 1848–1851', in Godechot, *La Presse ouvrière* (1966).

Gossez, R., 'La Résistance à l'impôt; les quarante-cinq centîmes', *Études, Bibliothèque de la Révolution de 1848*, 15 (1953), 89–131.

Goualt, J., *Comment la France est devenue républicaine. Les élections générales et partielles à l'Assemblée nationale 1870–1875* (Paris, 1954).

Gouges, Olympe de, *Déclaration des droits de la femme* (Paris, 1791).

Gouges, Olympe de, *Oeuvres*, new edn (Paris, 1986).

Gourden, J.M., *Le Peuple des ateliers. Les artisans au XIXe. siècle* (Paris, 1993).

Gourvitch, A., 'Le mouvement pour la réforme électorale', *La Révolution de 1848*, vols XI–XIV (1914–18).

Greenberg, L.M., *Sisters of Liberty. Paris and the Reaction to a Centralized State 1868–71* (Cambridge, Mass., 1971).

Griffiths, R., *Le Centre perdu. Malouet et les 'monarchiens' dans la Révolution française* (Grenoble, 1988).

Guépin, A., *Histoire de Nantes* (Nantes, 1837).

Guépin, A., *Philosophie du XIXe. siècle* (1854).

Guépin, A. and Bonamy, C.E., *Nantes au XIXe siècle* (Nantes, 1835).

Guillemin, H., *La Première Résurrection de la République* (Paris, 1967).

Guillon, E., *Les Complots militaires sous la Restauration* (Paris, 1912).

Guizot, F., *Des Moyens de gouvernement et des moyens d'opposition dans l'état actuel de la France* (Paris, 1821).

Guizot, F.P.G., *Histoire parlementaire de la France*, 5 vols ((Paris, 1863–4).

Guizot, F.P.G., *Mémoires pour servir à l'histoire de mon temps*, 8 vols (Paris, 1858–67).

Hanagan, M.P., *Nascent Proletarians. Class Formation in post-revolutionary France* (Oxford, 1989).

Hartmann, M., 'The sacrilege law of 1825 in France a study in anticlericalism and myth-making', *Journal of Modern History* (1972), 21–37.

Haury, P, 'Les commissaires de Ledru-Rollin en 1848', *La Révolution française*, LVII (1909), 438–74.

Hayward, J., *After the French Revolution. Six Critics of Democracy and Nationalism* (London, 1991).

Heywood, C., 'The revolutionary tradition in Troyes, 1789–1848', *Journal of Historical Geography*, 16 (1990), 108–20.

Heywood, O., *The Idea of Revolution in 1848* (unpublished PhD, University of London, 1975).

Higgs, D.C., *Ultra-royalism in Toulouse from its origins to the Revolution of 1830* (Baltimore, 1973).

Higgs, D.C., *Nobles in Nineteenth Century France. The Practice of Inegalitarianism* (Baltimore, 1987).

Higonnet, P., *Sister Republics. The Origins of French and American Republicanism* (Cambridge, Mass., 1988).

Hobsbawm, E., *Nations and Nationalism since 1780* (Cambridge, 1990).

Hodde, L. de la, *Histoire des sociétés secrètes, 1830–48 et du parti républicain de 1830 à 1848* (Paris, 1850).

Hoffman, R.L., *Revolutionary Justice: the Social and Political Theory of P.J. Proudhon* (Chicago, 1972).

Holtman, R.B., *The Napoleonic Revolution* (Philadelphia, 1967).

Howorth, J., 'The myth of Blanquism under the Third Republic 1871–1900', *Journal of Modern History*, 48 (1976).

Huard, R., *Le Mouvement républicain en Bas-Languedoc 1848–81* (Paris, 1982).

Huard, R., *Le Suffrage universel en France, 1848–1946* (Paris, 1991).

Hufton, O., *Women and the Limits of Citizenship during the French Revolution* (Toronto, 1992).

Hunt, L., 'The failure of the liberal republic in France 1795–1799; the road to Brumaire', *Journal of Modern History*, 51 (1979), 735–59.

Hunt, L., *Revolution and Urban Politics in Provincial France: Troyes and Reims 1686–90* (Stanford, 1978).

Hunt, L. and Sheridan, G., 'Corporatism, Association and the language of labor in France 1750–1850', *Journal of Modern History*, 58 (1986), 813–44.

Hutton, P.H., *The Cult of the Revolutionary Tradition. The Blanquistes in French Politics, 1864–1893* (Berkeley, 1981).

Ionescu, G. (ed.), *The Political Thought of Saint-Simon* (Oxford, 1976).

Jardin, A. and Tudesq, A.J., *Restoration and Reaction 1815–48* (Cambridge, 1983). Originally published as *La France des Notables 1815–48*, 2 vols (Paris, 1973).

Jaume, L., *Le Discours jacobin et la démocratie* (Paris, 1989).

Jaume, L., *Les Déclarations des droits de l'homme; du début 1789–1793 au préambule de 1946* (Paris, 1989).

Jennings, L.C., *France and Europe in 1848; A study of French Foreign Affairs in Time of Crisis* (Oxford, 1973).

Johnson, C.H., *Utopian Communism in France. Cabet and the Icarians 1839–51* (Ithaca, NY, 1974).

Johnson, C.H., 'Economic change and artisan discontent: the tailors' history, 1800–48', in R.D. Price, *Revolution and Reaction. 1848 and the Second French Republic* (London, 1975), pp. 87–113.

Johnson, D.W. (ed.), *French Society and the Revolution* (Cambridge, 1976).

Johnson, D.W., *Guizot. Aspects of French History 1787–1874* (London, 1963).

Jones, C., *The Longman Companion to the French Revolution* (London, 1988).

Jones, P.M., *Politics and Rural Society. The Southern Massif Central c. 1750–1880* (Cambridge, 1985).

Judt, T., *Marxism and the French Left* (Oxford, 1989).

Kelly, G.A., 'Liberalism and aristocracy in the French Restoration', *Journal of the History of Ideas* (1965).

Kent, S., *The Election of 1827 in France* (Cambridge, Mass., 1975).

Koepke, R.L., 'The failure of parliamentary government in France, 1840–48', *European Studies Review*, 9 (1979), 433–55.

Koepke, R.L., 'The short, unhappy history of progressive conservatism in France, 1840–1848', *Canadian Journal of History*, xviii (1983), 187–216.

Lamartine, A. de, *Histoire de la Révolution de février 1848*, 2 vols (Paris, 1849).

Langeron, C., *J. Demontry, sa vie et sa mort* (Brussels, 1850).

Langlois, C. and Tackett, T., 'A l'épreuve de la Révolution (1770–1830)', in F. Lebrun (ed.), *Histoire des catholiques en France du XVe. siècle à nos jours* (Paris, 1980).

Laponneraye, A. (ed.), *Oeuvres de Maximillien Robespierre* (Paris, 2 vols, 1832; 3 vols, 1840–2).

Laponneraye, A., *Réfutation des Idées Napoléoniennes* (Paris, 1839).

Latta, C., 'L'insurrection de 1839', in M. Agulhon, *Blanqui et les Blanquistes* (Paris, 1986).

Leclère, B. and Wright, V., *Les Préfets du IIe. Empire* (Paris, 1973).

[Ledru-Rollin] *Mémoire sur les événements de la rue Transnonain dans les journées des 13 et 14 avril 1834 par Ledru-Rollin, avocat* (Paris, 1834).

Lefebvre, G., *La Révolution française* (Paris, 1951).

Lefebvre, G., *The Great Fear of 1789: Rural Panic in Revolutionary France* (trans. London, 1973).

Leflon, J., *L'Église de France et la Révolution de 1848* (Paris, 1948).

Le Goff., T.J.A., *Vannes and its Region; a Study of Town and Country in Eighteenth-Century France* (Oxford, 1981).

Lequin, Y., *Les Ouvriers de la région lyonnaise, 1848 à 1914*, 2 vols (Lyon, 1977).

Leroux, P.H., *De la Ploutocratie* (Boussac, 1848).

Leuilliot, P., *L'Alsace au début du XIXe siècle. Essai d'histoire politique, économique et religieuse, 1815–30*, 3 vols (Paris, 1959–60).

Levy-Schneider, V., 'Correspondance de Martin Bernard, Commissaire général de la République à Lyon, avec sa famille', *Revue d'histoire de Lyon*, 12 (1913), 81–115, 179–216.

Lewis, G., *The Second Vendée* (Oxford, 1978).

Lewis, G. and Lucas, C. (eds), *Beyond the Terror, Essays in French Regional and Social History, 1794–1815* (Cambridge, 1983).

Lhomme, J., *La Grande Bourgeoisie au pouvoir 1830–1880* (Paris, 1960).

Lomenie, E. Beau de, *Les Responsabilités des dynasties bourgeoises*, 4 vols (Paris, 1964).

Loubère, L.A., *Louis Blanc; his Life and his Contribution to the Rise of French Jacobin Socialism* (Evanston, Ill., 1961).

Loubère, L.A., *Radicalism in Mediterranean France: its Rise and Decline* (Albany, NY, 1974).

Loustau, P., *Louis Blanc à la Commission de Luxemboug* (Paris, 1908).

Lovell, D.W., 'Early French socialism and class struggle', *History of Political Thought* (1988), 327–48.

Lovell, D.W., 'The French Revolution and the origins of socialism: the case of early French socialism', *French History*, 6 (1992), 185–205.

Lucas-Dubreton, J., *Le Culte de Napoléon. La Légende de l'Aigle dans l'opinion publique depuis Waterloo jusqu'à l'aurore du Second Empire* (Paris, 1960).

Luna, F. de, *The French Republic under Cavaignac* (Princeton, NJ, 1975).

Magraw, R., *History of the French Working Class*, 2 vols (London, 1991).

Magraw, R., 'Pierre Joigneux and socialist propaganda in the French countryside, 1849–1851', *French Historical Studies*, 10 (1987), 599–640.

Maistre, J. de, *Considérations sur la France* (Geneva, 1796).

Maitron, J., *Dictionnaire biographique du mouvement ouvrier français*, 3 vols (Paris, 1964–6).

Mandel, R.A., *J.B. André Godin and the Familistère of Guise, 1817–1888* (unpublished PhD, University of Toronto, 1978).

Mansel, P., *Louis XVIII* (London, 1981).

Mansel, P., 'How forgotten were the Bourbons in France between 1812 and 1814?' *European Studies Review*, 13 (1983), 13–37.

Manuel, F.E., 'The Luddite Movement in France', *Journal of Modern History*, x (1938), 180–211.

Manuel, F.E., *The New World of Henri Saint-Simon* (Cambridge, Mass., 1956).

Marchal, C., *Raspail* (Paris, 1848).

Marcilhacy, C., 'Les caractères de la crise sociale et politique de 1846 à 1852 dans le département du Loiret', *Revue d'histoire moderne et contemporaine*, 6 (1959), 5–59.

Margadant, T.W., *French Peasants in Revolt. The Insurrection of 1851* (Princeton, NJ, 1979).

Mariel, P., *Les Carbonari. Idéalisme et révolution permanente* (Paris, 1971).

Marrast, A., 'La presse révolutionnaire', *Paris Révolutionnaire*, 2 (1838).

Marrast, A., 'Les funérailles révolutionnaires', *Paris Révolutionnaire*, 3 (1838).

Marriott, J.A.R., *The French Revolution of 1848 in its Economic Aspect* (Oxford, 1913).

Marx, K., *The Civil War in France* (London, 1872).

Marx, K., *The Eighteenth Brumaire of Louis Bonaparte* (London, 1926).

Marx, K., *The Class Struggles in France 1848 to 1850* (Moscow n.d.; trans. from German edn 1895).

McKay, D.C., *The National Workshops. A Study in the French Revolution of 1848* (Cambridge, Mass., 1933).

McManners, J., *The French Revolution and the Church* (London, 1969).

McPhee, P., *A Social History of France 1780–1880* (London, 1992).

Mayeur, J.-M., *Les débuts de la IIIe République, 1871–1898* (Paris, 1973).

Mayeur, J.-M., *The Third Republic from its Origins to the Great War, 1871–1914* (Cambridge, 1987) (a translation of the preceding vols 9 and 10 of *Nouvelle Histoire de la France Contemporaine*).

Mazauric, C., *Babeuf et la Conspiration pour l'Egalité* (Paris, 1962).

Mazauric, C., *Babeuf* (Paris, 1988).

Mazauric, C., *Jacobinisme et révolution, autour du bicentenaire de Quatre-vingt-neuf* (Paris, 1984).

Mazoyer, L., 'Catégories d'âge et groupes sociaux. Les jeunes générations françaises de 1830', *Annales*, 10 (1938), 385–423.

Ménager, B., *Les Napoléons du peuple* (Paris, 1988).

Merriman, J., *The Agony of the Republic. The Repression of the Left in Revolutionary France 1848–51* (New Haven, Conn., 1978).

Merrriman, J. (ed.), *1830 in France* (New York, London, 1975).

Merriman, J., *The Red City. Limoges and the French Nineteenth Century* (Oxford, 1985).

Meuriot, P., *La Population et les lois électorales en France de 1789 à nos jours* (Paris, 1916).

Meyer, J. (ed.), *Histoire de Rennes* (Toulouse, 1972).

Michelet, J., *Histoire de la Révolution française*, 7 vols (Paris, 1847–53).

Mignet, *Histoire de la Révolution française depuis 1789 jusqu'en 1814*, 2 vols (Paris, 1827).

Mireaux, E., 'Un chirugien sociologue: Louis-Réné Villermé', *Revue des Deux-Mondes*, 2 (1962), 201–12.

Moissonnier, M., *La Première Internationale et la commune à Lyon* (Paris, 1972).

Moissonnier, M., 'La section lyonnaise de l'Intérnationale et l'opposition ouvrière à la fin du Second Empire, 1865–70', *Cahiers d'Histoire*, 10 (1965), 275–314.

Molinier, S., *Blanqui* (Paris, 1948).

Monnier, R., *Le Faubourg Saint-Antoine, 1789–1815* (Paris, 1981).

Moon, J., 'The *Association fraternelle et solidaires de toutes les associations'*, Western Society For French History, Annual Conference, October 1993).

Morange, G., *Les Idées communistes dans les sociétés secrètes et dans la presse sous la monarchie de juillet* (Paris, 1905).

Morère, P., 'La Révolution de 1848 dans un pays forèstier', *Révolution de 1848*, 12 (1916–17), 206–30.

Moses, C., 'Saint-Simonian men/Saint-Simonian women: The transformation of feminist thought in 1830s France', *Journal of Modern History*, 54 (1982).

Moss, B.H., *The Origins of the French Labour Movement: The Socialism of Skilled Workers, 1830–1914* (Berkeley, Cal., 1976).

Muller, P., 'Le Bas-Rhin de 1848 à 1852', *Revue de 1848*, 6 (1910), 353–66.

Nadaud, M., *Mémoires de Léonard, ancien garçon maçon* (Paris, 1895).

Napoleon-Louis, *Des Idées Napoléoniennes*, 1839, trans. B.D. Gooch, *Napoleonic Ideas* (New York, 1967).

Napoleon-Louis, *L'Extinction du paupérisme* (Paris, 1844).

Neely, S., *Lafayette and the Liberal Ideal, 1814–24. Politics and Conspiracy in an Age of Reaction* (Carbondale, Ill., 1991).

Neely, S., 'Rural politics in the Early Restoration; Charles Goyet and the liberals of the Sarthe', *European History Quarterly*, xvi (1986), 313–42.

Newman, E.L. (ed. with Simpson, R.L.), *Historical Dictionary of France from the 1815 Restoration to the Second Empire*, 2 vols (New York, 1987).

Newman, E.L., 'Lost illusions: the Regicides in France during the Bourbon Restoration', *Nineteenth-Century French Studies*, x (1981–2), 45–72.

Newman, E.L., *Republicanism during the Bourbon Restoration in France, 1814–1830* (unpublished PhD University of Chicago, 1969).

Newman, E.L., 'The Blouse and the Frock Coat', *Journal of Modern History*, 46 (1974), 26–59.

Newman, E.L., 'What the crowd wanted in the French Revolution of 1830', in J. Merriman, *1830 in France* (1975).

Nicolas, J. (ed.) *Mouvements populaires et consciences sociales, XVIe. au XIXe. siècles; Actes du colloque de Paris, 24–26 mai 1984* (Paris, 1985).

Nicolet, C., *L'Idée républicaine en France 1789–1924. Essai d'histoire critique* (Paris, 1981).

Nora, P., (*sous direction de*), *Les Lieux de Mémoire*, 3 vols (1984–93). vol. III *La France. 1. Conflits et partages 2. Traditions 3. De l'Archive à l'emblème* (Paris, 1993).

Nord, P., 'The party of conciliation and the Paris Commune', *French Historical Studies*, 15 (1987), 1–35.

Oeschlin, J., *Le Mouvement ultra-royaliste en France* (Paris, 1960).

Olivesi, A., *La Commune de 1871 à Marseille et ses origines* (Paris, 1950).

Orr, L., *Headless History. Nineteenth-century French Historiography of the Revolution* (Ithaca and London, 1990).

Ory, P. (ed.), *Nouvelle Histoire des idées politiques* (Paris, 1987).

Ory, P., *Une Nation pour mémoire. 1889–1939–1989 Trois jubilés révolutionnaires* (Paris, 1993).

Owen, R., *Report to the Country of Lanark* and *A New View of Society*, ed. by V.A.C. Gatrell (London, 1969).

Ozouf, M., *La Fête révolutionnaire, 1789–1799* (Paris, 1976).

Pagnerre, L.A., *Les Hommes du mouvement et les hommes de la résistance. Biographie politique des ministres, de tous les membres de la Chambre des Députés* (Paris, 1831).

Palau, P., *Histoire du département de la Côte-d'Or* (Dijon, 1978).

Palmer, R.R., *The Age of the Democratic Revolution*, 2 vols (Princeton, NJ, 1961, 1964).

Parent, F., 'Les cabinets de lecture dans Paris; pratiques culturelles et espace social sous la Restauration', *Annales*, 34 (1979), 1016–38.

Payne, H.C., *The Police State of Louis-Napoleon Bonaparte* (Seattle, Washington, 1966).

Paz, A., *Un Révolutionnaire professionel, Auguste Blanqui* (Paris, 1984).

Perreux, G., *Aux temps des sociétés secrètes. La Propagande républicain au début de la Monarchie de Juillet, 1830–35* (Paris, 1931).

Perreux, G., *Arbois, première cité républicaine* (Paris, 1932).

Perreux, G., 'Trois dates de l'histoire d'Arbois, 1830–1848–1851', *La Révolution de 1848*, 28 (1931), 193–216; 29 (1832), 34–50.

Pichois, C., 'Les cabinets de lecture à Paris durant la 1ère moitié du XIX siècle', *Annales: Economies, Sociétés, Civilisations*, 14 (1959), 521–34.

Pilbeam, P.M., *The 1830 Revolution in France* (London, 1991).

Pilbeam, P.M., *The Middle Classes in Europe 1789–1914; France, Germany, Italy and Russia* (London, 1990).

Pilbeam, P.M., 'Republicanism in early nineteenth-century France, 1814–35', *French History*, 5, 1 (1991), 30–47.

Pilbeam, P.M., 'Popular violence in provincial France after the 1830 revolution', *English Historical Review*, xci (1976), 278–97.

Pilbeam, P.M., 'The economic crisis of 1827–32 and the 1830 Revolution in provincial France', *Historical Journal* (June 1989), 319–38.

Pilbeam, P.M., 'The "liberal" revolution of 1830', *Historical Research*, lxiii (1990), 162–77.

Pilbeam, P.M., 'The emergence of opposition to the Orleanist Monarchy, August 1830–April 1831', *English Historical Review* (1970), 12–28.

Pilbeam, P.M., 'The growth of liberalism and the crisis of the Bourbon Restoration', *Historical Journal*, xxv, 2 (1982), 351–66.

Pilbeam, P.M., 'The "Three Glorious Days": the Revolution of 1830 in provincial France', *Historical Journal*, 26, 4 (1983), 831–44.

Pinkney, D.H., *Decisive Years in France 1840–47* (Princeton, NJ, 1986).

Pinkney, D.H., *The French Revolution of 1830* (Princeton, NY, 1972).

Pinkney, D.H., 'Les ateliers de secours à Paris (1830–31). Précurseurs des Ateliers Nationaux de 1848', *Revue d'histoire moderne et contemporaine*, 12 (1965), 65–70.

Plamenatz, J., *The Revolutionary Movement in France 1815–71* (London, 1952).

Plessis, A., *The Rise and Fall of the Second Empire 1852–1871* (Cambridge, 1987); trans. of *De la Fête impériale au mur des fédérés, 1852–71* (Paris, 1979).

Pommier, J., *Les Ecrivains devant la Révolution de 1848* (Paris, 1948).

Ponteil, F., *L'Opposition politique à Strasbourg sous la monarchie de juillet* (Paris, 1932).

Ponteil, F., *Les Institutions de la France de 1814 à 1870* (Paris, 1965).

Porch, D., *Army and Revolution, France 1815–48* (London, 1974).

Pouthas, C.H., 'La réorganisation du ministère de l'intérieur et la reconstitution de l'administration préfectorale par Guizot en 1830', *Revue d'histoire moderne et contemporaine*, ix (1962), 241–63.

Prévost–Paradol, L.A., *La France nouvelle* (Paris, 1868).

Price, R.D. (ed.), *Revolution and Reaction. 1848 and the Second French Republic* (London, 1975).

Price, R.D., *The French Second Republic: a Social History* (London, 1972).

Price, R.D., 'The French army and the Revolution of 1830', *European Studies Review*, 3 (1973).

Proudhon, P.J., *Confessions d'un révolutionnaire pour servir à l'histoire de la révolution de février* (Brussels, 1849).

Proudhon, P.J., *Idée générale de la Révolution,* trans. and ed. R. Graham (London, 1989).

Proudhon, P.J., *Oeuvres complètes*, 26 vols (Paris, 1867–70).

Proudhon, P.J., *Qu'est-ce que la propriété? ou recherches sur le principe du droit et du gouvernment* (Paris, 1840).

Proudhon, P.J., *Selected Writings*, ed. S. Edwards (London, 1969).

Proudhon, P.J., *Système des contradictions économiques ou philosophie de la misère* (Paris, 1846).

Quentin-Bauchart, A., *Etudes et souvenirs sur la deuxième République et le second Empire (1848–1870). Mémoires posthumes publiées par son fils*, 2 vols (Paris, 1901–2).

Quentin-Bauchart, P., *La Crise sociale de 1848. Les Origines et la Révolution de février* (Paris, 1920).

Quinet, E., *Le Christianisme et la Révolution française* (Paris, 1846).

Quinet, E., *La République* (Paris, 1872).

Raban, R., *Petite Biographie des députés* (Paris, 1826).

Rabbe, Vielle Boisjolin, St Preuve, de, *Biographie universelle et portative de contemporains*, 5 vols (Paris, 1834).

Rader, D., *Dubois of the Globe, Studies in Modern European History* (New York, 1956).

Rader, D.L., *The Journalists and the July Revolution in France* (The Hague, 1973).

Ramus, C.F., *Daumier. 120 Great Lithographs* (New York, 1979).

Raspail, F.V., *Réforme pénitentiare. Lettres sur les prisons de Paris* (Paris, 1839).

Rath, R.J., 'The carbonari: their origins, initiation rites and aims', *American Historical Review*, 69 (1963), 353–70.

Ravitch, N., *The Catholic Church and the French Nation, 1589–1989* (London, 1989).

Rémond, R., *L'anti-cléricalisme en France de 1815 à nos jours* (Paris, 1976).

Remusat, C.F.M. de (ed. C.H. Pouthas), *Mémoires de ma vie*, 5 vols (Paris, 1959).

Resnick, D., *The White Terror and the Political Reaction after Waterloo* (Cambridge, Mass., 1966).

Rials, S., *Révolution et contre-révolution au XIXe. siècle* (Paris, 1987).

Ribe, G., *L'Opinion publique et la vie politique à Lyon lors des premières années de la Seconde Restauration* (Paris, 1957).

Richard, G., 'La conspiration de l'Est, mai 1820', *Annales de l'Est*, (Nancy, 1958), 23–59.

Richard, G., 'Une famille de médecins révolutionnaires à Nancy sous la Monarchie de Juillet. Les docteurs Béchet', *Revue Médicale de Nancy* (Nancy, 1961), 867–98.

Richard, G., *Une Grande Figure médicale. Le Docteur Philippe Buchez* (Nancy, 1959).

Richardson, N., *The French Prefectoral Corps 1814–30* (Cambridge, 1966).

Richardson, N., *The Personnel of the French Prefectoral Corps under the Restoration* (PhD 4712, Cambridge, February 1964).

Rigaudias-Weiss, *Les Enquêtes Ouvrières en France entre 1830 et 1848* (Paris, 1936).

Robert, C., *Les Quatre sergents de la Rochelle* (Paris, 1849).

Roberts, J., *The Counter-Revolution in France 1787–1830* (London, 1990).

Roberts, J.M., *The mythology of the Secret Societies* (London, 1972).

Robin, R., *La Société française en 1789: l'exemple de Semur-en-Auxois* (Paris, 1970).

Rosanvallon, P., 'Les Doctrinaires et la question du gouvernement représentative', in F. Furet and M. Ozouf, *The Transformation of Political Culture 1789–1848*, vol. 3 of *The French Revolution and the Creation of Modern Political Culture* (Oxford, 1989).

Rose, R.B., *Gracchus Babeuf. The First Revolutionary Communist* (Stanford, Cal., 1978).

Rose, R.B., *The Enragés; Socialists of the French Revolution?* (Sydney, 1965).

Rougerie, J., *Le Procès des Communards* (Paris, 1964).

Rude, F., *L'Insurrection lyonnaise de novembre 1831: Le mouvement ouvrier à Lyon de 1827 à 1832* (Paris, 1969).

Rudé, G., *The Crowd in History 1730–1848* (New York, 1964).

Rudelle, O., *La République absolue. Aux Origines de l'instabilité constitutionnelle de la République, 1870–1889* (Paris, 1982).

Saint-Martin, J., *F.V. Raspail* (Paris, 1877).

Saint-Simon, H. de, *Catéchisme des industriels* (Paris, 1823–4).

Saint-Simon, H. de, *Le nouveau Christianisme*, ed. H. Desroche (Paris, 1969).

Saint-Simon, H. de, *New Christianity* (London, 1834).

Saint-Simon, H. de, *Oeuvres complètes* (Paris, 1966).

Sauvigy, G. de Bertier de, *La Restauration* (Paris, 1955).

Sauvigny, G. de Bertier de (ed. of documents), *La Révolution de 1830 en France* (Paris, 1970).

Sauvigny, G. de Bertier de, *Le comte Ferdinand de Bertier et l'énigme de la congrégation* (Paris, 1948).

Savigear, P., 'Carbonarism and the French army 1815–24', *History* (1969), 198–211.

Schiappa, J.A., *Gracchus Babeuf avec les Egaux* (Paris, 1991).

Schmidt, C., *Des Ateliers Nationaux aux barricades de juin* (Paris, 1948).

Schnerb, R., *Ledru-Rollin* (Paris, 1948).

Schulkind, E., *The Paris Commune: the View from the Left* (London, 1972).

Scott, J.W., *Glassworkers of Carmaux: French Craftsmen and Political Action in a Nineteenth-century French City* (Cambridge, Mass., 1974).

Scott, W., 'François Furet and democracy in France', *Historical Journal*, 34 (1991), 147–71.

Seignobos, C., *La Révolution de 1848 – le Second Empire (1848–59)*, vol. 4 of *Histoire de la France Contemporaine*, ed. E. Lavisse (Paris, 1921).

Sevrin, E., *Les Missions religieuses en France sous la Restauration: 1815–30*, 2 vols (Paris, 1948–59).

Sewell, W., 'La confraternité des prolétaires: conscience de classe sous la Monarchie de Juillet', *Annales: Economies, Sociétés, Civilisations* (1981), 650–71.

Sewell, W., 'Beyond 1793: Babeuf, Louis Blanc and the Genealogy of "Social Revolution" ', in F. Furet and M. Ozouf, *The French Revolution and the Creation of Modern Political Culture*, vol. 3 *The Transformation of Political Culture 1789–1848* (Oxford, 1989).

Sewell, W., 'Property, labor and the emergence of Socialism in France,

1789–1848', in Merriman, *Consciousness and Class Experience in Nineteenth-Century Europe* (New York, 1979).

Sewell, W., *Work and Revolution in France: the Language of Labour from the Old Regime to 1848* (Cambridge, 1980).

Sheridan, G.J., 'The political economy of artisan industry: government and the people in the silk trade of Lyon, 1830–1870', *French Historical Studies*, 11 (1979), 215–38.

Sheridan, Jr, G.J., *The Social and Economic Foundations of Association among the Silk Weavers of Lyon 1852–1870*, 2 vols (New York, 1981).

Sherwig, J.M., *Guineas and Gunpowder. British Foreign Aid in the Wars with France 1793–1815* (Cambridge, Mass., 1969).

Shorter, E. and Tilly, C., *Strikes in France, 1830–1968* (Cambridge, 1974).

Sibalis, M.D., 'The evolution of the Parisian labour movement 1789–1834', *Proceedings of the 10th Annual Meeting of the Western Society for French History* (Winnipeg, 1984).

Sibalis, M.D., 'The mutual-aid societies of Paris, 1789–1848', *French History*, 3 (1989), 1–30.

Sieyès, *Qu'est-ce-que le tiers état?* (Paris, 1788).

Simon, J., *Souvenirs du 2 décembre* (Paris, 1874).

Smith, W.H.C., *Napoleon III* (London, 1972).

Smith, W.H.C., *Second Empire and Commune: France 1848–1871* (London, 1985).

Snyder, D. and Tilly, C., 'Hardship and collective violence in France, 1830–1960', *American Sociological Review*, 37 (1972), 520–32.

Soboul, A., *Comprendre la Révolution; Problèmes politiques de la Révolution française 1789–97* (Paris, 1981).

Soboul, A., *Les Sans-culottes parisiens de l'An II* (Paris, 1958).

Soboul, A., *Problèmes paysans de la Révolution française 1789–1848* (Paris, 1976).

Soboul, A., *Précis historique de la Révolution française* (Paris, 1962; Eng. trans. 1975).

Spitzer, A.B., *Old Hatreds and Young Hopes. The French Carbonari against the Bourbon Restoration* (Cambridge, Mass., 1971).

Spitzer, A.B., *The French Generation of 1820* (Princeton, 1987).

Spitzer, A.B., *The Revolutionary Theories of Louis-Auguste Blanqui* (New York, 1957).

Spitzer, A.B., 'The elections of 1824 and 1827 in the Department of the Doubs', *French History*, 3, 2 (1989), 153–77.

Stendhal, *Lucien Leuwen* (1836).

Stendhal, *Le Rouge et le Noir* (1830; English trans. with introduction by Margaret R.B. Shaw).

Stewart-McDougall, M.L., *Artisan Republic: Revolution, Reaction and Resistance in Lyon 1848–1851* (Kingston and Montreal, 1984).

Strumingher, L.S., *Women and the Making of the Working Class* (Montreal, 1979).

Strumingher, L.S., 'The artisan family: traditions and transition in nineteenth-century Lyon', *Journal of Family History*, 2 (1977), 211–22.

Strumingher, L.S., 'Les jolies femmes d'Edouard de Beaumont', paper given at the annual conference of the Western Society for French History, October 1992.

Suratteau, J.R., *La République française: certitude et controverses* (Paris, 1972).

Sutherland, D.M.G., *The Chouans: the Social Origins of Popular Counter-revolution in Upper Brittany 1770-1796* (Oxford, 1982).

Sutherland, D.M.G., *France 1789–1815. Revolution and Counterrevolution* (London, 1985).

Sydenham, M.J., *The First French Republic 1792–1804* (London, 1974).

Tackett, T., *Religion, Revolution and Regional Culture in Eighteenth-Century France: The Ecclesiastical Wrath of 1791* (Princeton, NJ, 1985).

Taylor, K., *The Political Ideas of the Utopian Socialists* (London, 1978).

Taylor, K., *Henri Saint-Simon (1760–1825); Selected Writings* (London, 1975).

Ténot, E., *La Province en décembre 1851. Etude historique sur le coup d'état* (Paris, 1868).

Teste, C., *Projet de constitution républicaine et déclaration des principes fondementaux de la société* (Paris, 1833).

Thiers, A., *Histoire de la Révolution française*, 10 vols (Paris, 1823–7).

Thiessé, L., *Débats de la Convention Nationale*, 5 vols (Paris, 1828).

Thomas, E., *Histoire des Ateliers Nationaux* (Paris, 1848).

Thomson, D., *The Babeuf Plot: the Making of a Republican Legend* (London, 1947).

Thoré, T., *La Verité sur le parti démocratique* (Paris, 1840).

Thureau-Dangin, P., *Histoire de la Monarchie de Juillet*, 7 vols (Paris, 1884–92).

Thureau-Dangin, P., *Le Parti libéral sous la Restauration* (Paris, 1888).

Thureau-Dangin, P., *Royalistes et Républicains. Essais historiques sur des questions de politique contemporaine* (Paris, 1874).

Tilly, C., *The Contentious French. Four Centuries of Popular Struggle* (Cambridge, Mass., 1986).

Tilly, C. and Lees, L., 'Le peuple de Juin 1848', *Annales: Economies, Sociétés, Civilisations* (1974), 1061–91.

Tilly, L., 'La récolte frumentaire, forme de conflit politique en France', *Annales: Economies, Sociétés, Civilisations*, 27, I (1972).

Tocqueville, A. de, *The Old Regime and the French Revolution*, trans. S. Gilbert (New York, 1955).

Tocqueville, A. de, *Recollections*, trans. G. Lawrence (New York, 1971).

Tombs, R., 'Paris and the rural hordes; an exploration of myth and reality in the French Civil War of 1871', *Historical Journal* (1986).

Tombs, R., 'Prudent rebels: the 2nd *Arrondissement* during the Paris Commune of 1871', *French History*, 5 (1991), 393–413.

Tombs, R., *The War against Paris* (Cambridge, 1981).

Tombs, R., 'L'année terrible 1870–1871', *Historical Journal*, 35 (1992), 713–24.

Tonnesson, K.D., 'Les fédérés de Paris pendant les Cent-Jours', *Annales historiques de la Révolution Française*, 54 (1982).

Traugott, M., *Armies of the Poor. Determinants of Working-Class Participation in the Parisian Insurrection of June 1848* (Princeton, NJ, 1985).

Trélat, U., 'La Charbonnerie', *Paris Révolutionnaire*, II (1838), 275–341.

Trélat, U., *De la Constitution du corps des médecins et de l'enseignement médical* (Paris, 1828).

Tristan, F., *L'Union ouvrière* (first pub. 1844) (Paris 1967).

Tristan, F., *Le Tour de France. Etat actuel de la classe ouvrière sous l'aspect moral* (Paris, 1973).

Truant, C.M., 'Solidarity and symbolism among journeymen artisans: the case of compagnonnage', *Comparative Studies in Society and History*, 21 (1979), 217–20.

Truchon, D., 'La vie économique à Lyon 1814–30', *Revue d'histoire de Lyon*, XI (1912).

Tudesq, A.J., *Les Conseillers généraux en France au temps de Guizot 1840–1848* (Paris, 1967).

Tudesq, A.J., *Les Grands Notables en France 1840–1849. Etude Historique d'une psychologie sociale*, 2 vols (Paris, 1964).

Tudesq, A.J., 'La légende napoleonienne en France en 1848', *Revue Historique*, 81 (1957), 65–85.

Tudesq, A.J., *L'Election présidentielle du 10 décembre 1848* (Paris, 1965).

Viard, J. (ed.), *L'esprit républicain; colloque de l'université d'Orléans, 4–5 septembre 1972* (Paris, 1972).

Viard, J., *Pierre Leroux et les socialistes européens* (Avignon, 1983).

Viard, P., 'Les fédérés de la Côte-d'Or en 1815', *Revue de Bourgogne*, 16 (1926).

Vidalenc, J., 'La province et les journées de juin', *Etudes d'histoire moderne et contemporaine*, 2 (1948), 83–144.

Vidalenc, J., *Le Département de l'Eure sous la Monarchie Constitutionnelle 1814–48* (Paris, 1952).

Vidalenc, J., *Louis Blanc* (Paris, 1948).

Vidalenc, J., 'A propos de la campagne des banquets', *Congrès des sociétés savantes* (Rouen, 1956), *Section d'histoire moderne et contemporaine*, pp. 679–89.

Vigier, P., *La Séconde République dans la région alpine, 1845–52*, 2 vols (Paris, 1963).

Vigier, P., 'Les troubles forèstiers du premier moitié du XIX siècle française', *Revue Forèstiers Française*, 32 (1980), 128–35.

Villeneuve-Bargemont, J.P.A., *Economie politique chrétienne*, 4 vols (Paris, 1834).

Villermé, L.R., *Tableau de l'état physique et moral des ouvriers employés dans les manufactures*, 2 vols (Paris, 1840).

Vincent, K.S., *Pierre-Joseph Proudhon and the Rise of French Republican Socialism* (Oxford, 1984).

Vivier, R., 'Esprit d'opposition à Strasbourg sous la Monarchie de Juillet', *La Révolution Française* (1924), 230–47, 313–32 and (1925), 48–57.

Vovelle, M., *Les Images de la Révolution Française. Actes du colloque du 25–27 octobre 1985 à la Sorbonne* (Paris, 1988).

Vovelle, M., *La Mentalité révolutionnaire: société et mentalité sous la révolution française* (Paris, 1985).

Vovelle, M., *The Fall of the French Monarchy 1787–1792* (Cambridge, 1984); first published as *La Chute de la monarchie, 1787–1792* (Paris, 1972).

Vovelle, M., *The Revolution against the Church*, trans. from French (Cambridge, 1991).

Wahl, H., 'Les manifestations de l'opposition libérale et les complots militaires dans le Haut-Rhin sous la Restauration', *Revue d'Alsace*, 92 (1953).

Waresquiel, E. de, 'Les voyageurs français en Angleterre pendant la Restauration', Modern French History Seminar, *Institut Français*, London, 13 February 1993.

Weber, E., *Peasants into Frenchmen. The Modernization of Rural France 1870–1914* (London, 1977).

Weber, E., 'The Second Republic, politics, and the peasant', *French Historical Studies*, 11, 4 (1980), 522–50.

Weill, G., *Histoire du parti républicain en France de 1814 à 1870* (Paris, 1900).

Weill, G., 'Les mémoires de Joseph Rey', *Revue historique*, 156 (1928).

Weiner, D.B., *Raspail, Scientist and Reformer* (New York, 1968).

Williams, G.A., *Artisans and Sans-Culottes. Popular Movements in France and Britain during the French Revolution* (New York, 1969).

Winock, M. (*sous direction de*), *Histoire de l'extrême droite en France* (Paris, 1992).

Wocque, J. *Raspail* (Pàris, 1939).

Zeldin, T. (ed.), *Conflicts in French Society* (London, 1970).

Zeldin, T., *Emile Ollivier and the Liberal Empire of Napoleon III* (Oxford, 1963).

Zeldin, T., *France 1848–1945*, 2 vols (Oxford, 1977) (subseq. subdivided and reprinted as five paperbacks by OUP).

Zeldin, T., 'Government policy in the French general election of 1849', *English Historical Review* (1959).

Zeldin, T., *The Political System of Napoleon III* (London, 1958).

Zola, E., *La Fortune des Rougon* (Paris, 1981; first pub. 1871).

Index